DEFI Investment Made Easy

A Beginner's Guide to Investing in Decentralized Finance

By Dr. Liew

Disclaimer

The DEFI Handbook is an independent publication and is not affiliated with, nor has it been authorized, sponsored, or otherwise approved by any companies or organizations.

Trademarks

All trademarks referenced in the book belong to their respective owners.

Liability

The content of this book is to be used for educational and informational purposes only. It is of utmost importance for you to conduct your own research and analysis, as well as seek independent financial advice from a professional before making any investment in decentralized finance. Although every effort and care has been taken to make the information as accurate as possible, the author shall not be liable for any error and financial loss from using the instructions given in this book.

Copyright ® 2021 Liew Voon Kiong

All rights reserved. No part of this book may be reproduced in any form or by any means, without permission in writing from the author.

About the Author

Dr. Liew Voon Kiong holds a bachelor's degree in Mathematics, a master's degree in Management and a doctorate in Business Administration.

Dr. Liew is a sought-after **Blockchain Architect** by companies in the blockchain industry. He has played a lead role in designing and developing the native cryptocurrency of an incubation hub in Southeast Asia, as well as successfully getting it listed on a renowned exchange via an IEO campaign. He is also the Chief Strategy Officer of an Australian blockchain company that manages a crypto exchange.

Dr. Liew is also a blockchain researcher and has developed several use cases such as blockchain-powered supply chain management for the automotive and textile industries, building a blockchain-powered digital government, event, and ticketing DApps, and more. He is skilled in setting up blockchain networks such as private Ethereum networks, as well as writing smart contracts using Solidity and creating DApps. He has also created a blockchain blog titled Blockchain Guide for Everyone (http://www.blockchainguide.biz/).

He is a regular speaker in regional blockchain events and workshops.

Preface

DeFi and Yield Farming have been the most popular buzzwords among the crypto community in recent months. Some DeFi tokens can skyrocket to more than $10K in just a few days but drop back to near zero also in a matter of days! Besides that, people in the crypto community are talking about yield farming instead of mining nowadays.

Skeptics might argue that DeFi is merely hype, but the total value of digital assets locked in the DeFi platforms has reached an astounding $30 billion, thus creating huge DeFi economics. Indeed, DeFi has become an important investment tool that investors cannot ignore. However, the complexity of the DeFi protocols and DeFi coins that exist today and new ones that are emerging every day at a mind-boggling speed has created a huge challenge not only for newcomers but also seasoned crypto traders.

Therefore, I have authored this handbook with the mission to help you understand DeFi and know how to maximize returns from various DeFi tools. This book is written especially for beginners therefore I have minimized the jargons and included a lot of screenshots for easy learning. If you are an intermediate or advanced user, you may skip many of the steps and try out the DeFi platforms straightaway.

This handbook provides a comprehensive guide on how to use all the major DeFi platforms comprising decentralized exchanges, loan, savings markets, yield farming, DeFi applications and more. They include the likes of Uniswap, Sushiswap, Compound, dYdX, AAVE, YAM finance, Balancer, Bancor, MakerDAO, Harvest Finance, Sora Farm, InstaDapp, C.R.E.A.M Finance, Alpha Amora , Torque and more.

In addition, I have also included several topics that I think every reader should learn. The new topics include flash loan, a loan that you can borrow and repay in the same transaction. I explained the concept in detail and then guide you on how to execute a flash loan. Another topic is risk management. Although DeFi is an attractive investment opportunity, the risk is also high. In this topic, I explained how you can reduce risk due to smart contract failure, wallet security and more. Besides that, I showed you how to reduce or hedge risks by using the products and services offered by some of the DeFi platforms for buying and selling protection. The protection includes options trading and insurance.

Please check out other books by the author:

Blockchain and Cryptocurrency: A Blockchain and Cryptocurrency Guidebook for Everyone:

Paperback: https://www.amazon.com/dp/B089LJTNSG
Kindle Edition: https://www.amazon.com/dp/B089KC6B7Q

DeFi, NFT and GameFi Made Easy: A Beginner's Guide to Understanding and Investing in DeFi, NFT and GameFi Projects

Paperback: https://www.amazon.com/dp/B09HG7G751
Kindle Edition: https://www.amazon.com/dp/B09HP46CYW

Investing in DeFi and NFT Projects on Alternative Blockchains: A Beginner's Guide to Investing in DeFi and NFT Projects on Alternative Blockchains other than Ethereum"

Paperback: https://www.amazon.com/dp/B09B33RDCQ
Kindle Edition: https://www.amazon.com/dp/B09B69KXH5

How to maximize profit in DeFi- A Beginner's guide to yield farming and liquidity mining

Paperback: https://www.amazon.com/dp/B096CTX5XX
Kindle Edition: https://www.amazon.com/dp/B0969GHTKM
Hard Cover: https://www.amazon.com/dp/B096CX44TV

Table of Contents

Disclaimer 2

Trademarks 2

Liability 2

Preface 4

Chapter 1 11

Decentralized Finance-An Introduction 11

   1.1 DeFi Features 13

   1.2 The Advantages of DeFi 14

      1.2.1 Maintain Full Control of Your Own Digital Assets 14

      1.2.2 Increased Accessibility 14

      1.2.3 Opportunity to Own a Portion of An Expensive Asset 15

      1.2.4 Transparency 15

   1.3 Types of DeFi Products 15

      1.3.1 DeFi Lending and Borrowing 16

      1.3.2 Decentralized Exchange (DEX) 18

Chapter 2 20

DeFi Lending Platforms 20

   2.1 Compound-A DeFi Money Market 21

   2.2 MakerDAO-The Decentralized Credit Platform 28

      2.2.1 Lending DAI 30

      2.2.2 Opening a Maker CDP Vault 38

   2.3 AAVE-The Decentralized Lending and Borrowing Platform 41

   2.4 Idle Finance 45

   2.5 C.R.E.A.M. Finance 50

2.6 Fulcrum-A Lending and Trading Platform 53

2.7 Torque-A Borrowing Platform 57

2.8 dYdX, a Lending, Borrowing and Trading Platform 59

    2.8.1 Lending 60

    2.8.2 Borrowing 65

2.9 DeFi Saver-A One-Stop Lending and Borrowing App 69

    2.9.1 MakerDAO Dashboard 71

    I. Creating a CDP 72

    II. Automate a CDP 83

    2.9.2. Compound Dashboard 88

    2.9.3. Aave Dashboard 93

    2.9.4. Smart Savings 99

    2.9.4. Exchange 102

    2.9.5. Loan Shifter 103

    2.10 InstaDApp 105

Chapter 3 109

Decentralized Exchanges 109

    3.1 dYdX 109

        3.1.1 Margin Trade 109

        3.1.2 Perpetual Trading 121

    3.2 Uniswap- A Decentralized ER20 Token Exchange 127

    3.3 Balancer-An Automated Market Maker 132

    3.4 Radar Relay- A DEX Powered by DEX 137

    3.5 Bancor-A Non-Custodial Token Exchange 147

    3.6 Kyber Swap 150

- 3.7 Synthetix-A Platform for Trading Synthetic Assets.................. 154
- 3.8 Curve Finance-A DEX for Trading Stablecoins........................ 158
- 3.9 Fulcrum-A Tokenized Margin Trading Platform 163
  - 3.10 1inch-A Decentralized Exchange Aggregator 167
  - 3.11 Airswap-A Peer-to-Peer Trading Platform........................ 173
  - 3.12 Matcha-A DEX Powered by 0x.................................... 181
  - 3.13 Tokenlon-An Atomic Token Swap DEX.............................. 186
  - 3.14 Totle Swap-A DEX Aggregator.................................... 193
  - 3.15 DEX.AG-Another DEX Aggregator.................................. 196
  - 3.16 DDEX- A Decentralzied Margin Trading and Lending Platform 204
  - 3.17 Swerve Finance... 208

Chapter 4 210

Yield Farming 210

- 4.1 What is Yield Farming? 210
- 4.2 Yield Farming Platforms 212
  - 4.2.1 Harvest Finance 213
  - 4.2.2 Pickle Finance 222
  - 4.2.3 Liquidity Mining on Balancer.................................. 229
  - 4.2.4 Liquidity Mining on Unisawap 238
  - 4.2.5 Liquidity Mining with Bancor.................................. 243
  - 4.2.6 Synthetix- The Derivatives Liquidity Protocol 252
  - 4.2.7 Alpha Homora.. 256
  - 4.2.8 Curve Finance 257
- 4.3 Impermanent Loss 260

Chapter 5 Sora Farm-A Yield Farming Game............................... 263

5.1 Farming PSWAP 263

5.2 How to Farm PSWAP? 265

5.3 Sora Tokonomics(SORAnomics) 269

Chapter 6 DeFi Portfolio Management 271

6.1 Zapper.fi 271

6.2 Zerion 283

Chapter 7 288

DeFi Risk Management 288

7.1 Technical Risks 288

7.2 Financial Risk 289

7.3 Procedural Risks 289

7.4 DeFi Score 290

7.5 Swaprate.finance-Hegding Against Interest Rate Fluctuation. ... 296

7.6 Nexus Mutual 300

Chapter 8 303

DeFi Options Trading Protocols 303

8.1 Opyn- Buying Protection Via Options 304

8.1.1 Purchasing Put Options for Downside Protection 305

8.1.2 Purchasing Call Options for Upside Protection 309

8.1.3 Compound Deposit Protection 312

8.1.4 Selling Protections 314

8.1.5 What are oTokens? 321

8.2 Hegic-An On-chain Options Trading Protocol 329

8.2.1 Buying Options 330

8.2.1 Selling Options 334

  8.2.3 HEGIC Token 336

Chapter 9 Flash Loan 346

Glossary 356

Appendix A 360
 List of DeFi Platforms for Quick Reference 360
  I. Decentralized Finance 360
  II Decentralized Exchanges 361

Appendix B 364
 List of Top 20 DeFi Tokens 364

Appendix C 365
 Making a Claim (Exercising) on Opyn through Etherscan 365
 Exercise oETH 365
  1. Go to the 365

Appendix D 370
SORA TONONOMICS 370
 Token Bondage 372
 A New Token: VAL 378

References 381

INDEX 395

Chapter 1

Decentralized Finance-An Introduction

If 2017 was the tantalizing year of ICO for crypto projects fundraising, the year 2020 is the booming year of DeFi. Decentralized finance, popularly known as DeFi, means operating financial applications on a decentralized platform such as blockchain. Formerly known as Open Finance, DeFi is the new financial architecture that leverages decentralized networks and decentralized technologies like smart contracts to transform old financial products into trustless and transparent protocols that run without intermediaries.

Indeed, DeFi and Yield Farming have become the most popular buzzwords among the crypto community in the year 2020. Some DeFi tokens can skyrocket to more than 10K USD in just a few days but drop back to near zero also in a matter of days! Besides that, people in the crypto community are talking about yield farming instead of mining nowadays. Most of you might scratch your head and wonder, "what the heck is that"? Sceptics might assert that DeFi is merely hype, but the total value of digital assets locked in the DeFi platforms has reached an astounding $30 billion at the time of writing (as seen in Figure 1.1), creating huge DeFi economics (should I call it DeFiconomics?).

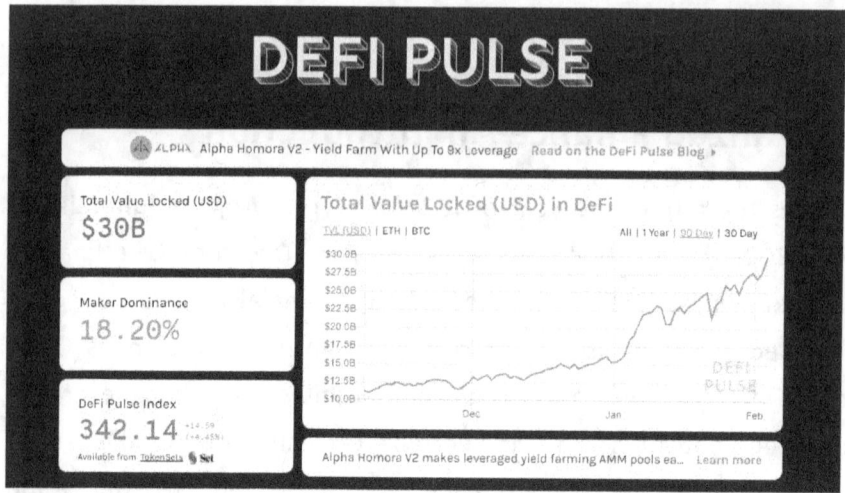

Figure 1.1 Source: https://defipulse.com/

As seen from Figure 1.1, DeFi has become an important investment tool that investors cannot ignore. However, the complexity of the DeFi protocols and DeFi coins that exist today and new ones that are emerging every day at a mind-boggling speed has created a huge challenge not only for newcomers but also seasoned crypto traders. Therefore, I have written this handbook with the mission to help everyone understand DeFi and know how to generate income from various DeFi protocols.

Generally, the trading of crypto assets is performed on centralized exchanges like Binance, Coinbase, Bittrex, Huobi and more. Though cryptocurrencies are minted based on decentralized ledger technology, trading on centralized exchanges does not allow you to have full control of your digital assets, as your private keys are in the custody of the centralized authorities and there is risk your digital funds could be misappropriated.

To mitigate the risk, truly decentralized platforms and associated new types of cryptocurrencies have emerged recently that allow investors to have full custody of their own digital assets and trade them on decentralized platforms without the need of centralized authorities.

In contrast, centralized finance means a single organization like a bank controls and manages the funds of the clients. This kind of centralized control has many weaknesses, including the abuse of funds and manipulation of personal data, fraud, single point of failure due to hacking, and more.

Most DeFi applications are built on top of Ethereum and features smart contracts, the core technology for decentralization and automation. However, there are notable DeFi projects are built on other blockchain protocols. One Notable project is SORA, it was developed using SORA V2 Network built using Polkadot's Substrate. DeFi applications use smart contracts to automatically execute transactions if certain conditions are met, thus allowing financial services to be accessible to anyone in the world with a smartphone and internet connection, without the intervention of a central authority.

1.1 DeFi Features

DeFi has unique features compared to CenFi (Centralised finance) and able to provide more convenient and seamless services, particularly for underserved people. Here are some of the features:

- P2P- Transactions are performed on peer-to-peer basis without the need for intermediaries
- No need for KYC- Anyone can open an account with a DeFi platform instantly and easily without going through the tedious and painful process of KYC
- No one holds your digital assets- DeFi platforms are non-custodian in nature which means they do not hold your private keys; you have full control of your own digital assets.

1.2 The Advantages of DeFi

1.2.1 Maintain Full Control of Your Own Digital Assets

The digital assets that you own on a DeFi platform solely belong to you and you have the freedom to use it in whatever ways you like, without the interference of an intermediary. There is no centralized authority, such as a bank, with the ability to freeze your account, seize your assets, or block your transactions.

1.2.2 Increased Accessibility

According to the World Bank, globally there are still approximately 1.7 billion unbanked adults. These people are at a disadvantage when it comes to pursuing many financial opportunities that could improve their socioeconomic status and lift them out of poverty.

Unfortunately, centralized financial institutions do not have an incentive to target this population. The revenue they would receive from providing services to the currently unbanked simply does not justify the costs of reaching them. In contrast, DeFi providers operate without expensive intermediaries. Hence, they are more willing to serve underprivileged people. Furthermore, DeFi is borderless and 'permissionless' hence everyone on earth particularly the unbanked population can access this form of affordable financial services. Therefore, DeFi has the potential to reduce the world's poverty.

1.2.3 Opportunity to Own a Portion of An Expensive Asset

Another DeFi application is tokenized assets. Tokenizing assets means creating digital tokens to represent the ownership of real assets that can be traded like securities such as shares. By creating tokenized assets that represent, say, a portion of a real estate investment, you open the investment for people who previously could not afford it, to having access from anywhere in the world. Almost anyone can trade tokenized assets as he or she is not required to commit to an entire high-value investment at once. Instead, he or she has the option to buy or sell just a portion of the asset.

1.2.4 Transparency

DeFi data is publicly available, enabling you to keep service providers honest. For instance, you can easily check the reserves of a DeFi protocol, shop around for accurate loan rates, or even track the transactions of public figures.

1.3 Types of DeFi Products

Popular DeFi products include decentralized exchanges, loan and savings markets, tokenized physical assets such as gold, derivatives, forecasting/betting markets, payment, insurance, asset management and more.

The complete list of DeFi products are as shown in Figure 1.2.

DeFi projects

Category	Count	Category	Count	Category	Count
Alternative Savings	4	Analytics	21	Asset Management Tools	
DAOs	7	Decentralized Exchanges	36	Derivatives	
Infrastructure & Dev Tooling	35	Insurance	4	KYC & Identity	
Lending & Borrowing	7	Margin Trading	5	Marketplaces	
Payments	12	Prediction Markets	4	Stablecoins	
Staking	13	Tokenization of Assets	11		

Figure 1.2 Source: DeFiprime(https://defiprime.com/)

1.3.1 DeFi Lending and Borrowing

DeFi loan and savings markets allow you to lend, borrow, or deposit money in a platform. Among the popular loan and savings platforms are Compound, Aave, MakerDAO, Fulcrum, dYdX, and more. DeFi lending platforms allows you to use your digital assets as a collateral to secure a loan and use that loan to invest in some other digital assets that you expect to gain higher return. The collateral is usually ETH but can be other cryptoassets such as DAI, USDT, USDC and more. The debt has an accruing interest which is to be paid off along with the principal.

You may further leverage on your collateral to secure more loans to purchase more assets with the expectation that the value of the assets will appreciate, not unlike real estate investment. Besides, you can lend your assets in a lending and borrowing market to earn more attractive interest than banks. In addition, you may contribute your assets to liquidity pools in the DeFi money market to earn rewards.

Since there is no intermediary in the DeFi lending protocol that manage the lending and borrowing process, how does DeFi lending and borrowing work? The simple answer is that it is done via a smart contract. When a lender sends his or her digital assets to a lending smart contract, the smart contract will issue the interest token to the lender as well as making the assets available for borrowing. The interest token can be redeemed when the lender withdraws the funds. Examples of interest tokens are cToken(cDAI, cUSDC, cETH etc.) issued by Compound, aToken(aETH, aDAI, aUSDT etc.) issued by AAVE, iToken(iUSDT, iDAI, iUSDC etc.) issued by Fulcrum and more.

Similarly, when a borrower initiates a loan application by supplying some collaterals to the protocol, the smart contract will issue the digital assets to the borrowers and create the loan interest and other fees (if any) that the borrowers must pay. By the way, there may be a limit that you can borrow, it depends on the amount of tokens available in the lending pool. This is especially true if you wish to borrow a large amount. For example, users often encounter such limit in MakerDAO when they want to borrow DAI to buy more ETH. When such limit has been reached, the message 'Global MakerDAO debt ceiling for used collateral has been reached' will be displayed. Another factor that limits your borrowing power is the amount of a collateral you supplied to the protocol, the more collateral you supply, the more you can borrow.

In addition, you may want to know how does interest rate in the form of APY(Annual Percentage Yield) calculated? Basically, the interest that the lenders will receive, and the borrowers must pay is calculated using the ratio between the supplied and borrowed tokens in a particular DeFi market. In addition, the APY usually varies according to the supply and demand of lending and borrowing for a specific token.

1.3.2 Decentralized Exchange (DEX)

Decentralized exchanges or DEXs are like stock exchanges but run by smart contracts on the Ethereum blockchain or other blockchain networks. While both allow you to trade assets, decentralized exchanges only trade cryptoassets and do not require centralized authorities to manage the trading. They run on autopilot 24/7. Therefore, it offers fantastic opportunity to anyone in the world to have access to invest in digital assets, particularly the unbanked and underserved.

Decentralized exchanges usually use automatic market maker to facilitate trading of digital assets. Indeed, automatic market maker (AMM) is one of the key components of the decentralized exchange(DEX) platform. Traditional exchanges and centralized digital exchanges rely on the order book to facilitate trading between buyers and sellers. In contrast, DEX employs an AMM algorithm that allows automated trading using a mathematical formula that determines the price of the tokens in a liquidity pool. In fact, AMM is a smart contract that is embedded in the liquidity pool of a decentralized exchange ecosystem.

Different DeFi protocols use different formulas in their AMM algorithms. Uniswap uses the formula $x*y=k$, where x is the amount of token X and y is the amount of token Y in the liquidity pool, and k is a constant. The equation implies that x and y will move inversely proportional to each other on a hyperbolic curve.

Let us examine the following example:

Assuming Uniswap has a pool comprising the ETH/USDT pair. Let say at a particular time the pool has 10000 ETH and the price of ETH was 1500 USDT, hence the total value of ETH was 15,000,000 USDT. As the ratio is 50:50, the total amount of USDT should be 15,000,000.

Based on the formula x*y=k, k=10000*15,000,000=150,000,000,000

Next, assuming now the amount of ETH has reduced to 8000, using the above equation: the amount of USDT should increase to 150,000,000,000/000=18,750,000.

Uniswap is the first truly decentralized AMM as it allows anyone to create a liquidity pool. Besides that, it allows anyone to provide liquidity to an existing pool.

Another popular DEX that employs AMM is Kyber Swap. However, it is not truly decentralized as it does not allow anyone to create a liquidity pool or provide liquidity to a pool. Kyber swap liquidity pools are deployed by professional market makers.

Other popular DEX that employed AMM are Balancer, Curve, Sushiswap and more.

Chapter 2

DeFi Lending Platforms

Lending and borrowing is a huge market in DeFi, and there are many platforms that were built for this market. In fact, it was one of the earliest markets that started with three renowned lending protocols: Compound, MarketDAO and AAVE. Judging from the TVL (Total Value Locked), these three protocols are the top three lending platforms in the DeFi space. At the time of writing, the TVL for MakerDAO is $2.80 billion, Compound is $1.79 billion and AAVE is $1.79 billion, as seen in Figure 2.1. You can see that the platforms that ranked fourth and below are far less in TVL than the top three platforms.

ALL | LENDING | DEXES | DERIVATIVES | PAYMENTS | ASSETS

DEFI PULSE	Name	Chain	Category	Locked (USD) ▼	1 Day %
1.	Maker	Ethereum	Lending	$2.80B	5.58%
2.	Compound	Ethereum	Lending	$1.79B	4.13%
3.	Aave	Ethereum	Lending	$1.79B	5.06%
4.	C.R.E.A.M. Finance	Ethereum	Lending	$170.0M	8.44%
5.	InstaDApp	Ethereum	Lending	$148.7M	9.06%
6.	Idle Finance	Ethereum	Lending	$139.5M	1.64%
7.	Alpha Homora	Ethereum	Lending	$121.0M	7.47%
8.	dYdX	Ethereum	Lending	$42.9M	6.39%
9.	bZx	Ethereum	Lending	$20.1M	6.74%
10.	ForTube	Ethereum	Lending	$17.9M	2.86%

Figure 2.1 Source: DeFiPulse (https://defipulse.com/)

Let us examine some of the more established DeFi lending platforms.

2.1 Compound-A DeFi Money Market

Compound is a protocol on the Ethereum blockchain that features a money market comprising a group of assets with algorithmically generated interest rates, based on supply and demand for those assets. The asset provider (lender) and borrower interact directly with the protocol, earning and paying floating interest rates, without having to negotiate conditions such as maturity, interest rates, or collateral with peers or business partners. In addition, Compound features its native utility token COMP that allows holders to govern its protocol.

Anyone can supply assets to Compound's liquidity pools and immediately begin earning perpetually compounding interest that varies with respect to supply and demand. Supplied asset balances are represented by cTokens: representations of the underlying asset that earn interest and serve as collateral. Each cToken can be convertible into an underlying asset, as interest accrues in the market. For example, if you supply DAI (a type of stable coin) to the protocol, you will earn cDAI and you can convert it back to DAI any time.

Users could borrow up to 50-75% of their cTokens' value, depending on the quality of the underlying asset. Users can add or remove funds at any time, but if their debt becomes undercollateralized, anyone can liquidate; a 5% discount on liquidated assets serves as incentive for liquidators. The Compound protocol sets aside 10% of interest paid as reserves; the rest goes to suppliers.

The protocol currently supports BAT, DAI, ETH, COMP, USDC, USDT, UNI, WBTC, and ZRX. Compound has been audited and formally verified. As of May 2020, Compound has transitioned to community governance; COMP token-holders and their delegates debate, propose, and vote on all changes to Compound.

To use Compound, you must access its website via the following link:

https://compound.finance/

Clicking on the link will direct you to its website, as shown in Figure 2.1.

Figure 2.1

To start using Compound, click 'App' at the top right corner of the screen to bring up the following webpage, as shown in Figure 2.2.

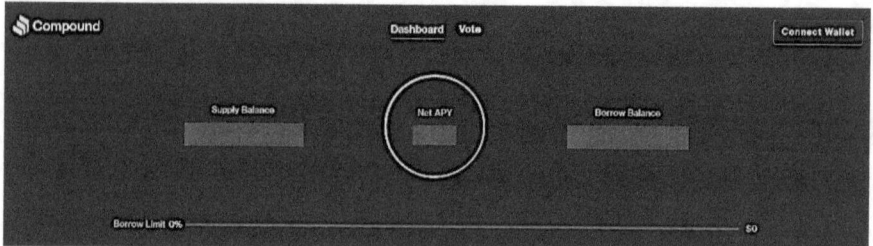

Figure 2.2

Next, click Connect Wallet to allow the Compound protocol to connect to your wallet, you can use MetaMask[1] or any other wallets supported by

---

[1] Please refer to my first book-*DeFi Handbook-A Comprehensive Guide to Decentralized Finance* on how to Install MetaMask and how to connect the wallet to the DeFi Platforms.

the platform. Trezor, a hardware wallet will be a good choice for top security.

Once your wallet is connected, the wallet address will appear on the top right corner of the web page, as shown in Figure 2.3.

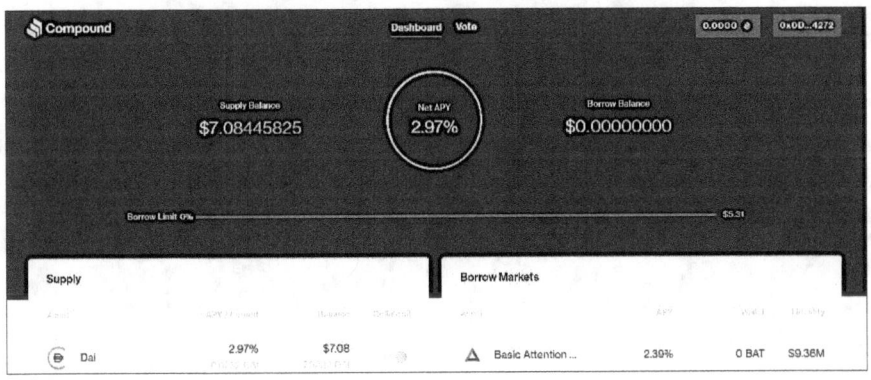

Figure 2.3

Now you can supply or borrow digital assets in Compound, as shown in Figure 2.4. The Figure also shows APY provided by each pool.

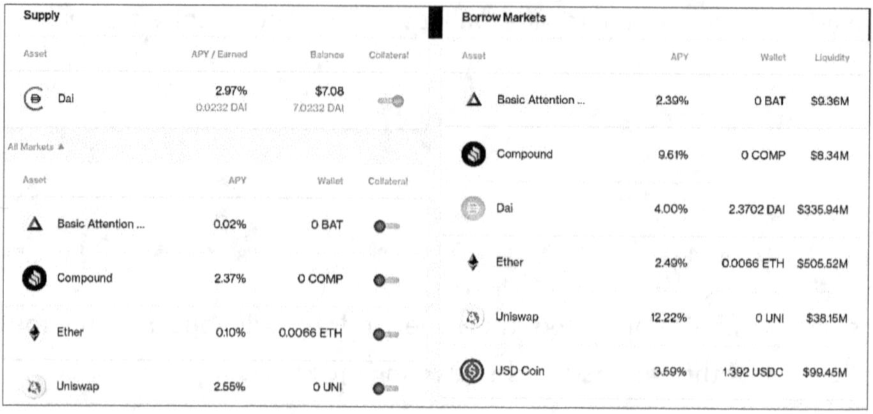

Supply					Borrow Markets			
Asset	APY / Earned	Balance	Collateral		Asset	APY	Wallet	Liquidity
Dai	2.97% 0.0232 DAI	$7.08 7.0232 DAI			Basic Attention ...	2.39%	0 BAT	$9.36M
All Markets					Compound	9.61%	0 COMP	$8.34M
Asset	APY	Wallet	Collateral		Dai	4.00%	2.3702 DAI	$335.94M
Basic Attention ...	0.02%	0 BAT			Ether	2.49%	0.0066 ETH	$505.52M
Compound	2.37%	0 COMP			Uniswap	12.22%	0 UNI	$38.15M
Ether	0.10%	0.0066 ETH			USD Coin	3.59%	1.392 USDC	$99.45M
Uniswap	2.55%	0 UNI						

Figure 2.4

To supply Dai, just click Dai and enter the amount you intend to supply, as shown in the following dialog box in Figure 2.5.

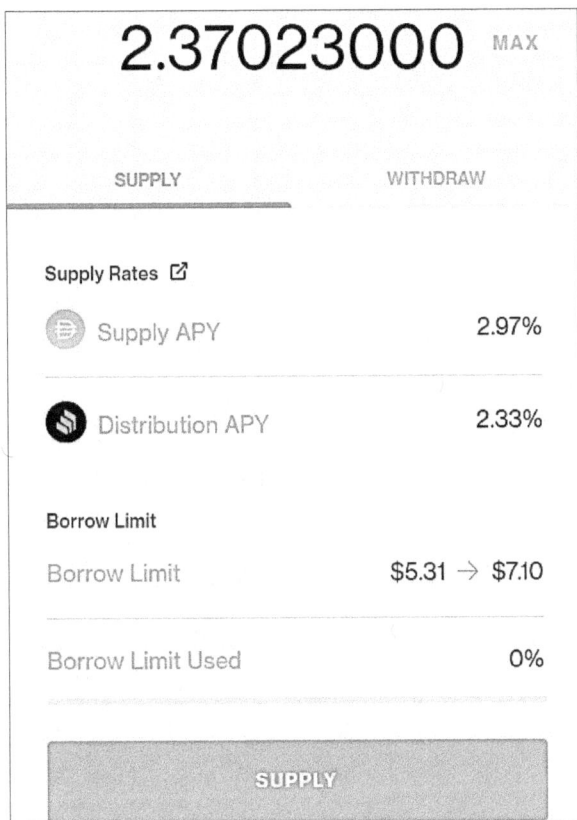

Figure 2.5

The dialog also shows you the supply APY and distribution APY (APY stands for Annual Percentage Yield, which simply means annual interest). Upon clicking supply, you will see your token appear on the Compound platform, as shown in Figure 2.6. The APY is 2.97% for Dai at the time of writing.

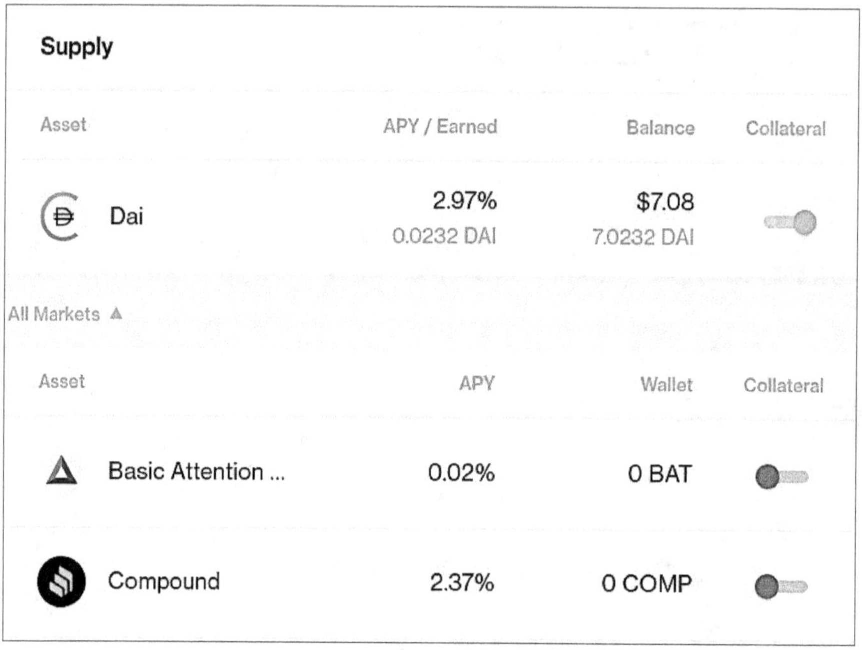

Supply			
Asset	APY / Earned	Balance	Collateral
Dai	2.97% 0.0232 DAI	$7.08 7.0232 DAI	⦿

All Markets ▲			
Asset	APY	Wallet	Collateral
Basic Attention ...	0.02%	0 BAT	○
Compound	2.37%	0 COMP	○

Figure 2.6

When you open your wallet, you will notice that you have earned cDAI,

You can also borrow digital assets from Compound. For example, you can borrow Ether by clicking on the Borrow button, as shown in Figure 2.7.

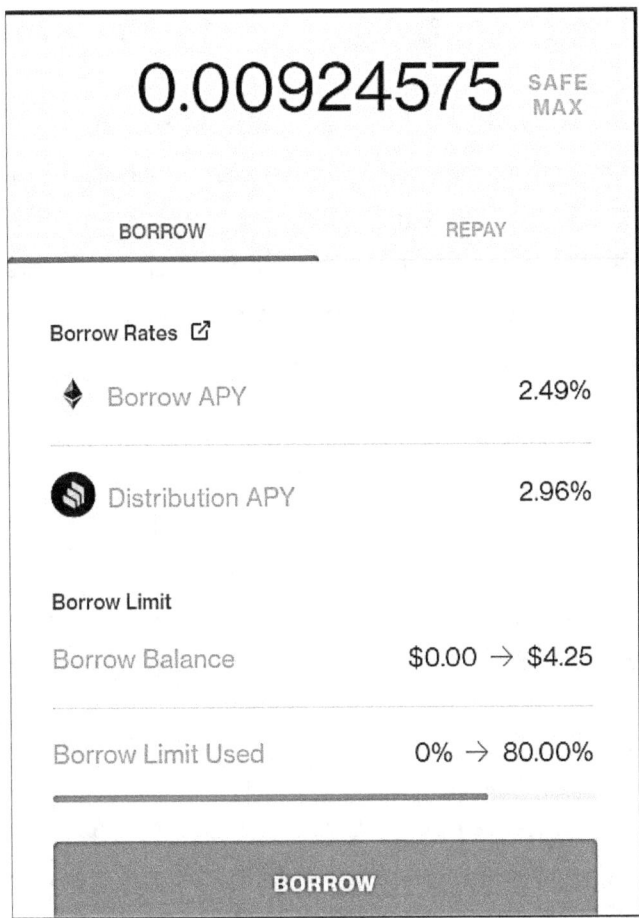

Figure 2.7

You must confirm your request for borrowing assets on Metamask to complete the transaction.

2.2 MakerDAO-The Decentralized Credit Platform

MakerDAO is a decentralized credit platform on Ethereum that supports DAI, a decentralized, unbiased, collateral backed stablecoin whose value is pegged to USD. The Maker Protocol which is known as Multi Collateral Dai (MSD) allows users to mint DAI by leveraging collateral assets approved by the Maker Governance. Maker Governance is a community organized and operated process of managing various digital assets of the Maker Protocol.

Anyone can use the Maker Protocol to open a Collateralized Debt Position (CDP), lock ETH as collateral, and generate DAI as a debt against that collateral. DAI debt incurs a stability fee (i.e., continuously accruing interest), which is paid in MKR (the governance token of MakerDAO) upon repayment of borrowed DAI. The MKR is burned, along with the repaid DAI.

Users can borrow DAI up to 66% of their collateral value (150% collateralization ratio). CDPs that fall below that rate is subject to a 13% penalty and liquidation (by anyone) to bring the CDP out of the vault. Liquidated collateral is sold on an open market at a 3% discount.

The Maker Protocol is one of the largest dApps on the Ethereum blockchain. It was the first DeFi application to gain significant adoption among the crypto communities. Since the release of Single Collateral Dai in 2017, user adoption of this stablecoin has increased dramatically. Indeed, it has become a driving force in the DeFi movement. The Maker Protocol is designed by a diverse group of individuals that include developers, external partners, and other entities. It is managed and governed by people who hold the governance token MKR through a system of scientific governance involving executing voting and governance polling.

Holders of MKR govern the system by voting on risk parameters such as the stability fee level. MKR holders also act as the last line of defence in case of a black swan event. If the system wide collateral value falls too low too fast, MKR is minted and sold on the open market to raise more collateral, diluting MKR holders.

To use MakerDAO services, you can access the Oasis App using the following link:

https://oasis.app/

The landing page is as shown in Figure 2.8.

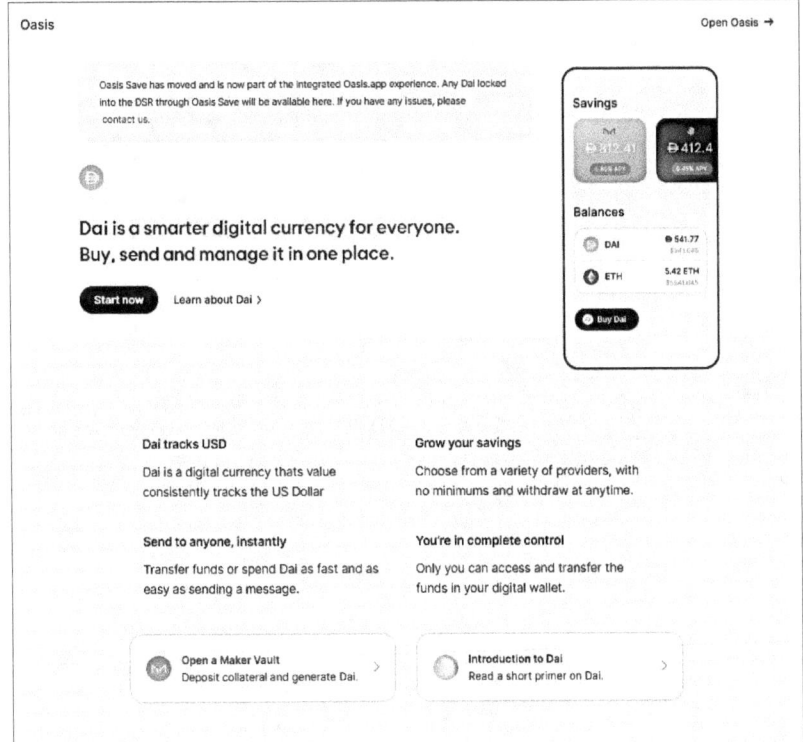

Figure 2.8

Oasis is a platform created by MakerDAO for decentralized finance. You can use it to borrow Dai and deposit DAI and earn savings — all in one place.

2.2.1 Lending DAI

Lending DAI means depositing DAI to earn interest. To deposit DAI, use the Oasis Save App by clicking 'Start Now' button or the Open Oasis link on the top right-hand corner. The Oasis Save App UI is as shown in Figure 2.9.

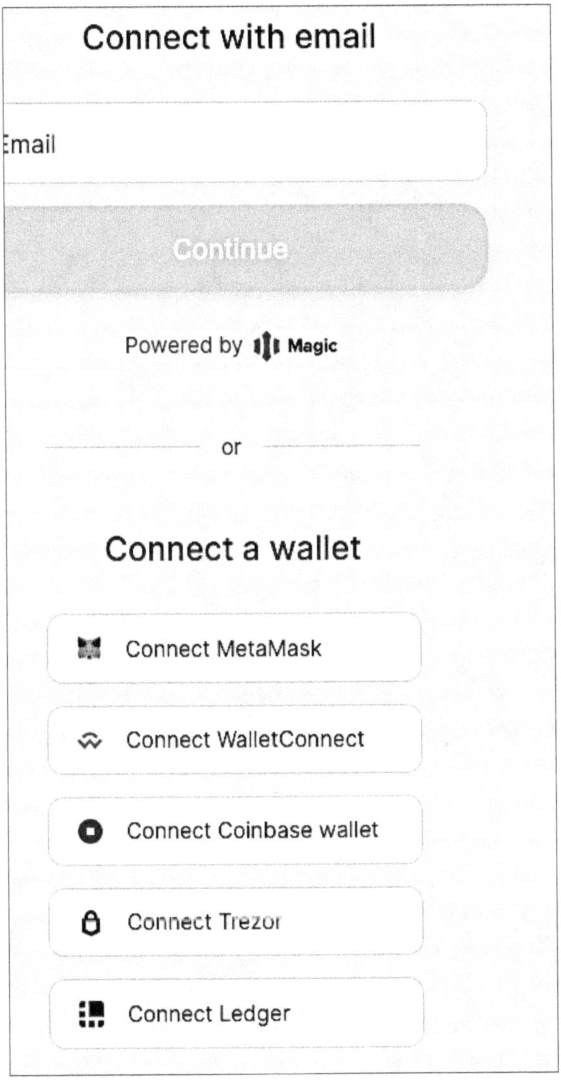

Figure 2.9

You can connect to the app via email or a wallet like MetaMask. After connected to the wallet, you can start using the Oasis app, as shown in Figure 2.10.

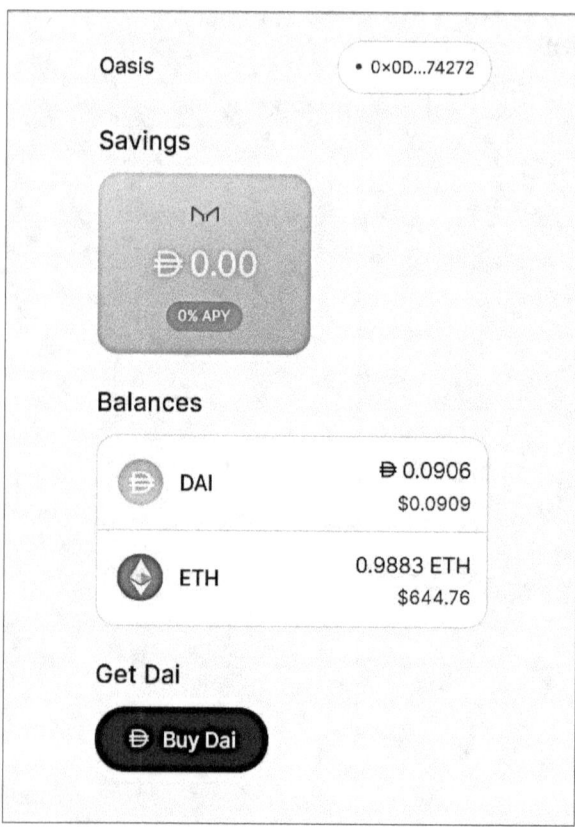

Figure 2.10

To deposit DAI , click the button under Savings to bring up the dialog box as shown in Figure 2.11.

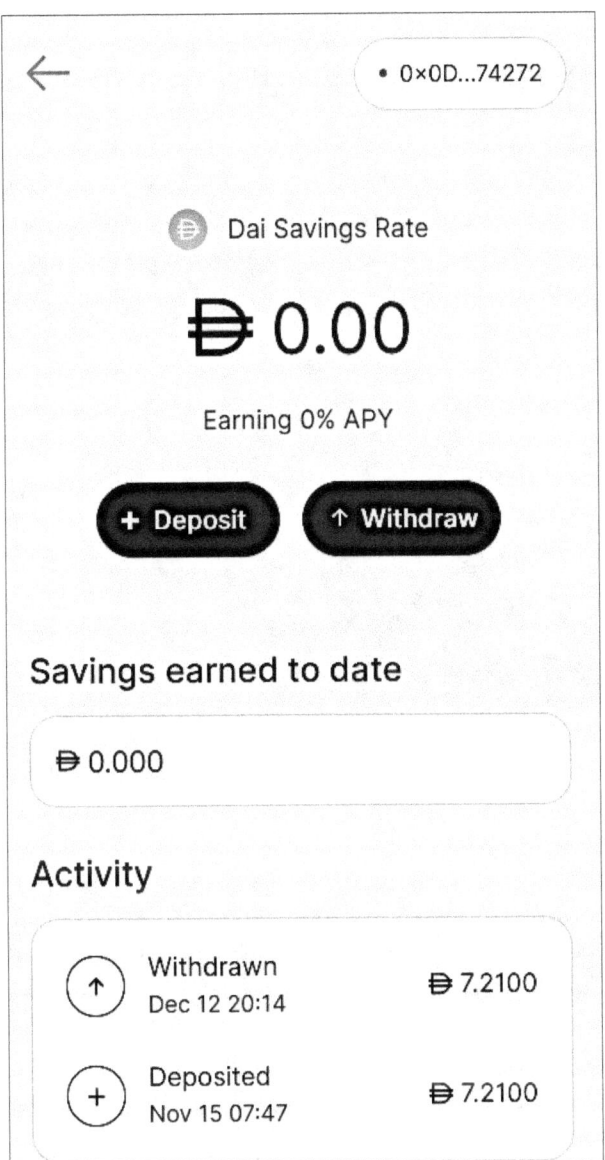

Figure 2.11

Next, click the Deposit button and enter the amount of DAI you wish to deposit, as shown in Figure 2.12.

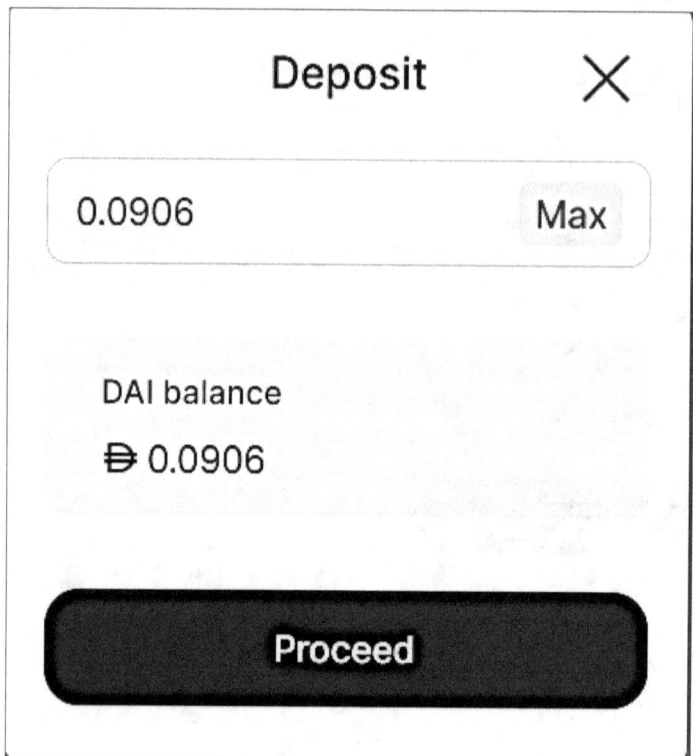

Figure 2.12

Finally, click the 'Proceed' button and confirm the transaction at MetaMask. You may withdraw your savings anytime by clicking the 'withdraw' button.

If you do not have DAI, you can purchase it at any Decentralized exchange like Uniswap or centralized exchange like Binance. However, you may also use fiat to buy DAI by clicking the 'BUY' button in Oasis app itself. When you click the'BUY' button, Oasis will direct you to the fiat to crypto exchanges, as shown in Figure 2.13.

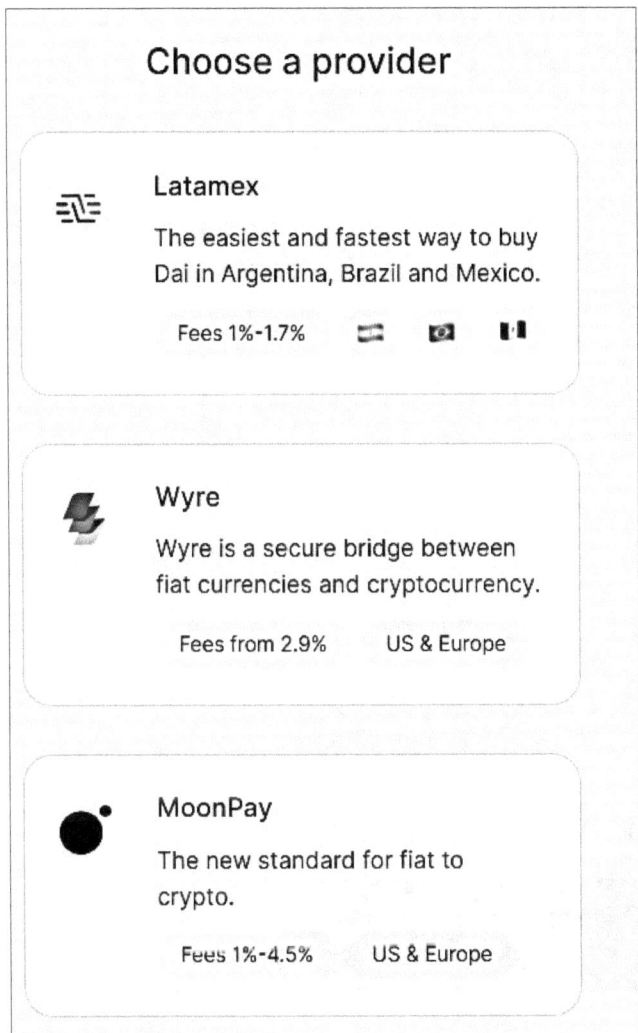

Figure 2.13

Let's say you wish to buy DAI from Wyre, click on it to launch the buying panel, as shown in Figure 2.14.

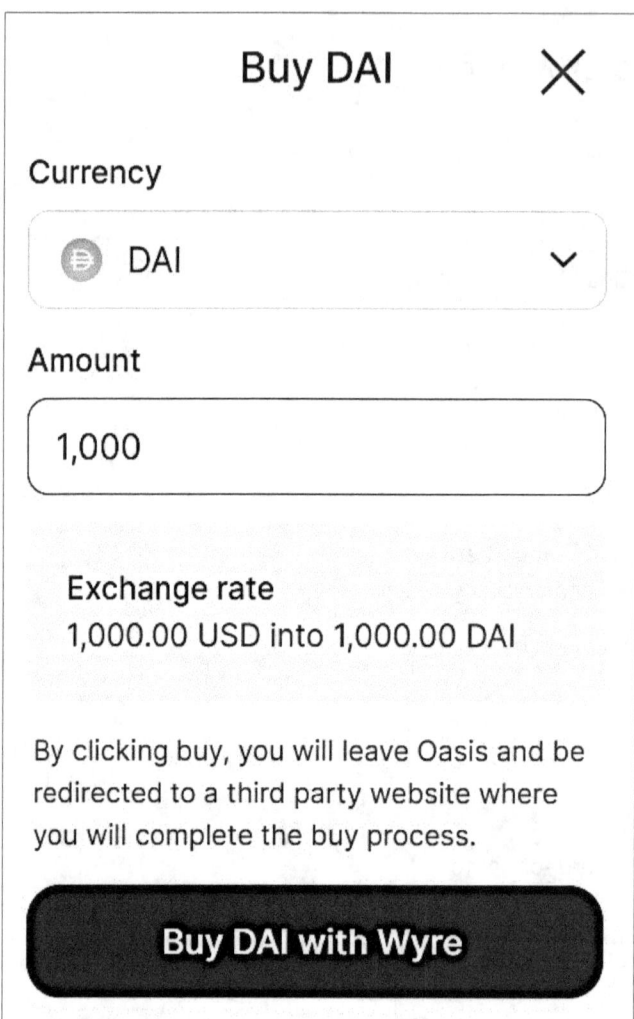

Figure 2.14

Next, click the 'Buy DAI with Wyrex' button to proceed to the Wyrex page, as shown in Figure 2.15. You may use ApplePay or Credit card to buy DAI.

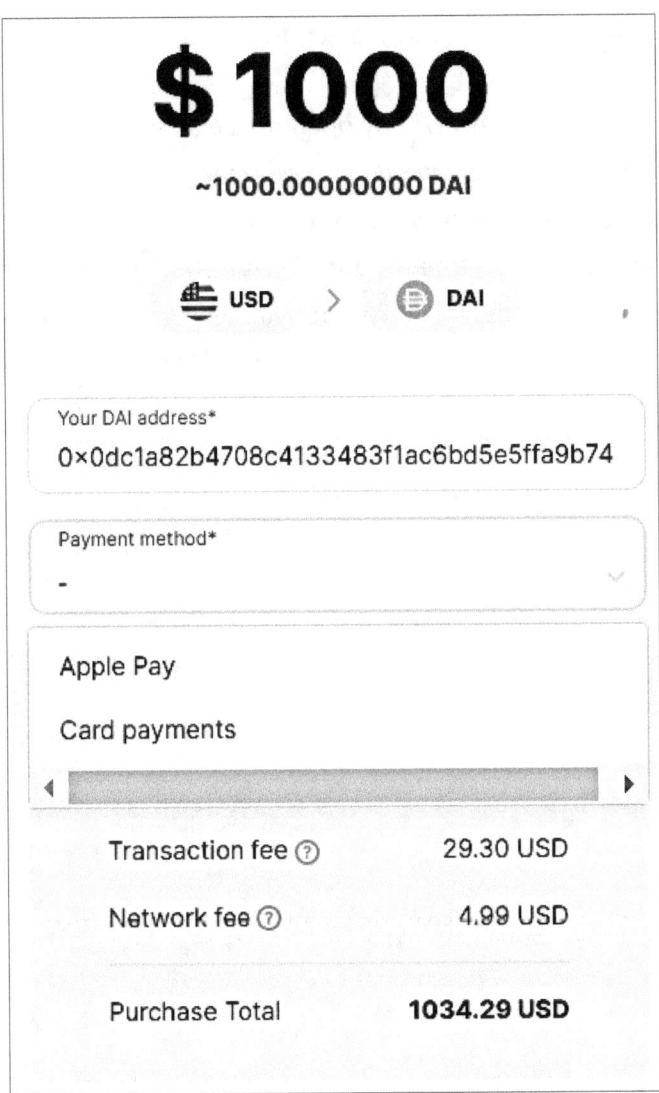

Figure 2.15

2.2.2 Opening a Maker CDP Vault

Besides lending, you can also borrow DAI by opening a Maker CDP[2] Vault. CDP is a core component of the Dai Stablecoin System whose purpose is to create Dai in exchange for collateral, which it then holds in escrow until the borrowed Dai is returned. Therefore, to borrow DAI, you must deposit a cryptoasset as a collateral in the vault. To open a CDP, click the 'Open a Maker Vault' button and connect the wallet to launch the borrowing page, as shown in Figure 2.16.

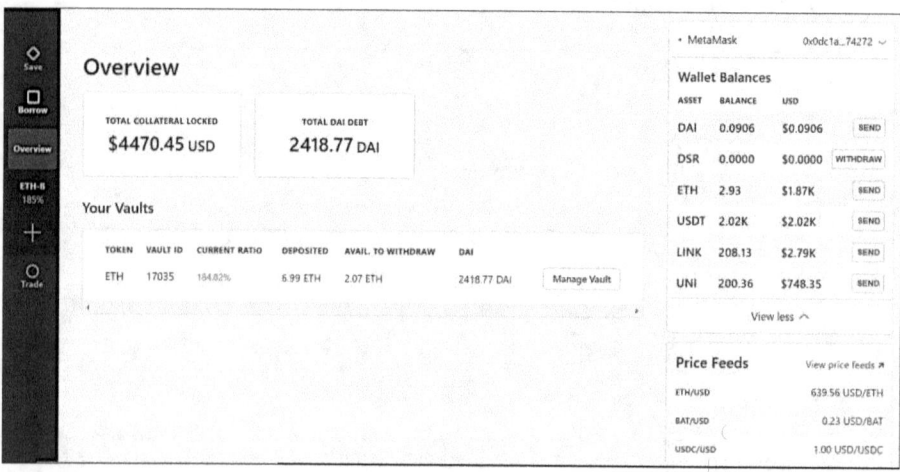

Figure 2.16

The page will show the current CDP and your wallet balances. To create a new CDP, click the + button on the left navigation menu to launch the collateral selection page, as shown in Figure 2.17. Currently Maker offers a dozen collateral types, the most popular one being ETH-A as can be seen from the whopping 130 million of ETH locked in the vault.

---

[2] CDP means Collateralized Debt Position. It is a representation of a debt position that is collateralized by an underlying pool of assets.

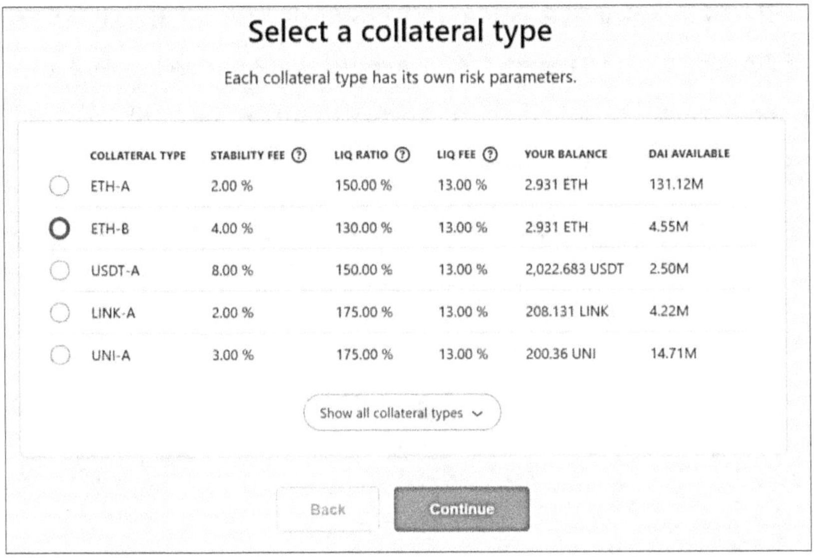

Select a collateral type

Each collateral type has its own risk parameters.

COLLATERAL TYPE	STABILITY FEE	LIQ RATIO	LIQ FEE	YOUR BALANCE	DAI AVAILABLE
ETH-A	2.00 %	150.00 %	13.00 %	2.931 ETH	131.12M
ETH-B	4.00 %	130.00 %	13.00 %	2.931 ETH	4.55M
USDT-A	8.00 %	150.00 %	13.00 %	2,022.683 USDT	2.50M
LINK-A	2.00 %	175.00 %	13.00 %	208.131 LINK	4.22M
UNI-A	3.00 %	175.00 %	13.00 %	200.36 UNI	14.71M

Show all collateral types

Back | Continue

Figure 2.17

Let select ETH-A and click 'Continue' to proceed with the opening of the vault. The vault is as shown in Figure 2.18.

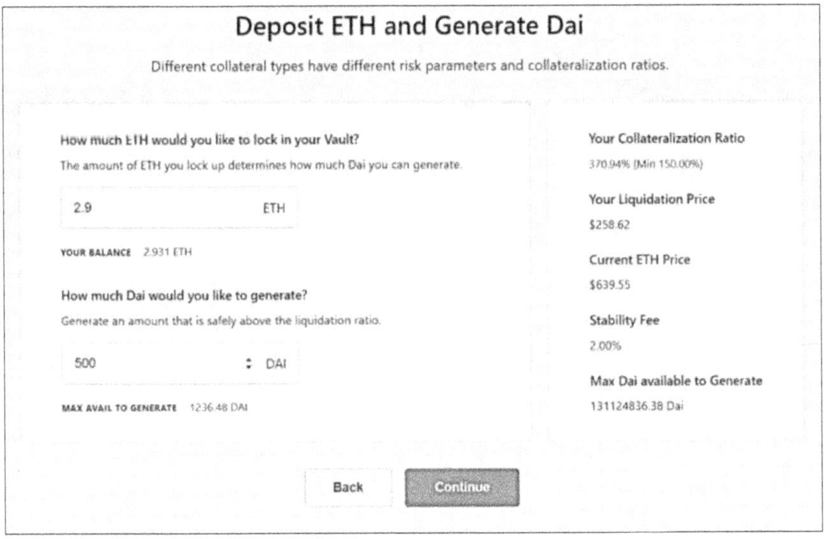

Deposit ETH and Generate Dai

Different collateral types have different risk parameters and collateralization ratios.

How much ETH would you like to lock in your Vault?
The amount of ETH you lock up determines how much Dai you can generate.

2.9 ETH

YOUR BALANCE 2.931 ETH

How much Dai would you like to generate?
Generate an amount that is safely above the liquidation ratio.

500 DAI

MAX AVAIL TO GENERATE 1236.48 DAI

Your Collateralization Ratio
370.94% (Min 150.00%)

Your Liquidation Price
$258.62

Current ETH Price
$639.55

Stability Fee
2.00%

Max Dai available to Generate
131124836.38 Dai

Back | Continue

Figure 2.18

Now enter the amount of ETH you wish to deposit as a collateral and the amount of DAI you wish to borrow. Please note that your collateralization ratio(collateral to debt ratio) must not be less than 130%. It will also show you the liquidation price and the stability fee you must pay.

After opening the CDP, you can view the details as shown in Figure 2.19.

Figure 2.19

2.3 AAVE-The Decentralized Lending and Borrowing Platform

Aave is a decentralized non-custodial money market protocol in which users can participate as depositors and borrowers. Depositors provide liquidity to the market to earn passive income, while borrowers can borrow in an overcollateralized or undercollateralized manner.

In layman terms, Aave enables users to lend and borrow a range of Ethereum-based cryptoassets. Borrowers can select from either stable or variable interest rates, and lenders can collect interest.

Aave began as ETHLend in 2017 after it successfully raised $16.2 million in an ICO to create a decentralized lending platform. ETHLend is a decentralized cryptocurrency credit platform and the world's first crypto lending marketplace that operates exclusively through Ethereum smart contracts. ETHLend also has a token known as the LEND token. It is the native ERC20 token of the ETHLend platform. Its token can be stored in any Ethereum wallet in a similar way as other ERC20 tokens.

However, after the recent approval in 2020 of the Aave Improvement Proposal, the protocol is requesting LEND token holders to migrate to the new AAVE token. At the time of writing, 89.65% of LEND tokens have been migrated to AAVE.

To use the service, you must deposit a certain amount of your preferred cryptocurrency. After depositing, you will earn passive income based on the market borrowing demand. Additionally, depositing digital assets allows you to borrow by using your deposited assets as a collateral. Any interest you earn by depositing funds helps offset the interest rate you pay by borrowing.

You can access the Aave App via the following link:

https://app.aave.com/markets

When you launch the App, it will prompt you to connect version 1 and version 2, as shown in Figure 2.20.

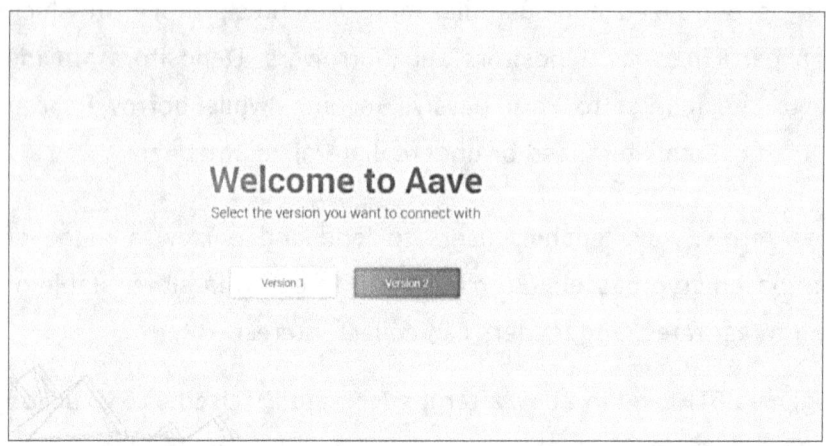

Figure 2.20

I suggest that you select version 2, the newer version. The landing page of AAVE version 2 is as shown in Figure 2.21.

Figure 2.21

The landing page displays the market size, the total borrowed, the deposit APY, variable borrow APY and stable borrow APY. Therefore, it is easy for you to choose tokens to deposit as well as borrow.

To start using the app, you must connect your wallet. After your wallet is connected, you may start to deposit or borrow the token of your choice. Let us deposit some USDT in Aave by clicking the USDT bar to enter the AAVE V2 market page, as shown in Figure 2.22.

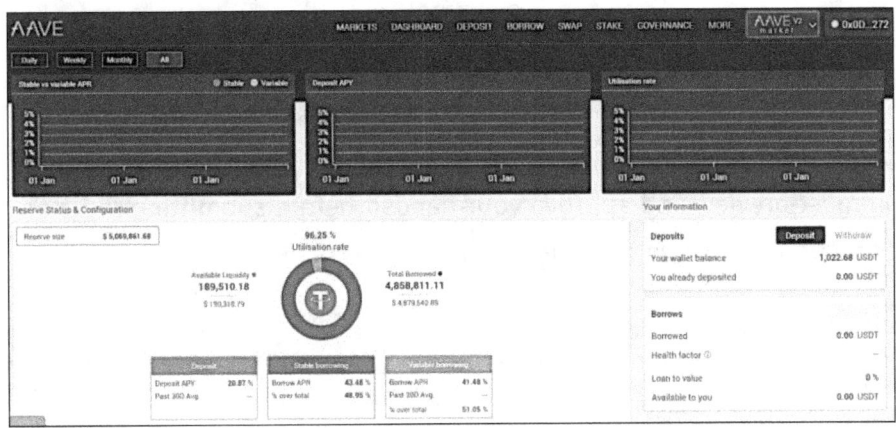

Figure 2.22

The page will show you some important information like available liquidity, total borrowed, deposit APY, variable borrow APY and stable borrow APY. The right panel will show you the amount of USDT you have in the wallet, the amount deposited as well as the borrow information.

Next, click the 'Deposit' button to deposit some USDT. Clicking the 'Deposit button' will launch the deposit page, when you will be presented with some detail information like utilization rate, available liquidity, deposit APY and more. If you are satisfied with the numbers, proceed to enter the amount you wish to deposit and click the 'Continue' button, as shown in Figure 2.23.

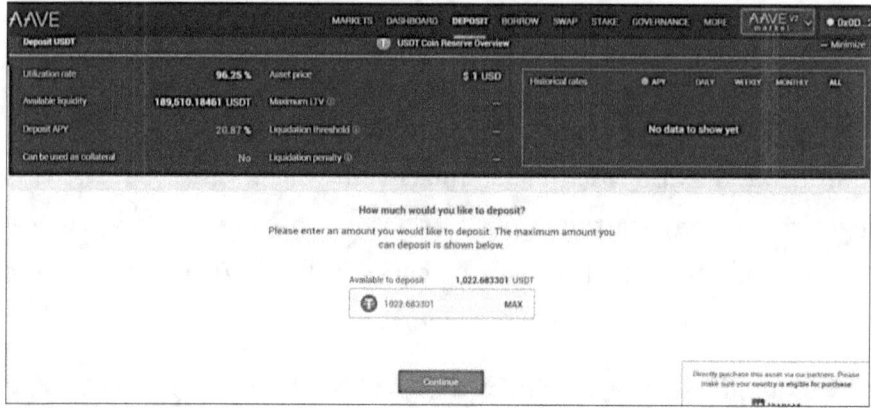

Figure 2.23

You must preview and approve your deposit before submitting the transaction, as shown in Figure 2.24.

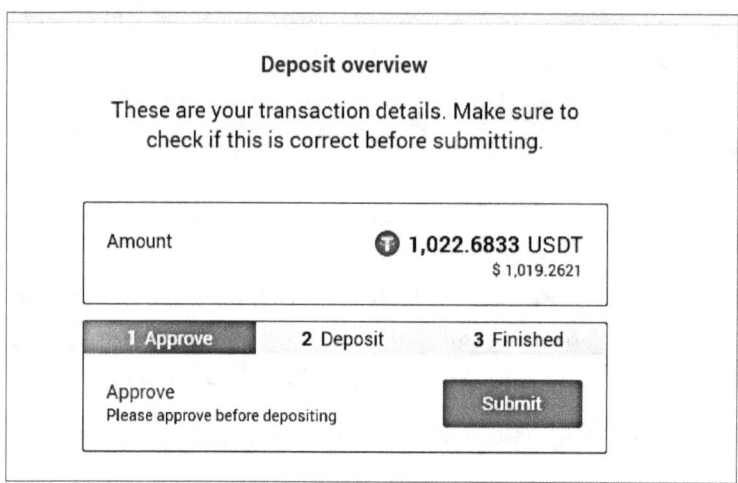

Figure 2.24

Once submitted and confirmed, you can view your position on the dashboard, as shown in Figure 2.25.

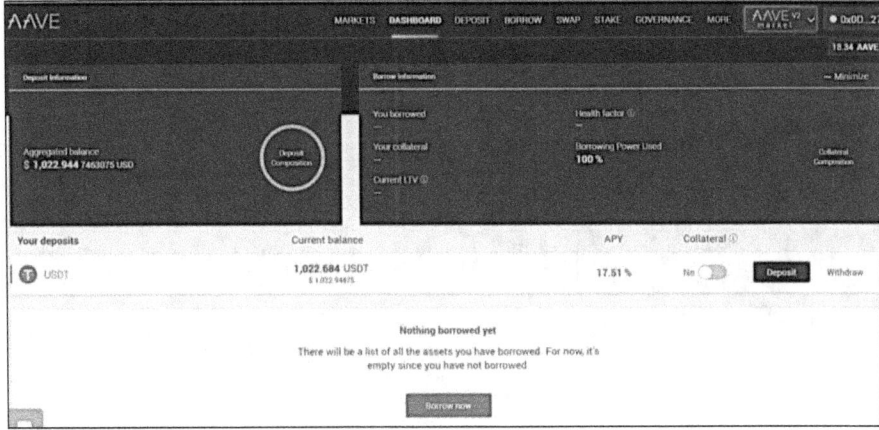

Figure 2.25

2.4 Idle Finance

Idle Finance is a decentralized lending protocol that allows users to manage their digital asset allocation automatically and algorithmically among different third-party DeFi protocols like Compound (Idle, n.d.). You can choose to maximize your interest rate returns through their Maximum Yield strategy or minimize your risk exposure through our Risk Adjusted allocation strategy.

The Idle protocol is governed by a DAO powered by the IDLE token which is responsible for the maintenance and improvement of Idle protocol.

To access Idle Finance, use the following link:

https://idle.finance/#/

The landing page is as shown in Figure 2.26.

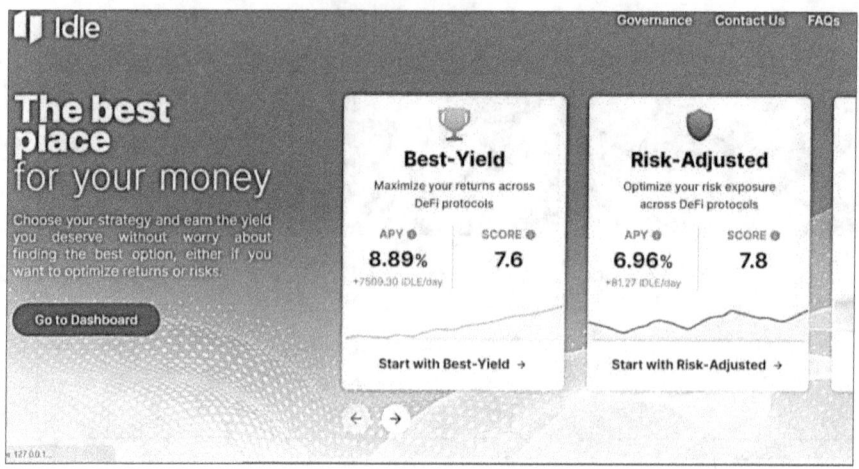

Figure 2.26

On the landing page, you can elect the best yield strategy, or the risk adjusted strategy. Let say you wish to invest using the best yield strategy, click the 'Start with Best-Yield' tab to launch the deposit page, as shown in Figure 2.27.

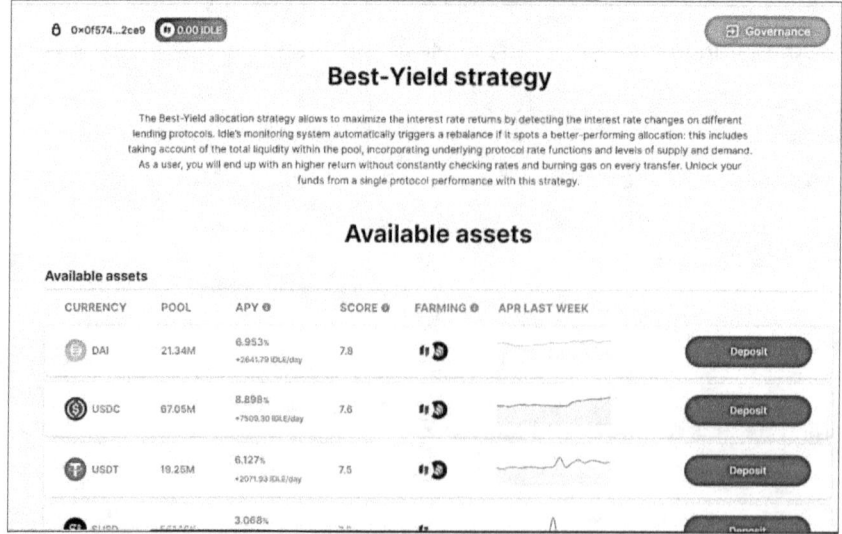

Figure 2.27

You can look at the APYs and decide to choose which pool to deposit funds. Currently only DAI, USDC, USDT, SUSD, TUSD and WBTC are available for best yield investment, as shown in Figure 2.28.

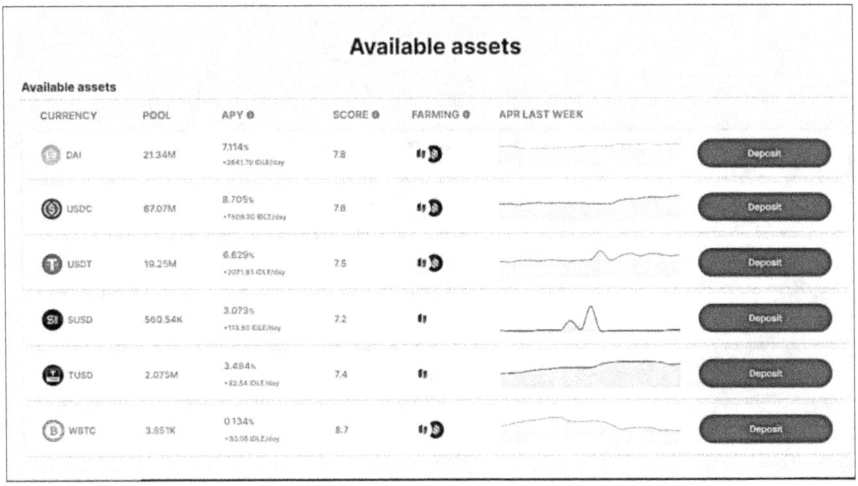

Figure 2.28

Let us choose DAI by clicking the 'Deposit' button to bring up the deposit panel, as shown in Figure 2.29.

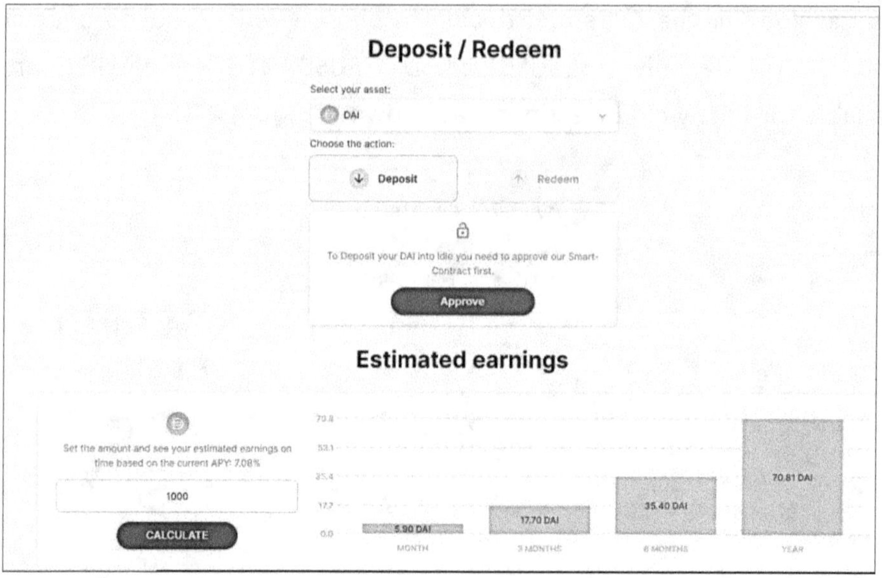

Figure 2.29

When you enter the amount you wish to deposit and click the 'Calculate' button, the app will calculate the estimated earnings for a month, three months, half a year and a year. You must approve the smart contract before you can deposit the crytpassets.

If you do not have DAI, you can purchase it via a bank account, a credit card or an Ethereum wallet, as shown in Figure 2.30.

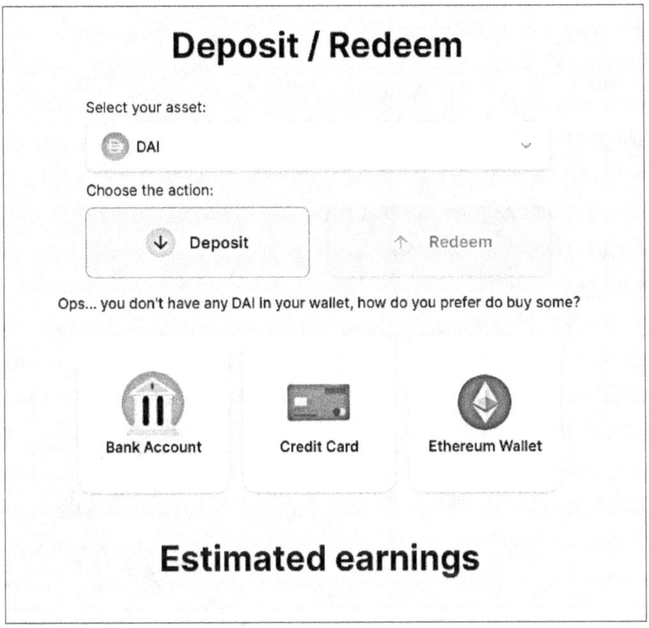

Figure 2.30

Currently, purchasing with a bank account or a credit card are only available in the following countries:

- UK
- Europe
- USA
- Australia
- Brazil
- China
- Mexico
- India
- Canada
- Hong Kong
- Russia
- South Africa

- South Korea

On the other hand, only three tokens are available for risk adjusted strategy, as shown in Figure 2.31.

Risk-Adjusted strategy

The Risk-Adjusted allocation strategy provides a way to earn the best rate at the lowest risk-level. The risk-management algorithm takes account of the total assets within a pool, incorporates underlying protocol rate functions and levels of supply and demand, skimming protocols with a bad score/rate mix, and finally determining an allocation that achieves the highest risk-return score possible after the rebalance happens.

Available assets

Currency	Pool	APY	Score	Farming	APR Last Week	
DAI	537.32K	7.118% +81.27 IDLE/day	7.8			Deposit
USDC	2.548M	9.591% +446.34 IDLE/day	7.4			Deposit
USDT	80.87K	7.413% +8.49 IDLE/day	7.8			Deposit

Figure 2.31

2.5 C.R.E.A.M. Finance

C.R.E.A.M. Finance is a decentralized peer to peer lending platform based on a fork of Compound Finance. C.R.E.A.M. bridges liquidity across underserved assets by providing algorithmic money markets to these underserved assets. Users can supply any supported assets and use these supplied assets as collateral to borrow any other supported assets.

To access C.R.E.A.M, use the following link:

https://app.cream.finance/

The landing page design is plain but easy to use. As usual, you must connect a wallet to use the app. The landing page lists the cryptoassets you can supply and the list of cryptoassets you can borrow as shown in Figure 2.32 and Figure 2.33.

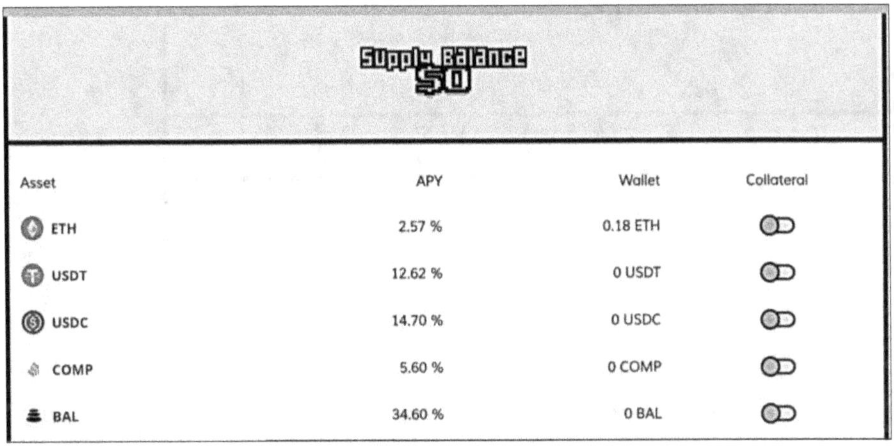

	Supply Balance $0		
Asset	APY	Wallet	Collateral
ETH	2.57 %	0.18 ETH	⚪
USDT	12.62 %	0 USDT	⚪
USDC	14.70 %	0 USDC	⚪
COMP	5.60 %	0 COMP	⚪
BAL	34.60 %	0 BAL	⚪

Figure 2.32

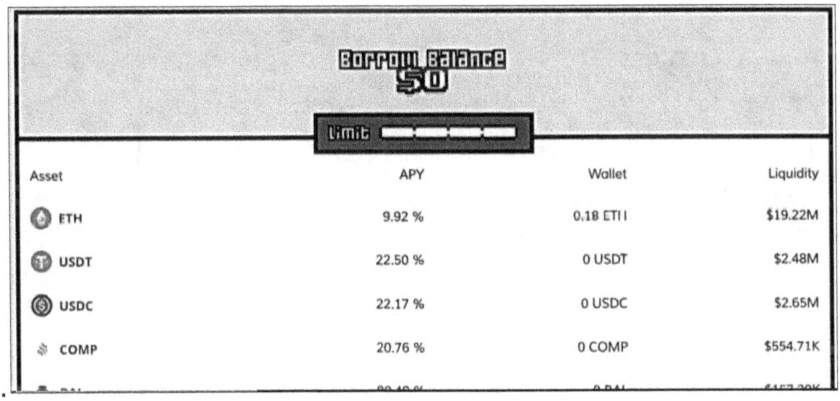

	Borrow Balance $0		
	Limit		
Asset	APY	Wallet	Liquidity
ETH	9.92 %	0.18 ETH	$19.22M
USDT	22.50 %	0 USDT	$2.48M
USDC	22.17 %	0 USDC	$2.65M
COMP	20.76 %	0 COMP	$554.71K

Figure 2.33

To supply an asset, simply click on the asset and proceed to deposit the asset, as shown in Figure 2.34. You must enable the cryptoasset you wish to supply before you can complete the depositing process.

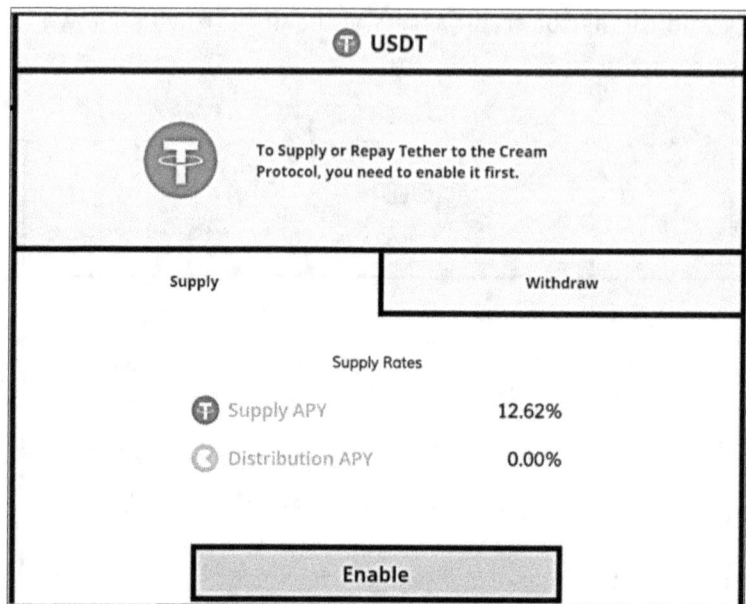

Figure 2.34

To borrow a cryptoasset like ETH, click the crypto asset to start the borrowing process. You must use the crypto assets that you have supplied to the protocol as a collateral before you can borrow the cryptosset, otherwise it will show insufficient funds, as shown in Figure 2.35.

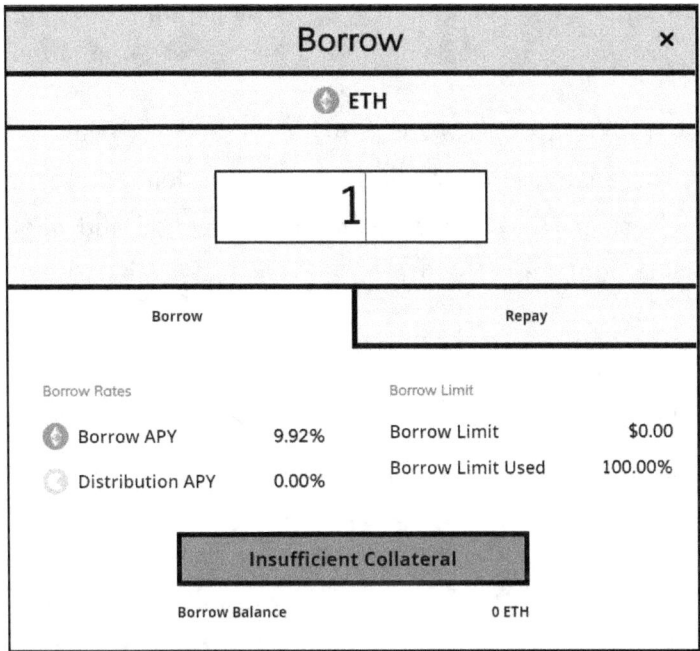

Figure 2.35

2.6 Fulcrum-A Lending and Trading Platform

Fulcrum is a tokenized lending and margin trading platform built with the bZx DeFi protocol. It allows users to lend assets to earn interest or enter short/leveraged positions (Defiprime, n.d.). Besides that, it features a governance native token $BZRX which is used to pay fees. We shall focus on lending first and discuss its trading platform in another chapter.

According to bZx (bZx, n.d.), lending on Fulcrum is powered by iTokens, which are global lending pools. Each asset has a single iToken equivalent (ETH has iETH, DAI has iDAI, USDT has iUSDT, USDC has iUSDC etc.), which means your assets are being tokenized. You can trade the iTokens just like any other ERC20 token. Besides that, each asset has an independent interest rate paid to lenders who have deposited funds in the contract. The interest earned is proportional to the amount of iTokens held by each lender.

According to bZx (bZx, n.d.), iTokens constantly accrue value and increase in price because its underlying assets are loaned out to borrowers. The interest of iTokens compounds each second and might drop if the underlying pool suffers a loss.

To access the Fulcrum platform, use the following link:

https://fulcrum.trade/

The website landing page is as seen in Figure 2.36.

Figure 2.36

To lend, click on the Lend button to load the Lend page, as seen in Figure 2.37.

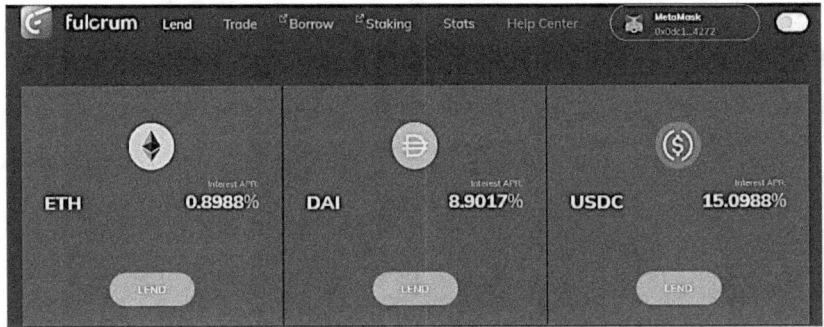

Figure 2.37

Let us proceed to lend some USDT, as shown in Figure 2.38.

Figure 2.38

As usual, you must confirm the transaction on your wallet. After confirmation, the transaction will be updated to the blockchain, as shown in Figure 2.39.

Figure 2.39

Upon confirmation, you can see that your fund is generating perpetual interest in real time, as shown in Figure 2.40.

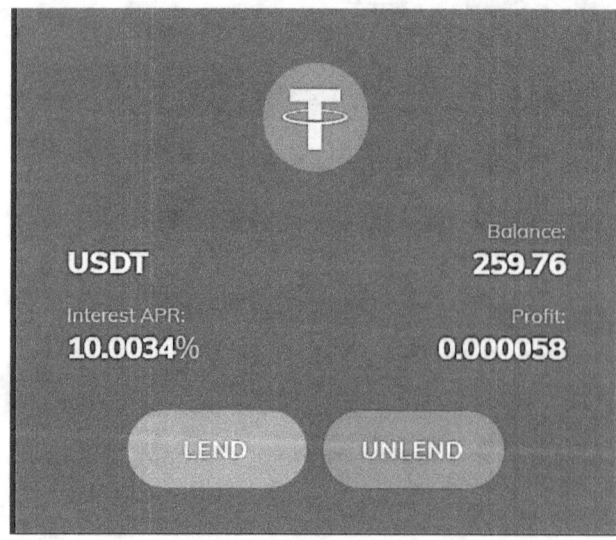

Figure 2.40

When you lend USDT, iUSDT is not automatically shown in your wallet. In MetaMask, you need to click the 'Add Token' button and paste the iUSDT contract address under the Custom Token tab and then click 'Add Token' to add it to your wallet. In addition, you can withdraw your deposit anytime by clicking the UNLEND button, as shown in Figure 2.41.

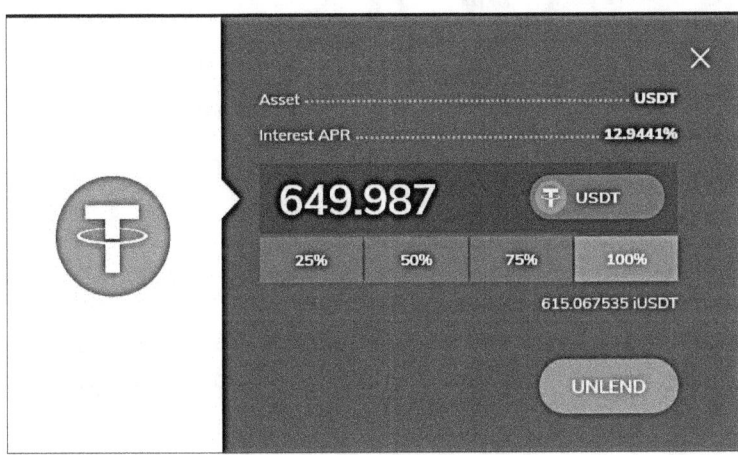

Figure 2.41

2.7 Torque-A Borrowing Platform

Torque is a DeFi platform built using bZx for borrowing assets with indefinite-term loans and fixed interest rates. The advantage is the platform is non-custodial and you can secure an instant, crypto-backed loan with no KYC or credit checks.

To access Torque, use the following link:

https://app.torque.loans/borrow

The landing page is as shown in Figure 2.42.

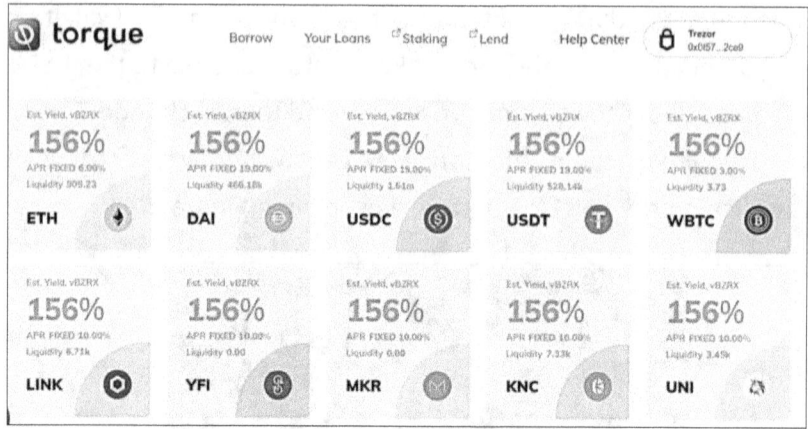

Figure 2.42

The landing page shows a dozen cryptcurrencies you can borrow. To borrow a certain cryptocurrency, you must deposit another cryptocurrency as a collateral, the minimum collateralization ratio is 150%. For example, let say you wish to borrow 1000 USDC, you must deposit 2.6613 ETH as a collateral, based on the price at writing, as shown in Figure 2.43. You can calculate the collateralization ratio as follows:

2.6613 ETH is approximately 1570 USDC

$$\text{Collateralization Ratio} = \frac{1570}{1000} \times 100 = 157\%$$

Which is more than the required 150%.

If you are satisfied with rate, you can click the 'Borrow' button to proceed, as shown in Figure 2.43.

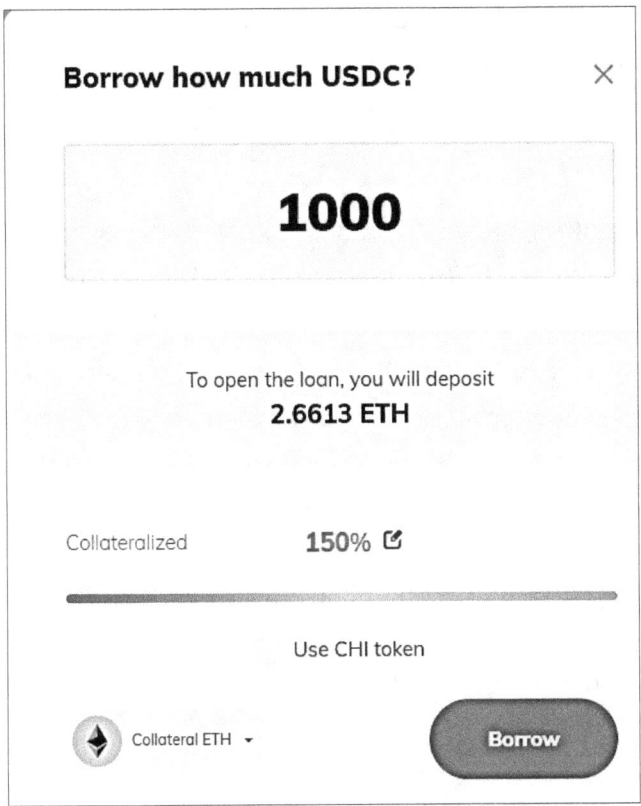

Figure 2.43

2.8 dYdX, a Lending, Borrowing and Trading Platform

dYdX is a decentralized platform that supports margin trading, spot trading, lending, and borrowing. The dYdX platform allows users to lend, borrow, or margin trade any supported asset like ETH, DAI, USDC, and more. Interest rates vary by asset and adjust with respect to supply and demand. Interest continuously accrues and is paid to lenders, minus 5% which is set aside for dYdX's insurance fund. In addition, dYdX allows users to borrow, lend and make bets on the future prices of popular cryptocurrencies. We shall focus on the lending and borrowing component of dYdX in this section and will discuss the trading component in another chapter.

On the dYdX platform, both lenders and borrowers interact with global lending pools via smart contracts (Hu, Getting Started With dYdX — Borrowing, n.d.). There is one global lending pool for each supported asset. When you deposit an asset on dYdX, your asset will be deposited into its corresponding lending pool, where borrowers can then borrow the same asset. This model allows borrowers and lenders on dYdX to deposit and withdraw assets at any time they wish.

To access dYdX platform, you can use the following link:

https://trade.dydx.exchange/margin/ETH-DAI

The website interface is as shown in Figure 2.44.

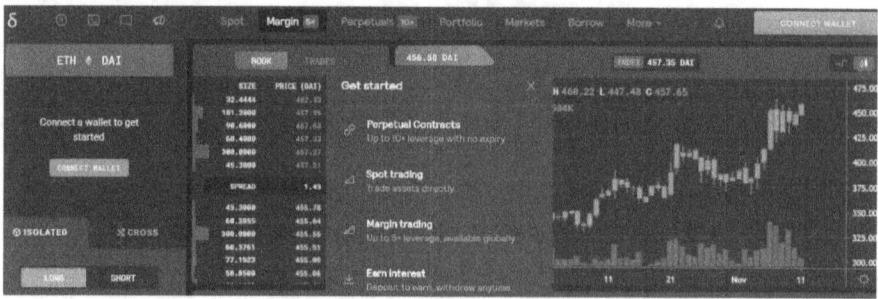

Figure 2.44

2.8.1 Lending

Lending on dYdX allows you to earn interest on your crypto assets in a passive way. This kind of investment is relatively low risk. By depositing crypto assets into your dYdX account, you will earn interest every second without having to perform any maintenance or worry about who are your borrowers (Hu, Getting Started With dYdX — Lending, 2019).

You may wonder how could dYdX afford to pay you interests perpetually? Where does the interest come from? Well, you do not have to worry. The interest you earn is paid by other users who are borrowing the same asset. As a matter of fact, dYdX will always ensure that borrowers always have enough collateral to be able to pay back their borrowed amount. If borrowers ever fall below a certain collateralization threshold, their collateral is automatically sold until they fully cover whatever amount they borrowed (Hu, Getting Started With dYdX — Lending, 2019).

Another good thing is while lending on dYdX, you have the freedom to withdraw your funds at any time. There is no lock up period, so as a lender you can deposit and withdraw funds whenever you wish.

Now, let us proceed to deposit some digital assets into dYdX. However, prior to that you must have installed the MetaMask wallet and purchased some supported cryptocurrencies. Currently dYdX only supports ETH, DAI and USDC. You can purchase them from any crypto exchange. Besides that, you must ensure that you have enough ETH in your wallet because every transaction requires gas fee.

To deposit some digital assets, click the 'portfolio' tab and click the 'balance' button as seen in Figure 2.44. You can choose to deposit in spot accounts, margin accounts as well as perpetual accounts. Depositing your asset into a spot account is a direct deposit, depositing into a margin account allows margin trading, and depositing into a perpetual account allows perpetual trading. Let us say we choose margin account. Next, click the Deposit button to bring up the Deposit dialog, as seen in Figure 2.45.

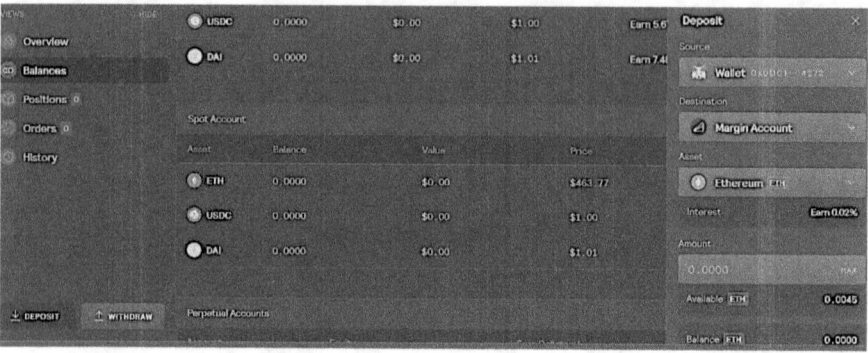

Figure 2.45

Now click Ethereum to view the drop-down list of tokens that you can deposit to earn interest. As you can see from Figure 2.46, only ETH, DAI and USDC are available.

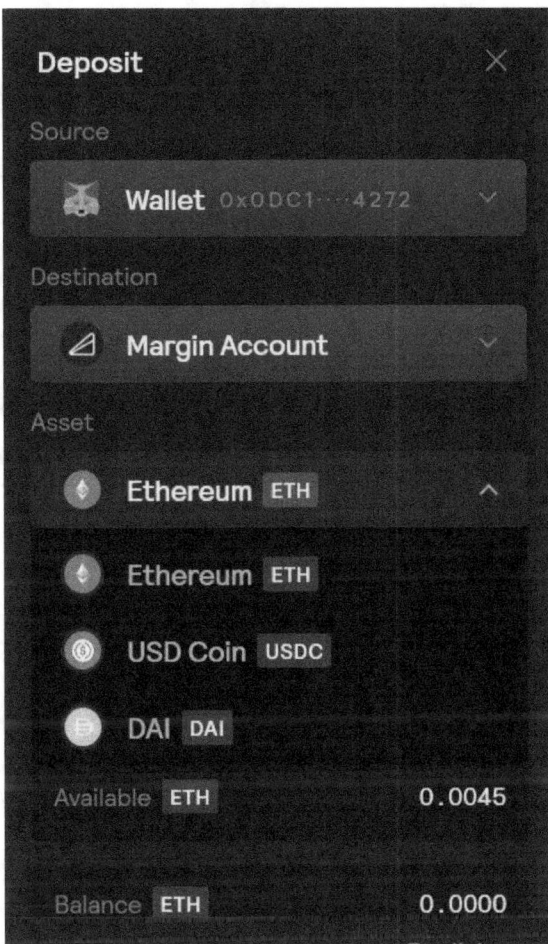

Figure 2.46

Let us click DAI to deposit it into dYdX. Clicking You must enable DAI for the first time and then confirm the transaction on the wallet.

I have deposited some DAI and I can see that I am earning 7.48% APY as shown in Figure 2.47. That is great! The good thing is you can withdraw your balance anytime, as shown in Figure 2.48, so it is relatively risk free.

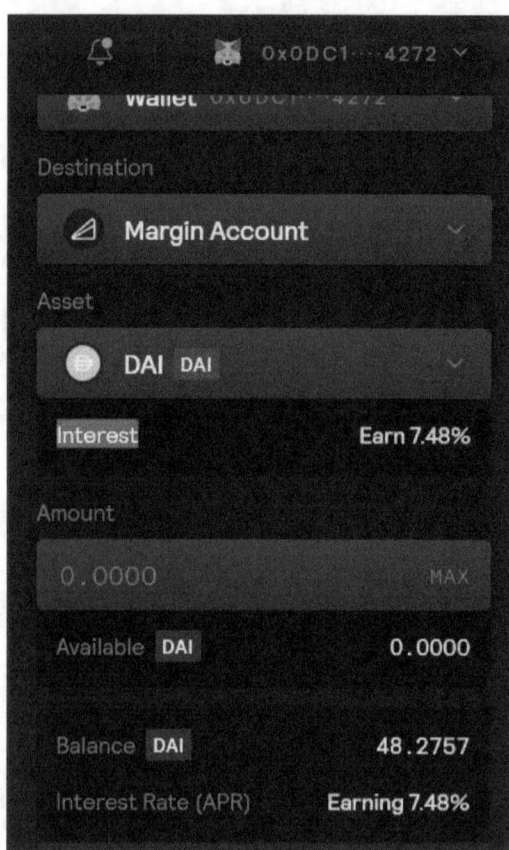

Figure 2.47

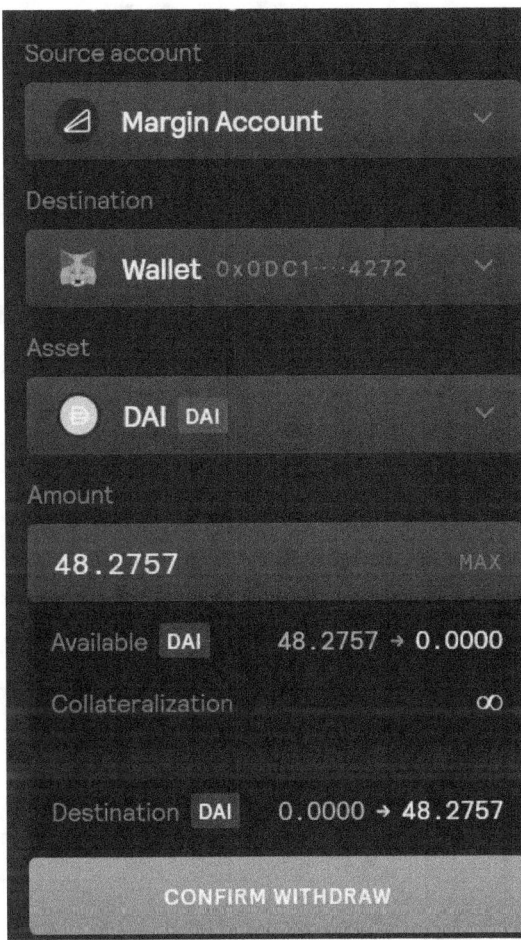

Figure 2.48

2.8.2 Borrowing

Borrowing allows you to hold your precious crypto assets such as ETH which you are not ready to liquidate yet and use them as collateral to obtain crypto funds to reap profits via trading, yield farming and more.

All borrowed funds must initially be collateralized with 125% of their value. Liquidation occurs if that ratio falls below 115% and comes with a 5% penalty. Traders can take leveraged long positions of up to 5x their collateral's value and 4x for shorts. Loans and margin trades can remain open for a max of 28 days, after which they are automatically closed out with a 1% expiration fee.

For example, let say your wallet balance has 0.9 ETH, which it is equivalent to about $400 at the price of $450 at the time of writing. You can then allow to borrow maximum up to $320 based on 125% collateral to debt ratio. This amount allows you to borrow 320 DAI.

The calculation is as follows:

Amount Borrowed (Debt) = 400/1.25 = 320 DAI

If one day the price of ETH falls to $409, the collateral becomes 0.9x$409 = $368. The collateral to debt ratio becomes 368/320 = 1.15 or 115%, which is below the liquidation threshold. Your collateral will be liquidated in the open market until you pay off your debt. On top of that, you must pay 5% liquidation fee. So, the final balance left will be as follows:

Assume 1 DAI = $1.00, then 320 DAI x $1.00 = $320

Balance After Liquidation = $368 - $320 = $68

Liquidation Fee = $320x5% = $16

Final Balance = $68 - $16 = $42 or 0.0103 ETH

To borrow from dYdX, navigate to the Borrow tab on its portal, as shown in Figure 2.49.

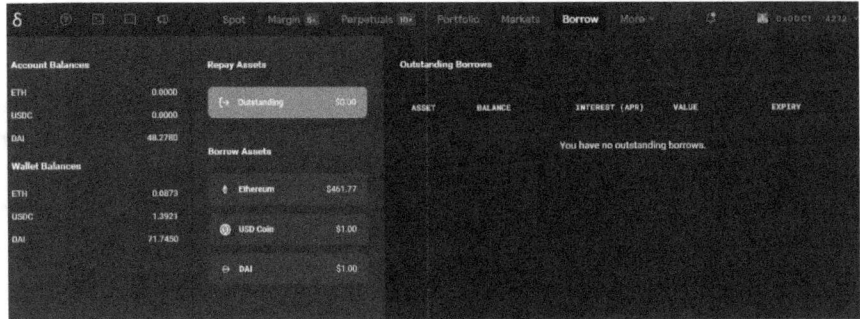

Figure 2.49

In this example, let us say you wish to borrow some DAI. Click DAI under 'BORROW ASSETS' and enter the amount you wish to borrow. The account collateralization will be displayed at the bottom. If the amount of ETH is not enough in your wallet, you need to top up the amount displayed at the bottom, as shown in Figure 2.50.

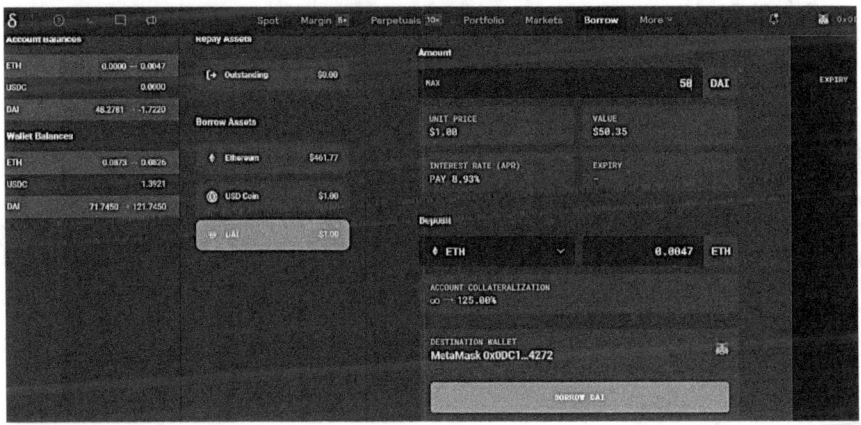

Figure 2.50

In the following example, let us borrow 50 USDC. Since the collateralization is 241.75%, which is more than the liquidation threshold of 125%, we do not need to top up ETH, as shown in Figure 2.51.

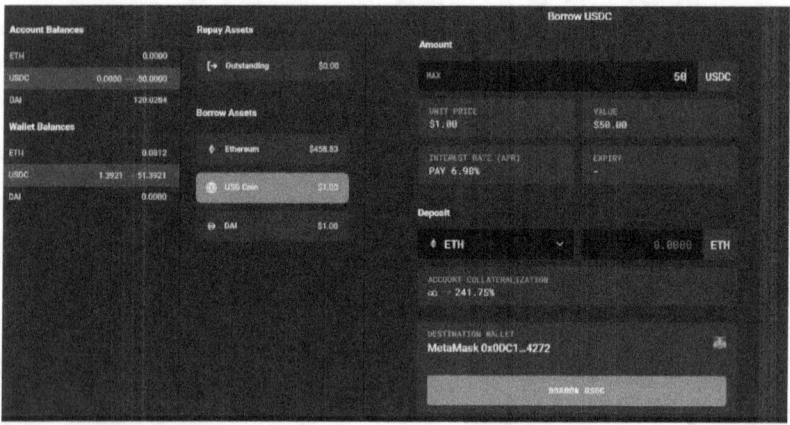

Figure 2.51

Once confirmed, your wallet will be funded with the amount of USDC you borrowed. This amount is also reflected in your balance as an outstanding amount (-50.0001), and the interest incurred is 7.44%, as shown in Figure 2.52.

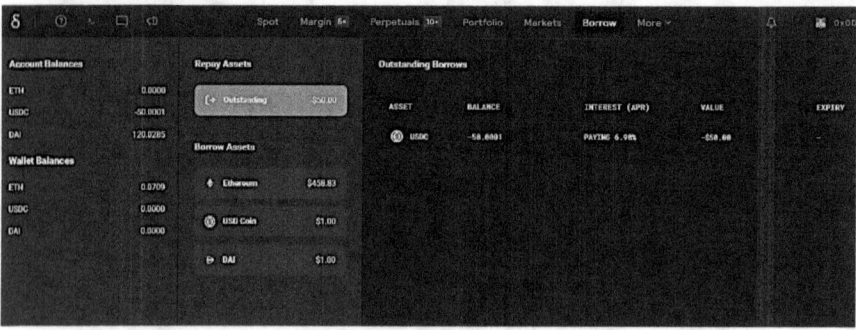

Figure 2.52

You can repay the amount anytime by hovering your mouse over USDC under 'OUTSTANDING BORROWS' and click the 'REPAY' button that pops up, as seen in Figure 2.53.

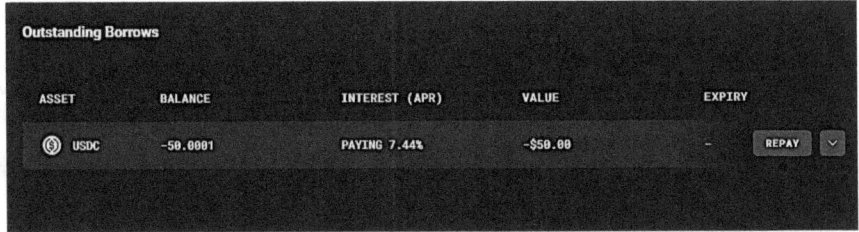

Figure 2.53

After repaying USDC, dYdX will show that you have no outstanding borrows, as seen in Figure 2.54.

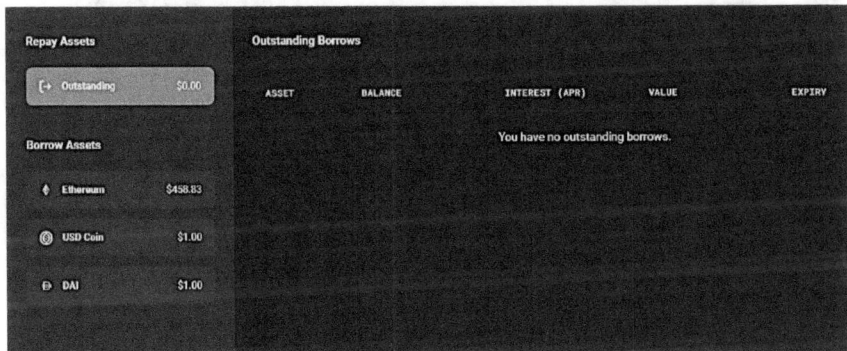

Figure 2.54

2.9 DeFi Saver-A One-Stop Lending and Borrowing App

DeFi Saver is a one-stop lending and borrowing decentralized finance protocols. It consolidates DeFi lending protocols comprising MakerDAO, Compound, dYdX and Aave (Defiprime, n.d.) all into one place. In addition, it provides a dozen of management tools for DeFi users. This provides users with a less fragmented, more streamlined experience.

To access Defi Saver, use the following link:

https://app.defisaver.com/

The landing page is as shown in Figure 2.55

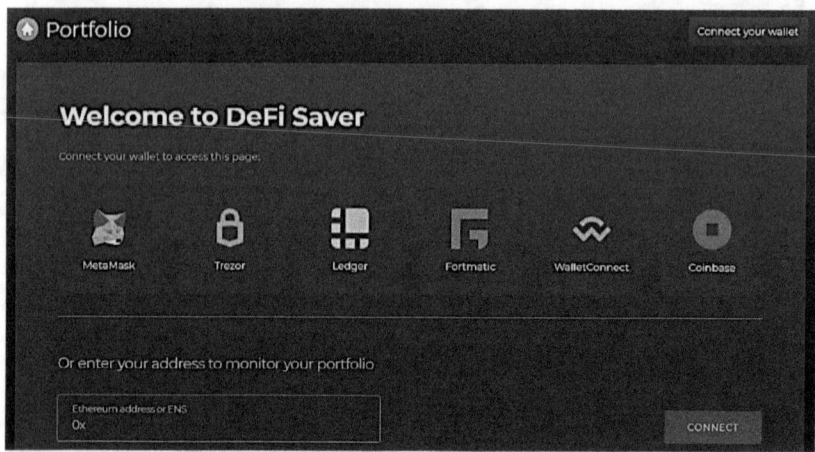

Figure 2.55

You are required to connect your wallet to continue. Once your wallet is connected, DeFi Saver will display your digital assets as well as your portfolio in MakerDAO, Compound and Aave, as shown in Figure 2.56.

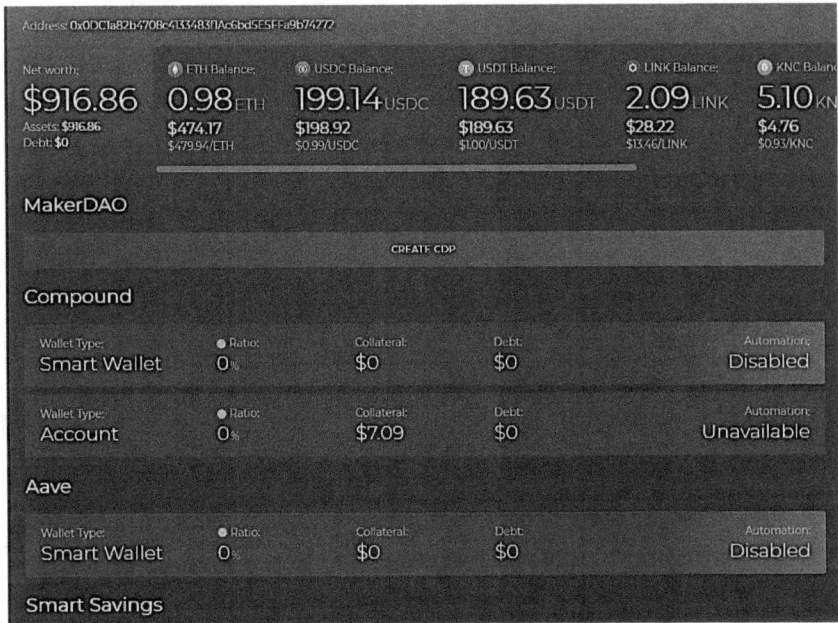

Figure 2.56

On the DeFi dashboard, you can manage and create your portfolio on any of the DeFi platforms directly without visiting those platforms. DeFi Saver has built the dashboard for every DeFi platform mentioned above. Let us explore them one by one.

2.9.1 MakerDAO Dashboard

We have learned about MakerDAO earlier in this chapter. Now, we shall deep dive into it to study how to create and interact with a Maker Vault.

Step 1 Create and Collateralize a Vault

We create a Vault by funding it with a specific type and amount of collateral that will be used to generate Dai (MakerDAO, n.d.). Once funded, a Vault will be collateralized.

Step 2 Generate Dai from the Vault

Having created the vault, you can generate Dai or you can leverage further by using the BOOST feature to add more collateral but at the same time increase our debts. The BOOST feature allows you to borrow more Dai to buy more ETH, this is akin to refinancing to buy another property. You are exposed to higher return with the expectation that the value of ETH will appreciate, but at the same time you are exposed to higher risk if the value of ETH goes down, not unlike the property market.

Step 3 Pay Down the Debt and the Stability Fee

You can withdraw a portion of all your collateral anytime. However, you must pay down or completely pay back the Dai plus the Stability Fee that continuously accrues on the Dai outstanding. Please note that the Stability Fee can only be paid in Dai.

Step 4 Closing the Position

Once you pay back all the Dai as well as the stability fee, you can retrieve your collateral. However, the Vault remains empty until you make another deposit. You can also close it completely.

I. Creating a CDP

To begin creating the vault, enter the MakerDAO dashboard by clicking the 'CREATE CDP' button. CDP means Collateralized Debt Position. There are several CDPs for you to choose from, as shown in Figure 2.57.

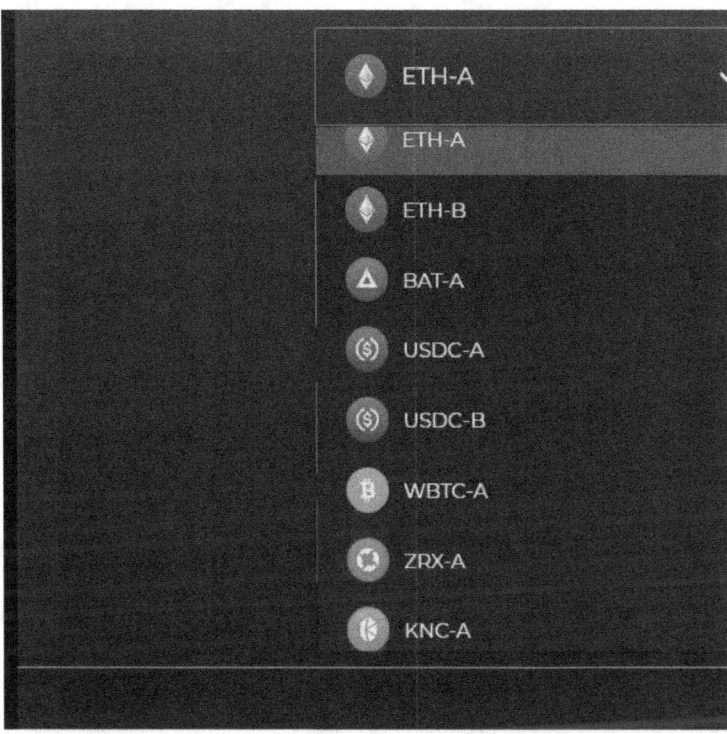

Figure 2.57

Our example is to create a CDP for ETH-DAI vault, as shown in Figure 2.58.

Figure 2.58

By depositing ETH as collateral, you can generate Dai. Notice that the liquidation ratio[3] is 150%. In addition, the collateralization ratio of 250% represents the collateral to debt ratio, which you can calculate based on the following formula:

$$\text{Collateralization Ratio} = \frac{Colleteral}{Debt} \times 100\%$$

Besides that, you need to pay 2.0% stability fee (i.e., continuously accruing interest). Generated Dai will be used to buy and add more ETH to the CDP and increase your leverage.

In addition, you can use leverage to open the position at CDP right away. It means MakerDAO allows you to supply ETH and generate DAI stablecoins to purchase more ETH for their position. This effectively

---

[3] [3] The Liquidation Ratio is the minimum required collateralization level for it to be considered undercollateralized and subject to liquidation (MakerDAO, n.d.).

created a Long ETH position where you would eventually earn more ETH in case its value went up. Previously you needed to generate 20 DAI minimum and then use Boost or generate Dai and use it to obtain ETH manually, but you do not have to do that now. Instead, all the generated Dai is instantly used to increase leverage and the interface will tell you just how much exposure you will gain. To open a leveraged CDP, check the Leveraged box, as shown in Figure 2.59.

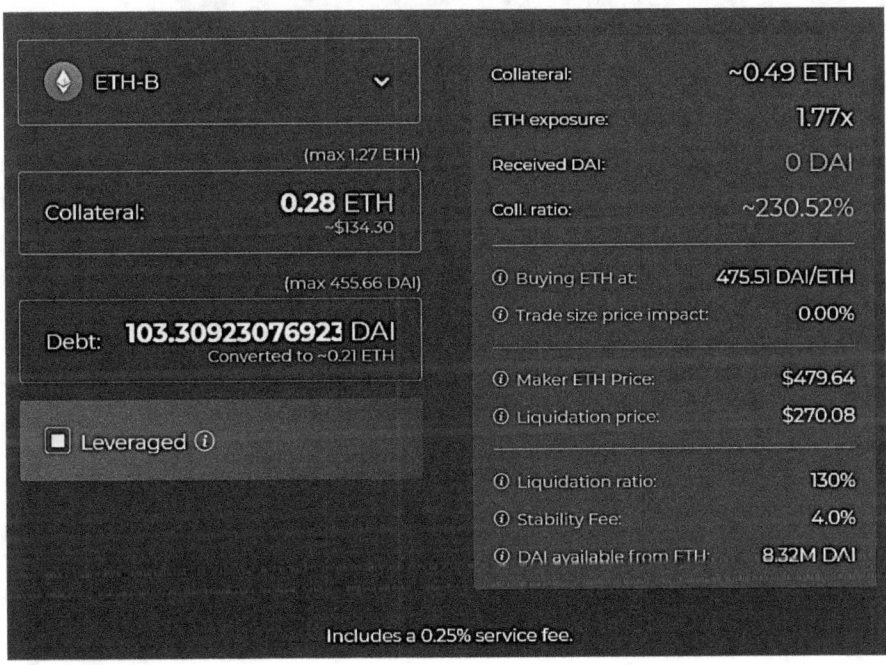

Figure 2.59

If you are satisfied with this position, click the 'CREATE' button to create the CDP. When you click the 'CREATE' button, you will receive a warning message, as shown in Figure 2.60. It tells you that the DAI generated will not be added to your wallet but will be used to buy additional collateral for your CDP to increase leverage.

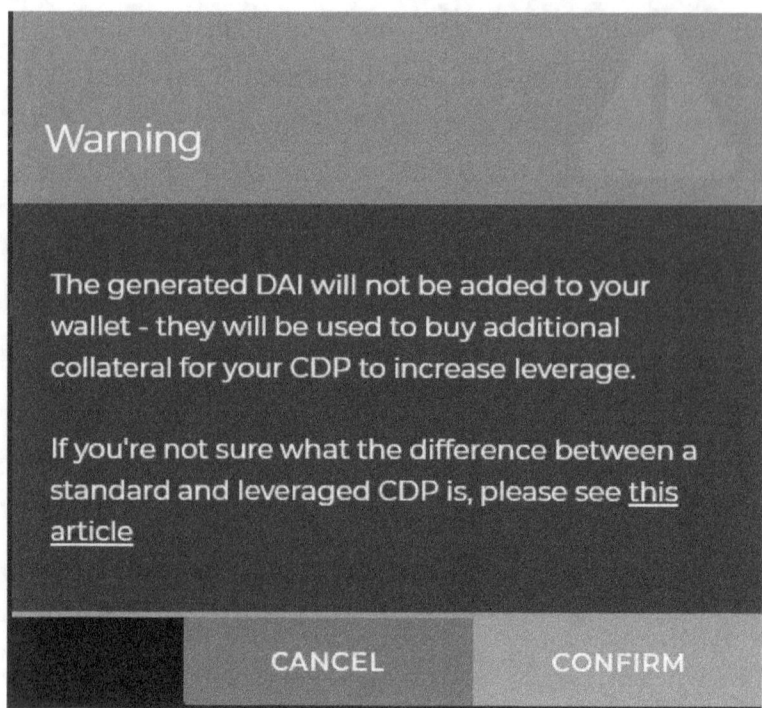

Figure 2.60

Next, you will be asked to confirm the transaction, as seen in Figure 2.61. It will show you the estimated gas fee.

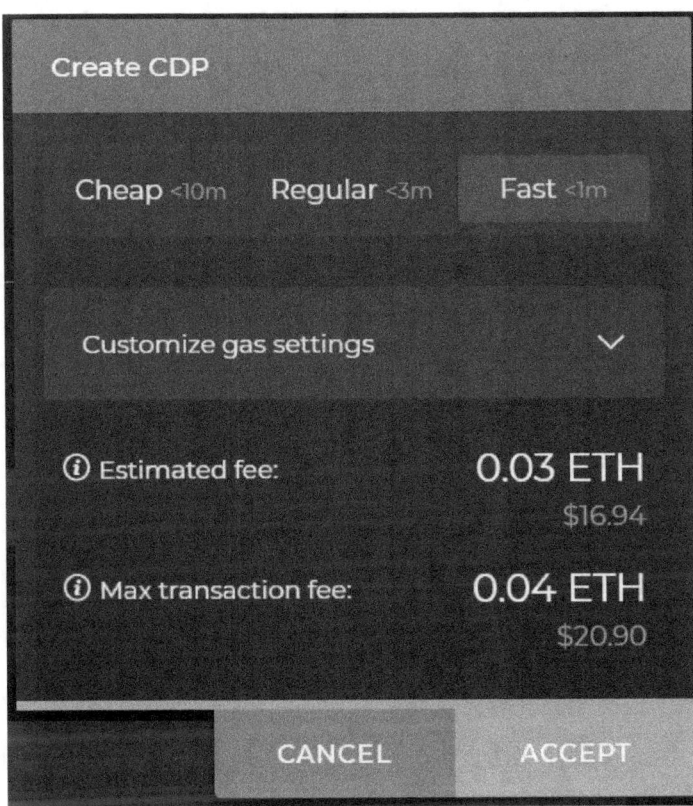

Figure 2.61

Once you accept the gas fee, click the 'ACCEPT' button and open your wallet to confirm the transaction. Once confirmed on the blockchain, you will be able to see your position as shown in Figure 2.62.

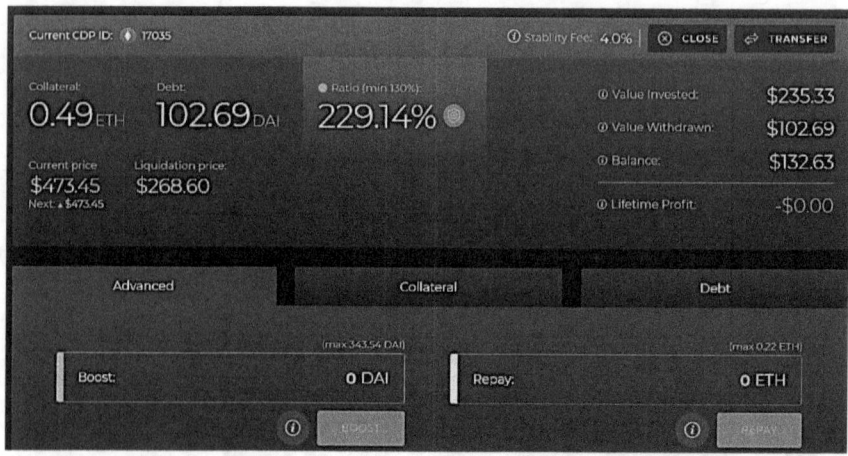

Figure 2.62

Now you can generate Dai by clicking the 'GENERATE' button, as shown in Figure 2.63.

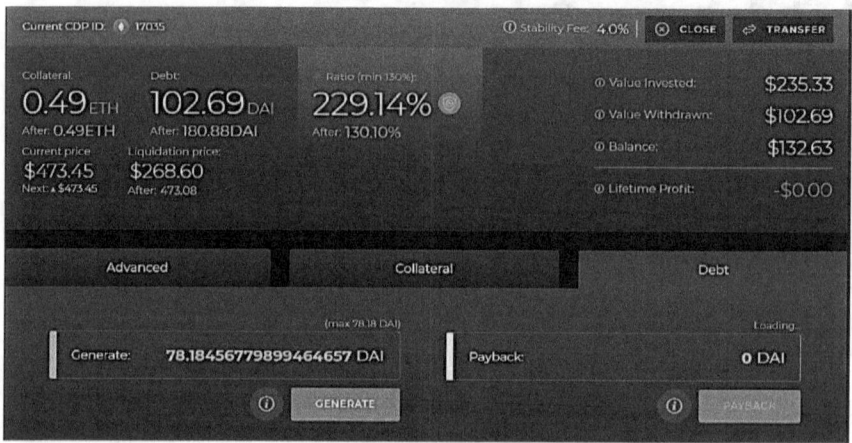

Figure 2.63

As usual you need to accept the transaction, as shown in Figure 2.64. It means you can short DAI, you will gain profit if the value of DAI depreciates when you pay back DAI. However, you may lose money if the price of DAI increases.

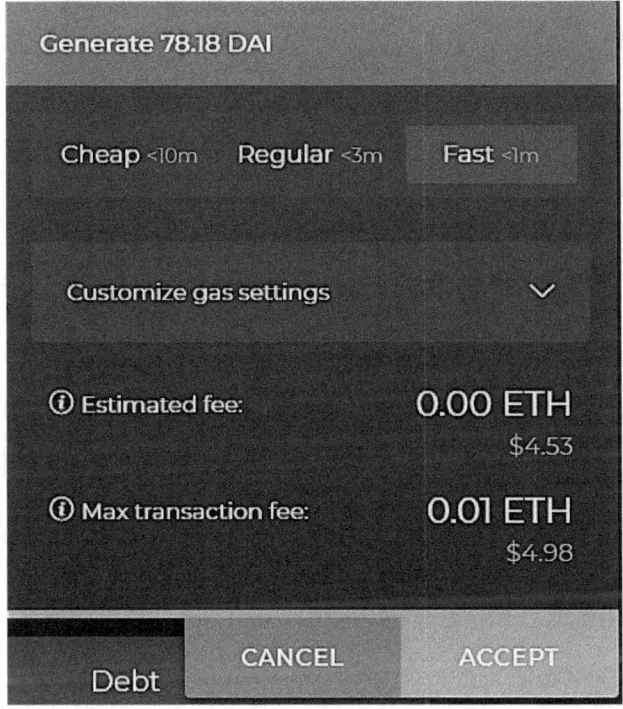

Figure 2.64

Finally, confirm the transaction on your wallet. Once the transaction has been verified, you can see that your wallet has been funded with Dai.

You can add collateral to avoid it falling below the liquidation ratio. I added 0.15 ETH to increase the value of collateral and now the ratio is well above the liquidation ratio, as shown in Figure 2.65.

Figure 2.65

Now you can use Boost to generate more Dai, use the Dai to buy ETH using multiple DEXs, and instantly add that ETH to your CDP vault. It will result in increased ETH exposure but a decrease in collateralization ratio. To boost, enter the amount of Dai and click the 'BOOST' button, as shown in Figure 2.66.

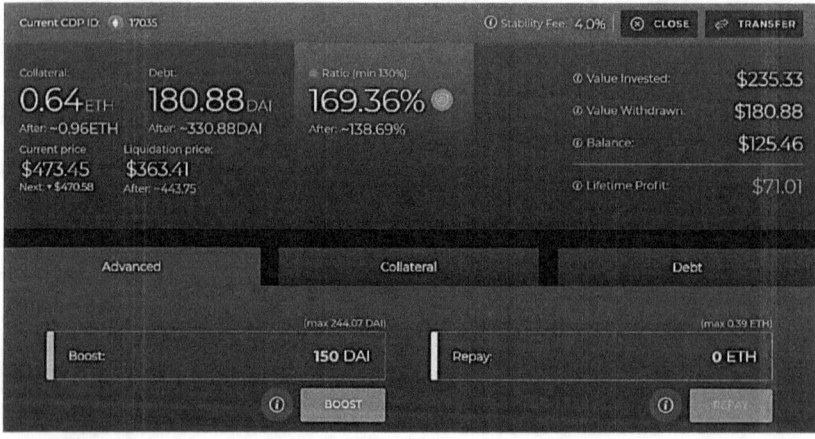

Figure 2.66

Clicking the BOOST button will bring up a message box (as shown in Figure 2.67) that presents some important messages like 'Boost generates Dai from your CDP to obtain more ETH. This increases your leverage at the cost of increasing your liquidation price and decreasing your collateralization ratio'. It will also show that it will sell your Dai at a few DEXs like 0x, Kyber, Uniswap and Oasis.

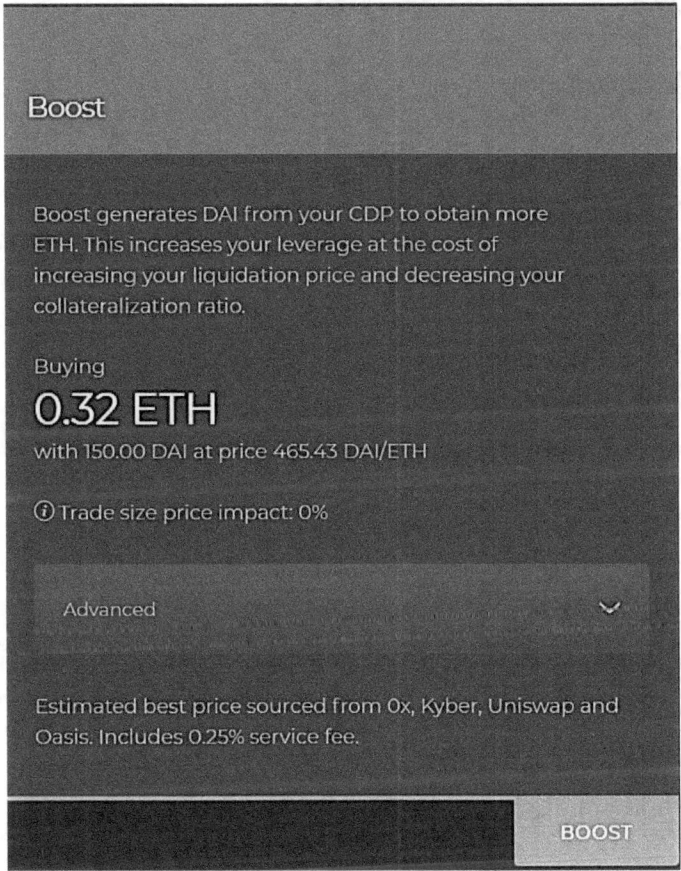

Figure 2.67

Next, click BOOST to continue. Subsequently you need to accept the gas fee you agree to pay, as seen in Figure 2.68.

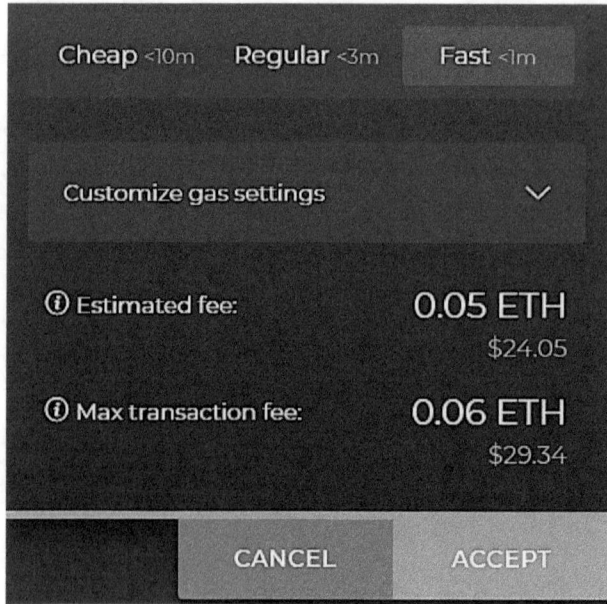

Figure 2.68

You can click repay button to pay off the debt together with the stability fee. The stability fee can be only be paid in Dai (MakerDao Whitepaper, n.d.). When you repay, it takes out a certain amount of ETH collateral, sells it for Dai and uses this Dai to instantly pay back your debt. It is a quick deleveraging, resulting in an increase in collateralization ratio and decreased debt. You can also close your position completely. If you pay back some Dai, your debt will be reduced and your collateralization ratio will increase, as seen in Figure 2.69.

Figure 2.69

II. Automate a CDP

In addition, if you have no time to maintain your CDP, you can opt for automation to avoid the risk of liquidation. Automation is a unique system built into MakerDAO that can automatically manage your collateralized debt position based on your configuration, effectively providing you with automatic liquidation protection and leverage increase (Jankovic, 2020).

Once automation is enabled, it will dynamically monitor your CDP and automatically increase or decrease leverage when price of the underlying collateral changes. Leveraging and deleveraging is done using the Boost and Repay functions.

Boost is applied once your ratio grows above the configured maximum ratio. When this happens, more DAI is generated and instantly used to obtain more ETH and add it to the CDP. This increases your ETH exposure, while also increasing your DAI debt and decreasing your ratio.

Repay is applied once your ratio drops below the configured minimum ratio. When this happens, part of the collateral from the CDP is taken out, instantly swapped for DAI and the DAI used to pay back debt. This increases your ratio, while decreasing your DAI debt as well as your ETH exposure.

Rest assured that automation will not use any funds in your Ethereum wallet account to pay for the gas fees. All adjustments are made solely using the collateral within the CDP Vault. To be eligible for automation, you must have at least 4000 DAI debt.

To set up automation, click the automate button to launch the CDP Automation Setup panel, as seen in Figure 2.70.

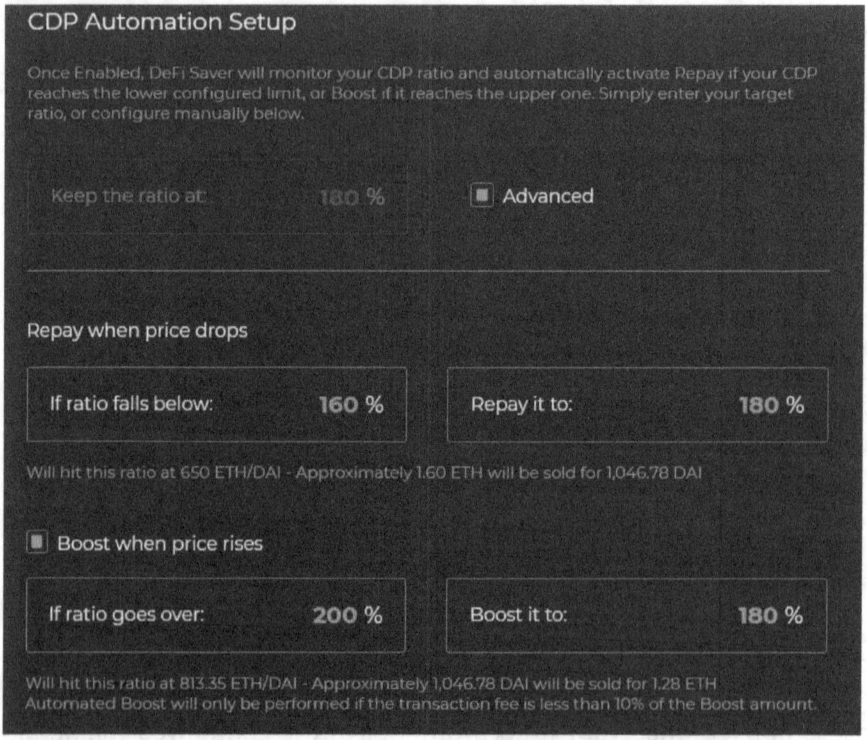

CDP Automation Setup

Once Enabled, DeFi Saver will monitor your CDP ratio and automatically activate Repay if your CDP reaches the lower configured limit, or Boost if it reaches the upper one. Simply enter your target ratio, or configure manually below.

Keep the ratio at: 180 %   ☐ Advanced

Repay when price drops

If ratio falls below: 160 %   Repay it to: 180 %

Will hit this ratio at 650 ETH/DAI - Approximately 1.60 ETH will be sold for 1,046.78 DAI

☐ **Boost when price rises**

If ratio goes over: 200 %   Boost it to: 180 %

Will hit this ratio at 813.35 ETH/DAI - Approximately 1,046.78 DAI will be sold for 1.28 ETH
Automated Boost will only be performed if the transaction fee is less than 10% of the Boost amount.

Figure 2.70

To configure automation, you must set your target collateralization ratio. In our example, we set it at 180%. First, set the ratio for repaying when price drop below a certain ratio to bring it back to 180%, in our case we set it at 160%. Secondly, we must set the ratio when you need boost when the price rises above a certain target, which we set it at 200%. After boosting it should bring back to 180%. The setting is as shown in Figure 2.71. Click enable button once you are satisfied.

If you are not sure how to set the ratios, you can use the simulation page to see your potential profit or loss by setting at various ratio. To access the simulator, click the following link:

https://defiexplore.com/simulation

The simulator is as shown in Figure 2.71.

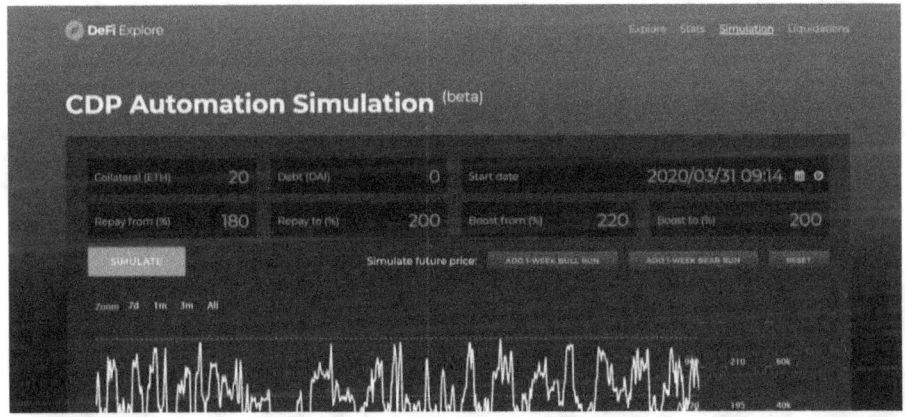

Figure 2.71

In the simulator, you can enter respective ratios and then see the outcomes below, as seen in Figure 2.72.

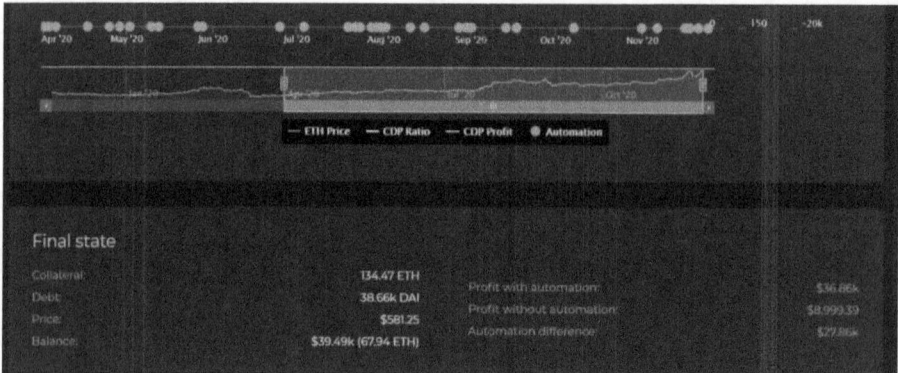

Figure 2.72

Once you are satisfied the outcomes you can then enter the ratios into the actual configuration panel. Once automation is enabled you can sit down and relax and see your profit grows. However, occasionally you must update the ratios particularly when the market is volatile.

You may check the automation activity history as shown in Figure 2.73.

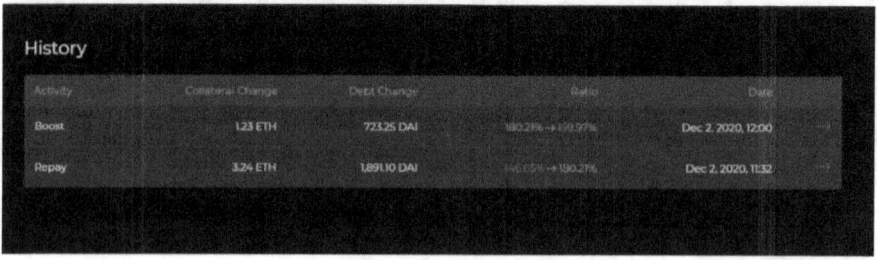

Figure 2.73

Clicking one of the activities will launch the detail transaction of the activity, as shown in Figure 2.74. It will show before and after the adjustment.

Figure 2.74

In addition, you can transfer your CDP to another wallet account by clicking the 'Transfer' button and key in the target wallet address, as shown in Figure 2.75. Besides that, you can close your CDP anytime.

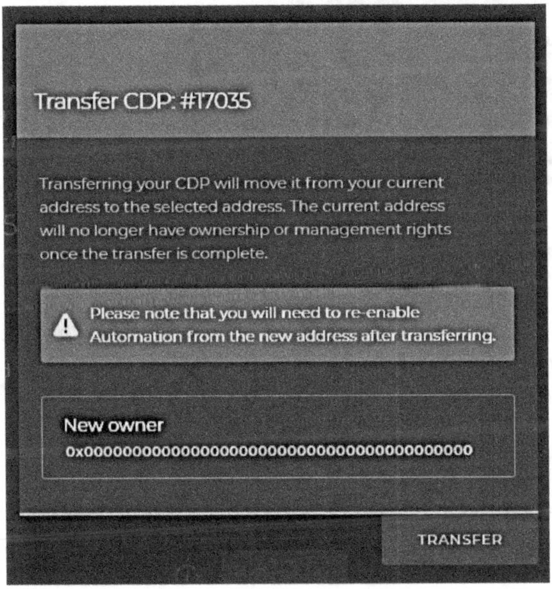

Figure 2.75

2.9.2. Compound Dashboard

Next, we move on to Compound by clicking the side tab. The Compound panel features a Smart wallet where you can open your position by depositing your asset as collateral and borrow other assets, as shown in Figure 2.76.

Figure 2.76

Let us deposit some UDSC as collateral. After clicking the 'SUPPLY' button, you are given the choice to select the gas fee and accept it, as shown in Figure 2.77.

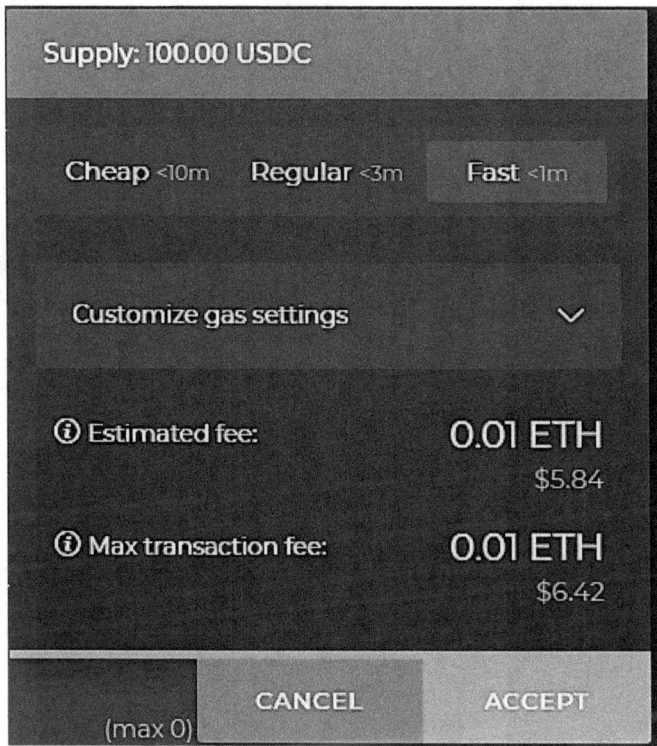

Figure 2.77

Clicking the ACCEPT button will launch your wallet and you must confirm the transaction. After your transaction is verified, you can view your position as shown in Figure 2.78.

Figure 2.78

Now let us use BOOST to buy more ETH, as shown in Figure 2.79.

Figure 2.79

Clicking the BOOST button will bring up a dialog box that shows you how many USDC you can buy, as seen in Figure 2.80. Click BOOST to continue.

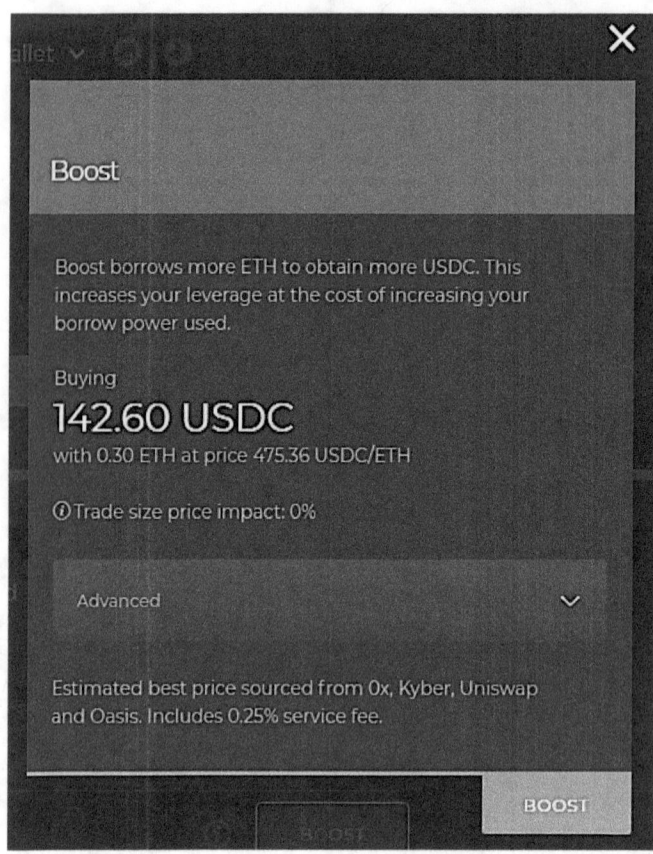

Figure 2.80

After boosting is confirmed, you can view your position as shown in Figure 2.81.

Figure 2.81

You can see that your supply now has increased to $250.07 and your collateralization ratio is 124.32%, still way above the liquidation ratio of 100%.

2.9.3. Aave Dashboard

Next, we move on to Aave. The UI is the same as the previous two. Let us supply USDC, as seen in Figure 2.82.

Figure 2.82

Click the 'SUPPLY' button to proceed. Next, select the gas fee you are comfortable with, as shown in Figure 2.83.

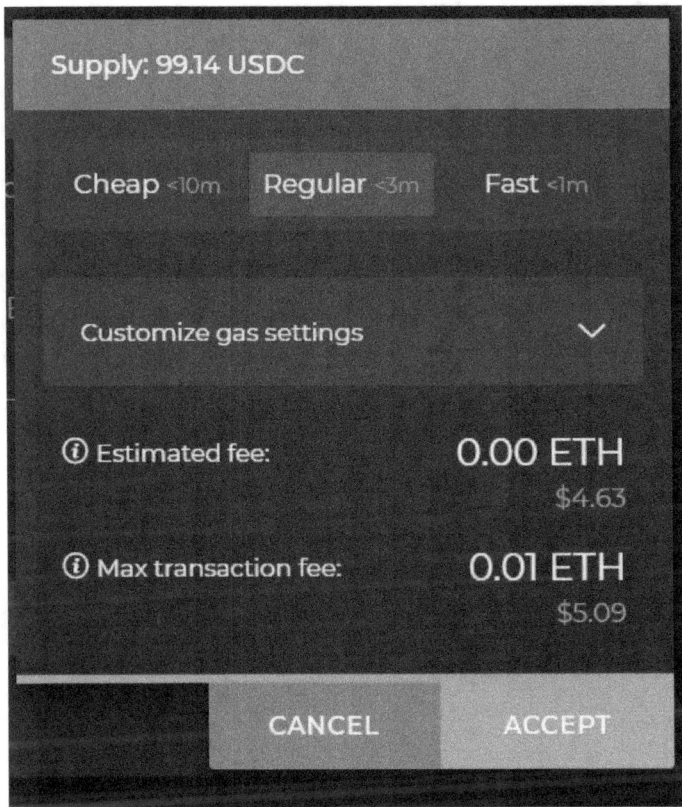

Figure 2.83

Subsequently, click 'ACCEPT' and confirm the transaction on your wallet. Once the transaction is confirmed you can view your position on the Aave dashboard, as shown in Figure 2.84.

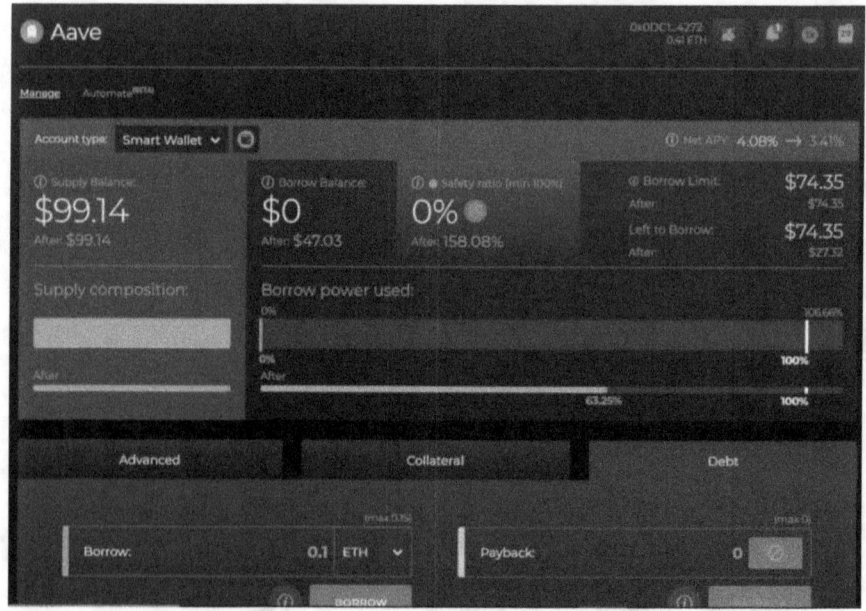

Figure 2.84

You may now proceed to create Debt via BOOST, let say ETH, as seen in Figure 2.84. Click 'BORROW" on the next screen as seen in Figure 2.85.

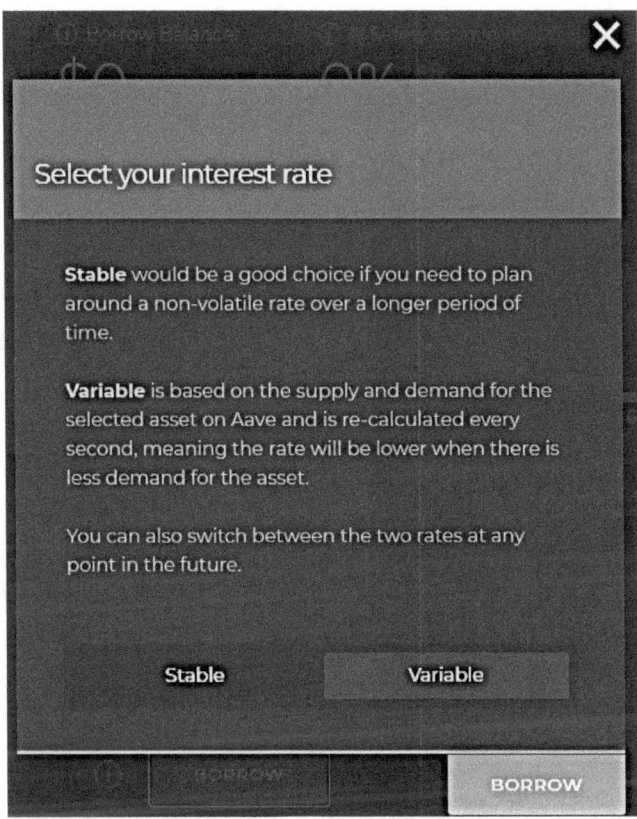

Figure 2.85

Next, accept the gas fee rate as seen in Figure 2.86.

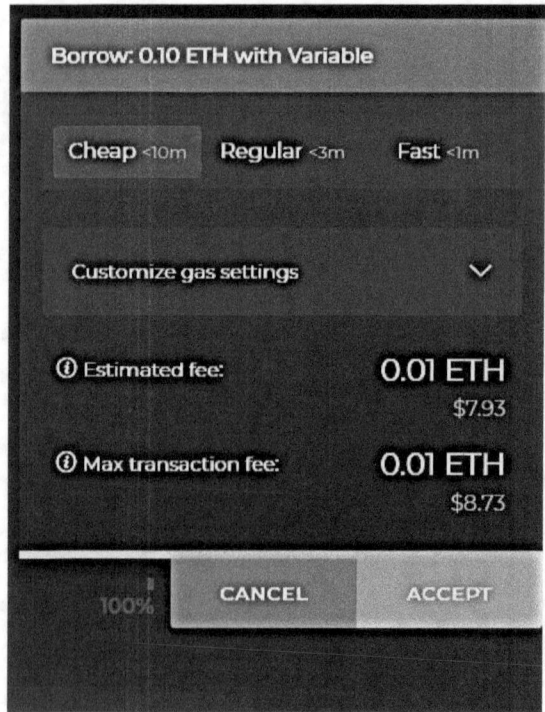

Figure 2.86

Finally, click on the 'CONFIRM' button to approve the transaction. Upon confirmation you can view your position as shown in Figure 2.87.

Figure 2.87

You can see your 'Borrow Balance' of $47.03 which is the price of 0.1 ETH that has been added to your wallet.

2.9.4. Smart Savings

Smart Savings allows you to deposit funds, move funds and view your balances, as shown in Figure 2.88.

Figure 2.88

You can choose to supply DAI to the protocols comprising Compound, dYdX, Maker DSR and AAVE and start earning interests. Once you have supplied DAI to any of the platforms, the deposited amount will be displayed, as shown in Figure 2.89.

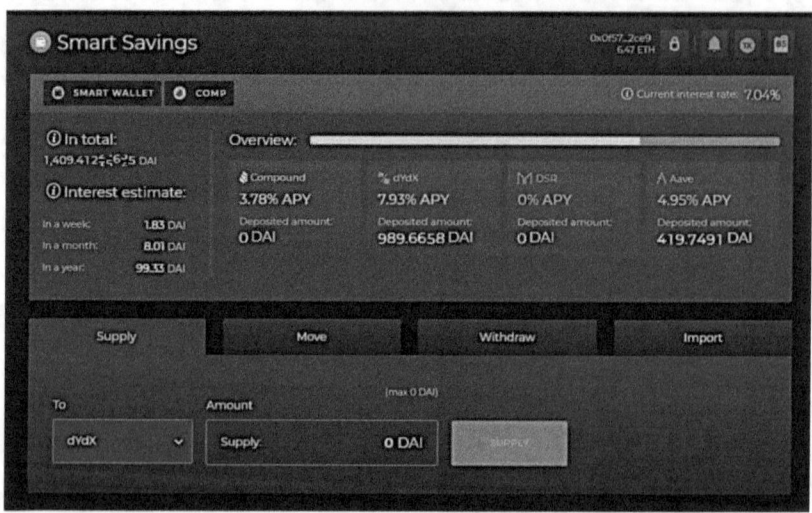

Figure 2.89

You will notice that interests will be added to the amount every second!

You may move the assets from one protocol to another by clicking the 'Move' button. For example, you may want to move all the DAI in AAVE to dYdX, as shown in Figure 2.90.

Figure 2.90

You may withdraw your assets in Smart Savings anytime from any of the protocols. Here I choose to withdraw all the Dai from dYdX, as shown in Figure 2.91.

Figure 2.91

2.9.4. Exchange

Besides that, you can swap token on DeFi Exchange, as seen in Figure 2.92.

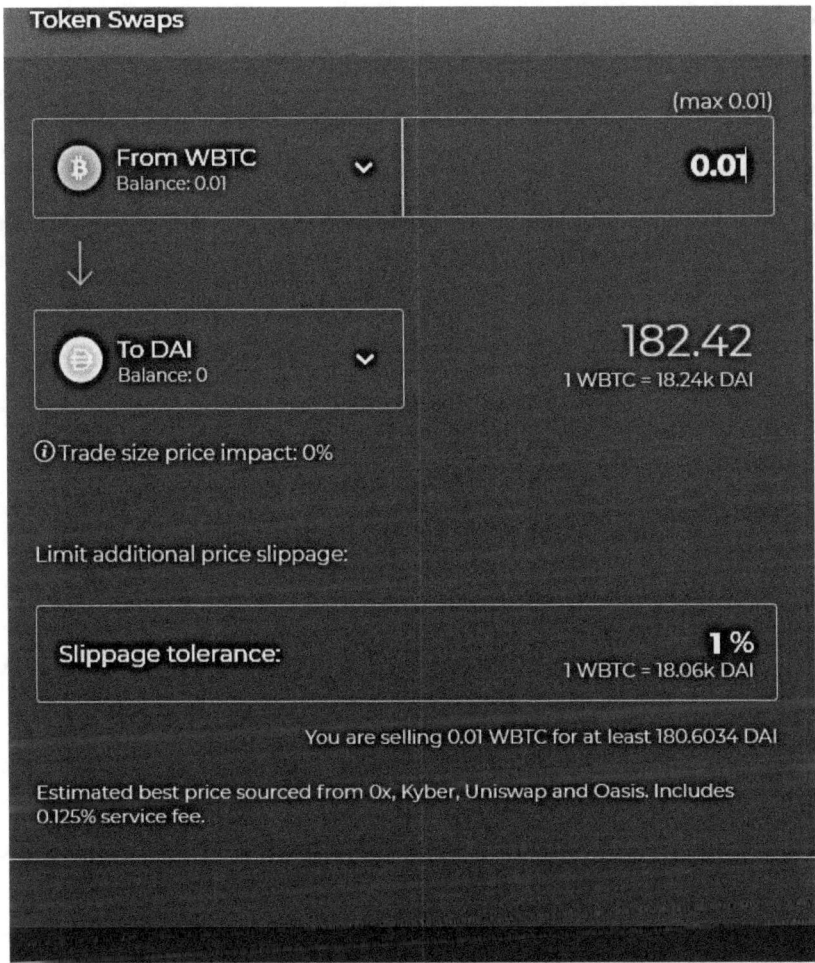

Figure 2.92

2.9.5. Loan Shifter

DeFi Saver also offers the 'Loan Shifter' for shifting your position between protocols or change your collateral and debt assets, a kind of rebalancing act. For example, you might want to shift your position from CDP #17035(ETH-B) to ETH-A CDP, you can select it from the drop-down list, as shown in Figure 2.93.

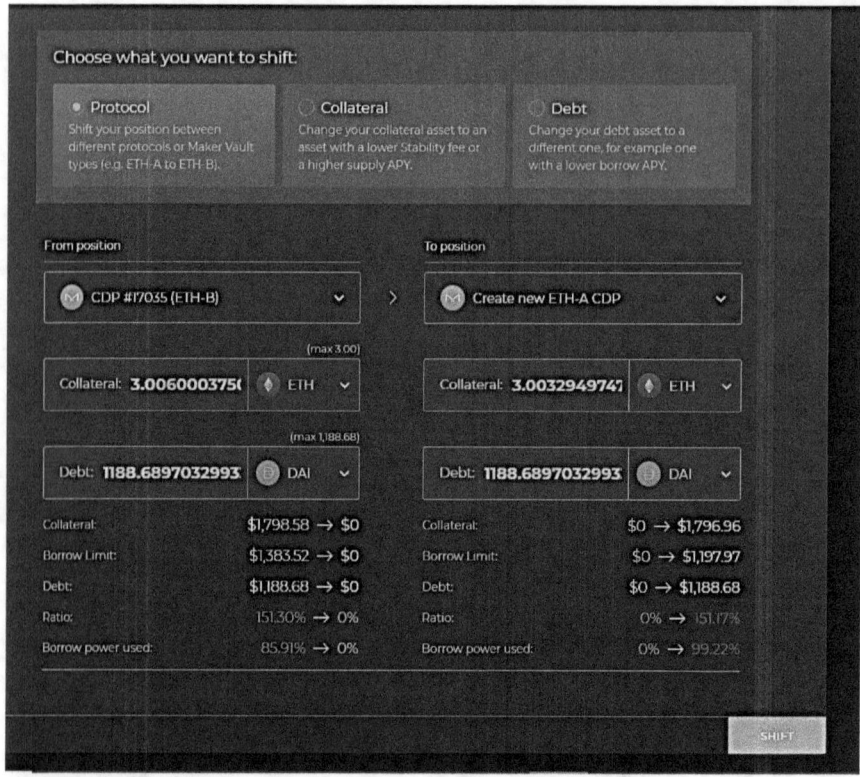

Figure 2.93

You can compare the collateral, borrow limit, debt, collateralized ratio and borrow power used before making your decision to shift. If you have decided to shift, just click the 'Shift' button to complete the action.

The following example is to shift your collateral from CDP ETH-B to USDC-A CDP, as shown in Figure 2.94.

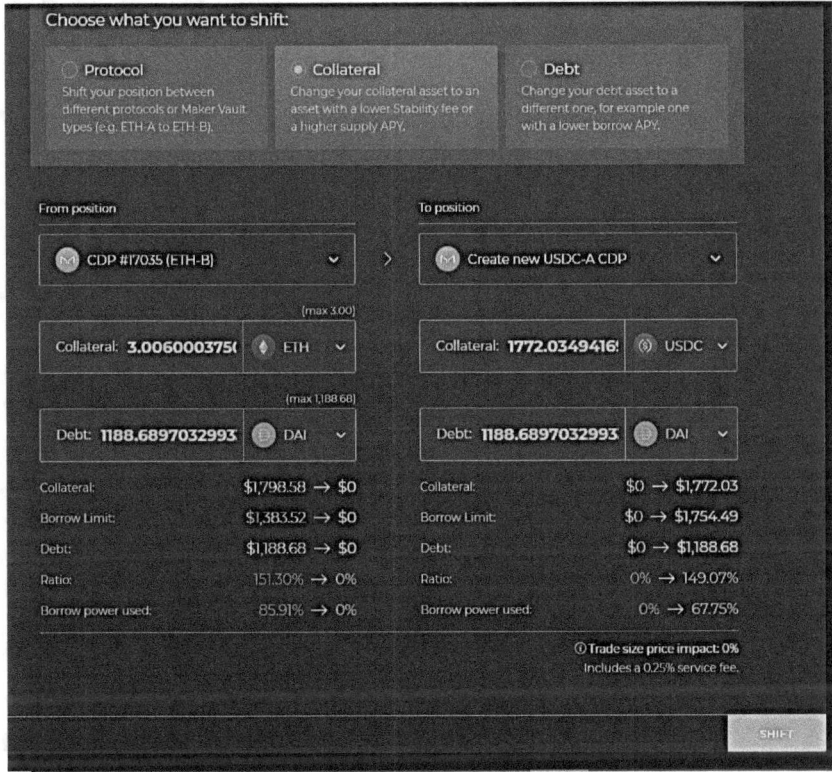

Figure 2.94

The Shift function is still at Beta stage so debt shifting is still not available.

2.10 InstaDApp

InstaDApp is a smart wallet built on top of popular DeFi projects like MakerDAO, Compound, Uniswap and more for managing assets. It is optimized for users who do not possess advanced technical or financial knowhow. InstaDApp allows users to perform complex actions like leveraging, or saving by buying or selling collateral in a single transaction. One of InstaDApp's most popular features is its Bridge which allows users to migrate debts between Maker Vaults and Compound Finance. Other features include the option to lend assets or add liquidity to Uniswap pools.

To access InstaDApp, use the following link:

htttps://defi.instadapp.io/

The dashboard is as shown in Figure 2.95.

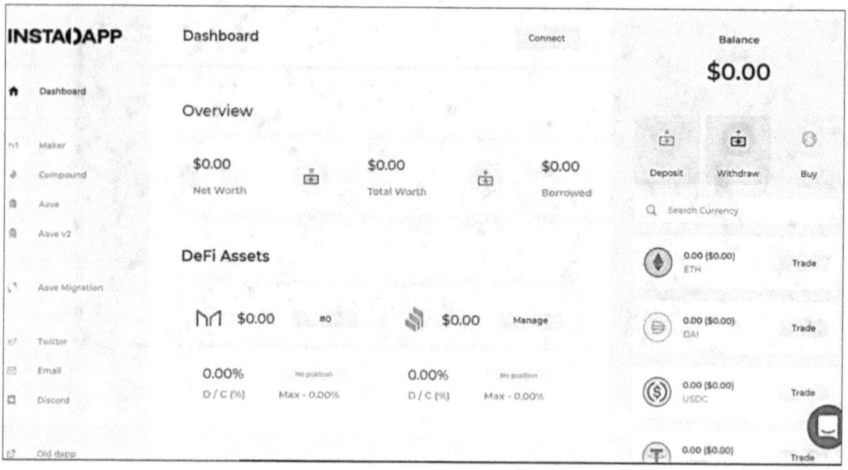

Figure 2.95

You can see that you can borrow or lend assets using Compound, Aave and Maker. You can even create a CDP on Maker. Let say you want to supply or borrow some assets on AAVE V2, just click the link to launch the dashboard, as shown in Figure 2.96.

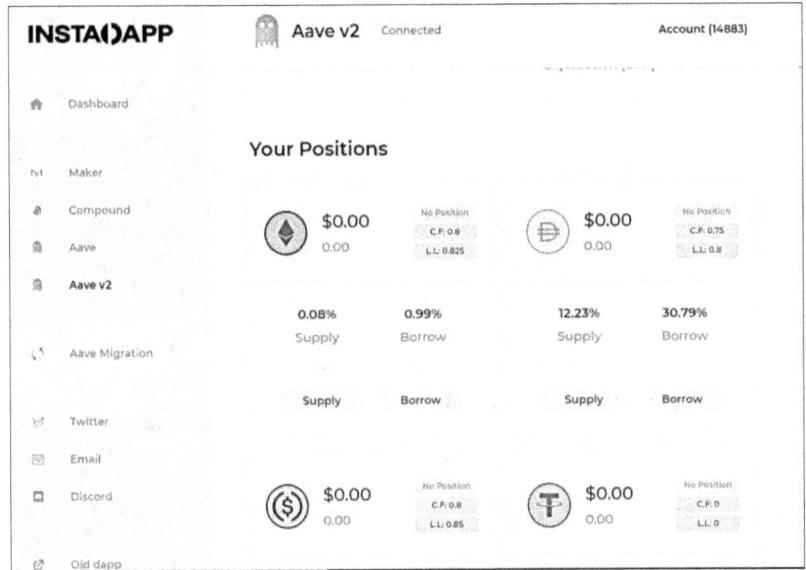

Figure 2.96

To create a CDP on Maker, select the collateral of your choice, as shown in Figure 2.97.

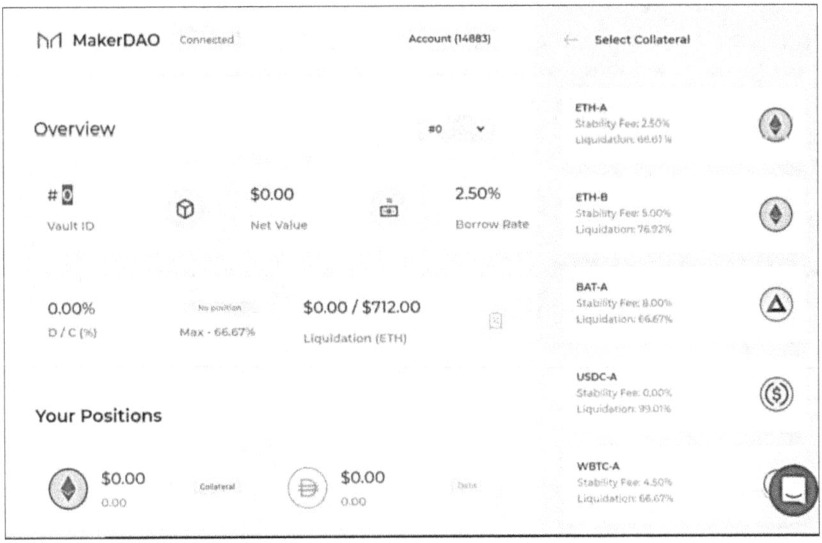

Figure 2.97

Next, click the collateral you wish to supply and enter the amount, as shown in Figure 2.98.

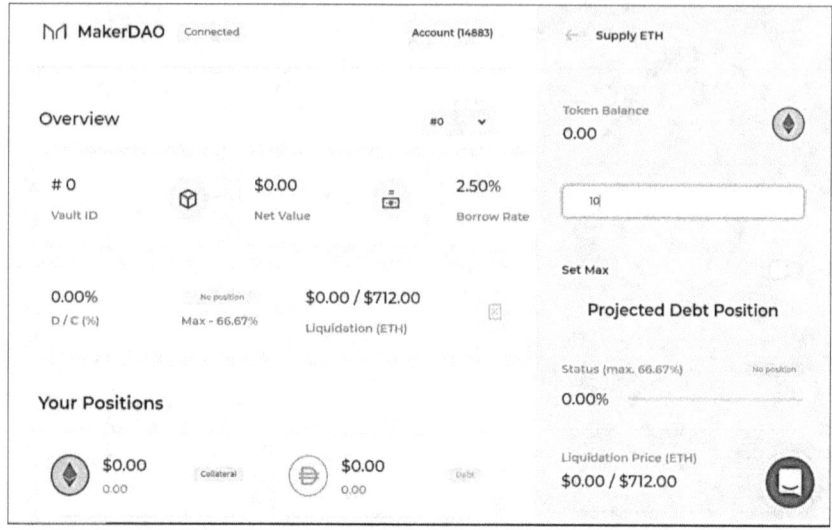

Figure 2.98

Once done you position will appear on the dashboard.

Chapter 3
Decentralized Exchanges

Numerous decentralized exchanges sprang up recently in tandem with craze of DeFi to cater for the needs of the investors. Decentralized exchanges or DEX are like stock exchanges but run by smart contracts on the Ethereum blockchain. While both allow you to trade assets, decentralized exchanges only trade cryptocurrencies and do not require centralized authorities to operate. Some of the popular exchanges are dYdX, Uniswap, Bancor, Kyberswap, Balancer, Sushiswap and more. Let us example some of the more popular decentralized exchanges.

3.1 dYdX

As we have learned in the previous chapter, dYdX is a decentralized platform that supports margin trading, spot trading, lending, and borrowing. The dYdX platform allows users to lend, borrow, or margin trade any supported asset like ETH, DAI, USDC, and more. We have learned how to lend and borrow, now let us delve into its trading component.

3.1.1 Margin Trade

Margin trade or rather buy on margin means to use money borrowed from a broker to purchase securities (Investopedia, n.d.). You must have a margin account to do so, rather than a standard brokerage account. A margin account is a brokerage account in which the broker lends the investor money to buy more securities than what they could otherwise afford with the balance in their account.

In dYdX, margin is the collateral amount being deposited by the users. Borrowed funds are collateralized by other digital assets like USDC, DAI or ETH and must be repaid with interest. There are two types of margin offers by dYdX, cross margin and isolated margin. Cross margin means trading using your account balances as collateral whilst isolated margin means opening a position independently collateralized from your account, usually from your wallet.

Additionally, dYdX offers up to 5x leverage when you conduct margin trading. You can create leverage when you trade margin. Leverage increases your buying power available to place a higher value trade than you could afford. However, while leverage increases the potential reward for you as a trader, it also increases the risk.

To begin margin trading, click the Margin tab to open the margin trading web page, as shown in Figure 3.1.

Figure 3.1

On the left panel of the trading webpage, you can see your MARGIN ACCOUNT BALANCES, the ISOLATED and CROSS buttons, the LONG and SHORT buttons, LEVERAGE selections, POSITION SIZE and more, as seen in Figure 3.2.

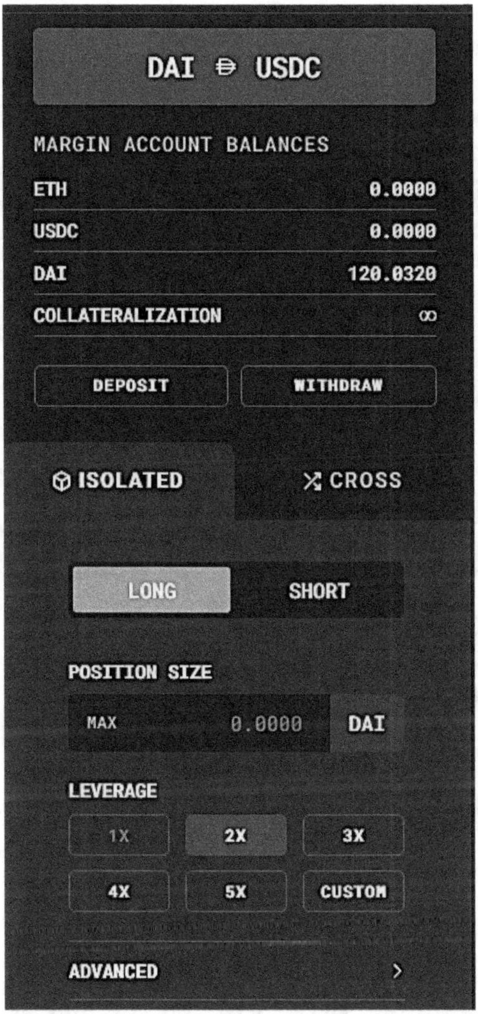

Figure 3.2

To open your position using ISOLATED margin, select the trading pairs you wish to trade. Currently dYdX offers three trading pairs comprising ETH-DAI, ETH-USDC and DAI-USDC, as seen in Figure 3.3.

Figure 3.3

Let us select DAI-USDC and go long to buy USDC with 300 DAI and 5x leverage. After entering your position size, you will notice the margin deposit is 60 DAI, as seen in Figure 3.4.

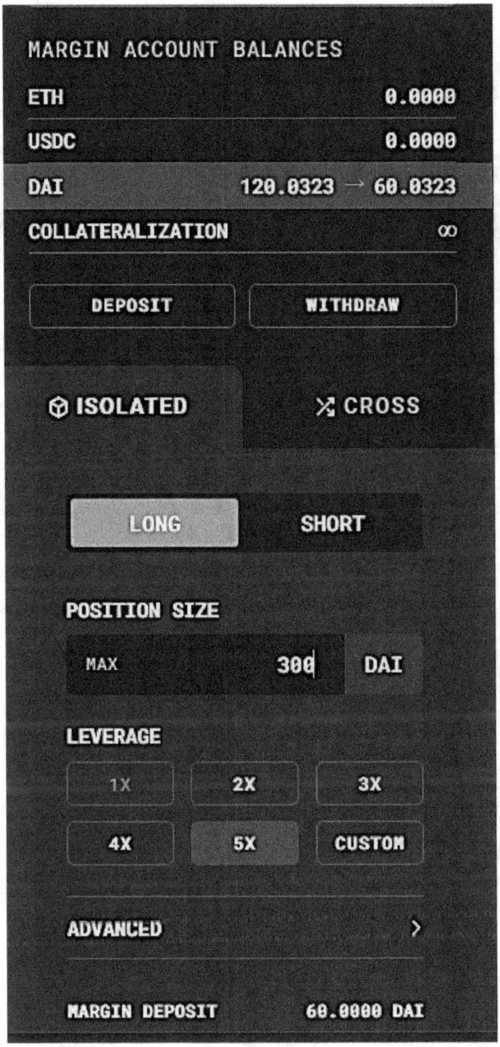

Figure 3.4

When you scroll down the trading pane, you can view other fields such as TRADE AMOUNT, EXPECTED PRICE, LIQUDATION PRICE and more, as seen in Figure 3.5.

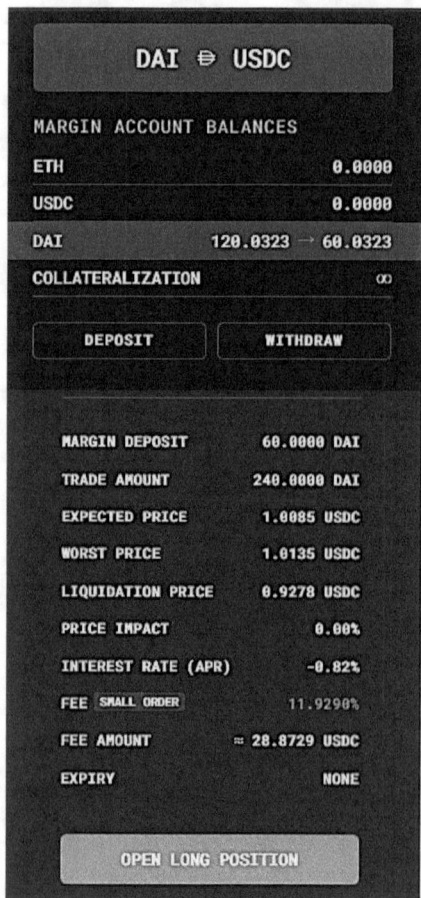

Figure 3.5

Margin deposit is your own personal stake deducted from your balance, which is 60 DAI as seen in Figure 3.5. On the other hand, trade amount is the remaining portion of your position which is 240 DAI, consisting of borrowed funds. Adding up both equals to your position size, which is 300 DAI.

Although borrowing funds allows you to gain more exposure to the market than you normally would be able to, you are also exposed to additional risk compared to trading with your own funds. In the event your collateralization ratio gets dangerously low and crosses the liquidation threshold, your position will get liquidated. Upon liquidation, collateral in your position will be sold until all your negative balances are zero, and a 5% liquidation fee will be taken. The liquidation fee is calculated based on the liquidation price as indicated in Figure 3.5.

Interest rate is the average interest rate your position will pay or earn depending on the market rates: you earn interest on the collateral locked in your position and pay interest on the amount borrowed. A negative interest rate indicates you will be paying interest, whilst a positive interest rate means you will be earning interest. In our case, you will pay an interest of 0.82%. The interest rate changes based on supply and demand; you can always track each individual asset interest rate on the markets page.

You also need to pay the fee that will cover the transaction. All trades on dYdX are resolved on-chain, and dYdX covers 100% of the gas fees for each trade.

You will notice that there is no expiration date. However, this is not true for US citizens. US regulations require all margin trades to have a 28-day expiration.

After clicking OPEN LONG POSITION, it will bring up your MetaMask wallet which requires you to sign the transaction. Upon signing the 'SIGN' button, the long position will be successfully opened. Once your position is opened, you have the option to close it anytime.

Once your position is confirmed, it will be shown in your portfolio, as shown in Figure 3.6.

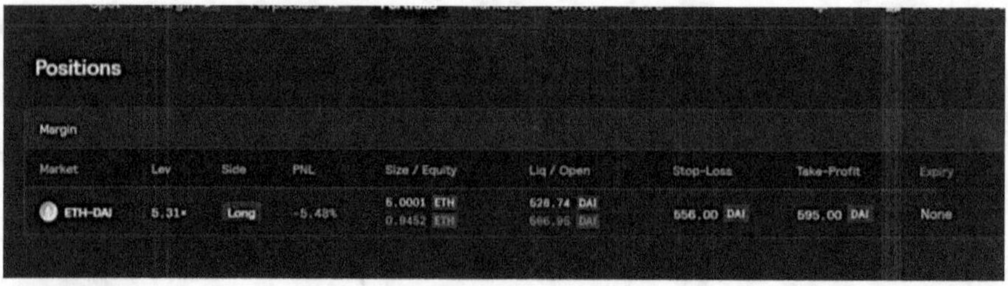

Figure 3.6

You can also add a stop loss price and a take profit price, as shown in Figure 3.7. Besides that, you may close your position anytime.

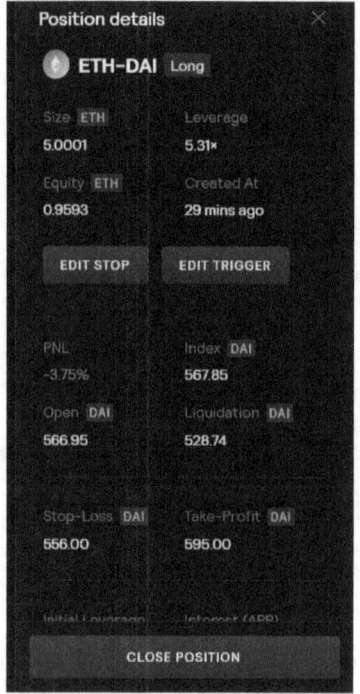

Figure 3.7.

To go short, you go through the same process. Just click the 'SHORT' button, and enter the amount you wish to go short, as shown in Figure 3.8.

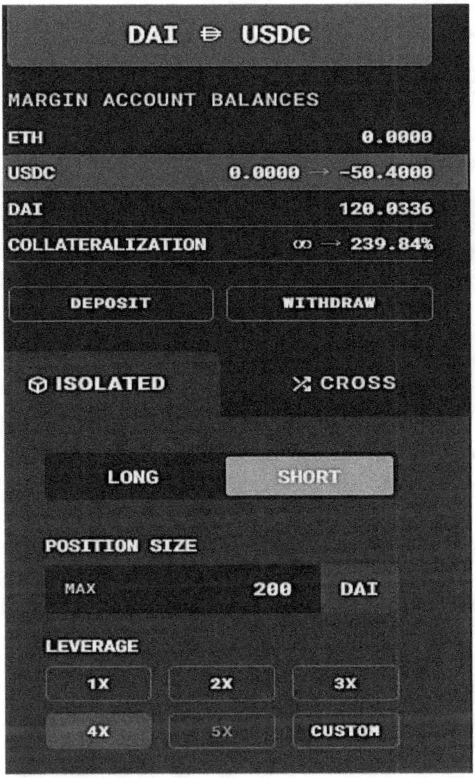

Figure 3.8

The margin deposit, trade amount, expected price, interest and more are shown in Figure 3.9.

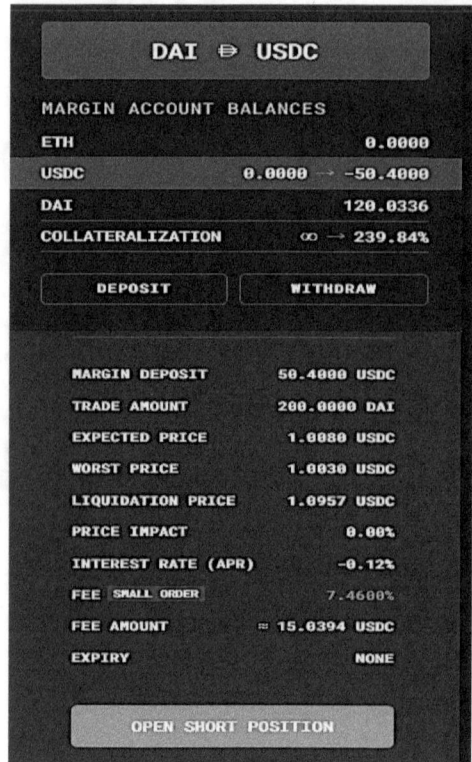

Figure 3.9

Cross margin trading utilizes all assets in your dYdX account balance as collateral. Cross margin trades are subject to the same collateralization rules as borrowing and lending on dYdX. All positive balances earn interest, and all negative balances pay interest. To start buying and selling using cross margin, click the 'CROSS' button and place your order, whether buying or selling, as shown in Figure 3.10. The process is the same as trading using Isolated Margin.

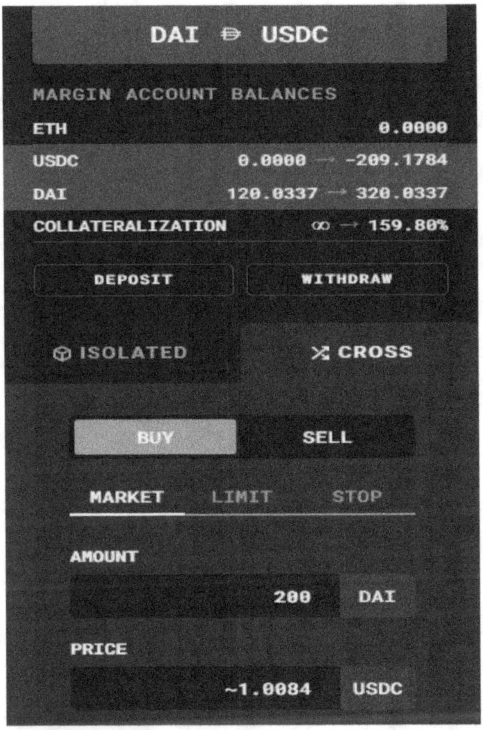

Figure 3.10

The following is an example of a short position, as shown in Figure 3.11 and Figure 3.12.

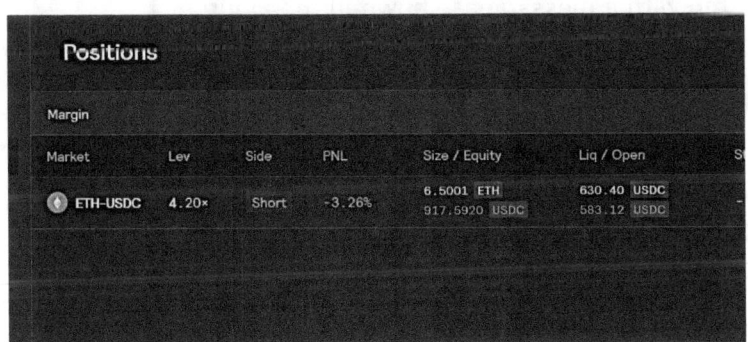

Figure 3.11

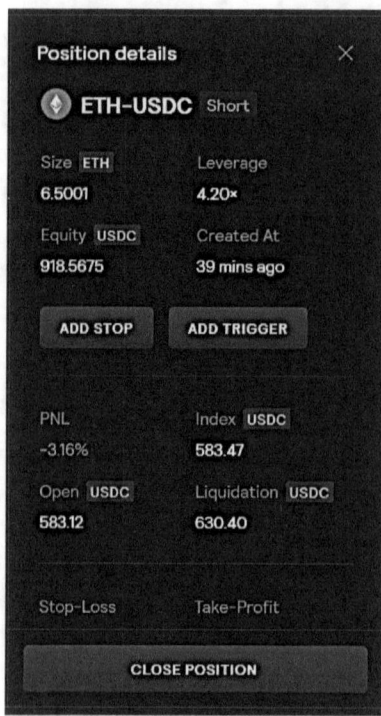

Figure 3.12

You may add stop loss or add trigger to take profit. However, if the price is within 5% of the liquidation price, you are not allowed to add stop loss. You will be alerted with a message as shown in the Figure 3.13.

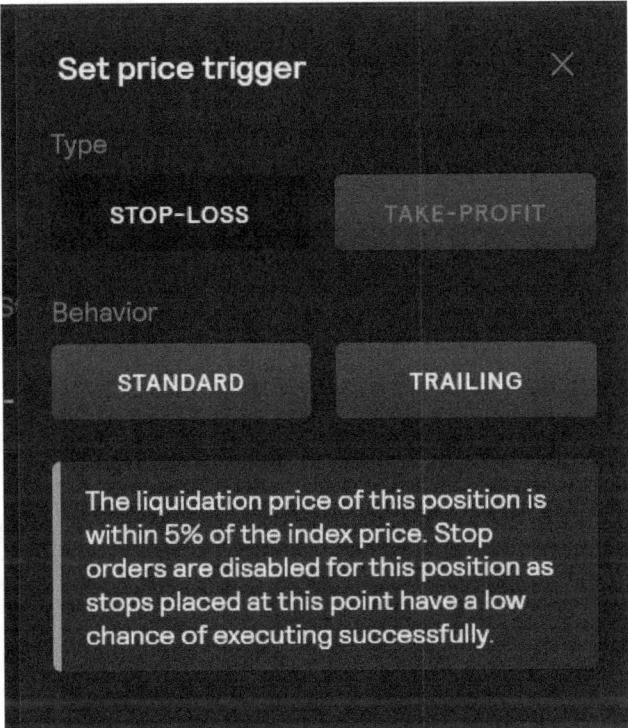

Figure 3.13

3.1.2 Perpetual Trading

When we talk about perpetual contracts trading, we must understand the concept of futures trading first. According to Investopedia, futures or rather futures contracts allow traders to lock in a price of the underlying asset like shares and cryptocurrencies or commodity like gold and oil. These contracts have expiration dates and set prices that are known upfront.

A perpetual contract is a special type of futures contract (Binance Academy, 2020). However, in contrast to the traditional form of futures, it does not have an expiry date. Therefore, you can hold a position for as long as you wish. In addition, the trading of perpetual contracts is based on an underlying Index Price. The Index Price consists of the average price of an asset, according to major spot markets and their relative trading volume.

One the other hand, spot trading refers to the purchase or sale of a foreign currency, financial instrument, or commodity for instant delivery on a specified spot date (Investopedia, n.d.). In the case of dYdX, spot trading involves buying and selling crypto assets instantly.

Perpetual Contract Markets are powered by the dYdX Perpetual Contracts Protocol. They are synthetic trading markets on Ethereum that allow for exposure to digital assets using ERC20 tokens as collateral.

Like existing perpetual contracts, the price of the contract is tied to the price of the underlying asset by a dynamic interest rate. An on-chain price oracle is used for liquidation purposes. However, the order book for the market is off-chain, allowing for faster price movements and better liquidity.

I must point out that the contract's underlying asset does not have to already exist as a token. For each account trading the perpetual, profits and losses are exchanged using the collateral ERC20 token. This allows investors to trade assets that do not actually exist on Ethereum if a sufficient price oracle exists. For example, a BTC–USDC perpetual contract can exist if a BTC–USDC oracle exists. Only USDC would be used as margin deposit for all parties; tokenized BTC is not required. By the way, an oracle is a way for a blockchain or smart contract to interact with external data. With blockchains being deterministic one-way streets, an oracle is the path between off-chain and on-chain events.

On dYdX, equity is the trading capital a trader has at stake for perpetual contracts. In the case of the BTC-USD Perpetual offering, the margin and settlement asset are USDC, so USDC is the equity type for this contract. The amount of equity a trader has available determines their margin level, which is found by dividing equity by the amount of margin used. Each perpetual market has its own account that is separate from your main margin account.

In Perpetual trading, users must collateralize their perpetual accounts separately from their margin trading accounts. In addition, free collateral is the amount of collateral a perpetual trader can withdraw per their ongoing positions. To trade Perpetual Futures, navigate to the Perpetual tab, as seen in Figure 3.14.

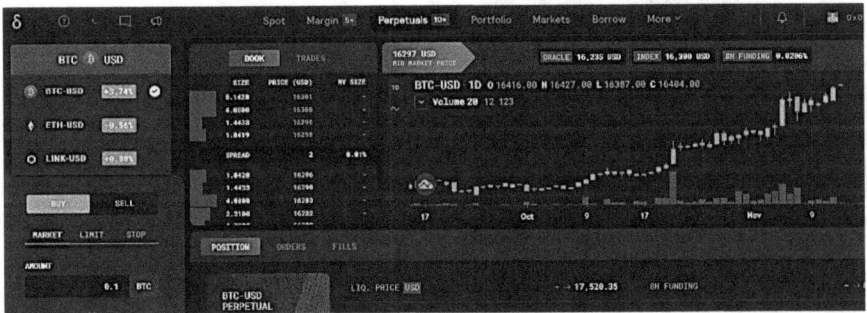

Figure 3.14

dYdX allows you to trade perpetual futures for BTC-USD, ETH-USD and LINK-USD, as seen in Figure 3.15.

Figure 3.15

Bear in mind that your dYdX perpetual accounts must be collateralized so you must deposit the trading capital you wish to put as stake into your perpetual accounts first before you place any orders. To proceed, click the 'DEPOSIT' button at the "Equity" and "Free Collateral" dashboard, as seen in Figure 3.16.

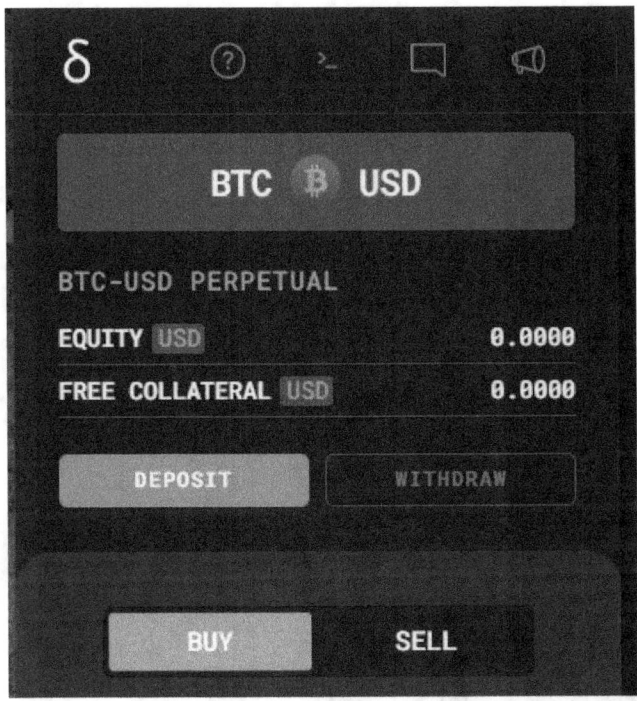

Figure 3.16

Upon clicking the DEPOSIT button, you will be prompted to deposit your USDC or USDT from your MetaMask wallet, as shown in Figure 3.17.

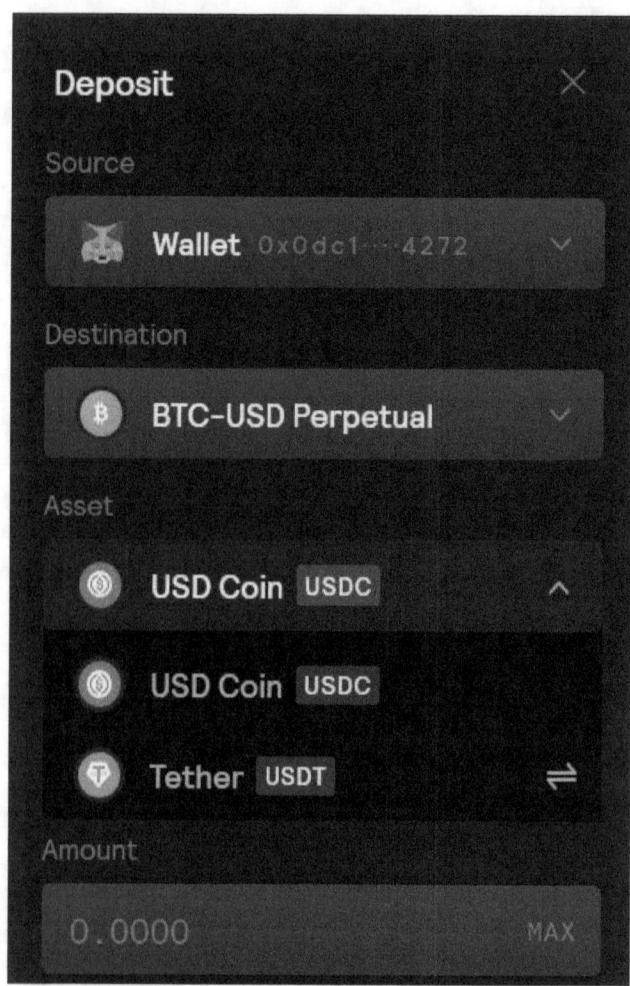

Figure 3.17

You must enable USDC and USDT before you can deposit funds in your account. After depositing the fund, you may start perpetual futures trading.

In addition, dYdX also offers spot trading.

3.2 Uniswap- A Decentralized ER20 Token Exchange

Uniswap is a decentralized ERC20 token exchange that supports Ethereum and ERC20 tokens. The advantage of Uniswap is that you can swap ERC20 tokens in a decentralized way. No companies involved, no KYC, and no intermediaries.

The Uniswap platform is unique in that it does not use an order book to derive the price of an asset or to match buyers and sellers of tokens. Instead, Uniswap uses the Liquidity Pool which comprises a group of tokens managed by smart contracts. The liquidity pool ensures enough tokens for users to exchange with each other using Ethereum as a channel.

Technically speaking, Uniswap is an automated liquidity protocol powered by a constant product formula and implemented in a system of smart contracts on the Ethereum blockchain. Each Uniswap smart contract or pair manages a liquidity pool made up of reserves of two ERC20 tokens.

The beauty of this system is that anyone can become a liquidity provider for a pool by depositing an equivalent value of each underlying token in return for pool tokens. These tokens track pro-rata LP shares of the total reserves and can be redeemed for the underlying assets at any time.

Whenever new ERC20 tokens are added to a Uniswap liquidity pool, the contributor receives a "pool token", which is also an ERC20 token (Decrypt, n.d.). In fact, pool tokens are created whenever funds are deposited into the pool and as an ERC20 token. Pool tokens can be freely swapped, transferred, and used in other dApps. When funds are reclaimed, the pool tokens are burned. Each pool token represents a user's share of the pool's total assets and share of the pool's 0.3% trading fee.

To access Uniswap platform, click the following link:

https://uniswap.org/

The platform website is as seen in Figure 3.18.

Figure 3.18

To start using Uniswap services, click the Launch App button on the top right corner. The app interface is as seen in Figure 3.19.

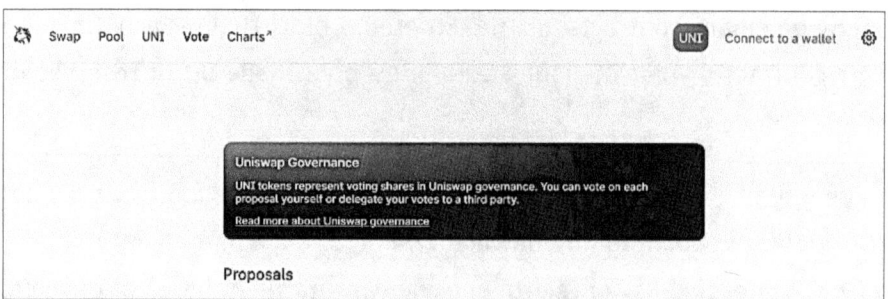

Figure 3.19

In the app, you can swap tokens, add tokens to liquidity pool, vote, as well as view charts. However, you must connect Uniswap app to your wallet.

When your wallet is connected, you will see your wallet address appear on the top right corner of the page, as shown in Figure 3.20.

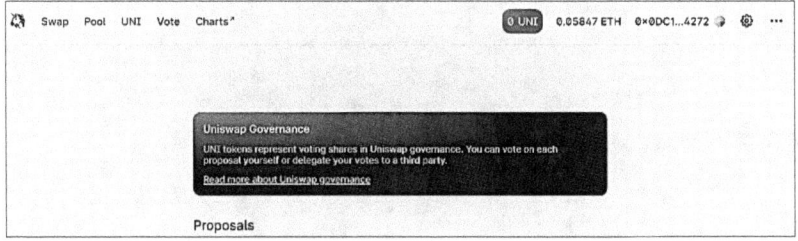

Figure 3.20

To swap tokens, click the Swap tab and use your token to swap for another token. In our example, I swap ETH for USDC, as shown in Figure 3.21.

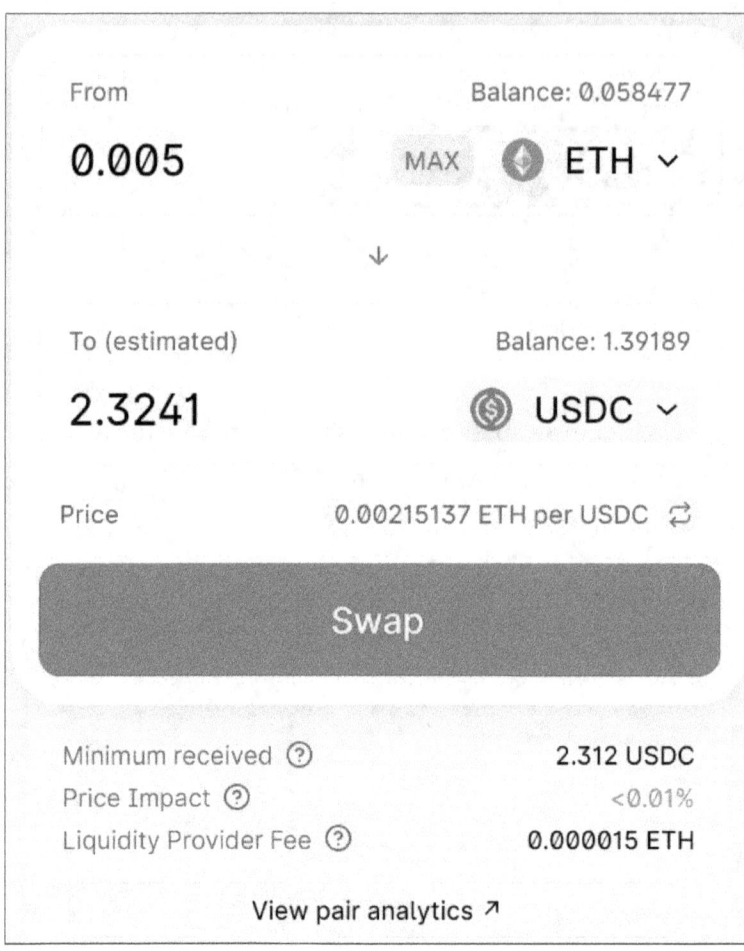

Figure 3.21

After clicking the swap button, you will be shown the following dialog box, as seen in Figure 3.22.

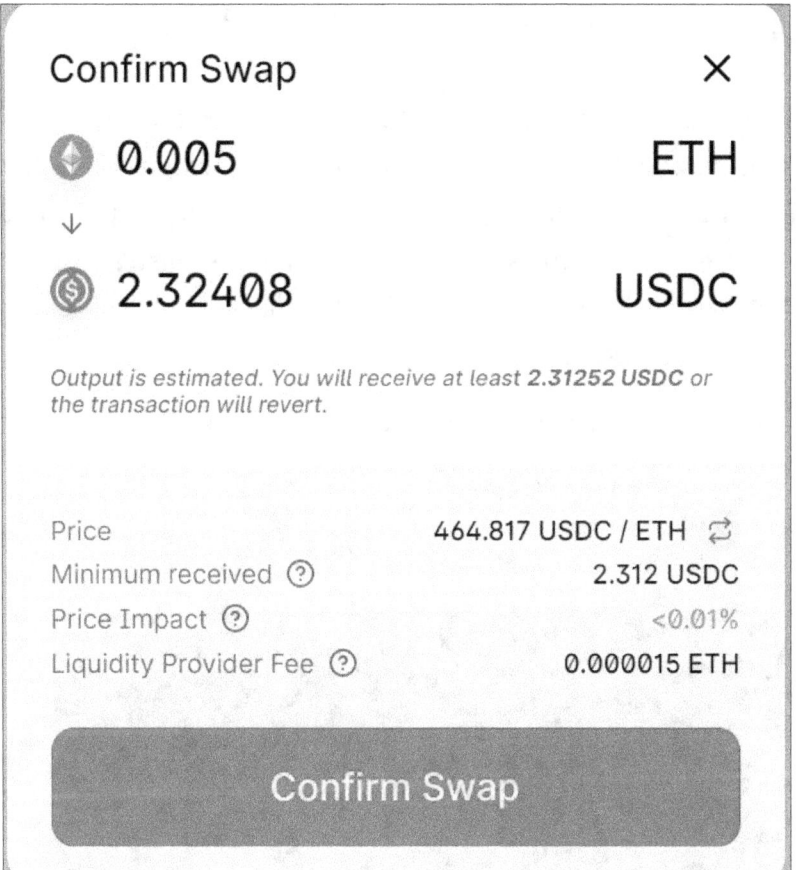

Figure 3.22

Next step is to click the Confirm Swap button to confirm the swap. Clicking the Confirm Swap button will launch your MetaMask wallet prompting you to accept and confirm the swap. It also shows how much gas fee you must pay. Finally, clicking the Confirm button to proceed with the transaction. When the swap is confirmed, USDC will appear in your wallet.

3.3 Balancer-An Automated Market Maker

Balancer is a decentralized crypto exchange that allows you to swap ERC20 tokens. In addition, Balancer is also an automated market-maker (AMM) built on Ethereum blockchain. It allows anyone to create or add liquidity to customizable pools and earn trading fees. Instead of the traditional AMM model, Balancer's formula allows any number of tokens in any weights or trading fees.

To access the Balancer exchange, click the following link:

https://balancer.exchange/#/swap

The exchange interface is as seen in Figure 3.23.

Figure 3.23

Before you start to buy and sell tokens, click the Connect Button to connect to your wallet of choice, as seen in Figure 3.24.

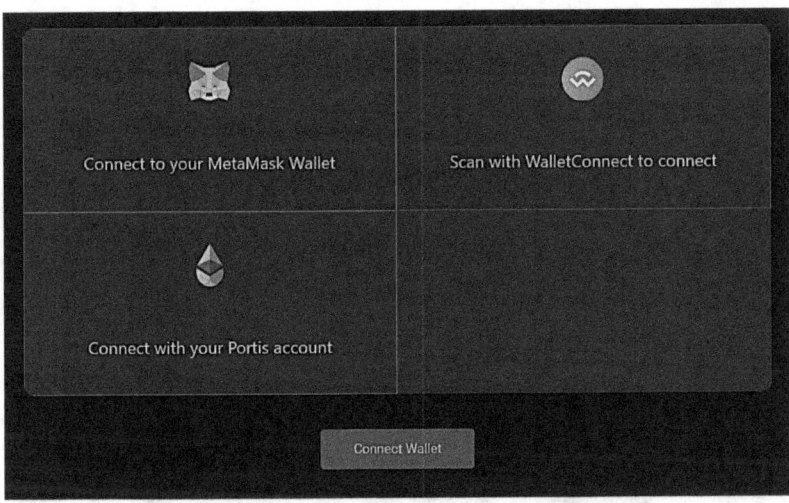

Figure 3.24

When the Connect button is clicked, your wallet will be connected to Balancer exchange, as seen in Figure 3.25.

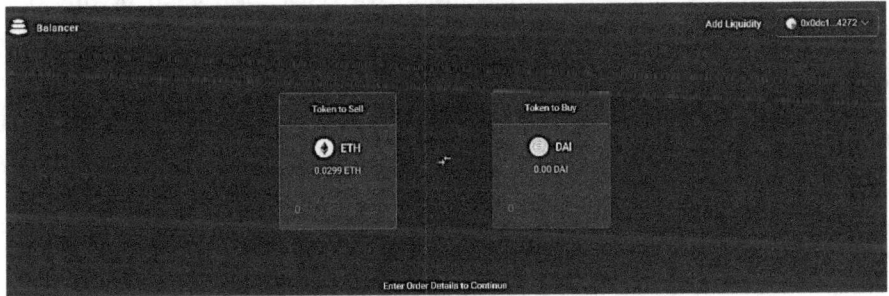

Figure 3.25

Now you can start to buy or sell tokens. Clicking the 'Token to Buy' button will reveal a basket of tokens you can select to buy, as seen in Figure 3.26.

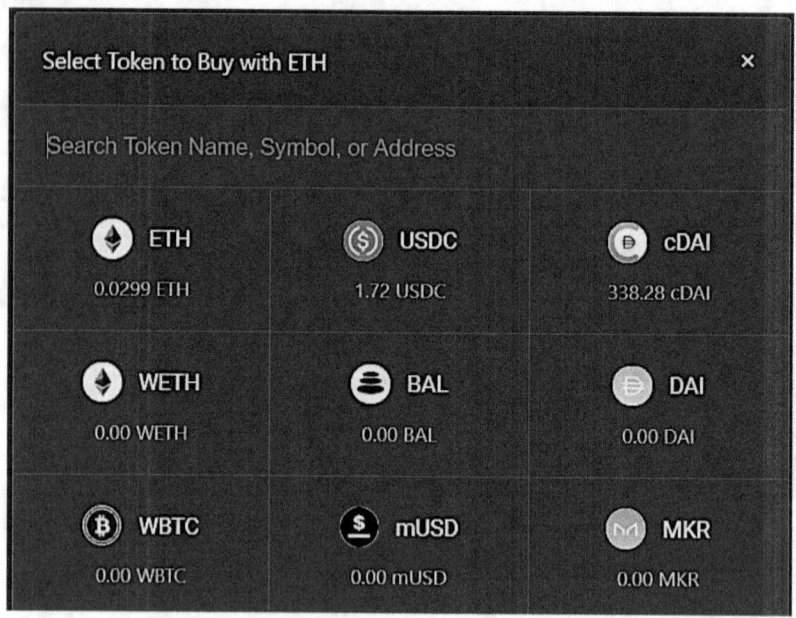

Figure 3.26

You must have ETH to buy the tokens. For instance, if you wish to buy 10 USDC, select USDC and enter the amount of USDC you wish to buy, as seen in Figure 3.27. It also shows the expected price slippage which refers to the difference between the expected price of a trade and the price at which the trade is executed.

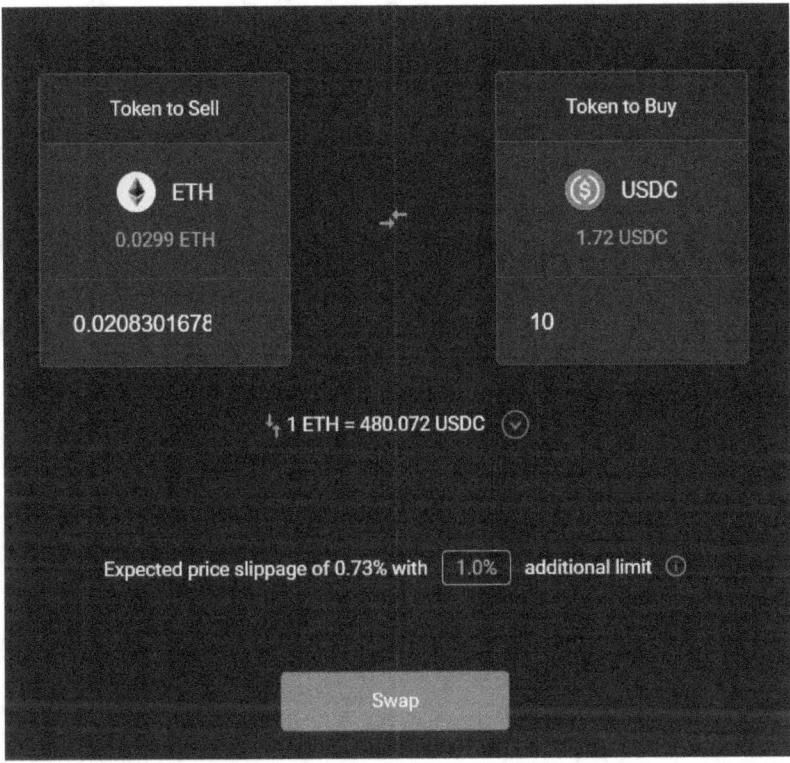

Figure 3.27

Next, click the 'Confirm' button to submit the request to the Ethereum mainnet for approval. Once approved you will be able to see that your wallet has been funded with USDC, as shown in Figure 3.28.

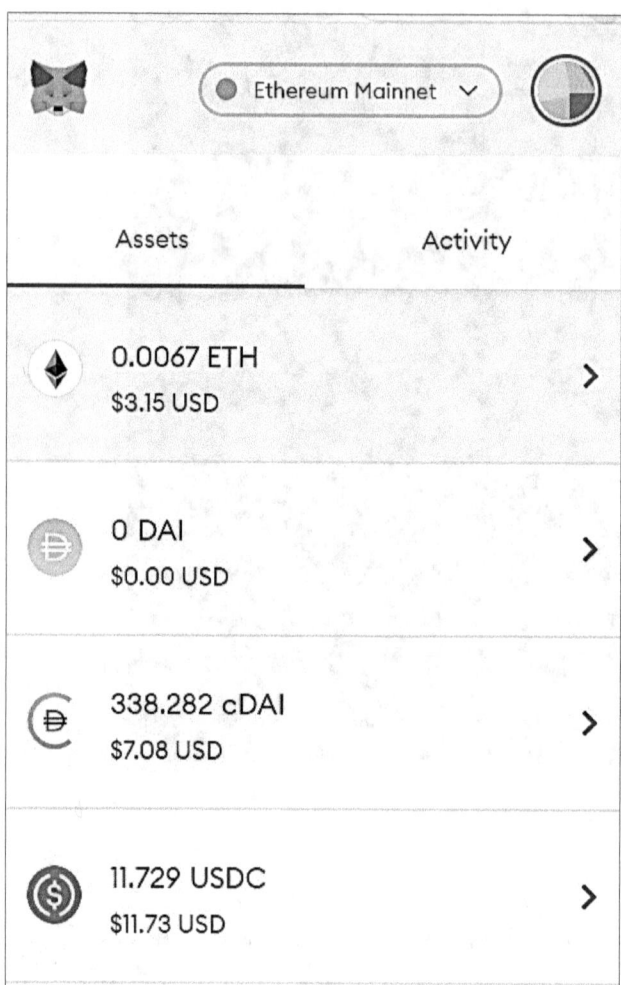

Figure 3.28

Besides buying and selling tokens on Balancer, you can also monetize your digital assets by depositing them into Balancer's liquidity pools. We shall discuss this function under yield farming chapter.

3.4 Radar Relay- A DEX Powered by DEX

Radar Relay is a decentralised token exchange that provides a wallet-to-wallet trading platform for Ethereum tokens (De, 2018). You can connect your wallet to the platform to exchange tokens directly, without the need of an intermediary. Radar Relay works on 0x protocol. 0x protocol allows the trading of ERC20 tokens on the Ethereum blockchain.

To start trading on Relay Radar DEX, use the following link:

https://relay.radar.tech/

The trading platform is as shown in Figure 3.29.

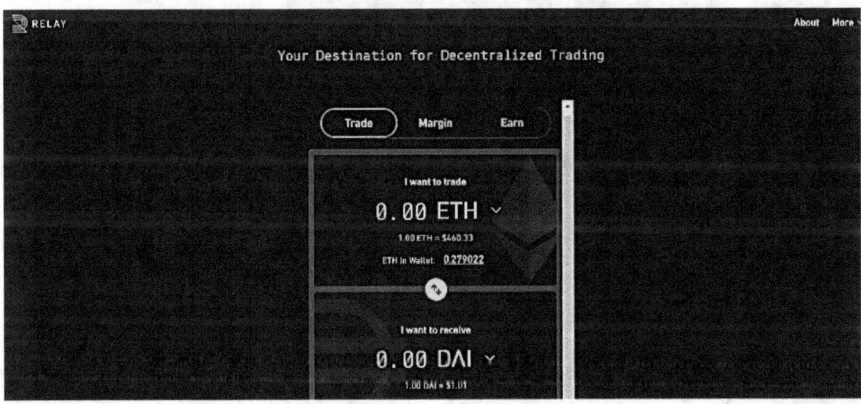

Figure 3.29

You must connect your wallet to the platform to be able to trade. Once your wallet is connected, you will notice that on the app, as shown in Figure 3.30.

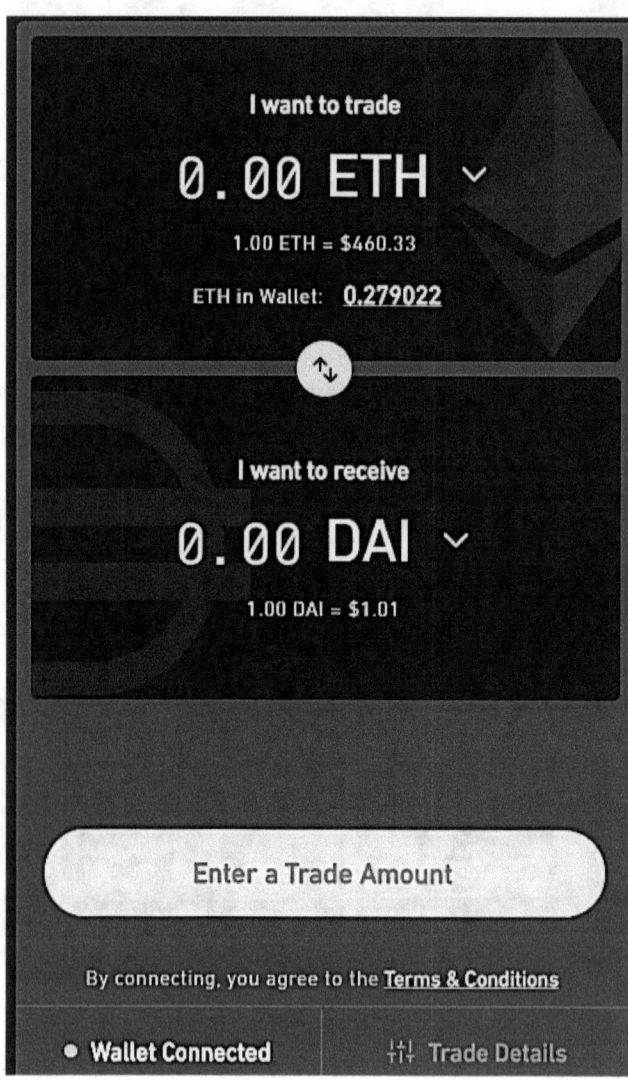

Figure 3.30

To buy DAI using ETH, just enter the amount of DAI you wish to receive, as shown in Figure 3.31.

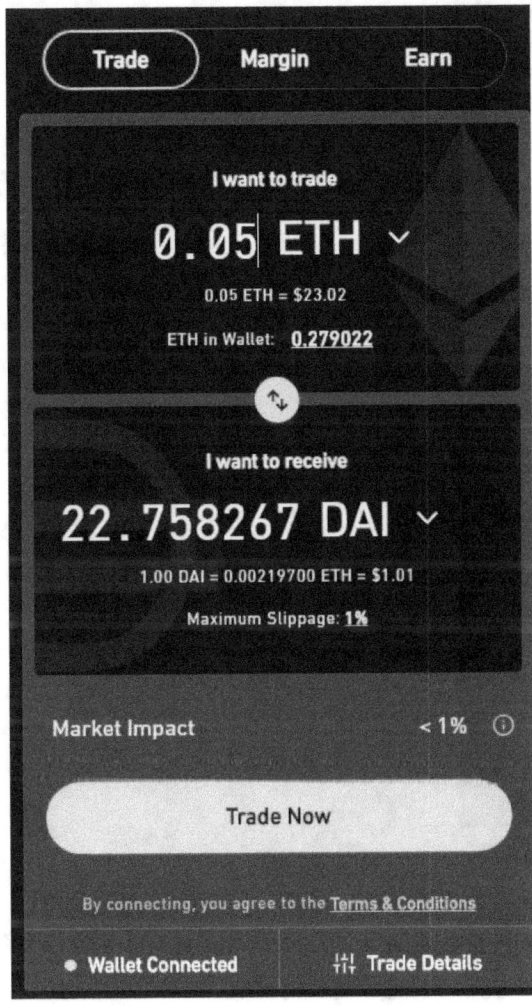

Figure 3.31

After you click the Trade Now button, you will need to confirm your transaction on your wallet. Once verified your wallet will be funded with DAI.

Besides swapping tokens, you can also go for margin trade by opening a long position or a short position, as shown in Figure 3.32.

Figure 3.32

If you believe the future price will increase, you go for long while if you believe the future price will decrease, you go for short.

Let say we wish to open a long position for ETH-DAI with 5x leverage with a margin deposit of 1 ETH, as shown in Figure 3.33.

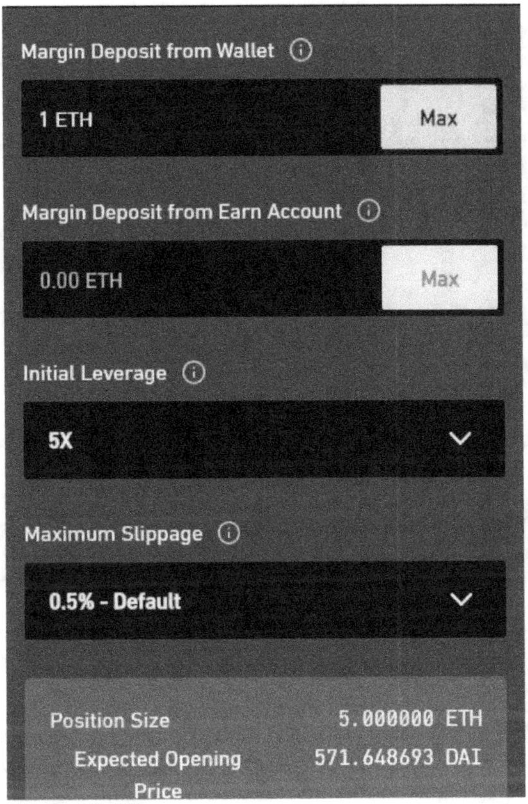

Figure 3.33

You can scroll down to see the details of your position that show your position size, expected opening price, liquidation price, interest rate and expiration date, as seen in Figure 3.34.

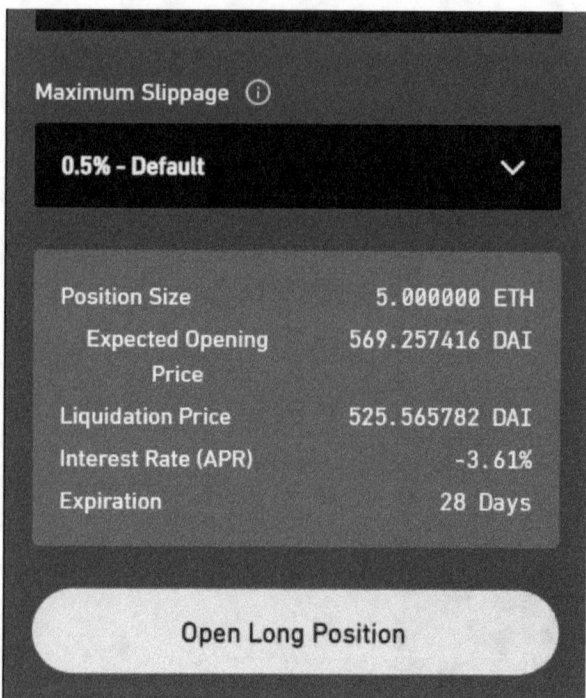

Figure 3.34

If the price falls below the liquidation price, your position will be liquidated. You may use your Earn Account or your wallet as the margin deposit.

In addition, you can also earn interest by depositing your crypto assets into Relay Radar DEX by clicking the Earn tab, as shown in Figure 3.35.

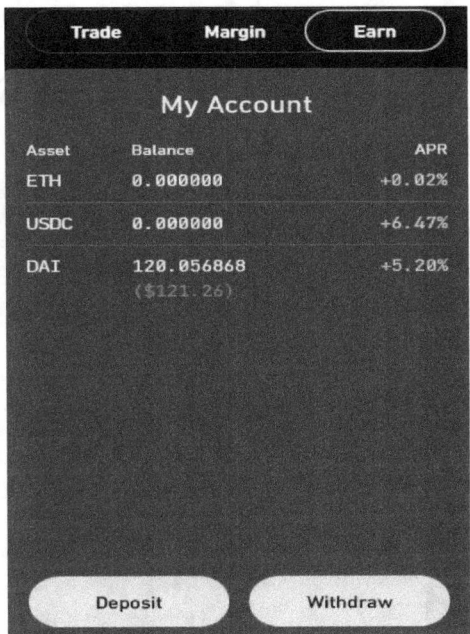
Figure 3.35

To deposit funds, click the Deposit button, as shown in Figure 3.36.

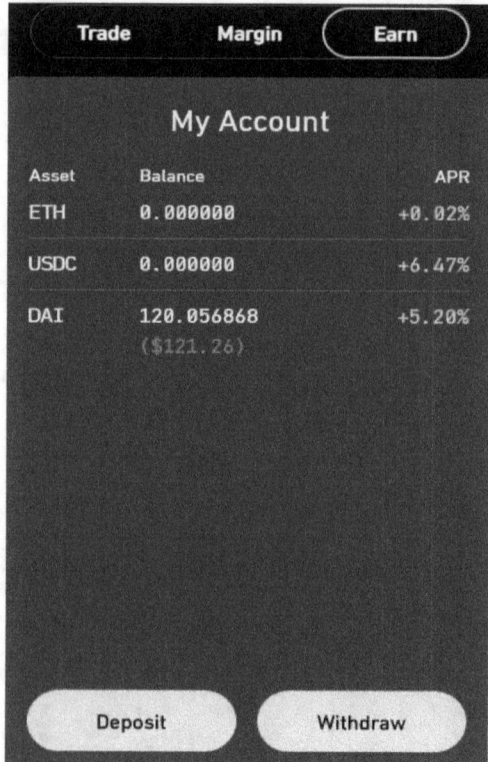

Figure 3.36

Upon clicking the Deposit button, you can choose the type of funds in your wallet to deposit. I chose USDC because it offers the highest APY of 6.47%., as shown in Figure 3.37.

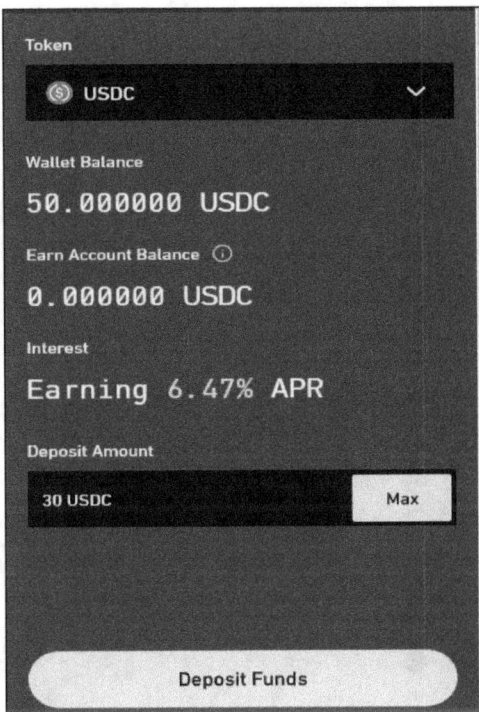

Figure 3.37

As usual you must confirm the transaction. Once confirmed your money will start earning interest, as shown in Figure 3.38.

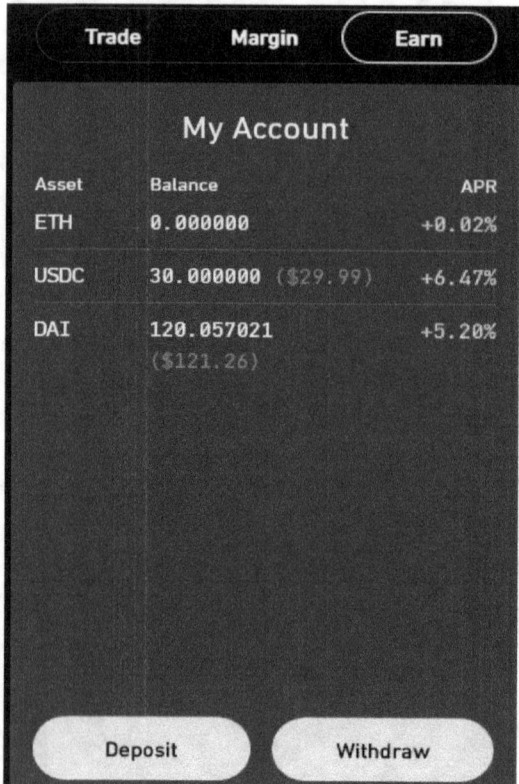

Figure 3.38

3.5 Bancor-A Non-Custodial Token Exchange

Bancor is a protocol on Ethereum for non-custodial token exchange using pooled liquidity. Bancor does not use order books. Instead, it uses an algorithmic market-making mechanism using smart contracts. This will ensure liquidity and accurate prices by maintaining a fixed ratio among connected tokens and adjusting their own supply.

The Bancor platform has expanded beyond Ethereum to offer an exchange with EOS and POA Network. It also features a native token known as BNT (Bancor Network Token), which serves as a Smart Token hub that connects all other tokens on the Bancor Network, enabling instant trades among any asset supported by Bancor.

You can swap tokens in Bancor as well as adding token pairs to its liquidity. To access Bancor network, click the following link:

https://app.bancor.network/

The website interface is as seen in Figure 3.39.

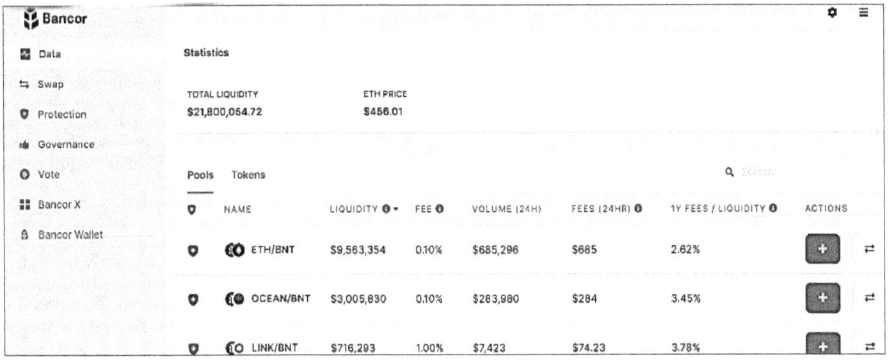

Figure 3.39

To swap tokens, click the 'Swap' link on the sidebar. You must connect the platform to your wallet to be able to swap. In our example, let us swap ETH with BNT, the native token of Bancor, as seen in Figure 3.40.

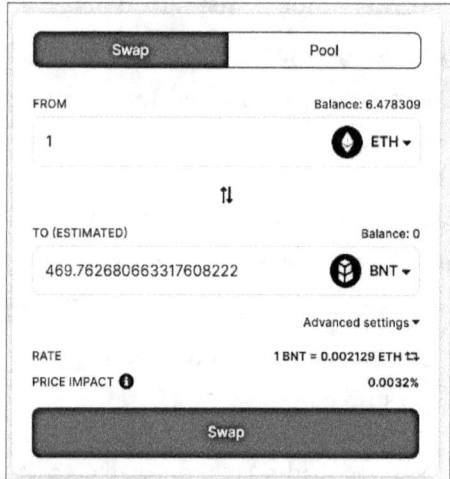

Figure 3.40

Next, enter the amount of ETH you wish to swap. The amount of BNT will automatically show based on the current price. If you are satisfied with the rate, click the 'Swap' button, and confirm the transaction as seen in Figure 3.41.

Figure 3.41

The final step is to conform the transaction on your wallet.

3.6 Kyber Swap

Kyber is a blockchain-based liquidity protocol that aggregates liquidity from a wide range of reserves into a single pool, which provides the best rates for users. It allows instant and secure token exchange in any decentralized application (Kyber Network, n.d.). Besides that, Kyber does not use order books; when a user initiates a trade, Kyber returns the best price across all reserves.

The Kyber Network can be integrated into dApps to enhance user experience. In addition, vendors and wallets can also use the Kyber Network to allow users to transact using their token of choice in a single transaction. Moreover, Kyber has a native token called KNC which is used to provide ecosystem incentives. Holders can stake KNC to participate in governance and earn rewards, reserve managers pay fees and receive rebates in KNC, and DApp integrators receive a portion of fees.

To access the Kyber Swap network, follow this link:

https://kyberswap.com/swap

The landing page is as shown in Figure 3.42.

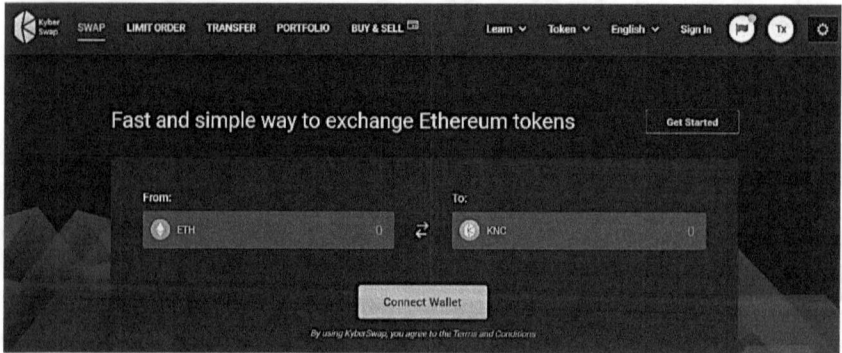

Figure 3.42

As usual, you must connect Kyber Swap to your wallet by clicking the 'Connect Wallet' button and subsequently confirm the request on the wallet. Once the request has been verified you will be able to see your wallet balance in Kyber Swap, as seen in Figure 3.43.

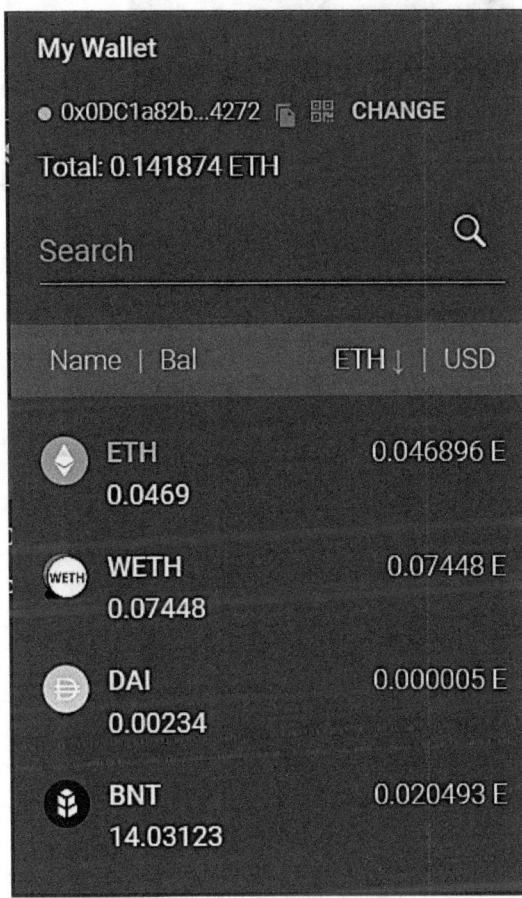

Figure 3.43

You can view your portfolio in Kyber as shown in Figure 3.44.

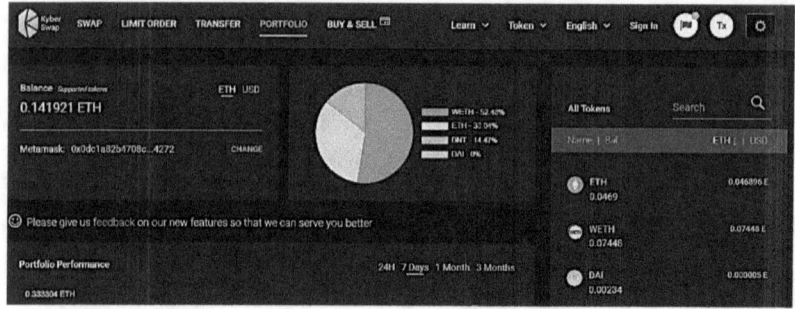

Figure 3.44

Next, you can start swapping for the tokens you wish to own, as seen in Figure 3.45.

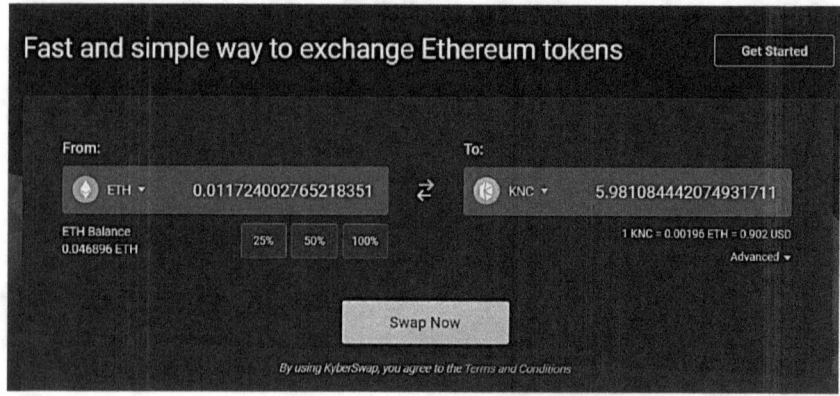

Figure 3.45

Clicking the 'Swap Now' button invokes a dialog box that prompt you to confirm the request, as shown in Figure 3.46.

Figure 3.46

Clicking 'Confirm' will invoke your wallet and you must confirm the transaction in the wallet. When your transaction is verified, KNC will be deposited In your wallet.

3.7 Synthetix-A Platform for Trading Synthetic Assets

Synthetix.Exchange is a platform that allows anyone to access crypto-backed synthetic assets[4] (a.k.a Synths) without a counterparty. It provides an interface for converting between Synths seamlessly without liquidity restrictions. The Synthetix network's distributed collateral pool (provided by SNX holders) allows unbanked and crypto-native users to gain exposure to different assets that they might not otherwise have access to.

In 2019, Synthetics launched the synthetic Bitcoin (sBTC) on the Ethereum blockchain (businesswire, 2019). This release allows Ethereum users to gain non-custodial exposure to Bitcoin, which means they do not need to trust an intermediary to hold the underlying asset. The beauty of sBTC is that it provides access to the value of Bitcoin without the need to own a Bitcoin wallet or hold it. Moreover, it be used within the Ethereum ecosystem to trade and swap ERC20 tokens.

Besides sBTC , Synthetix.Exchange also allows anyone to access a wide variety of assets without a counterparty. Synths are backed by crypto assets. Synthetix is decentralized and trustless, and liquidity is much easier because it does not require a party to hold the underlying asset.

Trading on Synthetix.Exchange is relatively simple. Just choose a Synth you are currently holding and choose a Synth to convert into (Synthetix.Exchange Overview, 2019). All conversions are on-chain, and currently generate a 0.30% fee that are distributed to locked SNX holders.

---

[4] Synthetic asset refers to a mix of assets that have the same value as another asset (Kuznetsov, 2020).

To access Synthetix.Exchange, use the following link:

https://syntnetix.exchange/#/markets

The Exchange platform is as seen in Figure 3.47.

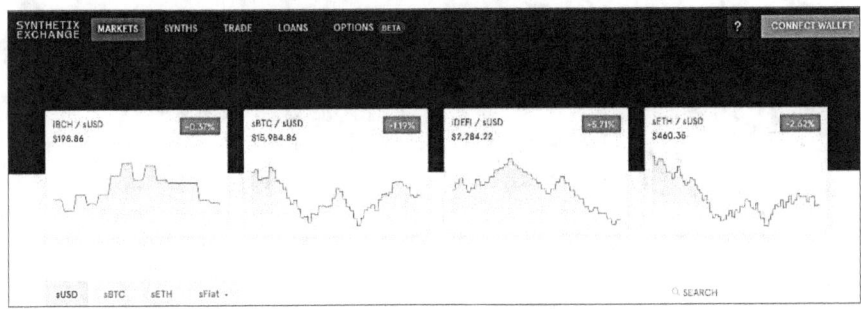

Figure 3.47

You must connect your wallet to the platform before starting to trade. Click the 'Connect Wallet' button to connect. It will request you to select wallet to connect. Once your wallet is connected you will be able to see your wallet address on the top right-hand corner of the website, as shown in Figure 3.48.

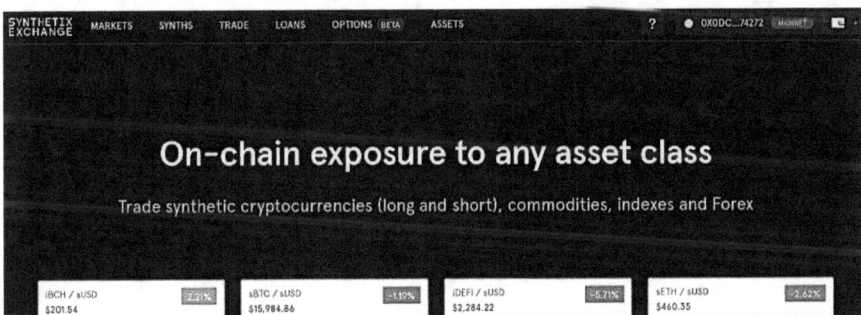

Figure 3.48

You can view the markets, synths that are available, trade tokens and more. Bear in mind that Synthetix only allows you to trade synths like sBTC, sETH and more. For example, you can buy sETH with sUSD, as seen in Figure 3.49.

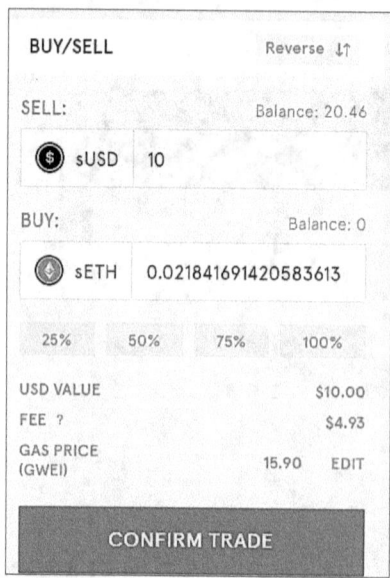

Figure 3.49

If you do not have any of the synths, you can borrow it from Synthetix or buy it from centralized exchanges such as Huobi, Coinsquare or swap ETH for sETH at Uniswap. To borrow sBTC, click the Loans tab and borrow sUSD using ETH as a collateral, as seen in Figure 3.50.

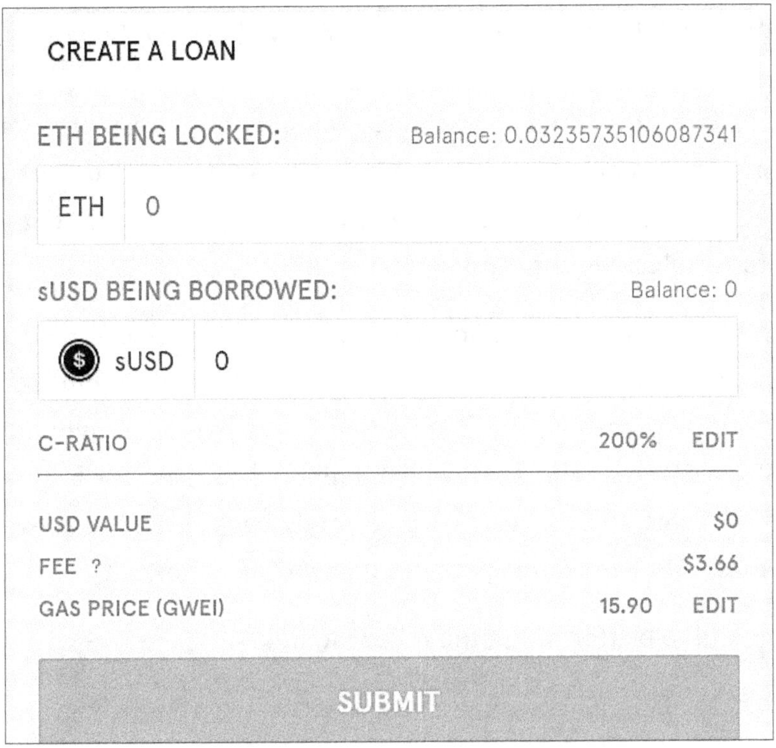

CREATE A LOAN		
ETH BEING LOCKED:		Balance: 0.03235735106087341
ETH	0	
sUSD BEING BORROWED:		Balance: 0
$ sUSD	0	
C-RATIO		200% EDIT
USD VALUE		$0
FEE ?		$3.66
GAS PRICE (GWEI)		15.90 EDIT
	SUBMIT	

Figure 3.50

Since I have 20.46 sUSD in my wallet which I have got it from Uniswap, let us buy sETH with sUSD, as shown in Figure 3.48. As usual, you need to confirm the transaction on your wallet. When the transaction is confirmed, you can view your sETH in your wallet. If you cannot see sETH, do not worry, just click Add Token and search for sETH. It will appear in your wallet.

3.8 Curve Finance-A DEX for Trading Stablecoins

Curve Finance is a decentralized exchange liquidity pool on Ethereum designed for trading stablecoins (Curve Finance, n.d.). It allows users to trade stablecoins with low slippage, a low fee algorithm designed specifically for stablecoins and earning fees.

Besides that, the tokens held by Curve's liquidity pools are also supplied to the Compound Protocol or yearn.finance to generate more income for liquidity providers. Currently, there are seven Curve pools: Compound, PAX, Y, BUSD, sUSD, ren, and sBTC which support swapping for a wide variety of stablecoins and assets. Curve currently has released a native token known as CRV. Each Curve pool has its own ERC20 token.

To access the Curve platform, use the following link:

https://www.curve.fi/

When you visit the website, you will be asked to connect your wallet first, as shown in Figure 3.51.

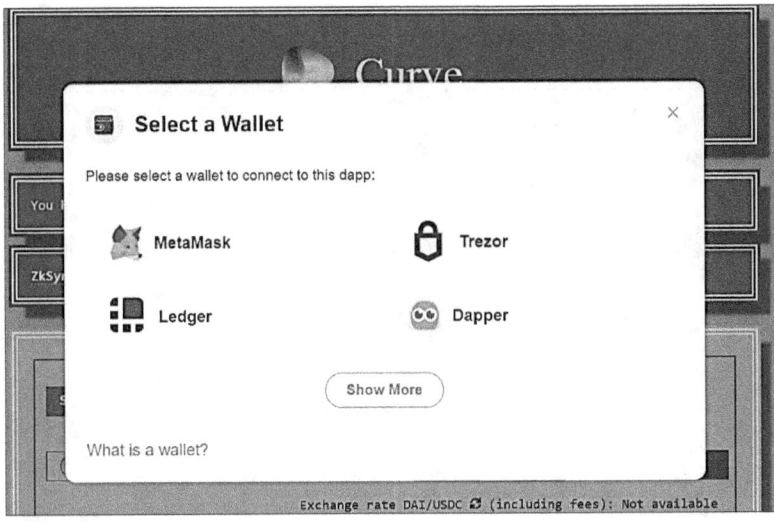

Figure 3.51

Once the wallet is connected, you can start swapping tokens, as shown in Figure 3.52.

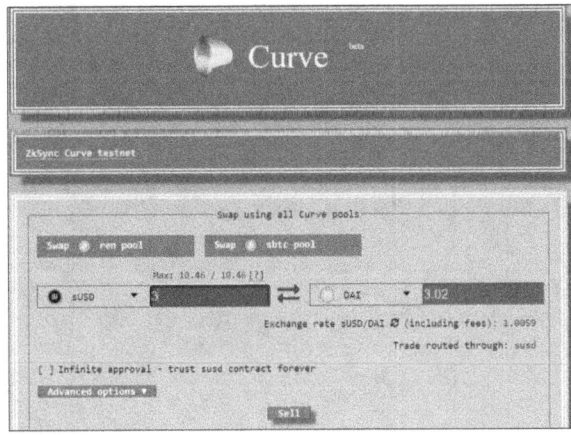

Figure 3.52

You can swap many types of tokens from the Curve pool, as shown in Figure 3.53.

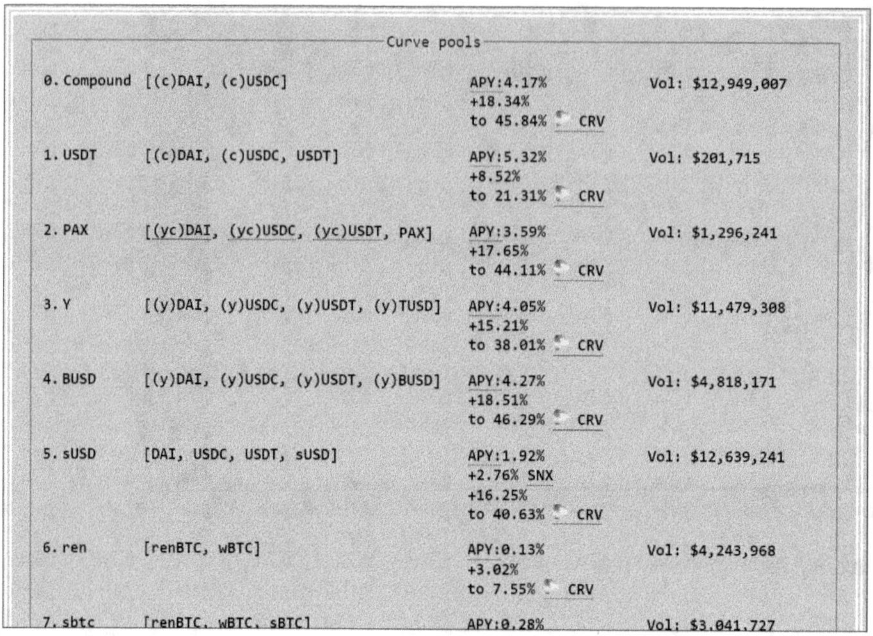

```
┌─────────────────────── Curve pools ───────────────────────┐
│ 0. Compound  [(c)DAI, (c)USDC]              APY:4.17%        Vol: $12,949,007
│                                             +18.34%
│                                             to 45.84%  CRV
│ 1. USDT      [(c)DAI, (c)USDC, USDT]        APY:5.32%        Vol: $201,715
│                                             +8.52%
│                                             to 21.31%  CRV
│ 2. PAX       [(yc)DAI, (yc)USDC, (yc)USDT, PAX]  APY:3.59%   Vol: $1,296,241
│                                             +17.65%
│                                             to 44.11%  CRV
│ 3. Y         [(y)DAI, (y)USDC, (y)USDT, (y)TUSD]  APY:4.05%  Vol: $11,479,308
│                                             +15.21%
│                                             to 38.01%  CRV
│ 4. BUSD      [(y)DAI, (y)USDC, (y)USDT, (y)BUSD]  APY:4.27%  Vol: $4,818,171
│                                             +18.51%
│                                             to 46.29%  CRV
│ 5. sUSD      [DAI, USDC, USDT, sUSD]        APY:1.92%        Vol: $12,639,241
│                                             +2.76% SNX
│                                             +16.25%
│                                             to 40.63%  CRV
│ 6. ren       [renBTC, wBTC]                 APY:0.13%        Vol: $4,243,968
│                                             +3.02%
│                                             to 7.55%  CRV
│ 7. sbtc      [renBTC, wBTC, sBTC]           APY:0.28%        Vol: $3,041,727
```

Figure 3.53

Let us swap sUSD with DAI, as shown in Figure 3.53.

Click the 'Sell' button to bring up your wallet which requires you to confirm the transaction on the wallet.

Once confirmed, you can see that your wallet is funded with DAI and your sUSD was deducted.

You can also deposit your preferred tokens and earn interest, as shown in Figure 3.54.

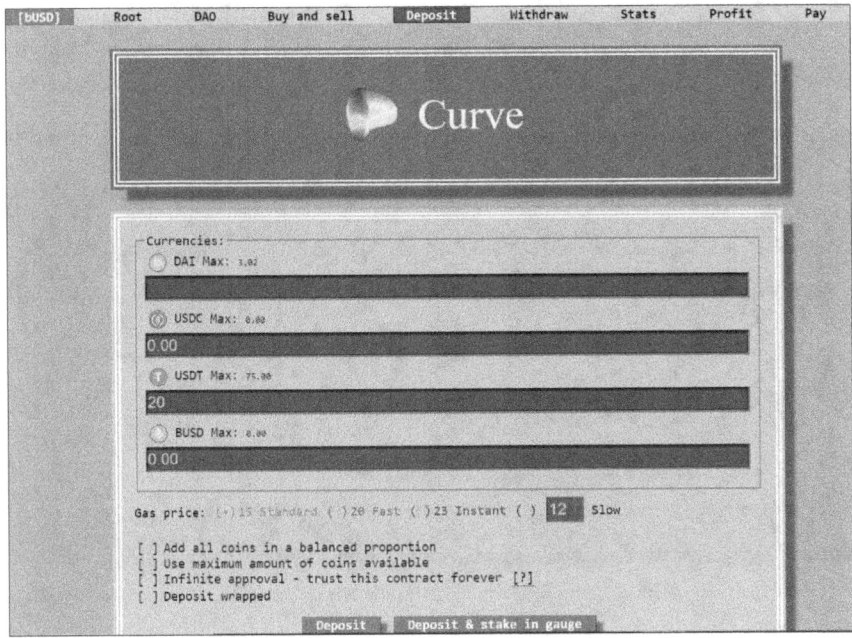

Figure 3.54

Let's say you wish to deposit 20 USDT into the pool, you enter the amount and click the Deposit button and confirm the transaction on your wallet.

After your deposit has been approved, you may view it at the bottom of the Curve homepage, as shown in Figure 3.55.

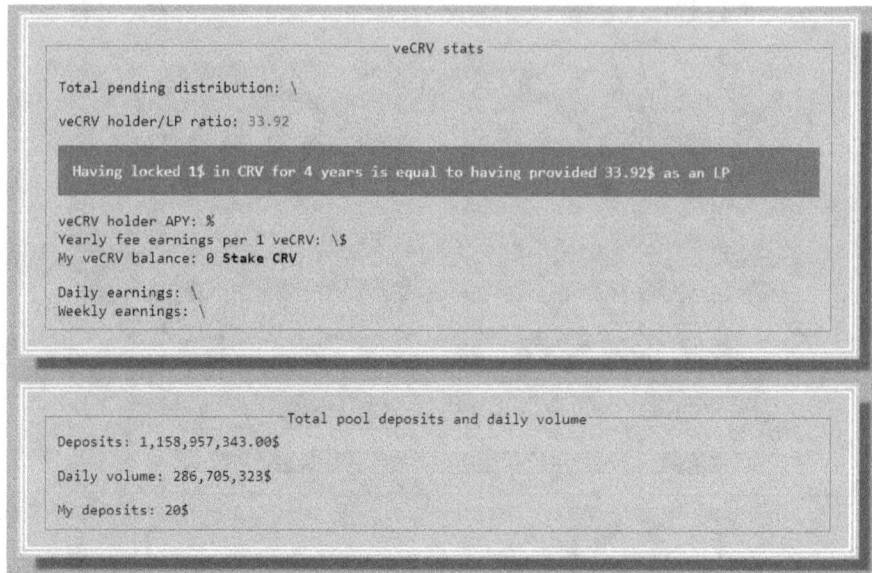

Figure 3.55

Curve is also an established platform of liquidity mining and yield farming. Many platform aggregators like Harvest Finance, Zerion, Zapper and more for liquidity mining and yield farming. We will discuss liquidity mining on Curve in the next chapter.

3.9 Fulcrum-A Tokenized Margin Trading Platform

As we have learned earlier, Fulcrum is a platform for tokenized margin lending and trading. Since we have learned lending, let see how to trade on Fulcrum.

To start trading or lending on Fulcrum, use the following link:

https://fulcrum.trade/

The website landing page is as seen in Figure 3.56.

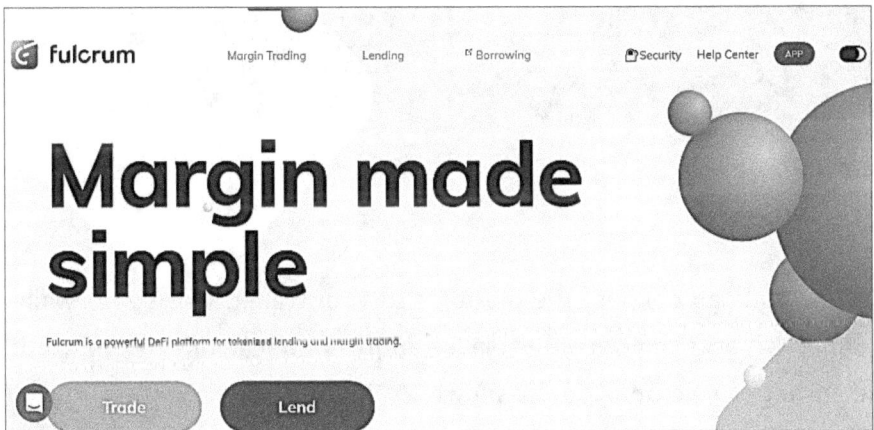

Figure 3.56

Click the 'App' button on the top right-hand corner of the website to enter the trading app, where you can trade or lend. Alternatively, you can click the 'Trade' button at the bottom to enter the app.

The Fulcrum app will prompt you to connect to the wallet of your choice from the list of wallets available, as shown in Figure 3.57.

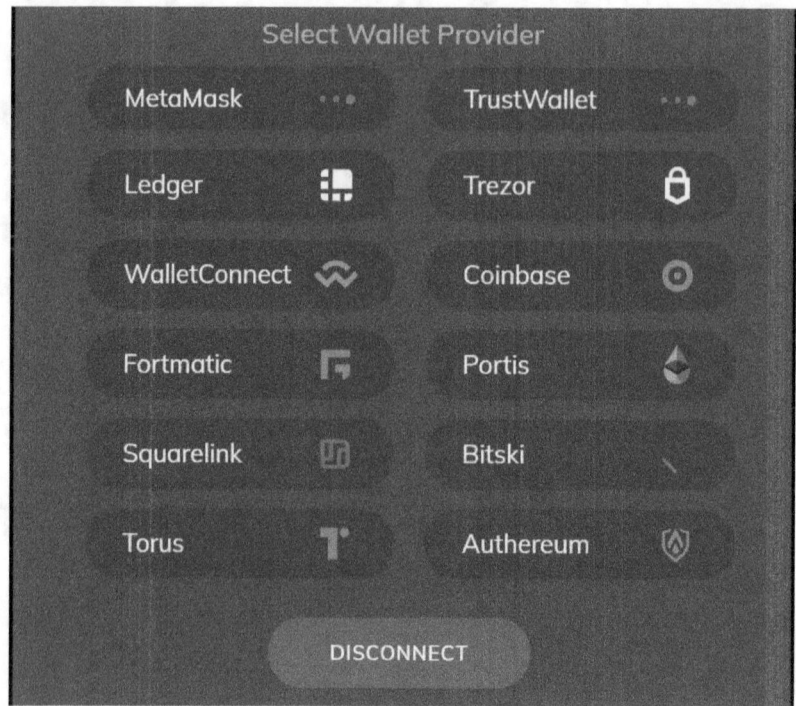

Figure 3.57

As usual, you can connect the platform to your wallet. Once your wallet is connected, you can see your wallet address appear on the top right-hand corner of Fulcrum App, as shown in Figure 3.58.

Figure 3.58

Once your wallet is connected, you can proceed to trade. To trade, click the trade tab and select the market to trade. We select ETH-USDT, as seen in Figure 3.59.

Figure 3.59

The next step is to select the leverage you desire for a long or short position, as shown in Figure 3.60.

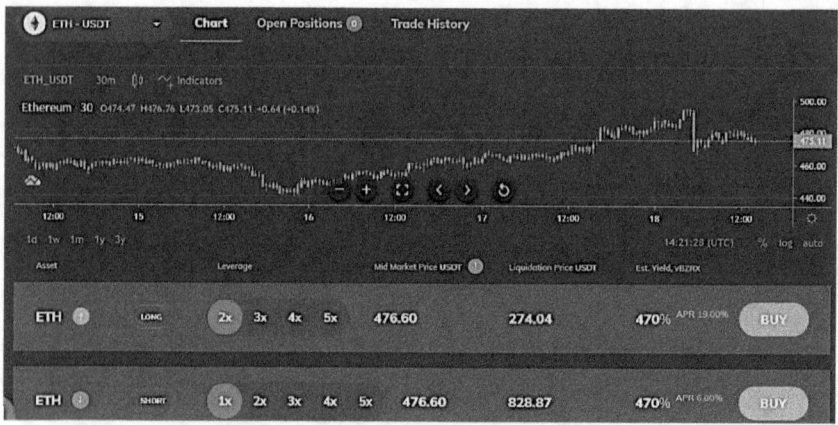

Figure 3.60

Let us open long position with 2x leverage. After selecting your leverage, click the 'Buy' button and then set your position size in the panel that appears, as shown in Figure 3.61.

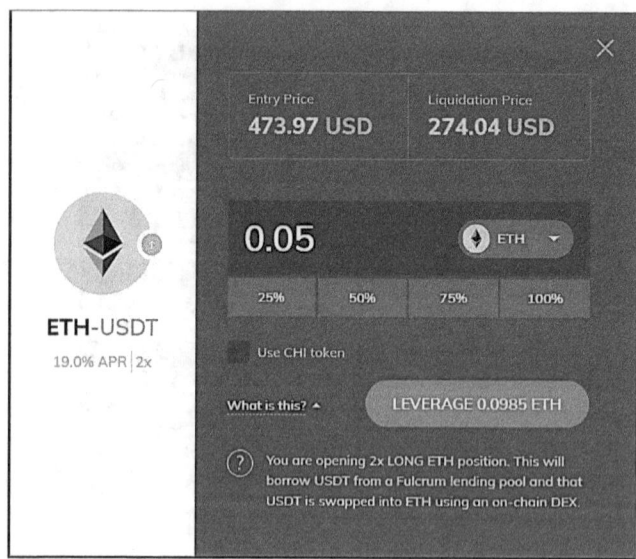

Figure 3.61

Next, click the LEVERAGE1.04 LINK to submit the request. You must confirm the transaction on your wallet. After confirmation, your position will be viewable on the Fulcrum dashboard.

3.10 1inch-A Decentralized Exchange Aggregator

According to its blog (1inch, n.d.), 1inch is a decentralized exchange aggregator that offers the best prices on the market. It achieves best rates by splitting orders among multiple decentralized exchanges in one single transaction. It claims that its gas price is also lower.

To access 1inch, use the following link:

https://1inch.exchange/#/

The landing page is as seen in Figure 3.62.

Figure 3.62

You must connect your wallet to start trading on 1inch. Click the 'Connect Wallet' button and choose the wallet to connect, as shown in Figure 3.63.

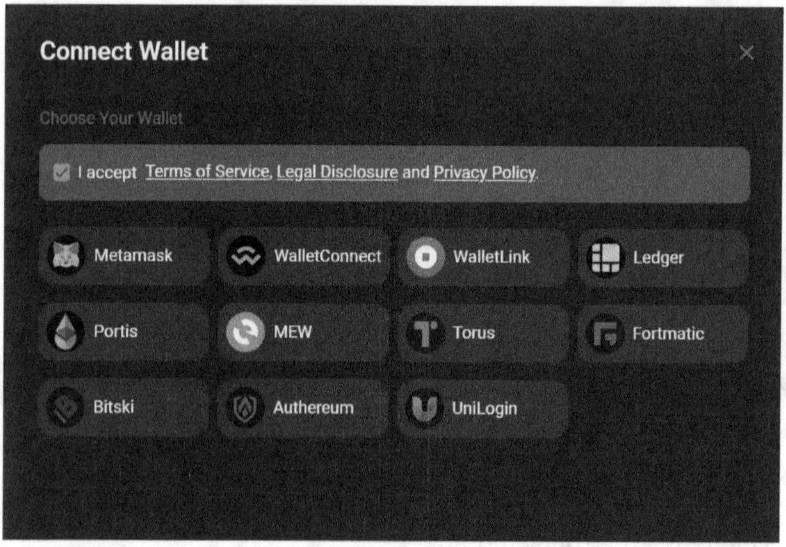

Figure 3.63

After your wallet is connected, you can see your wallet address appears on the top right-hand corner of your landing page, as shown in Figure 3.64.

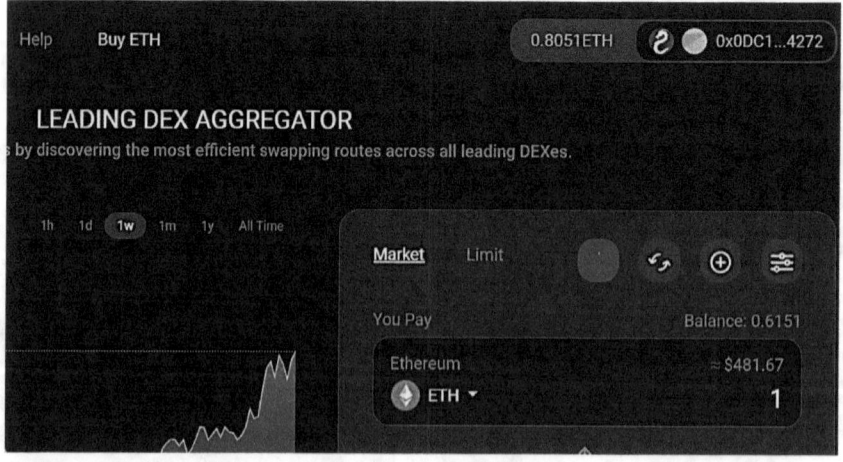

Figure 3.64

Now you may start trading tokens. Let's say we wish to swap Dai with LINK. Enter the amount of Dai you wish to trade, as shown in Figure 3.65.

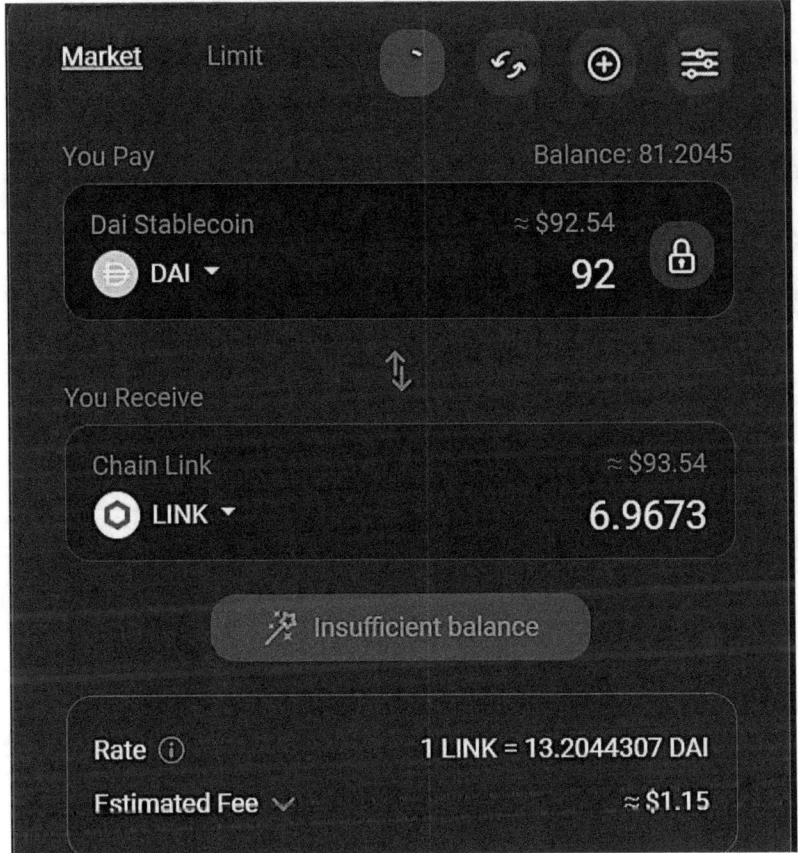

Figure 3.65

You must unlock your Dai to trade, as shown in Figure 3.66.

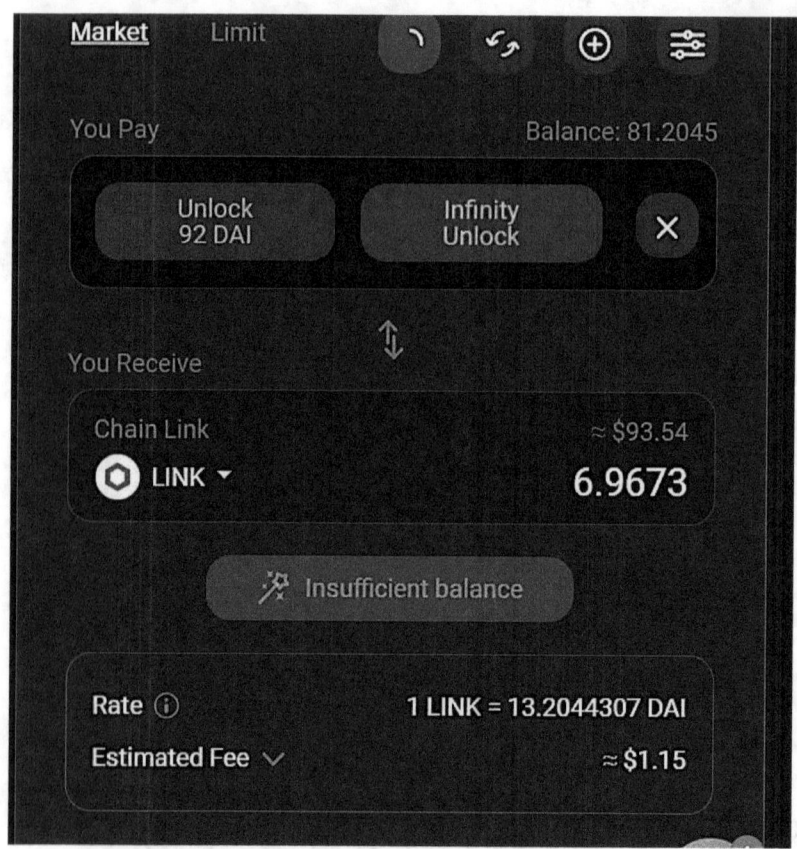

Figure 3.66

After unlocking your Dai, you must agree to let 1inch spend your Dai, as seen in Figure 3.67.

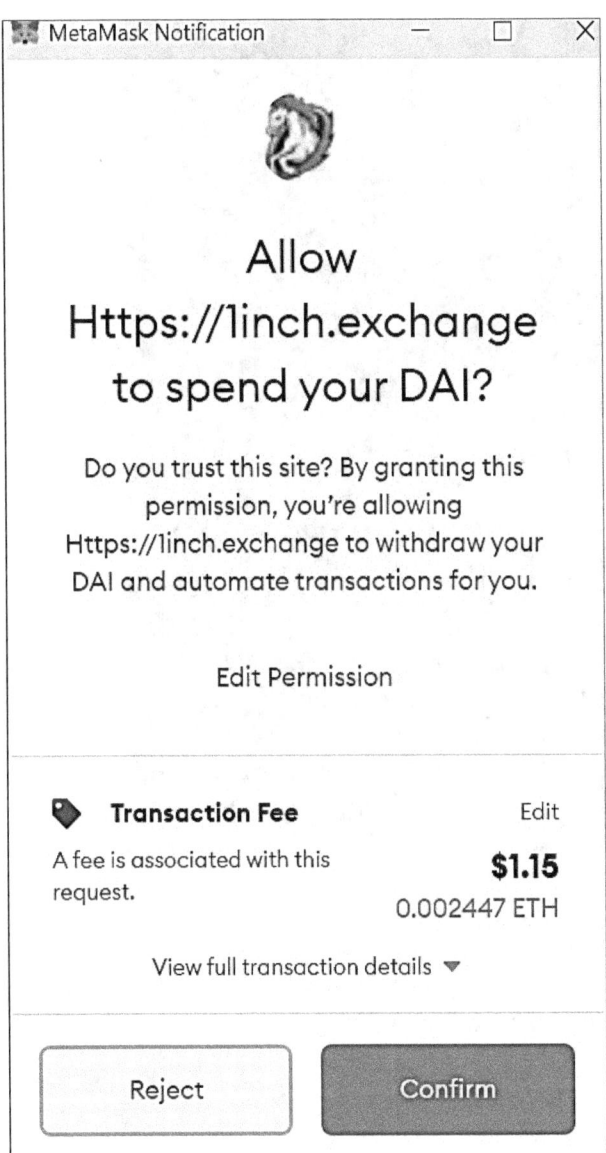

Figure 3.67

Finally, click the SWAP Token button to proceed, as seen in Figure 3.68.

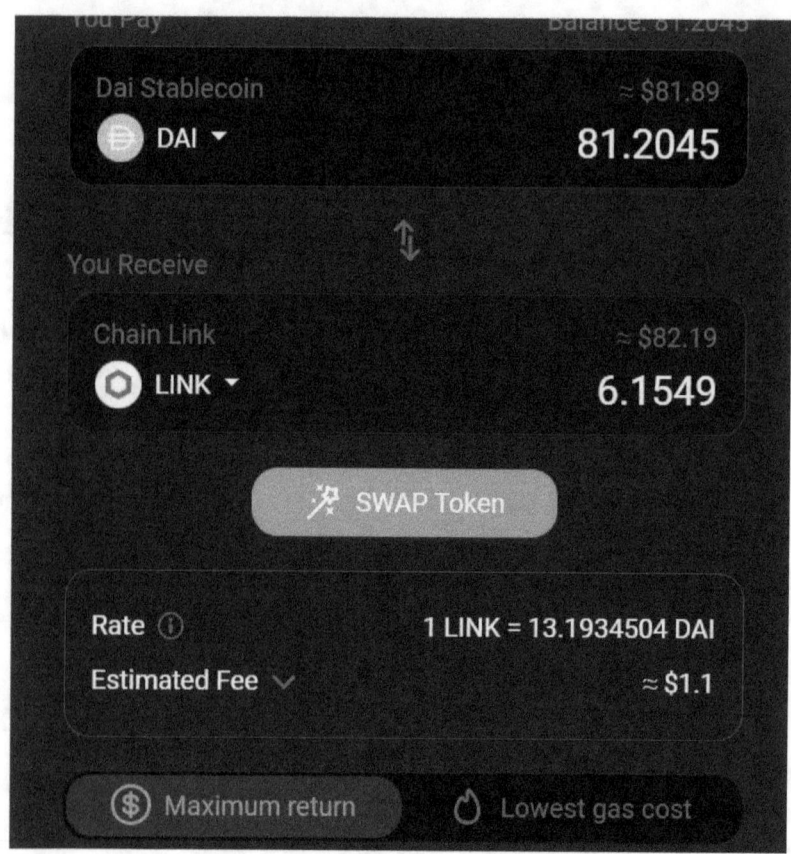

Figure 3.68

You must confirm the swap, as seen in Figure 3.69.

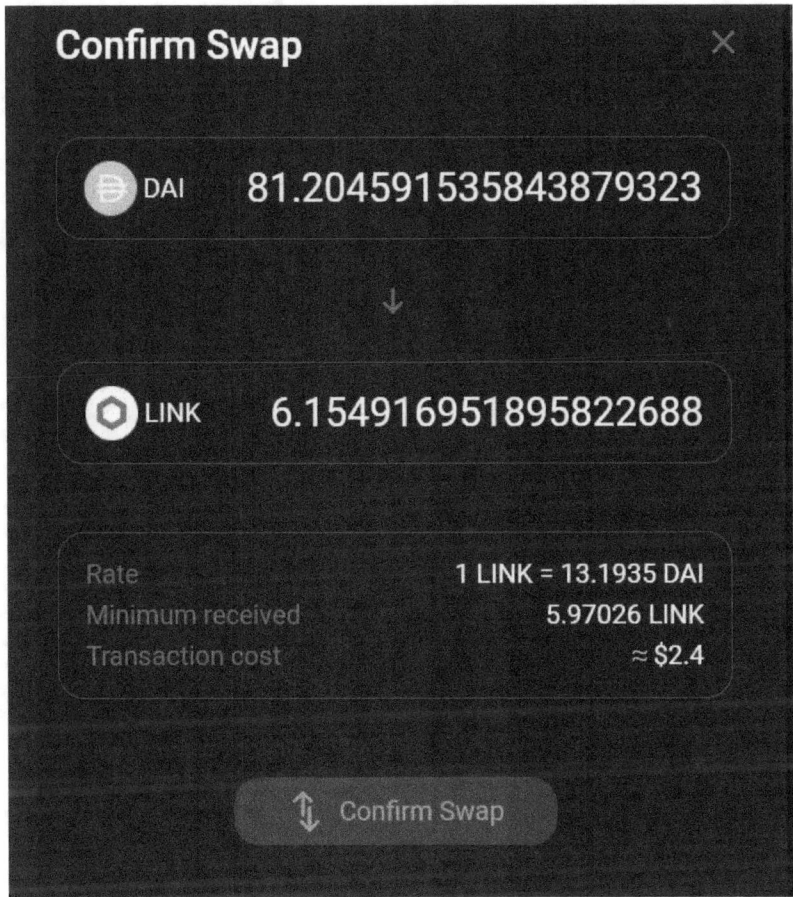

Figure 3.69

Finally, confirm the swap on your wallet. Now you will see your wallet is funded with Link.

3.11 Airswap-A Peer-to-Peer Trading Platform

According to Decrpt (Tran K. C., 2019), AirSwap is a peer-to-peer trading platform for ETH and ERC20 tokens. Users trade their tokens directly with each other without any intermediary. The platform is decentralized because AirSwap does not control the users' funds and trading execution is done via smart contracts.

The AirSwap platform works by having users communicate with each other what tokens they wish to exchange and at what price. When both parties are ready to complete the exchange, the Swap Protocol, which is an Ethereum smart contract, then executes the trade.

To access Airswap, use the following link:

https://www.airswap.io/

The landing page is as seen in Figure 3.70.

Figure 3.70

You have the option to choose 'Trade Now' or 'Swap OTC'. Trade Now allows p2p trading whilst Swap OTC allows you to advertise your offer price and let users bid for your offer.

Let us proceed to trade by clicking the 'Trade Now' button. The Trade Now UI is as shown in Figure 3.71. As usual, you must connect your wallet to be able to trade. Let us say you wish to buy 20 DAI.

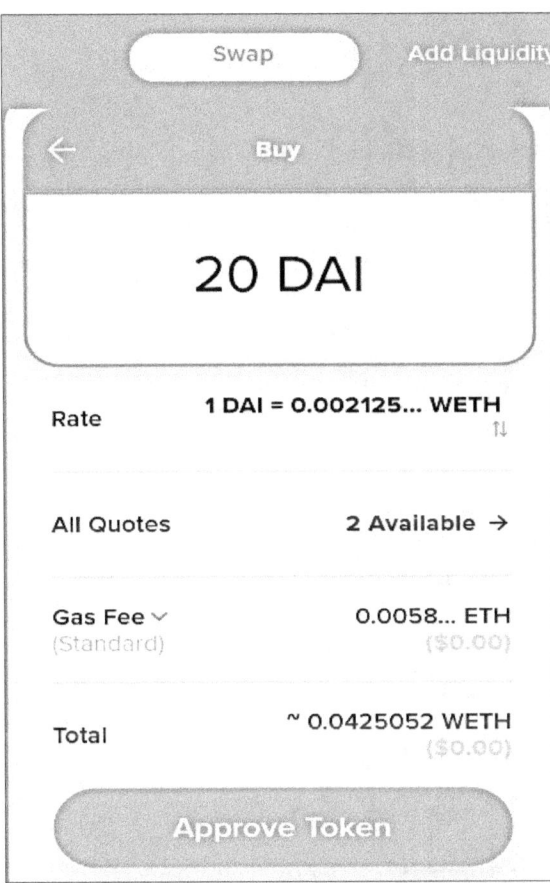

Figure 3.71

Next, click the 'Get Quotes' to get the best rate offered by peers, as seen in Figure 3.72.

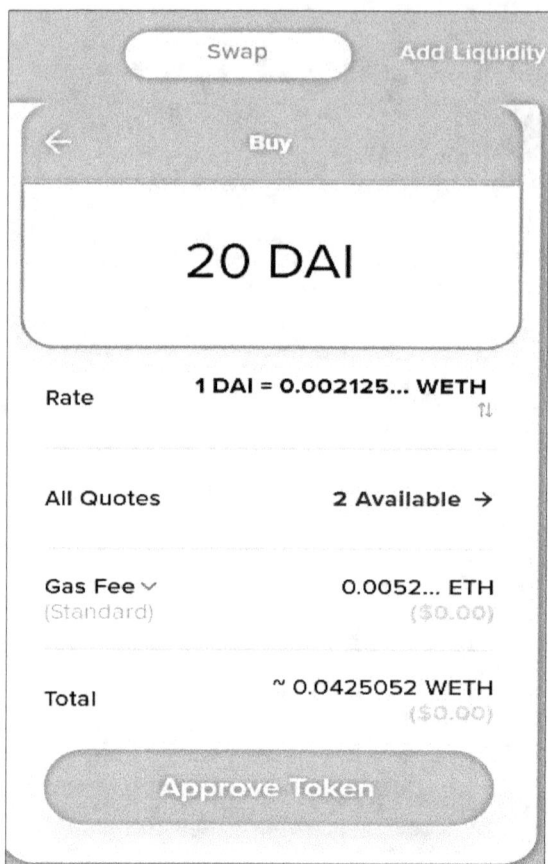

Figure 3.72

The next step is to approve swap or approve wrapper. Approve wrapper is only needed for ETH trading as it will automatically wrap or unwrap your ETH. Subsequently confirm your trade on your wallet.

Next, you might want to create your offer by using the Swap OTC feature. Let us say you wish to create an offer to swap USDT with DAI. You can set up your offer as seen in Figure 3.73.

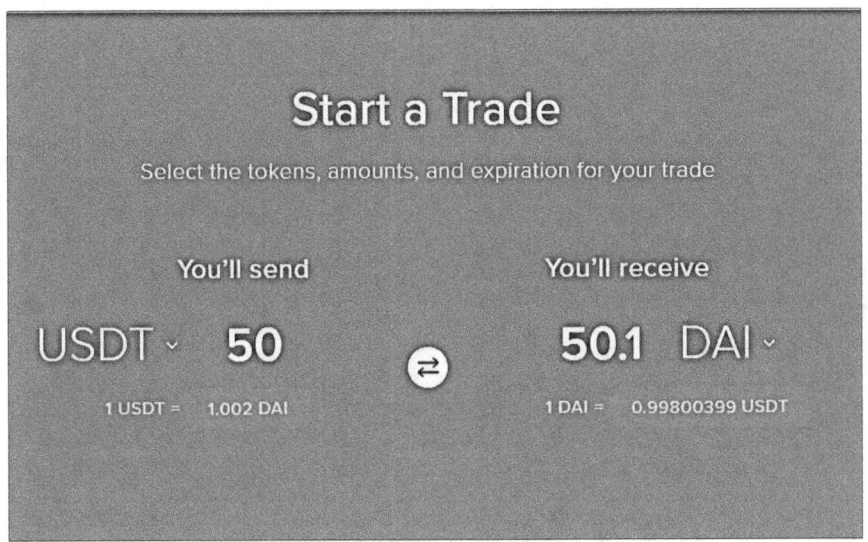

Figure 3.73

After clicking the Create button you must connect your wallet to Airswap, as shown in Figure 3.74.

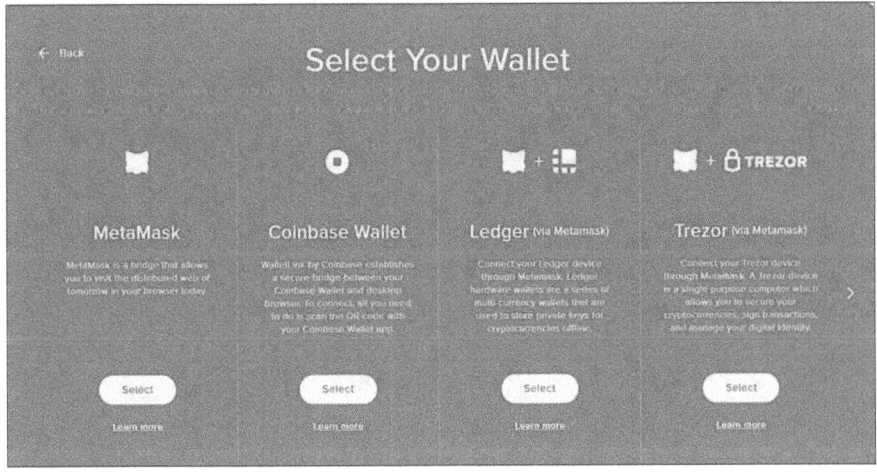

Figure 3.74

You must give AirSwap's smart contract permission to swap USDT. You only need to do this once for each token, as seen in Figure 3.75.

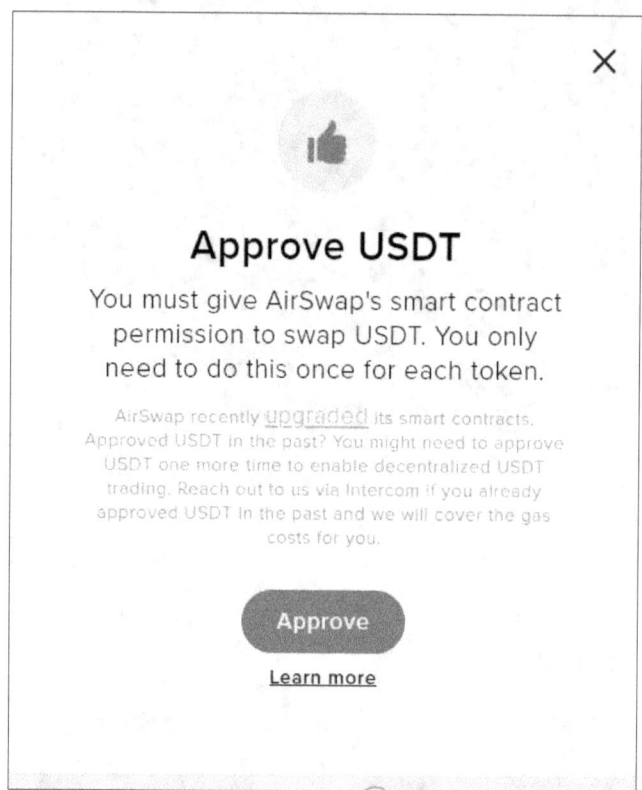

Figure 3.75

You must confirm the approval of the smart contract at your wallet, as shown in Figure 3.76.

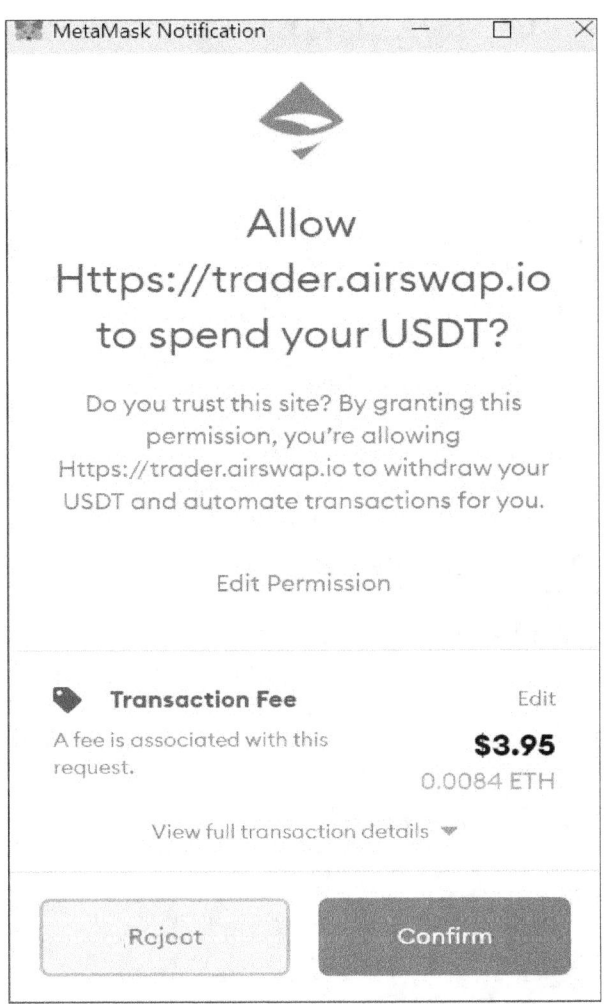

Figure 3.76

Upon confirmation you need to sign the request, as seen in Figure 3.77.

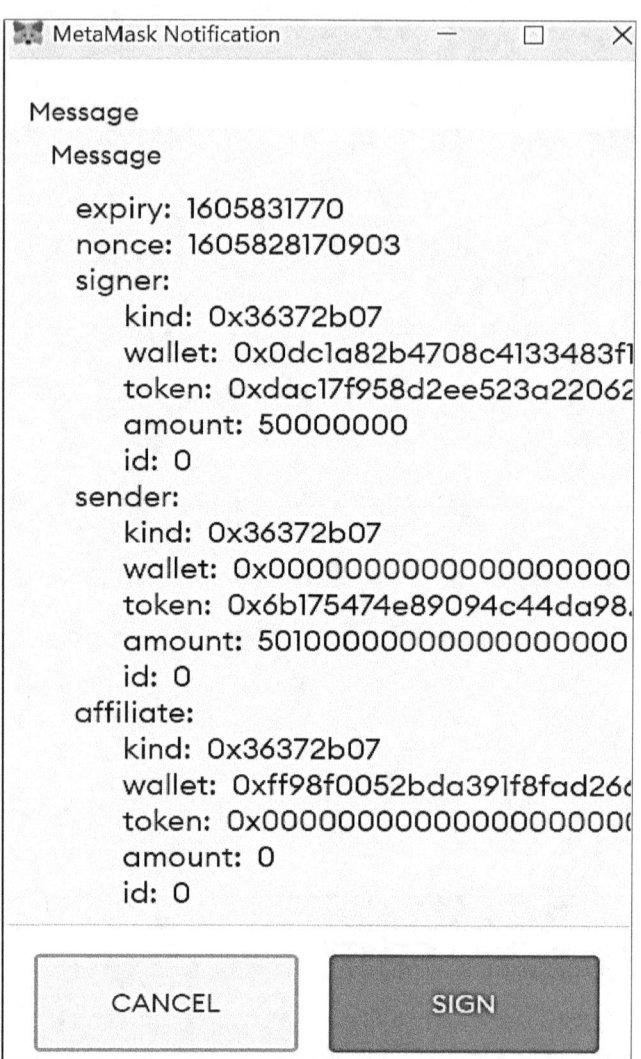

Figure 3.77

Finally, share your link to start trading at Airswap, as seen in Figure 3.78.

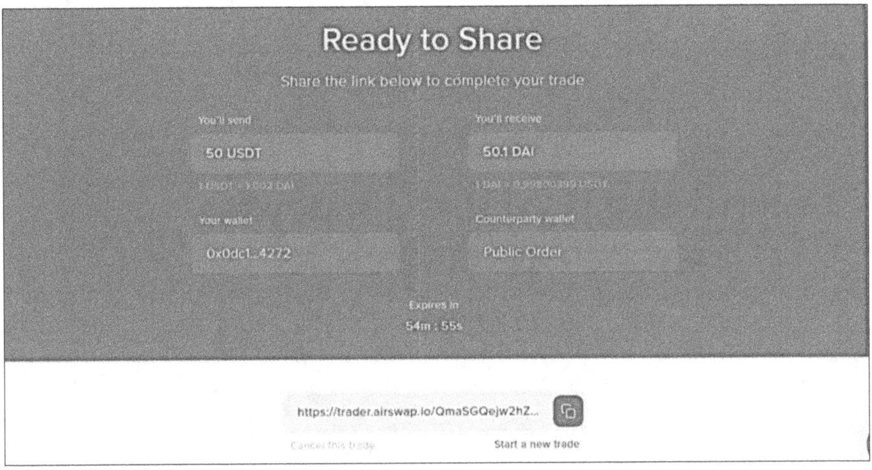

Figure 3.78

3.12 Matcha-A DEX Powered by 0x

Matcha is a decentralized exchange powered by the 0x protocol. Matcha is different from other decentralized exchanges in that it splits trades across 0x Mesh, Kyber, Uniswap, Curve, Oasis, and its own proprietary liquidity sources to find the best prices for traders (Kalani, 2020).

To access Matcha, use the following link:

https://matcha.xyz/

The landing page is as shown in Figure 3.79.

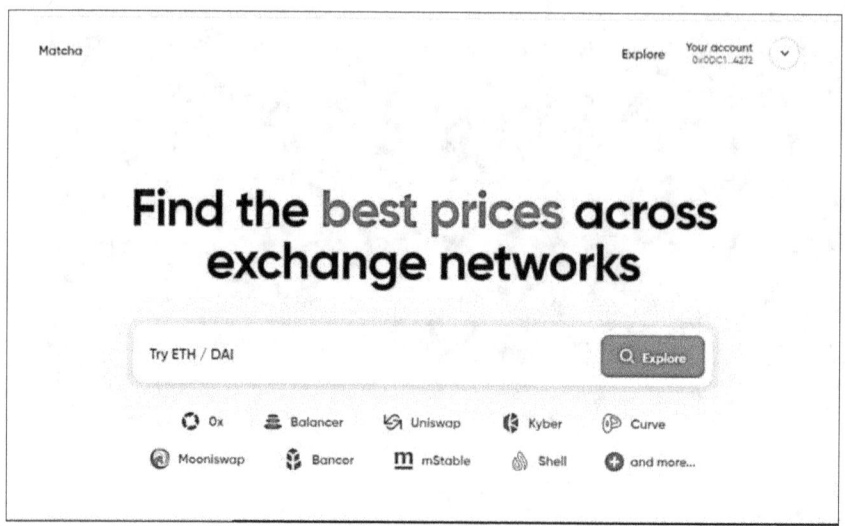

Figure 3.79

You must connect your wallet to start trading on Matcha. To start trading, click Explore to proceed. Matcha allows you to select from different categories of tokens, as seen in Figure 3.80.

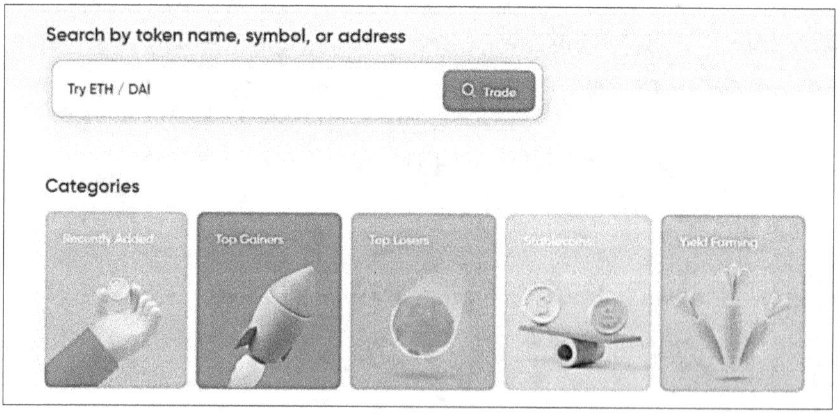

Figure 3.80

Let us select the 'Top Gainers' category and view the tokens in this category, as seen in Figure 3.81.

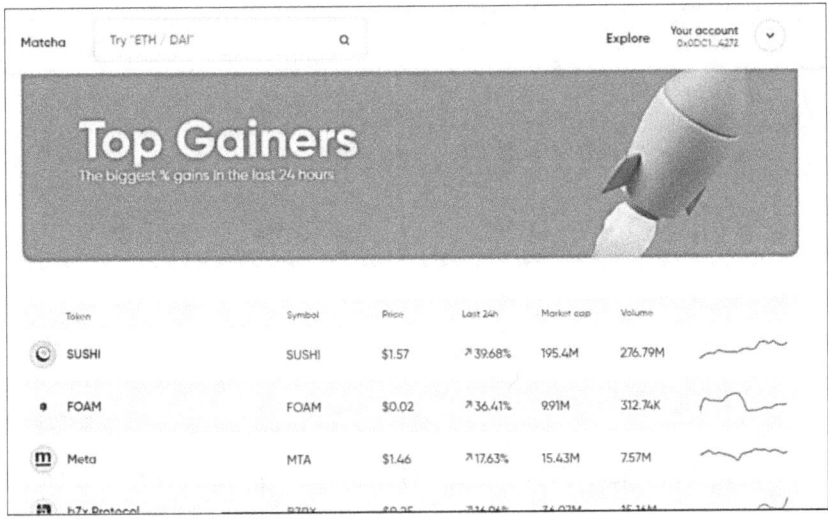

Figure 3.81

To trade a token, click on the token to launch the trading panel, as seen in Figure 20.4. Notice that the market information is also displayed on the trading page. Our example here is SUSHI token. Let us buy SUSHI with USDT, as shown in Figure 3.82.

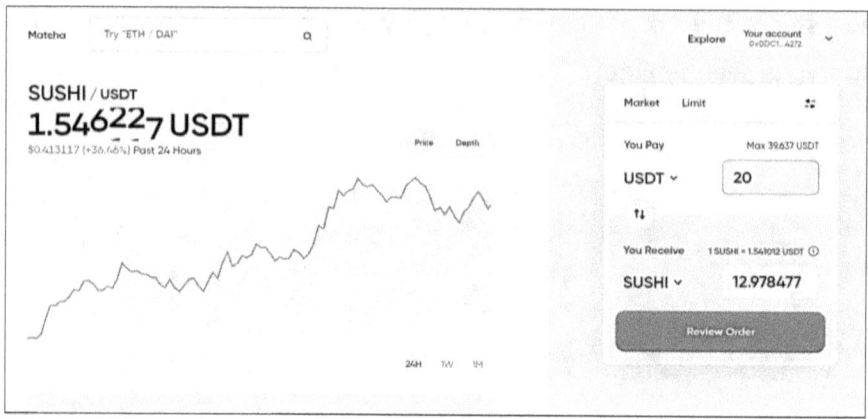

Figure 3.82

You are required to review your order before placing the order, as shown in Figure 3.83.

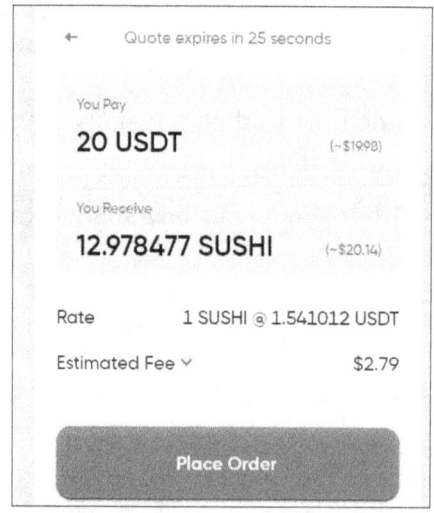

Figure 3.83

If you are satisfied with the quote, you can proceed to place the order and confirm the request at MetaMask, as shown in Figure 3.84.

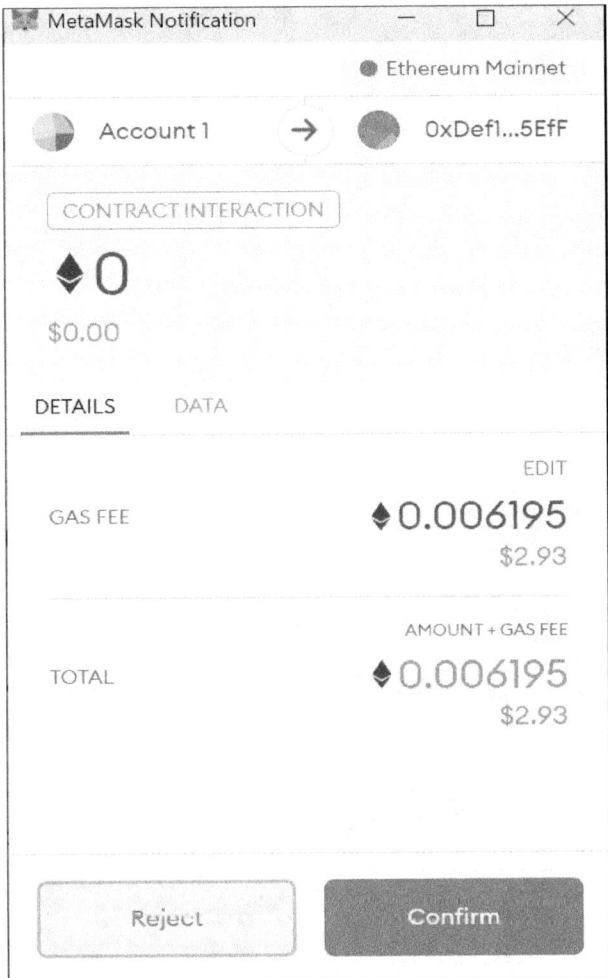

Figure 3.84

Upon successful confirmation, you will be notified by Matcha, as shown in Figure 3.85.

Figure 3.85

You will see that your wallet has been funded with the SUSHI token.

3.13 Tokenlon-An Atomic Token Swap DEX

Tokenlon is a decentralized exchange based on 0x protocol that enables decentralized atomic token exchange. It claims that it can provide instant token swapping as it operates at high speed (Tokenlon, 2020). Besides, it also offers better pricing for using its services.

To use Tokenlon, visit the following site:

https://tokenlon.im/instant#/

Its landing page is as seen in Figure 3.86.

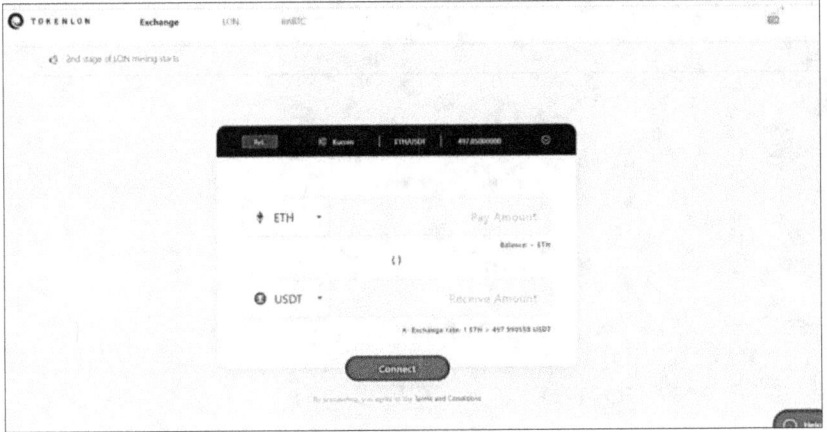

Figure 3.86

It should prompt you to connect your wallet upon loading the page. Otherwise, you must click on the Connect button to connect your wallet. Clicking the Connect button will prompt you to select a wallet, as shown in Figure 3.87.

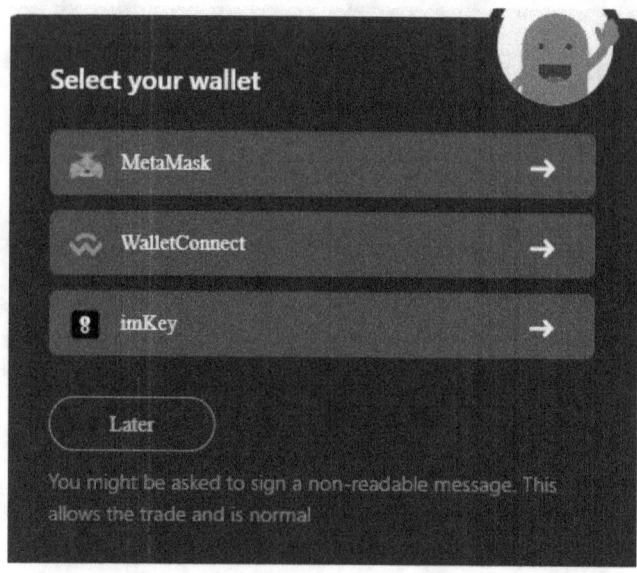

Figure 3.87

When your wallet is connected, you can see your wallet balance, as seen in Figure 3.88.

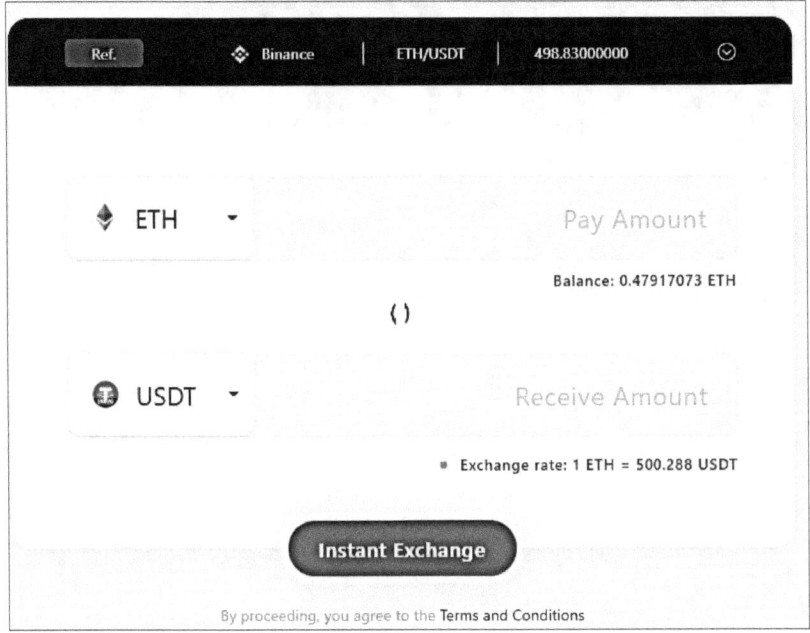

Figure 3.88

Let say you want to swap USDT to LINK, as seen in Figure 3.89. The reason the Instant Exchange button is blurred is because you must give TokenIon permission to spend your USDT.

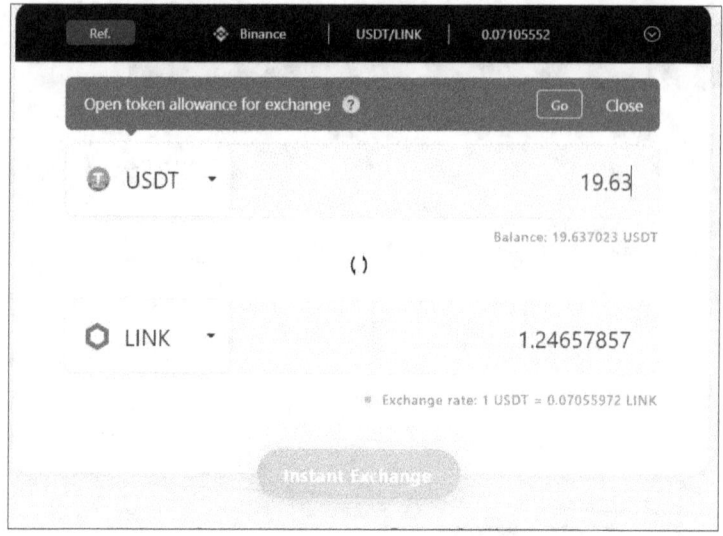

Figure 3.89

Next, click the Go button to authorize TokenIon to spend your USDT, as shown in Figure 3.89. Click the Confirm button on your wallet to finalize the authorization. Once authorized you will see the following message, as seen in Figure 3.90.

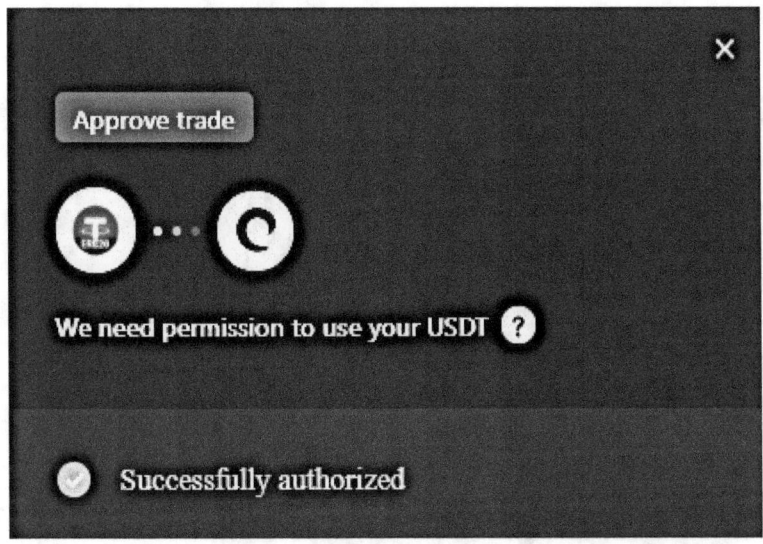

Figure 3.90

Once your USDT is authorized you may start swapping your token, as seen in Figure 3.91.

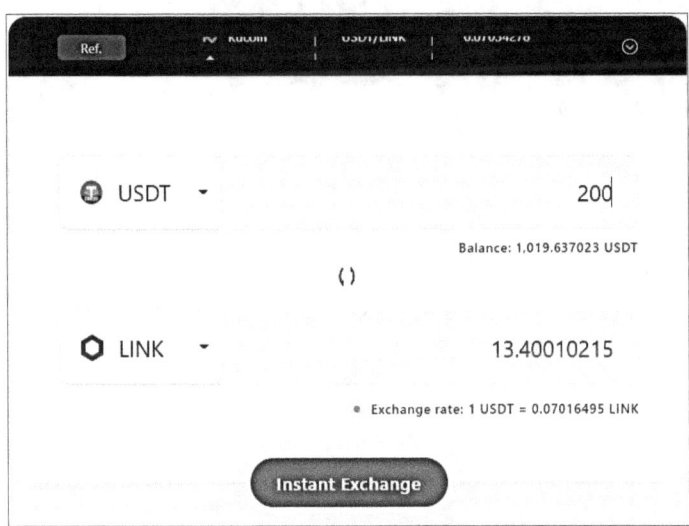

Figure 3.91

Upon clicking the Instant Exchange button, you will see your transaction has been submitted and that the transaction is pending, as seen in Figure 3.92.

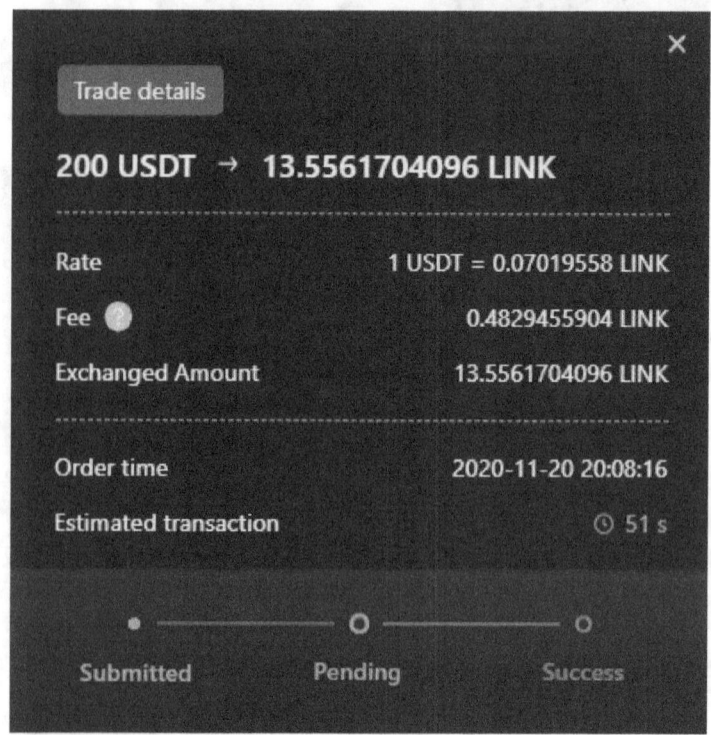

Figure 3.92

Once the transaction is successful, you can see the details such as gas fee and the amount of LINK you received, as shown in Figure 3.93.

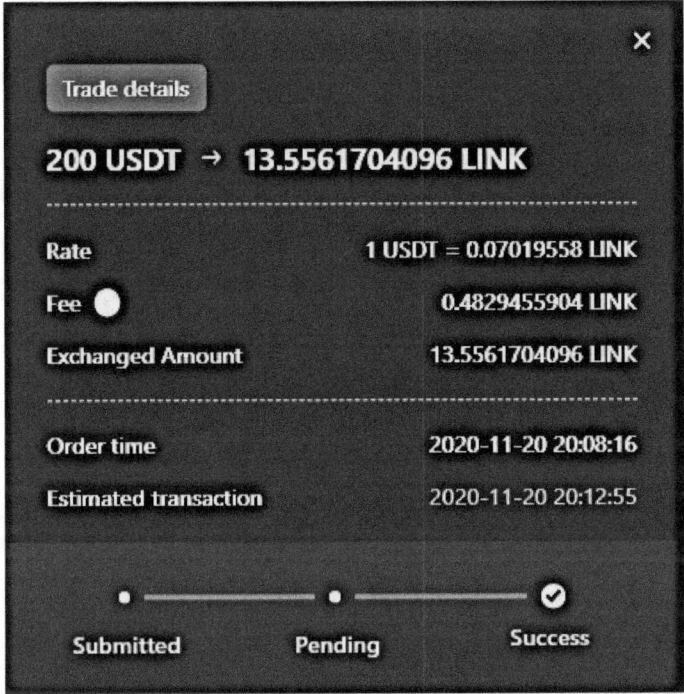

Figure 3.93

3.14 Totle Swap-A DEX Aggregator

Totle Swap is another DEX aggregator that makes decentralized exchanges and synthetic asset providers into a set of tools that makes it easy to trade DeFi assets at the best price.

To access Totle Swap, visit:

https://www.totle.com/

The landing page is as seen in Figure 3.94.

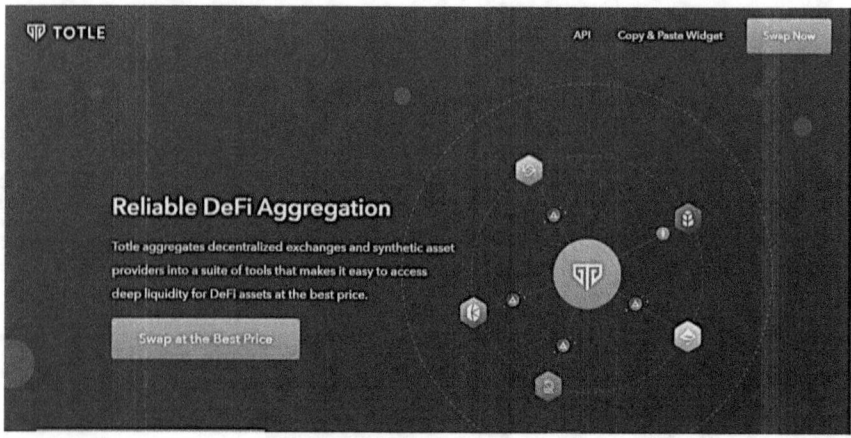

Figure 3.94

Next, click the 'Swap Now' button or 'Swap at the Best Price' to enter the exchange dashboard, as shown in Figure 3.95.

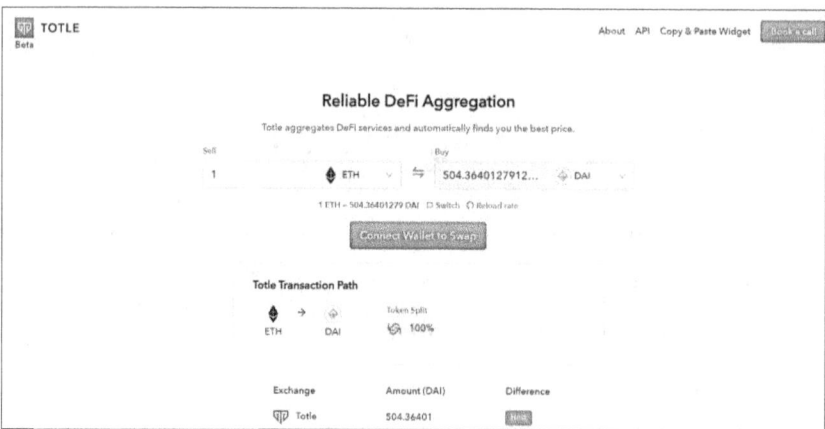

Figure 3.95

You must connect your wallet to swap tokens. Choose the wallet you wish to connect, as seen in Figure 3.96.

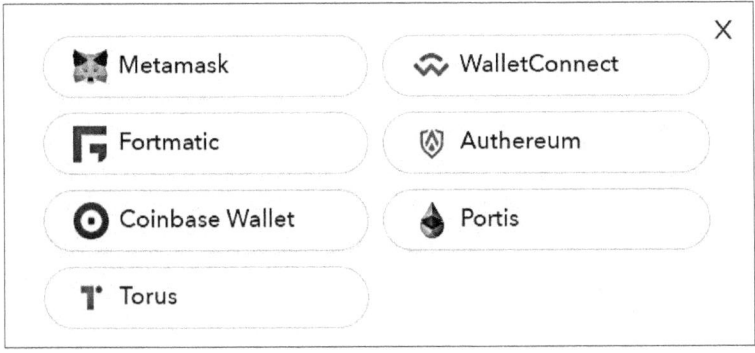

Figure 3.96

Once your wallet is connected you can start trading in Totle. Let us buy some UNI with USDT, as shown in Figure 3.97.

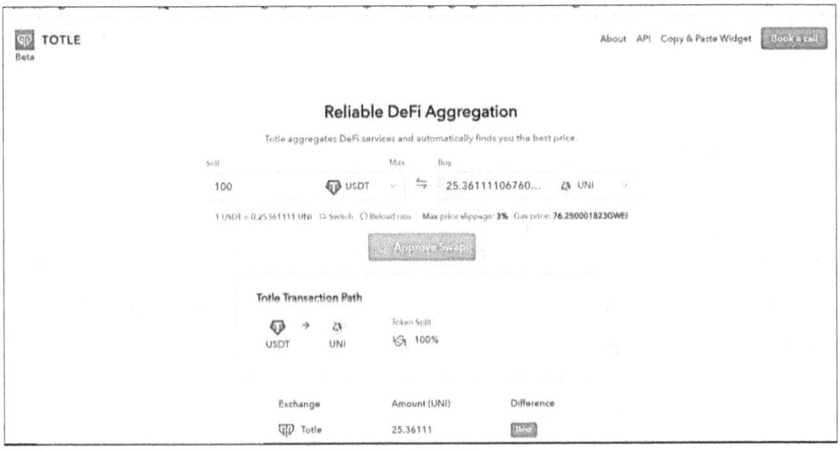

Figure 3.97

Click the 'Approve Swap' button to proceed and click 'Confirm' on your wallet to permit Totle to spend your USDT. Once the permission to spend USDT is approved you can proceed to swap the token, as seen in Figure 3.98.

Figure 3.98

Next, click the 'Submit Swap' button followed by the 'Confirm' button on your wallet. Once confirmed, UNI will be deposited in your wallet.

3.15 DEX.AG-Another DEX Aggregator

Dex.ag is another DEX aggregator that has aggregated some popular decentralized exchanges comprising Uniswap, Oasis, 0x, Kyber Swap, Curve, Balancer, Bancor and more (DeBank, n.d.).

To access its website, use the following link:

https://dex.ag/

The landing page is as shown in Figure 3.99.

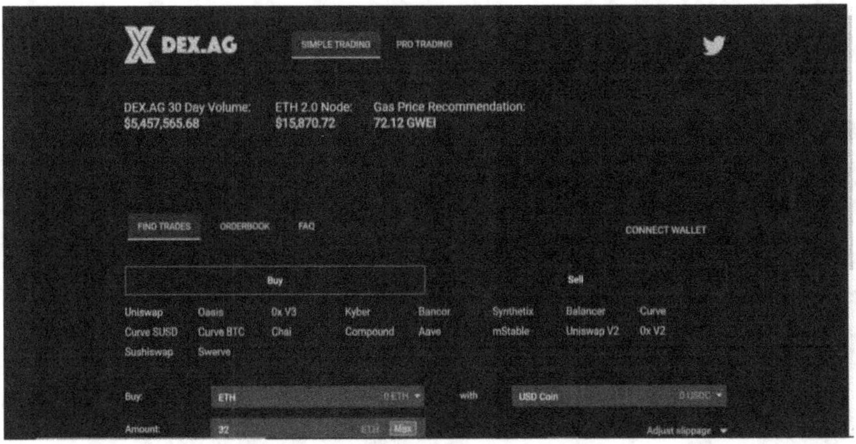

Figure 3.99

You must connect your wallet to start trading in Dex.ag. When the connection is established, your wallet address will appear, as seen in Figure 3.100.

Figure 3.100

You may choose simple trading or pro trading. For simple trading, just pick the token you wish to buy, and which token you wish to sell.

When you pick the token you wish to sell, you can see the availability of each token in your wallet, as seen in Figure 3.101.

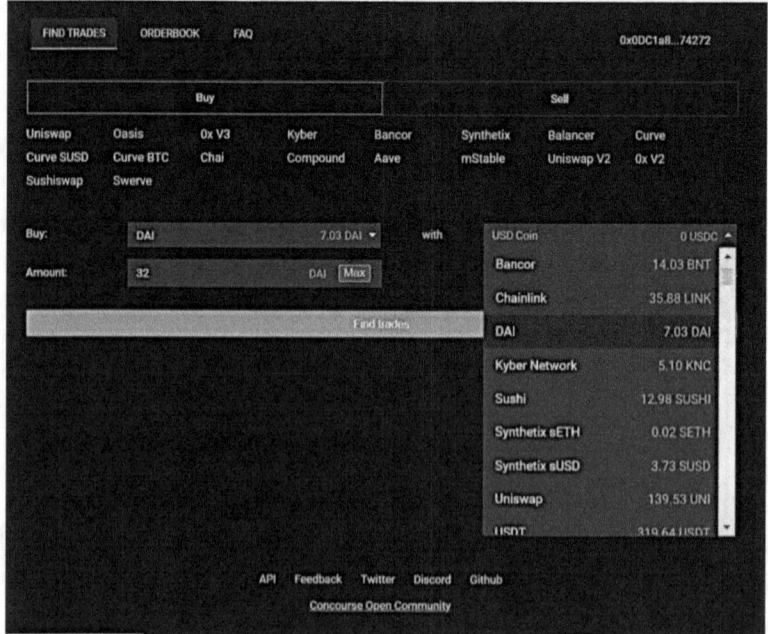

Figure 3.101

After you have selected your tokens to buy and sell, you can click the Find Trades button to find the best rates, as shown in Figure 3.102.

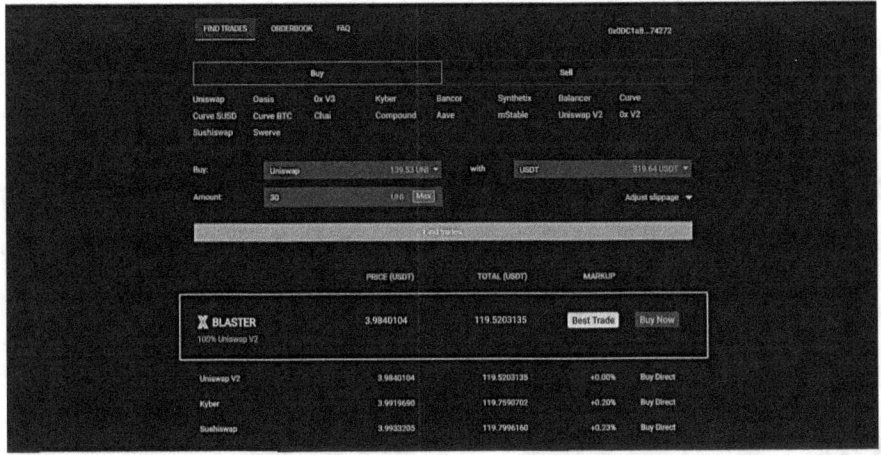

Figure 3.102

When you are satisfied with the rate, click the 'Buy Now' button to grant permission to Dex.ag to spend your USDT. Next, confirm the trade on your wallet if you are satisfied with the gas fee.

In Pro Trading, you can buy and sell tokens using limit order. To access Pro Trading, click the Pro Trading tab and launch the real-time trading portal, as shown in Figure 3.103.

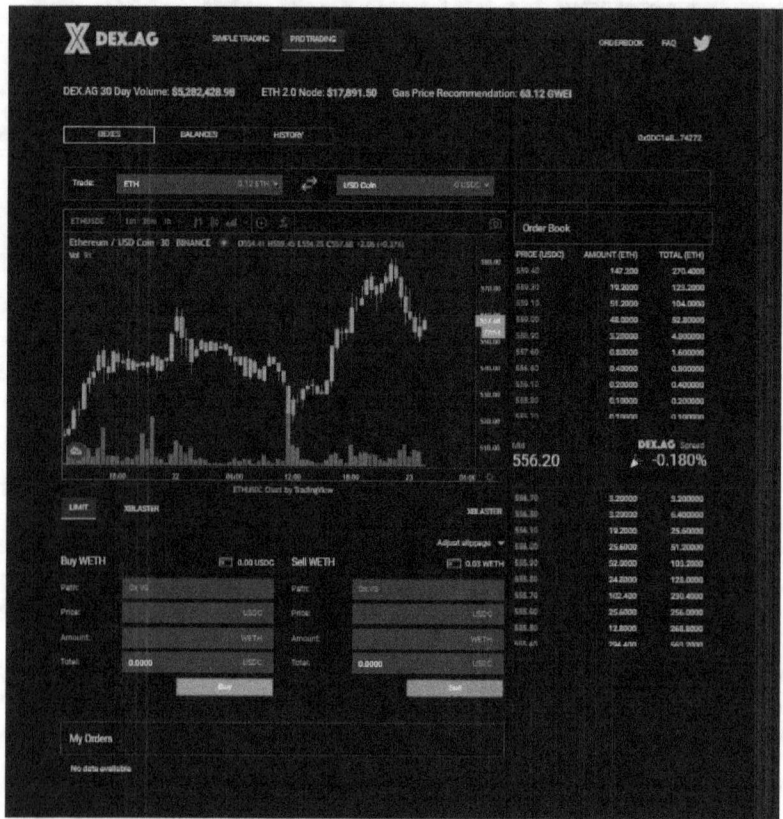

Figure 3.103

In the trading page, you can also view the charts, your balances, and your trading history.

To start trading, you must choose the token pair. The default is ETH/DAI, but you can choose any other pair by clicking the drop-down button, as seen in Figure 3.104.

Figure 3.104

By the way, Dex.ag use WETH to trade instead of ETH. Therefore, if you only have ETH, you must wrap it first before trading. To wrap your ETH, click the 'Balances' tab to access the Balances page. Under the 'Actions' column next to ETH, click 'Wrap' and enter the amount of ETH you wish to wrap and press the 'Go!' button, as shown in Figure 3.105.

Figure 3.105

Next, confirm the transaction on your wallet. Once your transaction is confirmed, the WETH will be shown under your balances page. Unwrapping WETH back into ETH is as simple as clicking the 'Unwrap' next to WETH under 'Balances', entering the amount you want to unwrap, and submitting your transaction, as shown in Figure 3.106.

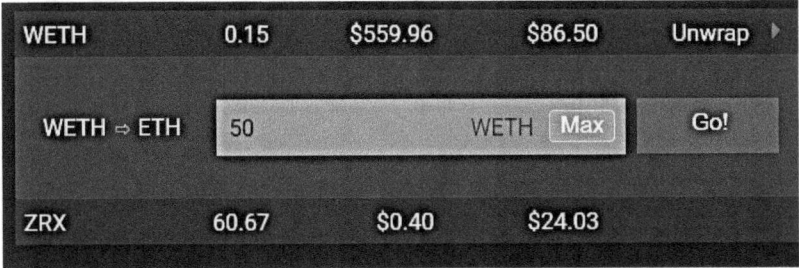

Figure 3.106

To start trading, place the limit order by setting a target price and the amount you wish to buy or sell, as seen in Figure 3.107.

Figure 3.107

This trade order is placed on the 0x order books where it can be filled by 0x trades on DEX.AG. Please note that placing a limit order costs 0 gas fees because the trader who fills your limit order pays the gas to submit the transaction.

3.16 DDEX- A Decentralzied Margin Trading and Lending Platform

DDEX is another decentralized exchange that allows margin and spot trading, as well as lending and borrowing. DDEX is a unique platform because it uses a hybrid of two protocols (hydro and 0x) offering matching that is done off-chain, and settlement that is done on-chain.

It claimed that it is the first exchange that offers off-chain matching, giving it an advantage over other platforms with higher speed and liquidity. The hybrid approach has enabled DDEX exchange to operate 50 times faster than its competitors, and with less fees. To start margin trade, open the link below:

https://ddex.io/margin/ETH-USDT

The margin trade landing page is as shown in Figure 3.108.

Figure 3.108

With margin trade, you can either go long or short with leverage. Let say you wish to long 10 ETH with 5x leverage, you must deposit 2 ETH to borrow USDT to buy ETH, as show in Figure 3.109.

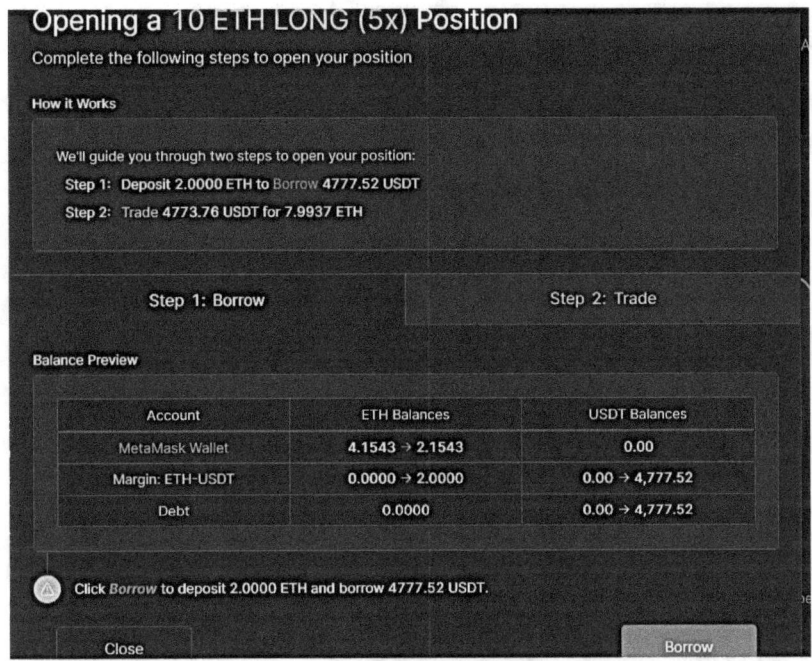

Figure 3.109

On the other hand, if you wish to go short for 10 ETH with 5x leverage, you need to have margin deposit of 1186.24 USDT(=2ETH) based on the current price of ETH at 593.05, as shown in Figure 3.110.

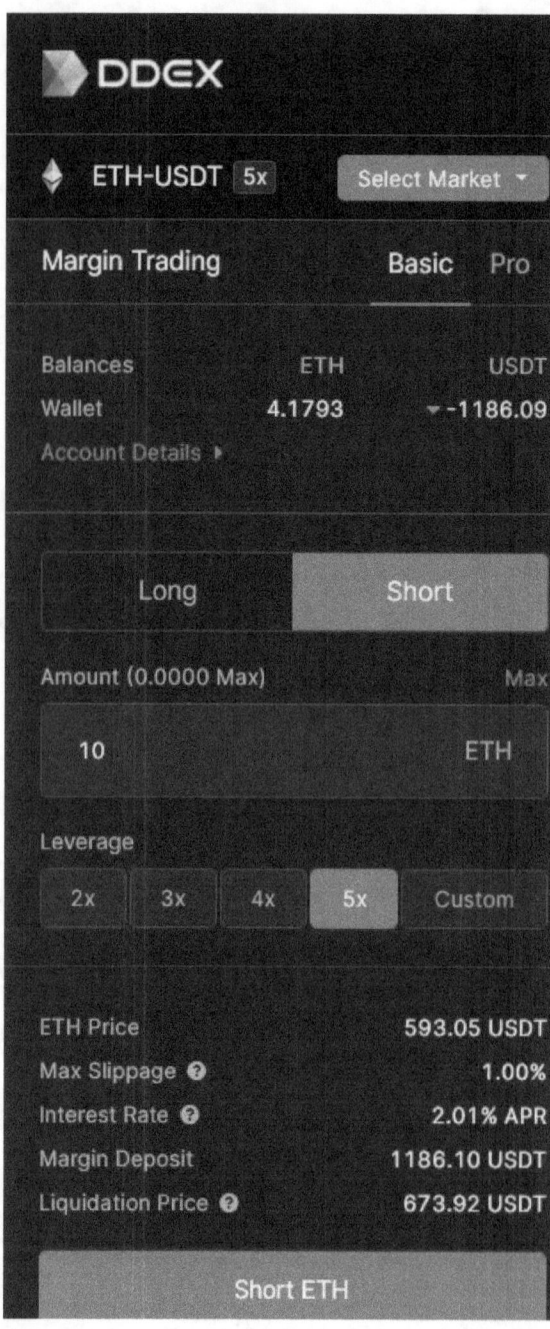

Figure 3.110

After you opened a position, you can close it anytime you wish. You can view your position real time, as shown in Figure 3.111.

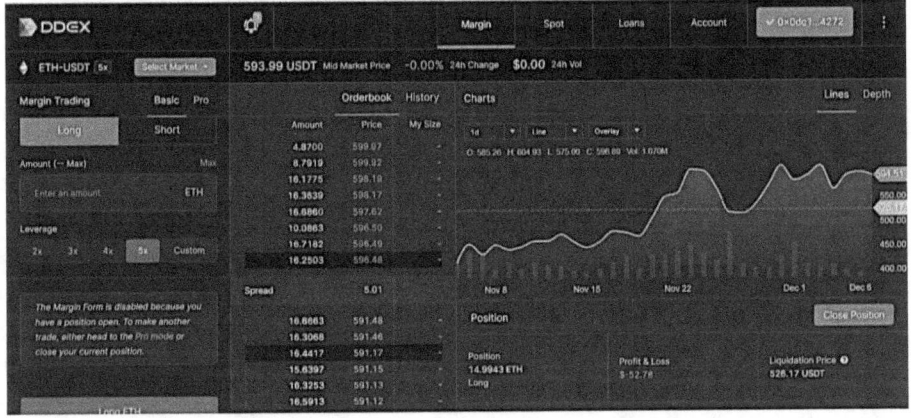

Figure 3.111

It will show your profit and loss real time as well as the liquidation price.

Besides margin trading, you can also do spot trading as shown in Figure 3.112.

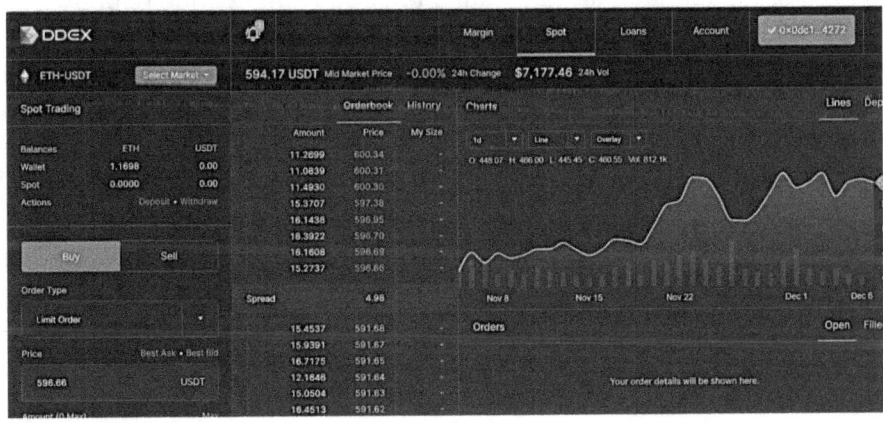

Figure 3.112

In addition, you can also lend and borrow on DDEX platform, as shown in Figure 3.113.

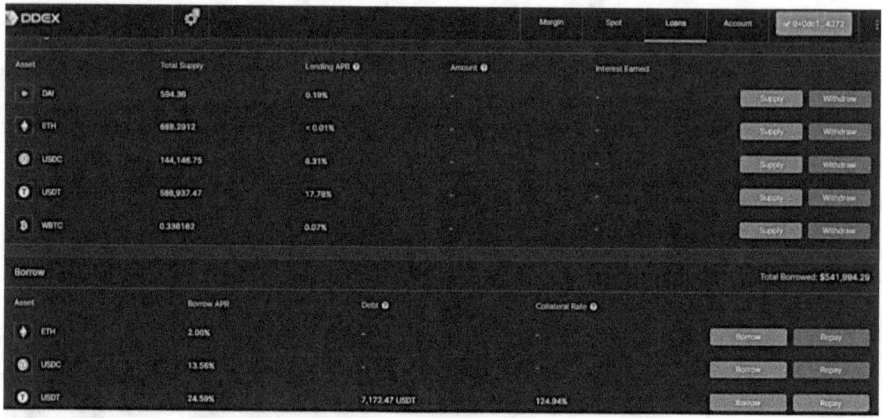

Figure 3.113

3.17 Swerve Finance

Swerve is a community-owned and governed fork of Curve Finance, an AMM-based decentalized exchange specializing in efficient stablecoin swaps. Swerve was originally launched in 2020 with just one pool of stablecoins (DAI, USDC, USDT and TUSD) which allowed Swerve to cut gas costs down dramatically for interactions.

When users provide liquidity to Swerve, they receive swUSD tokens which can be staked in the Swerve DAO to earn SWRV tokens. 100% of SWRV tokens were distributed and "farmed" by the community. Swerve DAO members propose and vote on protocol changes such as adding new liquidity pools.

To access Swerve Finance, use the following link:

https://swerve.fi/

At the landing page, click the 'SWERVE APP' button to enter the app page where you can swap tokens in the pools, as shown in Figure 3.114

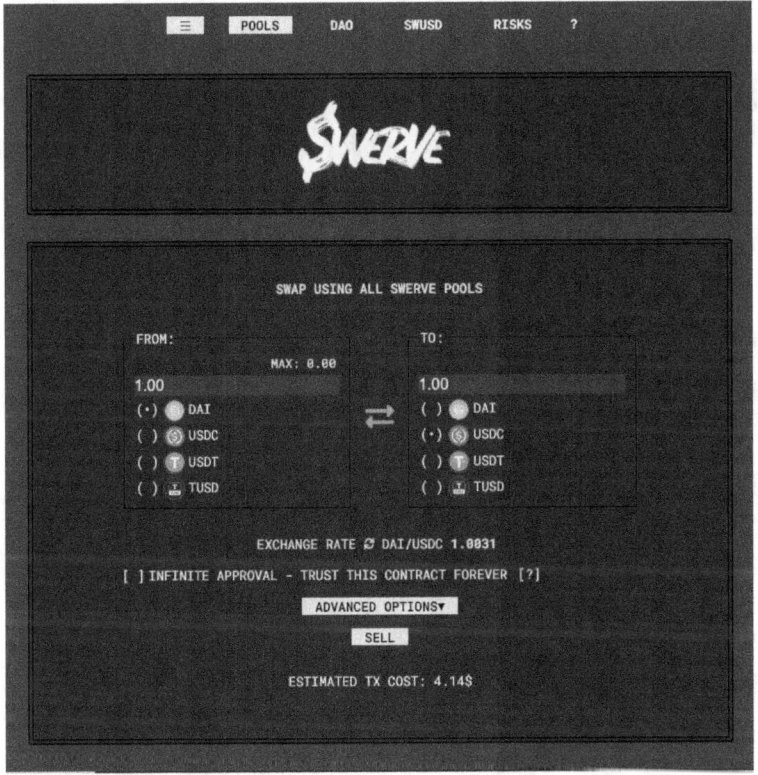

Figure 3.114

Chapter 4
Yield Farming

4.1 What is Yield Farming?

Yield farming is an activity that uses crypto assets to maximize return on those assets. Yield farming rewards users for providing digital assets to liquidity pools or providing other value-added services to a decentralized application's ecosystem (Chainlink, 2020). The money used to pay the yield farmers comprises trading fees within a decentralized exchange and interest from lending in a money market. Yield farming is also known as liquidity mining.

Yield farmers are usually paid pro rata in an application's native governance token, allowing the user to earn a higher Annual Percentage Yield (APY). In addition, some projects also include yield farming rewards for other services, such as user participation on the platform or supporting community, marketing, or developer initiatives.

To gain more profit, yield farmers can continually chase after pools that seemingly offer the best APY (Annual Percentage Yield). This may involve moving to risky pools from time to time and yield farmers must mitigate the risk.

In some sense, yield farming is like staking but is much more complex. In many cases, it works with users called liquidity providers (LP) that add funds to liquidity pools. For example, a yielding farmer puts 100,000 USDT into the Compound. In return, he or she will get a token for the stock, called cUSDT.

Let us say he or she gets 100,000 cUSDT back. He or she can then put the cUSDT into a liquidity pool that uses cUSDT in Balancer, an AMM (auto market maker) that allows users to set up a crypto index fund that is rebalanced every now and then. Usually, yield farmers can earn a small amount of transaction fees in this way. This is the basic idea of yield farming. Yield farmers are looking for sophisticated cases in the system to produce as many results as possible in as many products as possible.

Yield Farming has two main objectives. First, it is to incentivize users to deposit and lock up their liquidity into a DeFi protocol and grow the Total Value Locked (TVL), and building the supply side of the ecosystem (Chainlink, 2020). More liquidity will reduce slippage for users and stimulates growth in the demand side of the DeFi ecosystem.

Second, Yield Farming attempts to fairly distribute a DeFi application's governance token to protocol users who absorb the opportunity cost of not depositing their funds elsewhere (impermanent loss). The fair distribution of tokens enshrines decentralized governance as none of the supplied digital assets is set aside for privileged entities.

The pioneer of Yield Farming was Synthetix, a decentralized derivatives protocol powered by Chainlink price feeds (Chainlink, 2020). In 2019, Synthetix launched a liquidity mechanism to reward sETH/ETH liquidity providers on Uniswap. Users who staked their tokenized sETH/ETH liquidity pool shares from Uniswap into a staking contract earned a proportional amount of SNX.

To increase the liquidity incentivization and ensure fair distribution of tokens in Yield Farming, smart contract developers have leveraged additional infrastructure to further improve upon these goals. One of such infrastructure providers is Chainlink which provides price feeds powered by decentralized oracle networks. Chainlink Price Feeds are used widely in Yield Farming.

All the protocols we have discussed so far involve some kind of yield farming, but there are a few DeFi protocols that are specifically geared towards yield farming. They are Yearn Finance, Yam Finance and Sushi Swap, which we shall examine in later chapters.

Be incredibly careful when you invest via yield farming. It can be very risky. Fortunately, you can assess the yield farming risk by visiting the following website hosted by CoinMarketCap:

https://coinmarketcap.com/yield-farming/

This website displays APY as well as impermanent loss rating of all the DeFi pools, whether high or low, as shown in Figure 4.1. You are advised to do your own research before investing in any yield farming project.

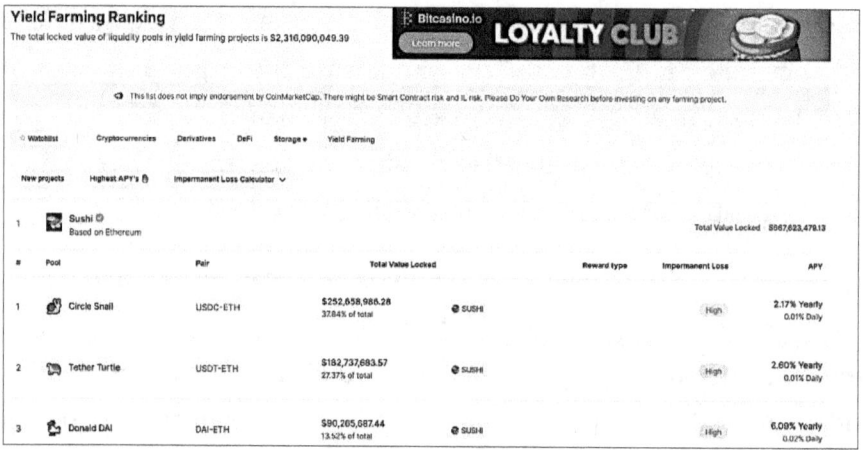

Figure 4.1

4.2 Yield Farming Platforms

Most of the DeFi platforms and protocols in previous chapters involve in some kinds of yield farming. The better ones among are Compound, MakerDAO, Synthetix, Aave, Uniswap, Curve Finance, Yearn Finance and Balancer.

However, all the above platforms require manual rebalancing and management. Fortunately, there are some yield farming platform that allows auto yield farming, they are Harvest Finance and Pickle Finance.

4.2.1 Harvest Finance

Harvest was created for those looking for a convenient way to farm the latest projects that are producing yield for users. When you deposit your tokens to Harvest.Finance, they are put to work in high-yield farming opportunities and you receive an fTokens (fDAI, fUSDC, fWBTC, fUSDT etc) that earns a proportional share of the farming revenue. Besides that, you will also be rewarded with its native FARM token by staking the fTokens.

Furthermore, holders of the FARM token can profit share in the yield farming revenue, receive incentives for providing liquidity in Uniswap, and vote to help decide the direction of the cooperative.

The greatest advantage is Harvest lowers the barrier to entry for people who do not have time to track DeFi 24/7, pay gas costs to harvest regularly and move funds between opportunities and more. Harvest handles the APY tracking, strategy development and auditing, gas costs, and regular harvesting to ensure that returns compound.

To enter Harvest Finance, use the following link:

https://harvest.finance/

The landing page is as shown in Figure 4.2.

| Farm | Stake | FAQ | Dashboard | Wiki | 策略 | Claim |

Your hard work is about to become easier with Harvest 🚜
It ain't much, but it's honest work.

| Deposits in Harvest: 469,960,859.12 USD
Annual Profits to Farmers: 34,726,043.89 USD | Weekly Emission Drop
03 Days 15:48:10.69
BUY FARM | 🚜 FARM price: 104.41 USD
FARM staking APY: 132.95%
Market cap: 35.56M USD
FARM staked: 77% |

Deposit and farm your assets

Amount		Asset	Harvest APY	Deposits ($)	Your balance
0	MAX	♦ WETH	2.14% 🞄 🚜	31.02M	0.000000000
0	MAX	🚜 FARM	132.95% 🚜	19.02M	0.000000000

▼ Stablecoins	🟡 YCRV	🔵 3CRV	🟢 CRV:COMPOUND	APY: 4.29% – 38.94%
	🔵 CRV:BUSD	🟣 CRV:USDN	ⓤ USDC	Deposits($): 123.82M
	🟠 USDT	ⓣ TUSD	◆ DAI	Rewards: 🞄 ⓞ 🚜

Amount		Asset	Harvest APY	Deposits ($)	Your balance
0	MAX	🟡 YCRV	34.19% 🞄 🚜	24.92M	0.000000000
0	MAX	🔵 3CRV	19.31% 🞄 🚜	28.13M	0.000000000
0	MAX	🟢 CRV:COMPOUND	19.92% 🞄 🚜	21.96M	0.000000000
0	MAX	🔵 CRV:BUSD	38.94% 🞄 🚜	13.67M	663.120126835
0	MAX	🟣 CRV:USDN	37.47% 🞄 🚜	13.38M	0.000000000
0	MAX	ⓢ USDC	9.00% ⓞ 🚜	10.09M	0.000000000
0	MAX	🟠 USDT	8.30% ⓞ 🚜	6.99M	0.000000000
0	MAX	ⓣ TUSD	29.05% 🚜	1.49M	0.000000000
0	**MAX**	◆ DAI	4.29% ⓞ 🚜	3.14M	0.000000000

Figure 4.2

You must connect your wallet to use the service. Harvest Finance offers many types of tokens that you can start farming immediately. The APYs are show side-by-side with the tokens. Both native tokens and LP tokens are available for farming. If you do not own a specific token, you can purchase from DEXs like Uniswap or you can follow the link provided by Harvest Finance to obtain the token by staking. For example, if you wish to get CRV-BUSD, just hover you mouse over the token and the link will appear, as shown in Figure 4.3.

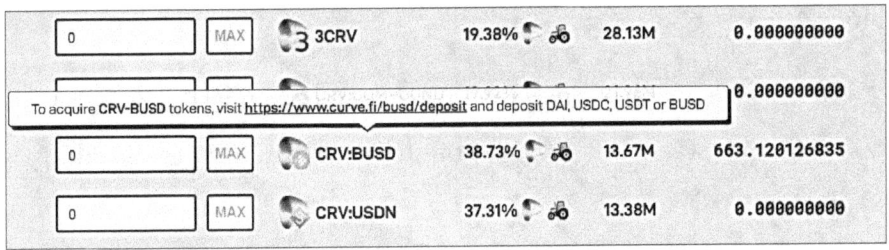

Figure 4.3

If you already own the token, you can deposit or deposit and stake to earn interest. There is a different between deposit and deposit and stake. Harvest Finance will pay you native APY if you just deposit your tokens, you also get the LP tokens (fTokens) which will be deposited in your wallet. However, if you deposit and stake, you will earn the native APY as well as the FARM token rewards.

In this example, the trader already has the LP token CRV-BUSD which was minted when stable coins were deposited in Curve's liquidity pool. The user can again earn APY by depositing and staking CRV-BUSD in Harvest Finance liquidity pool. If the trader just deposited the tokens without staking, Harvest Finance will alert the trader to stake the token to earn better APY, as shown in Figure 4.4.

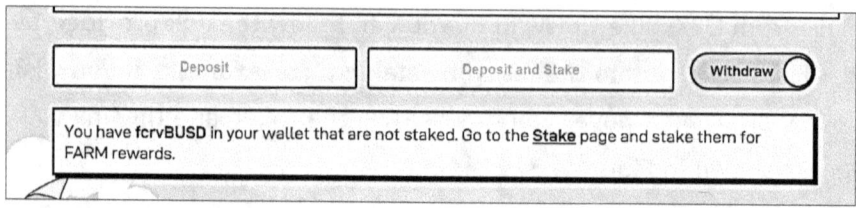

Figure 4.4

Let us click the 'Stake' link to stake the token fcrvBUSD at the staking page in Figure 4.5.

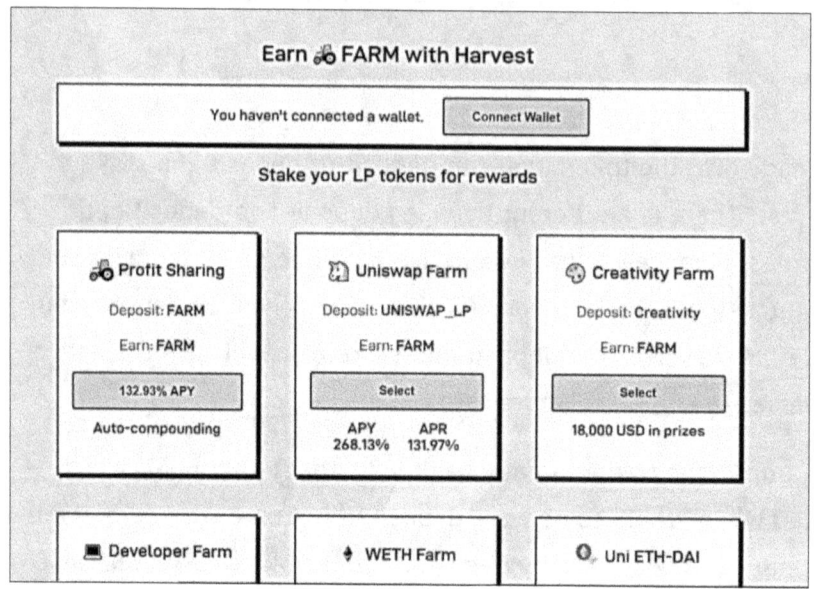

Figure 4.5

Next, select the Farm that you have already deposited FCRV-BUSD, as shown in Figure 4.6

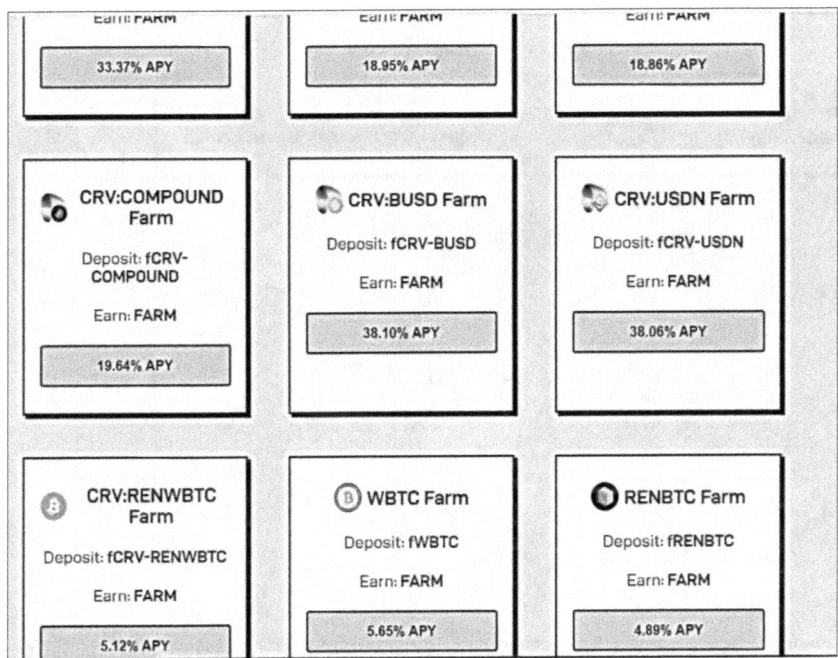

Figure 4.6

Now click the box and you can stake your LP token FCRV-BUSD as shown in Figure 4.7. You can stake any amount or maximum number of tokens.

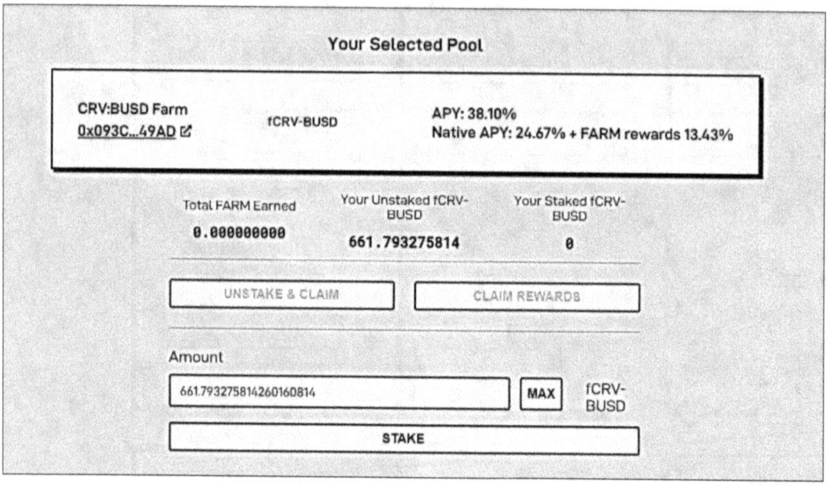

Figure 4.7

To proceed, click the 'STAKE" button and confirm it on your wallet. Once approved, the staked FCRV-BUSD will appear, as shown in Figure 4.8. It also shows that you have earned some FARM rewards.

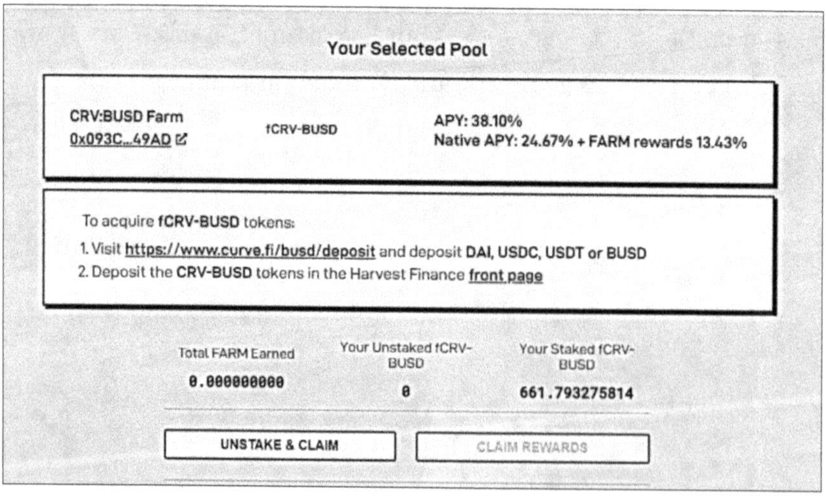

Figure 4.8

If you wish to stake more CRV-BUSD, you need to stake it in CRV or you can add it directly from Zapper, as shown in Figure 4.9.

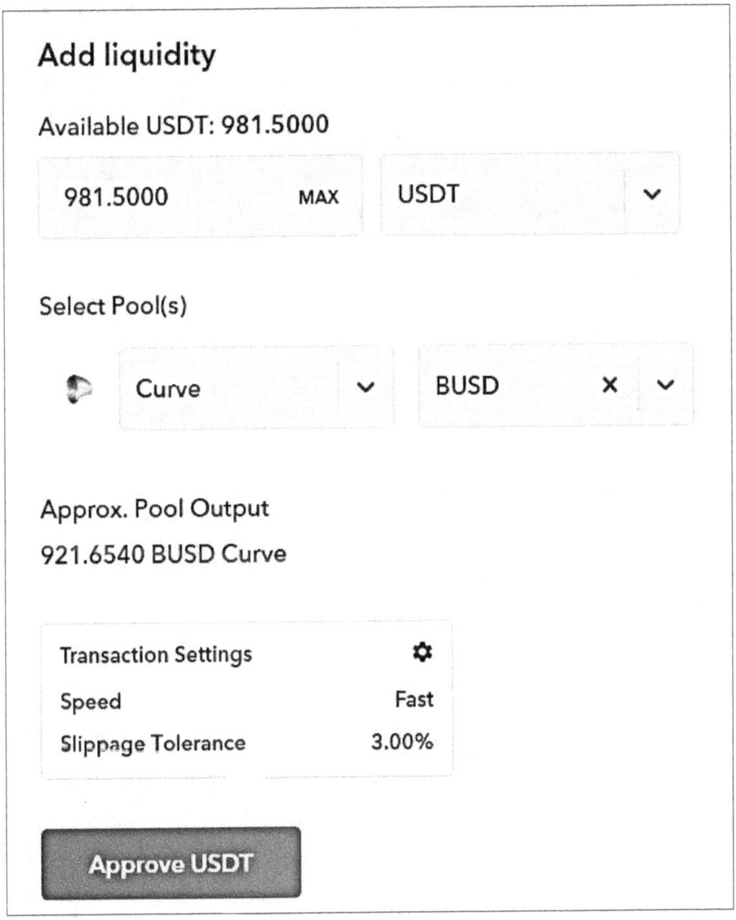

Add liquidity

Available USDT: 981.5000

| 981.5000 | MAX | USDT ⌄ |

Select Pool(s)

| Curve ⌄ | BUSD × ⌄ |

Approx. Pool Output
921.6540 BUSD Curve

Transaction Settings	⚙
Speed	Fast
Slippage Tolerance	3.00%

Approve USDT

Figure 4.9

Once approved your pool tokens will appear on Zapper, as shown in Figure 4.10

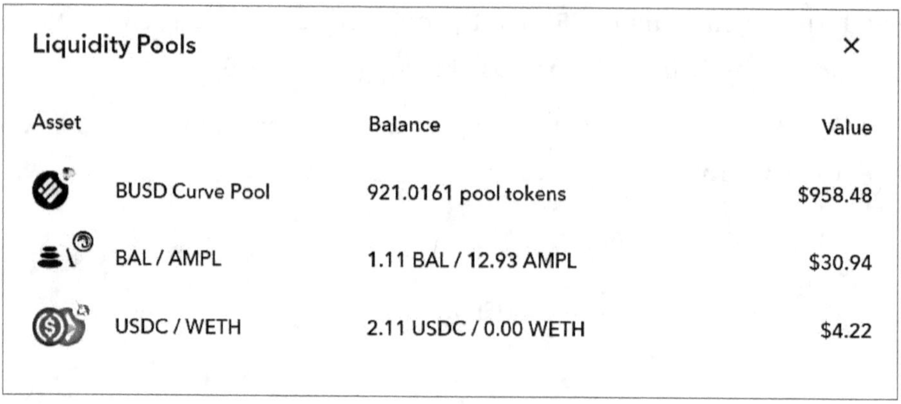

Liquidity Pools
Asset
Balance
Value
BUSD Curve Pool
921.0161 pool tokens
$958.48
BAL / AMPL
1.11 BAL / 12.93 AMPL
$30.94
USDC / WETH
2.11 USDC / 0.00 WETH
$4.22

Figure 4.10

It will also be shown in your wallet with the token symbol syDAI+yUSD+yUSDT+yBUSD, as seen in Figure 4.11.

Ethereum Mainnet
Assets
Activity
$0.00 USD
0 BPT
SyDAI+yUSDC+yUSDT+yBUSD
$1,140.12 USD

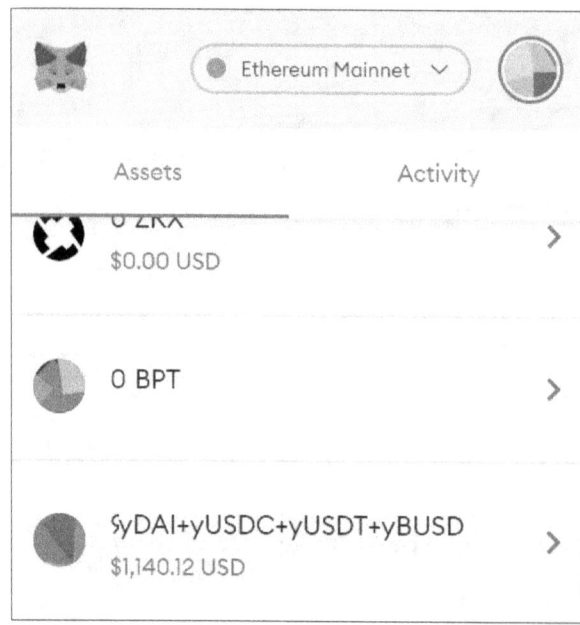

Figure 4.11

Now you can stake more CRV-BUSD in Harvest's farm, and the new amount as well as the rewards will be reflected in your account, as shown in Figure 4.12.

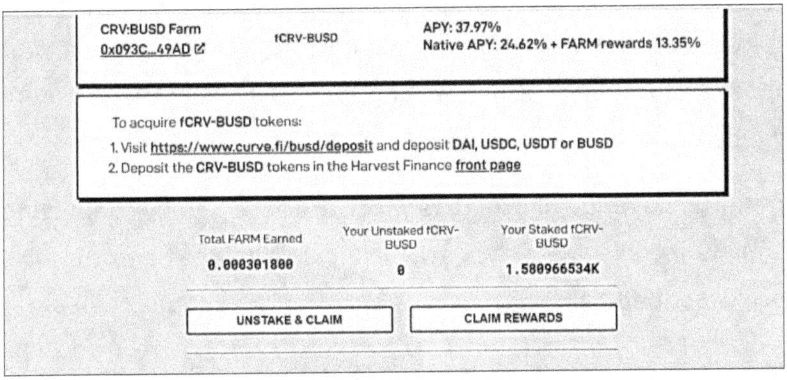

```
CRV:BUSD Farm                              APY: 37.97%
0x093C...49AD        fCRV-BUSD             Native APY: 24.62% + FARM rewards 13.35%

To acquire fCRV-BUSD tokens:
1. Visit https://www.curve.fi/busd/deposit and deposit DAI, USDC, USDT or BUSD
2. Deposit the CRV-BUSD tokens in the Harvest Finance front page

              Total FARM Earned    Your Unstaked fCRV-    Your Staked fCRV-
                                         BUSD                   BUSD
                 0.000301800              0                1.580966534K

                    UNSTAKE & CLAIM           CLAIM REWARDS
```

Figure 4.12

It is also updated in your Zapper account, as seen in Figure 4.13.

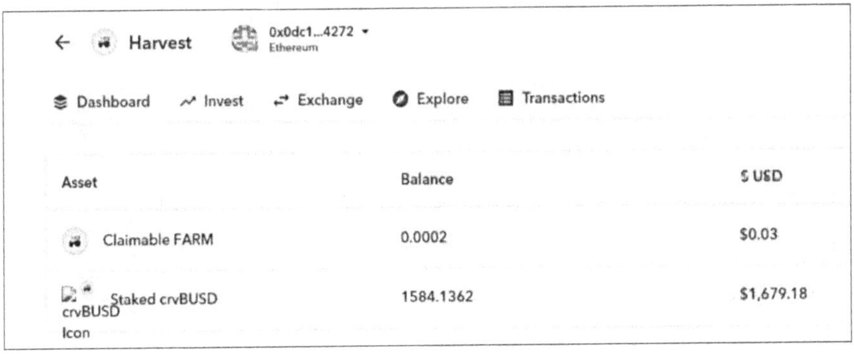

```
  ←   Harvest      0x0dc1...4272 ▾
                   Ethereum

  Dashboard    Invest    Exchange    Explore    Transactions


  Asset                        Balance                        $ USD


     Claimable FARM            0.0002                         $0.03


     Staked crvBUSD            1584.1362                      $1,679.18
  crvBUSD
  Icon
```

Figure 4.13

4.2.2 Pickle Finance

Pickle Finance is another interesting DeFi protocol that provide good attractive yield to the investors via yield farming activities. It claims that its mission is to be a one-stop shop for maximizing yield earning on your cryptoassets. As of the time of this writing, people have entrusted more than $150 million dollars with Pickle.

The platform offers a range of products which are accessed by connecting an Ethereum wallet like MetaMask to the Pickle Finance platform. The products are described below:

a) Pickle Jars

Pickle Jars allow users to deposit tokens from liquidity pools such as Uniswap, and then execute sophisticated strategies that benefit the depositor. For example, the series 0.69 Jars auto-harvest the Uniswap UNI token, sell those tokens, and purchase more Uniswap liquidity tokens on behalf of the user.

b) Pickle Farms

Pickle Farms allow users to deposit a variety of tokens and earn PICKLE tokens, which they can harvest at any time. Currently, there are two types of farms—one that provides a generous allocation of PICKLE rewards to participants of the PICKLE/ETH liquidity pool at Uniswap, and secondly, farms which allow Pickle Jar users to additionally earn PICKLE!

c) Pickle Staking

People who stake their PICKLE tokens at Pickle Finance receive profits earned by the project. Currently, that is all Treasury funds more than $500,000.

d) Pickle Jar Swap

This product allows you to swap jars. For example, you are earning APY in a BTC-related Jar, and due to a surge in BTC price, you might want to switch into USD. You can do that directly at Pickle by swapping from one Jar to another, free of charge!

To start farming in Pickle, visit the website using the following link:

https://app.pickle.finance/

The landing page is as shown in Figure 4.14

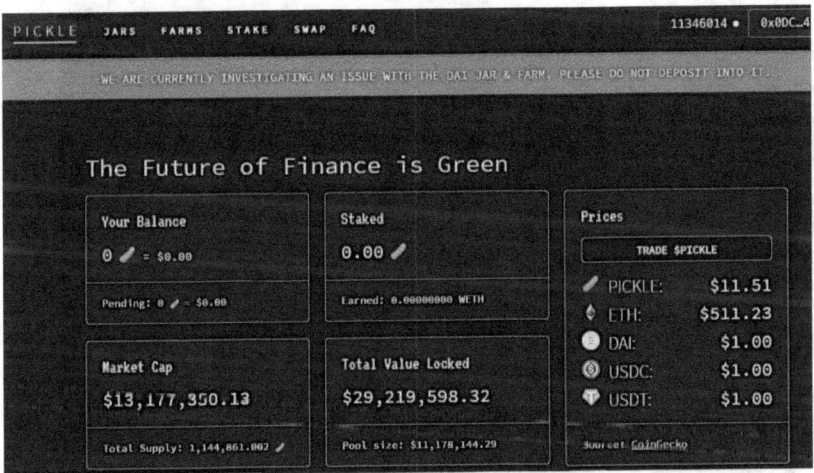

Figure 4.14

At the time of writing, we are advised not to use the DAI Jar and Farm and as there is an issue they must rectify. As usual, you must connect it to your wallet.

If you wish to deposit some funds and earn interest, you can explore various jars that provide good APY, as shown in Figure 4.15.

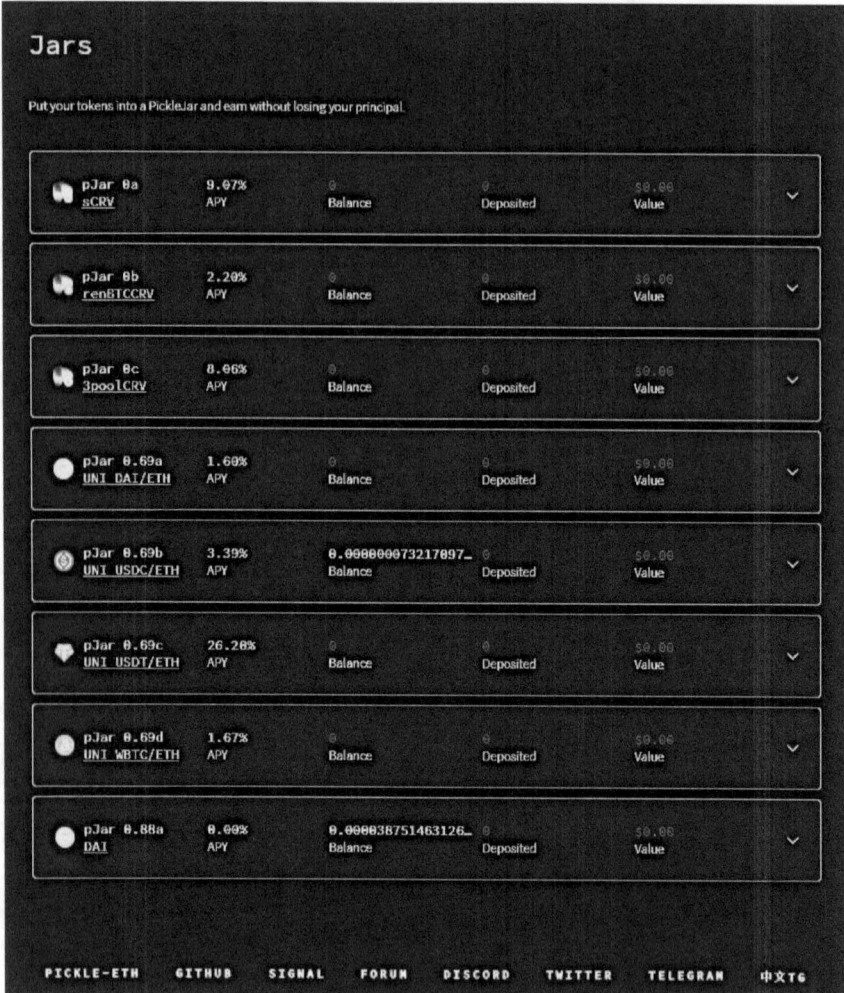

Figure 4.15

You must obtain your LP tokens from several platform particularly Curve Finance and Uniswap. Since I have some LP tokens in UNI USDC/ETH pool, I can deposit some of it in the Jars, as shown in Figure 4.16.

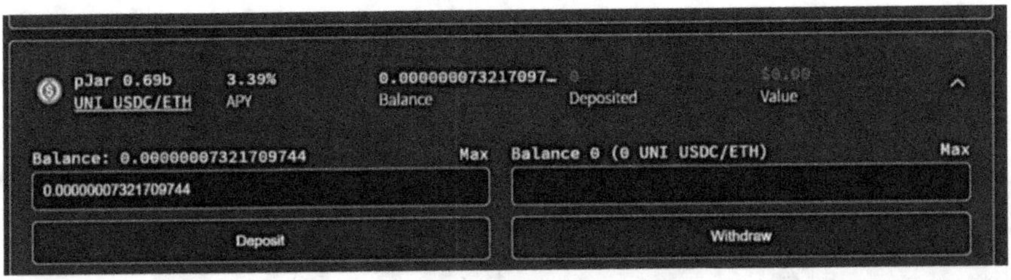

Figure 4.16

After clicking the 'Deposit' button, you must confirm it on your wallet.

Besides that, you can earn income from its farms, as shown in Figure 4.17.

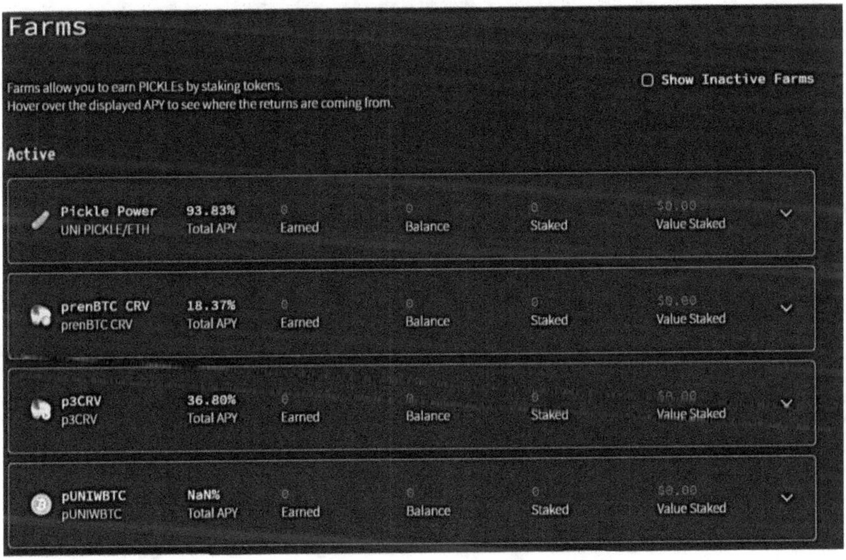

Figure 4.17

Before you can start farming, you must acquire the pool tokens from other platforms. For example, you might want to invest in Pickle Power, then you need to obtain the UNI PICKLE/ETH pool token from Uniswap, as shown in Figure 4.18.

Figure 4.18

Next, click the 'Add Liquidity link' to add ETH and PICKLE to the pool, as shown in Figure 4.19.

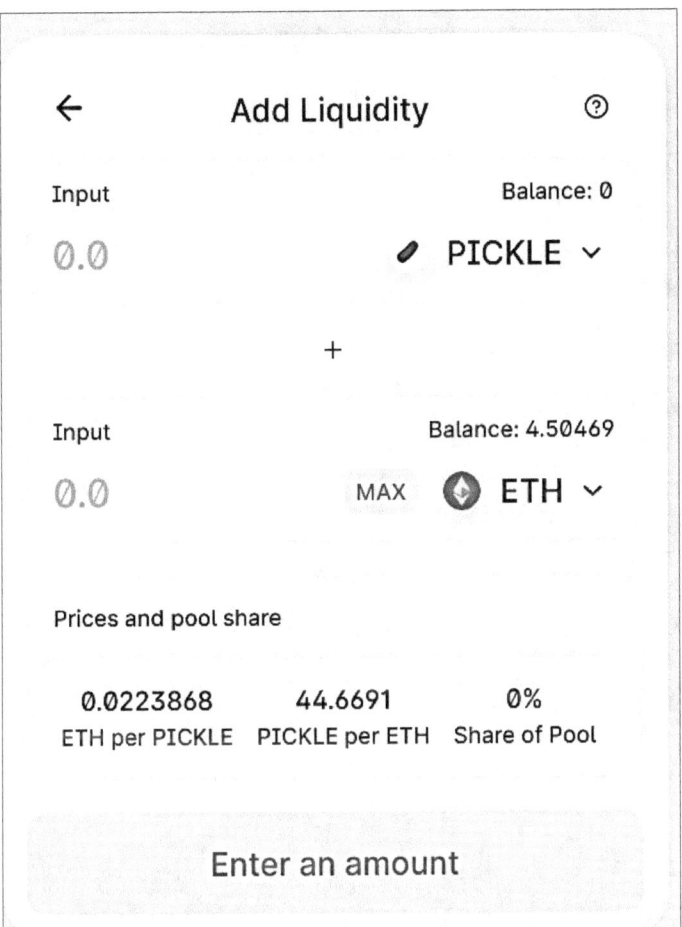

Figure 4.19

However, you must have both ETH and PICKLE to add liquidity to the pool. You can buy PICKLE directly from MetaMask, as shown in Figure 4.20

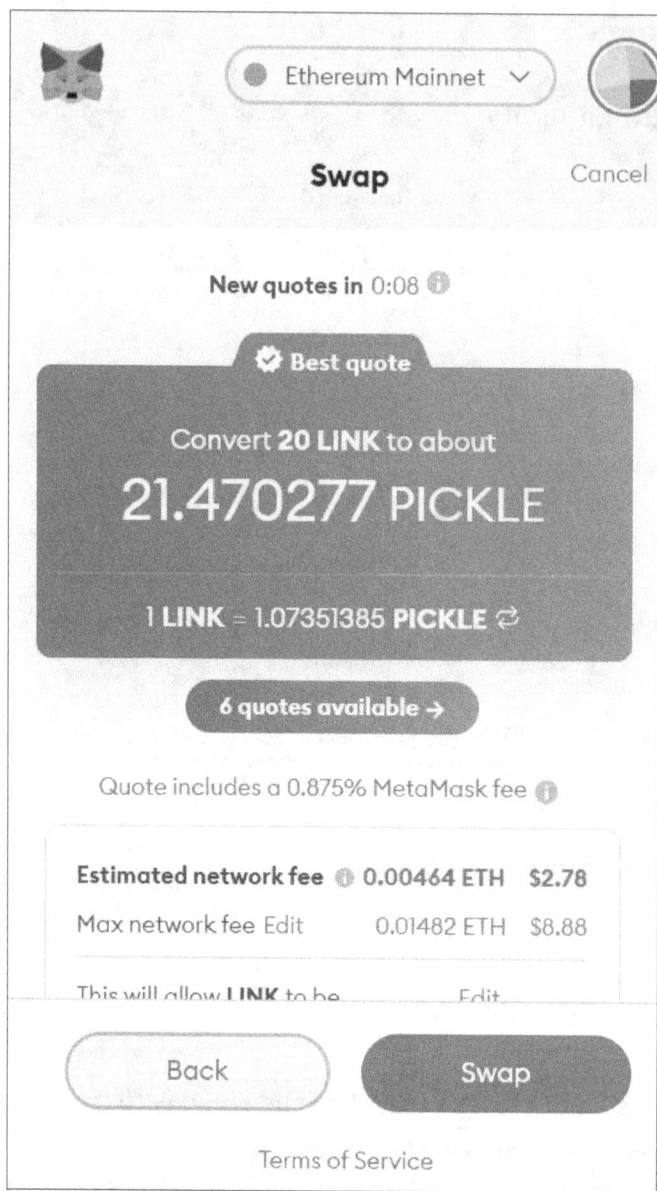

Figure 4.20

Once you have purchased the PICKLE token and you have ETH, you can add the pair to Uniswap to obtain the LP token, subsequently you can start farming on the PICKLE POOL. In addition to farming, you may also stake and swap your tokens.

4.2.3 Liquidity Mining on Balancer

Besides functioning as a decentralized exchange which we have learned in the previous chapter, Balancer also allow liquidity mining. To add liquidity, click the 'Add Liquidity' button on the top right corner of its landing page, as shown in Figure 4.21.

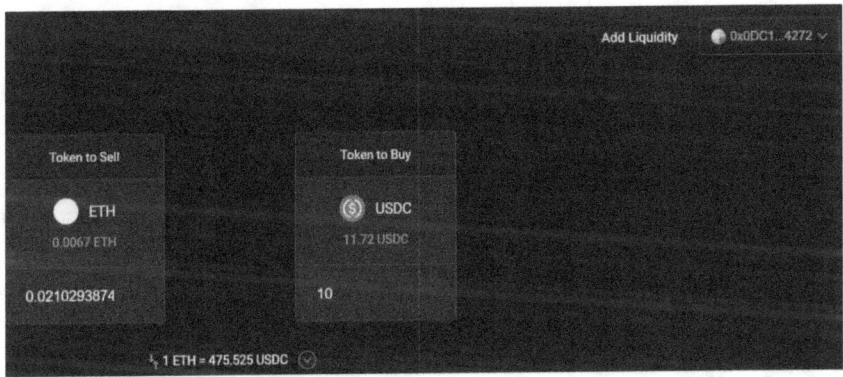

Figure 4.21

Clicking the 'Add Liquidity' button will direct you to the liquidity pool dashboard where you can see pools that are available, as shown in Figure 4.23.

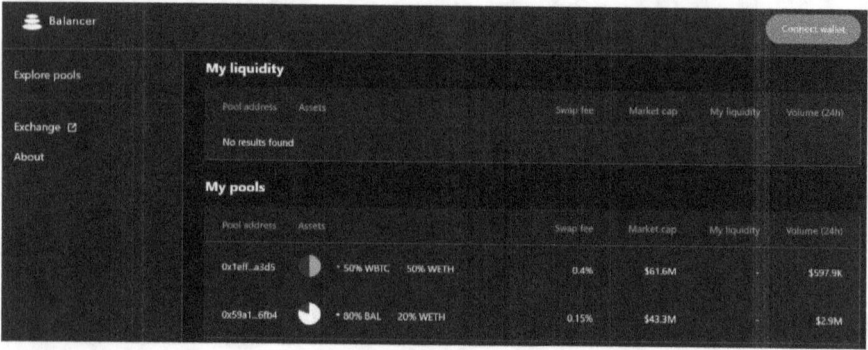

Figure 4.22

You must connect your wallet to deposit funds in the liquidity pool, so proceed to click the 'Connect wallet' button located on the top right-hand corner of the dashboard.

Clicking the 'Connect wallet' button will trigger a dialog box that prompts you to select the wallet of your choice, as shown in Figure 4.23.

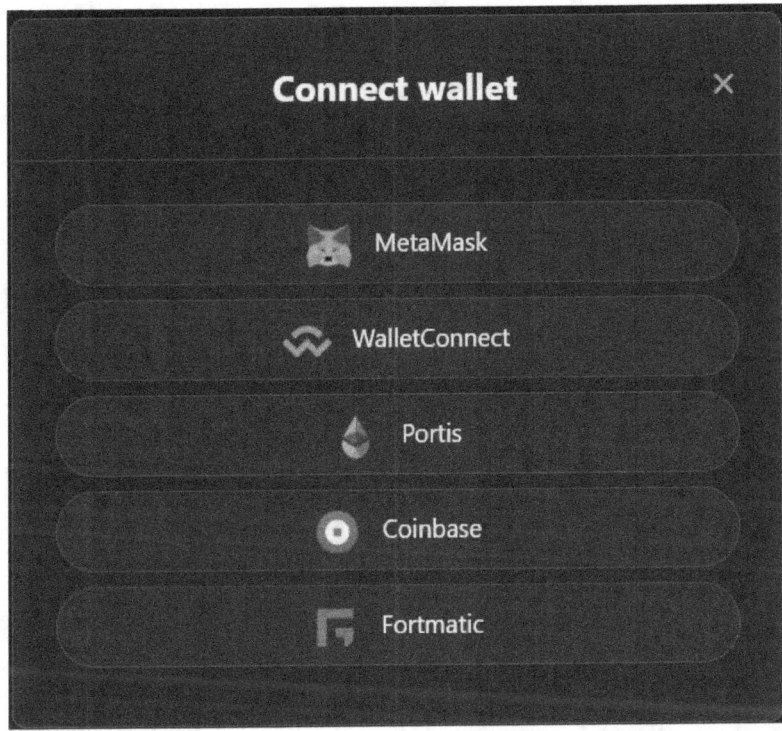

Figure 4.23

When your wallet is connected, you can view your liquidity pool, as shown in Figure 4.24. The pool is still empty as you have not added any tokens yet.

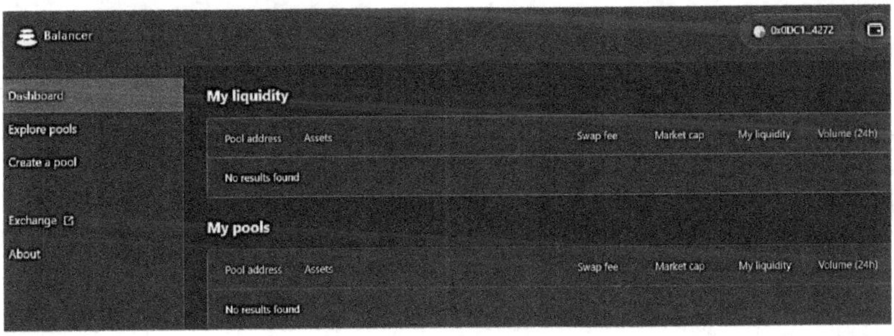

Figure 4.24

To explore the pool, you may click the 'Explore pools' tab to view the available pools, as seen in Figure 4.25.

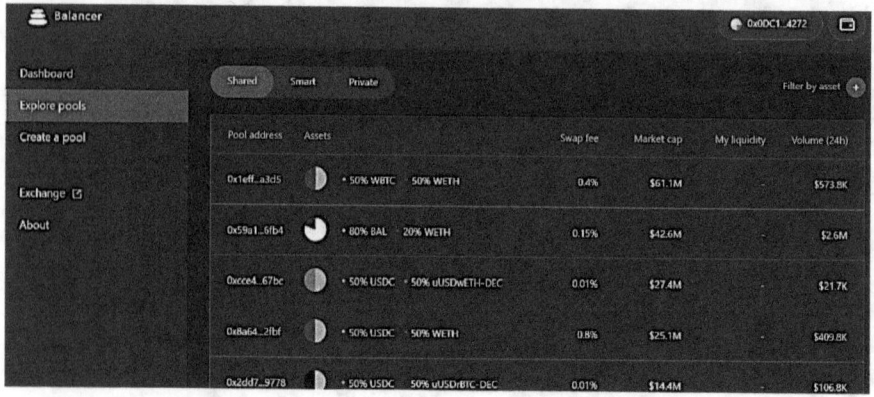

Figure 4.25

Balancer offers three types of pools:

1) Private Pools where only the owner can contribute liquidity using any of its parameters.

2) Anyone can add liquidity to shared pools and the ownership of the pool's liquidity is tracked with a specific token called BPT – Balancer Pool Token.

3) A Smart Pool is a variation of a private pool where the controller is a smart contract which allows any arbitrary logic/restrictions on how pool parameters can be changed. Smart pools may also accept liquidity from anyone and issue BPTs to track ownership. You may also create a new pool by clicking the Create a pool button.

To add liquidity, you may choose token pairs that you prefer. You may notice that WBTC and WETH are featured in the pools. WBTC stands for wrapped BTC, which is an Ethereum token that represents Bitcoin (BTC) on the Ethereum blockchain (Coinbase, 2020). One Bitcoin can be converted to one Wrapped Bitcoin, and vice-versa. WBTC was created to allow Bitcoin holders to participate in decentralized finance ("DeFi") apps that are popular on Ethereum blockchain. WBTC is an ERC20 token. Similarly, WETH represents wrapped ETH, which refers to the ERC20 compatible version of Ether (ADolmatov, n.d.). WETH is created by sending ETH to a smart contract where the ETH is placed on hold, in turn receiving the WETH ERC20 token at a 1:1 ratio.

You can buy WBTC from crypto exchanges such as Binance. As for WETH, you can get it from Balancer itself or from exchanges like Relay Radar. The good thing about Relay Radar is that it can wrap and unwrap your ETH. I will discuss Relay Radar in the next chapter.To wrap your ETH in Balancer, click the wallet icon on the top right corner of the dashboard and bring up the dialog box as shown in Figure 4.26.

Figure 4.26

Next, click Wrap to WETH to wrap your ETH. If you do not have ETH, you need to buy it from exchanges. Clicking the 'Wrap to WETH 'button will bring up the following dialog box as shown in Figure 4.27.

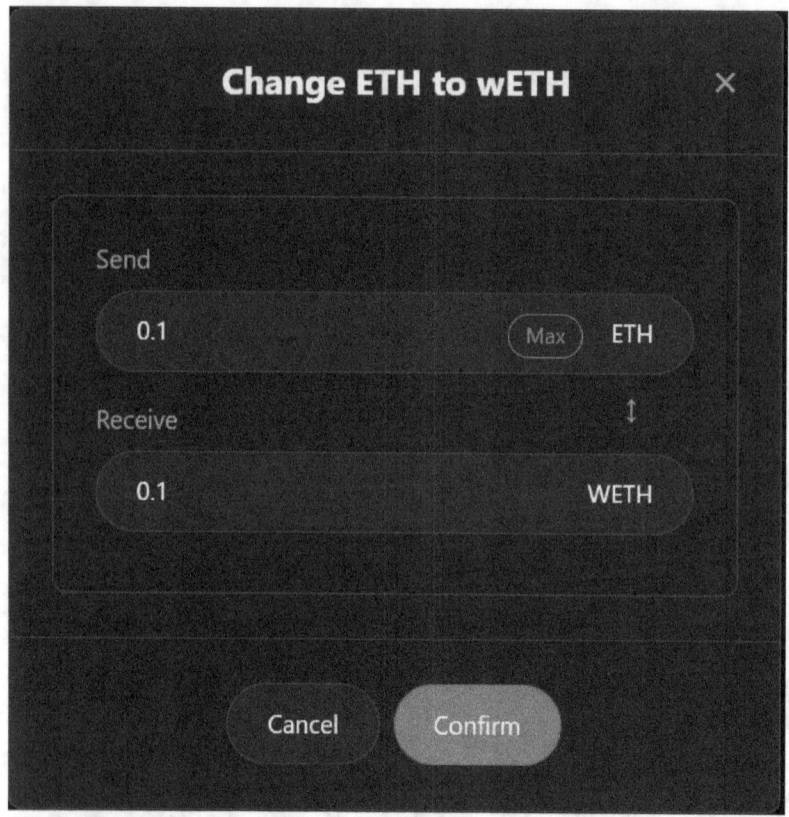

Figure 4.27

Next, click the 'CONFIRM' button to wrap the ETH. You will be asked to confirm the transaction on your wallet. Once confirmed you will see that WETH has been added to your wallet.

Additionally, your wallet in Balancer also shows WETH and you can unwrap it anytime, as shown in Figure 4.28.

Figure 4.28

To add to the liquidity, you need to set up the proxy, as shown in Figure 4.29.

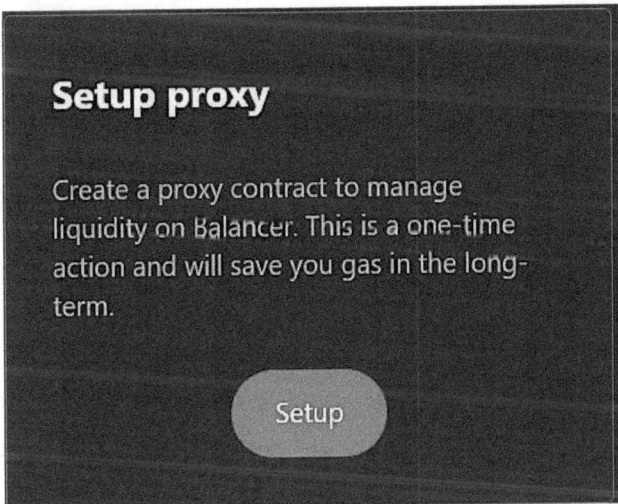

Figure 4.29

You must have enough ETH in your wallet. Once confirmed, the proxy will be successfully set up. Now you can proceed to add liquidity to a pool. Let us choose WETH/USDC pair, as shown in Figure 4.30.

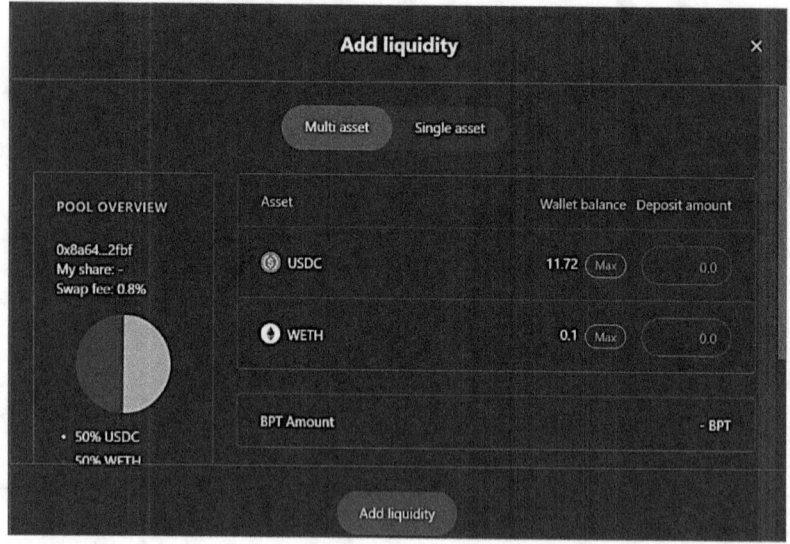

Figure 4.30

You may choose multi asset or single asset. Let us choose multi asset and click Max for USDC to deposit all USDC. You will notice that you will be rewarded with 2.892 BPT, as shown in Figure 4.31.

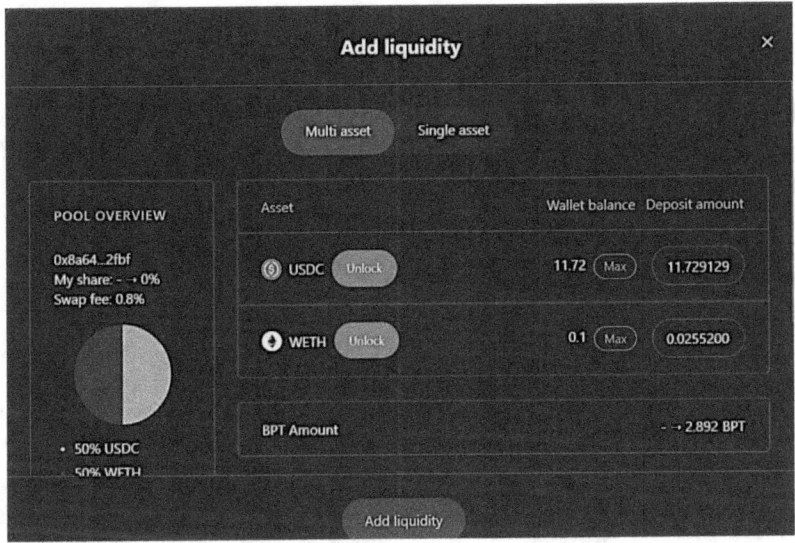

Figure 4.31

You must unlock your USDC and your WETH to complete the transaction. You must be aware that all transactions incur some gas fees.

After successfully adding your tokens, your liquidity will be displayed on the Balancer dashboard, as shown in Figure 4.32.

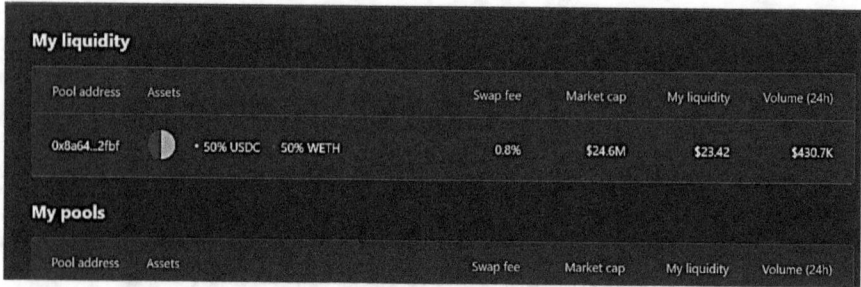

Figure 4.32

4.2.4 Liquidity Mining on Unisawap

Besides token swap, Uniswap allows you to participate in liquidity mining. To add ERC20 tokens to the liquidity pool, click the Pool tab. The Pool page is as shown in Figure 4.33.

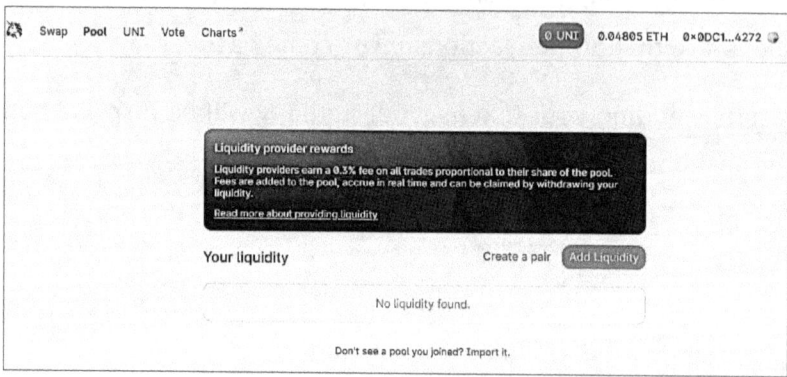

Figure 4.33

Now, click 'Create a Pair' button or the 'Add Liquidity' button to add your token pair. In our example, we add USDC and ETH to the pool, as shown in Figure 4.34.

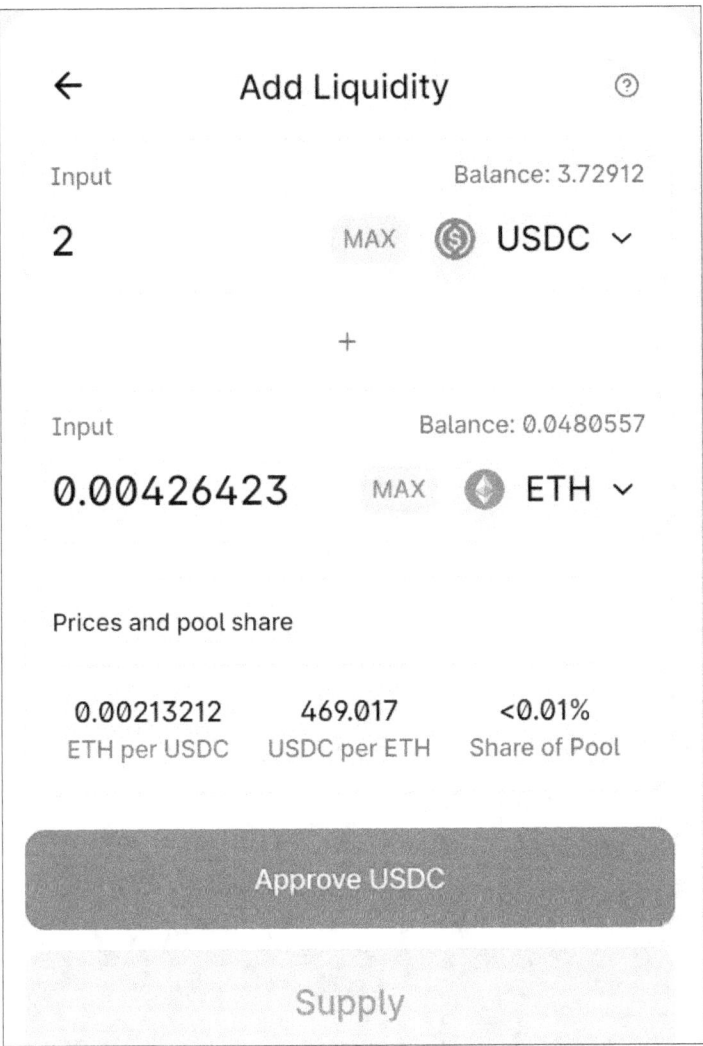

Figure 4.34

Proceed to click the 'Approve USDC' button and subsequently confirm the transaction on your wallet.

Once approved, you can click the supply button as shown in Figure 4.35.

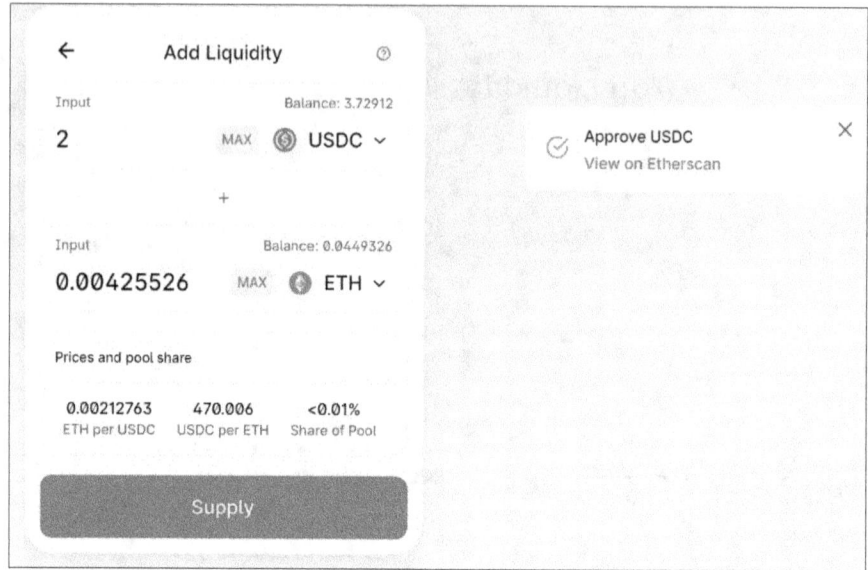

Figure 4.35

Clicking the 'Supply' button will bring up the subsequent dialog box that shows how much pool tokens you will receive, and you must confirm the supply, as seen in Figure 4.36.

Figure 4.36

After the transaction is approved, you will be able to see your pool liquidity details which include the pool tokens, as shown in Figure 4.37.

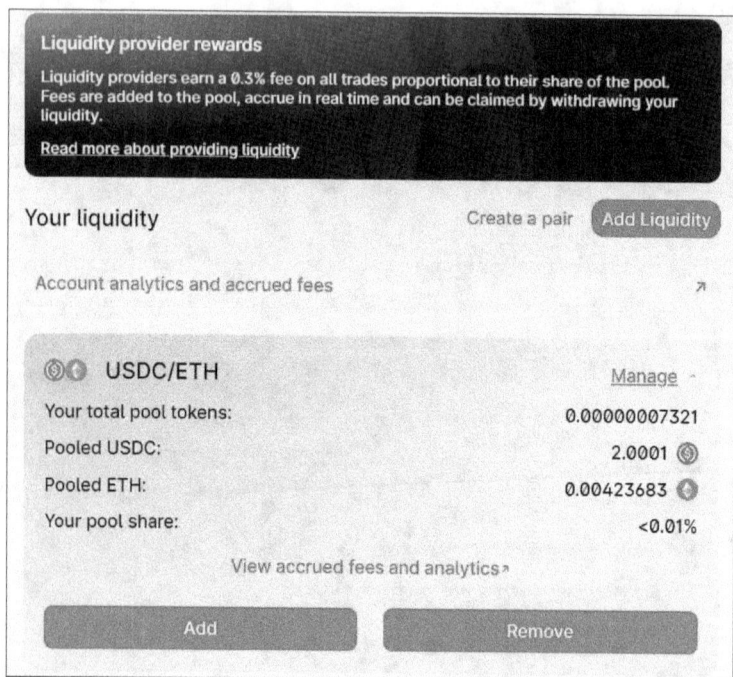

Figure 4.37

To view the amount of fees you earn, click View accrued fees and analytics link. You will see your liquidity and earnings as shown in Figure 4.38.

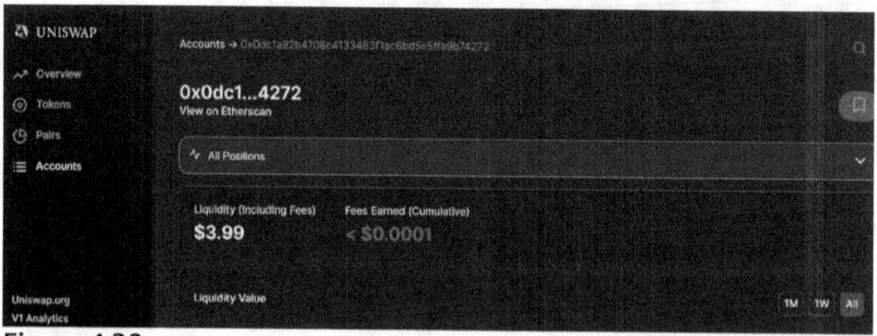

Figure 4.38

4.2.5 Liquidity Mining with Bancor

Bancor also offers liquidity mining besides token swap. The Bancor network lists various token pairs in the pool. According to Bancor, by joining a pool, liquidity providers earn a percentage fee on all trades proportional to their share of the pool. Fees are added to the pool, accrue in real time, and can be claimed by withdrawing your liquidity (Bancor, n.d.).

To add tokens to the liquidity pool, simply click the plus button under the ACTIONS column, as shown in Figure 4.39.

Statistics

TOTAL LIQUIDITY	BNT PRICE	VOLUME (24HRS)	TOTAL BNT STAKED
$111,876,011	$1.15	$9,111,539	50.27%

	NAME	LIQUIDITY	REWARDS	FEE	VOLUME (24H)	FEES (24HR)	APR	ACTIONS
	ETH/BNT	$26,817,933	BNT 160.59% ETH 32.49% (46d 21h 9m 51s)	0.10%	$3,603,954	$3,604	4.91%	+ ⇌
	WBTC/BNT	$14,137,106	BNT 251.32% WBTC 48.46% (46d 21h 9m 52s)	0.40%	$543,671	$2,175	5.61%	+ ⇌
	LINK/BNT	$12,578,512	BNT 211.84% LINK 70.18% (46d 21h 9m 52s)	0.50%	$788,052	$3,940	11.43%	+ ⇌
	USDT/BNT	$10,797,474	BNT 248.41% USDT 75.63% (46d 21h 9m 52s)	0.20%	$820,804	$1,854	6.27%	+ ⇌
	DAI/BNT	$10,609,384	BNT 271.20% DAI 75.33% (46d 21h 9m 52s)	0.10%	$910,584	$911	3.13%	+ ⇌

Figure 4.39

Clicking the plus button will bring up the dialog box as shown in Figure 4.40.

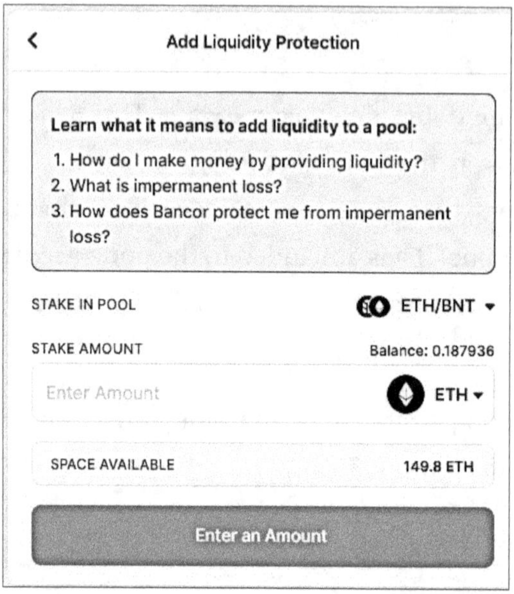

Figure 4.40

You can select a pool from pools shown in a drop-down list when you click the inverted triangle beside the tokens pair. The list of pools is as shown in Figure 4.41.

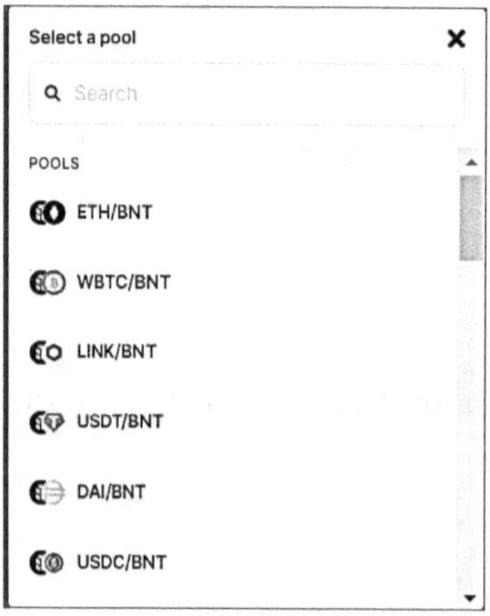

Figure 4.41

To stake in the pool, enter the amount of ETH you wish to add to the pool. Once you enter an amount, the 'Enter and Amount' button becomes 'Stake and Protect', as seen in Figure 4.42.

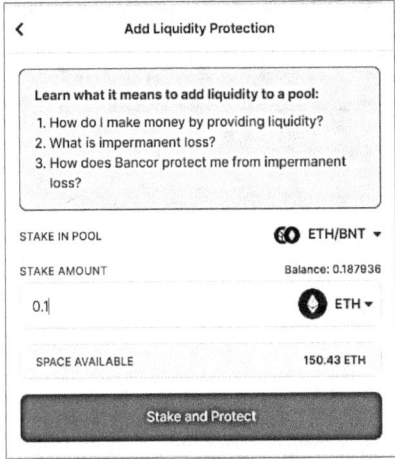

Figure 4.42

Upon clicking the 'Stake and Protect', you must confirm it in the message box appears, as shown in Figure 4.43.

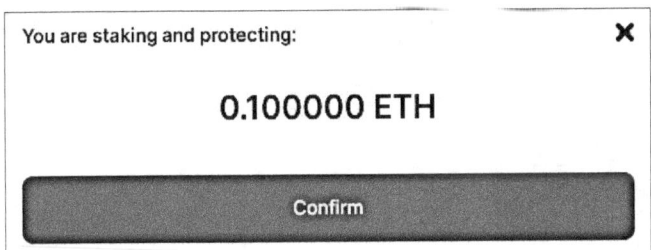

Figure 4.43

Next, you must confirm the transaction on your wallet to complete the transaction.

Boncor is the only platform that offers protection against impermanent loss (which I shall explain in the last section of this chapter) by providing the option of choosing single-sided protection, which means you only deposit one token into the pool. In this way, you will not suffer impermanent loss.

To access this feature, click the 'Protection' tab on the sidebar and select 'Add Single Liquidity' then click the 'Stake' button to launch the staking panel, as shown in Figure 4.44.

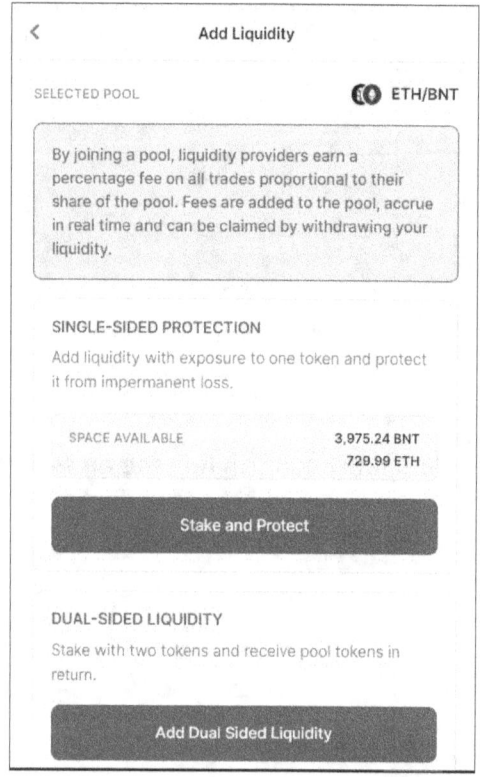

Figure 4.44

You have already learned how to stake a single token as shown in Figure 4.43. Now let us stake two tokens into a pool. To contribute two tokens to a particular pool, click 'Add Dual Side Liquidity' to bring up the dialog as shown in Figure 4.45.

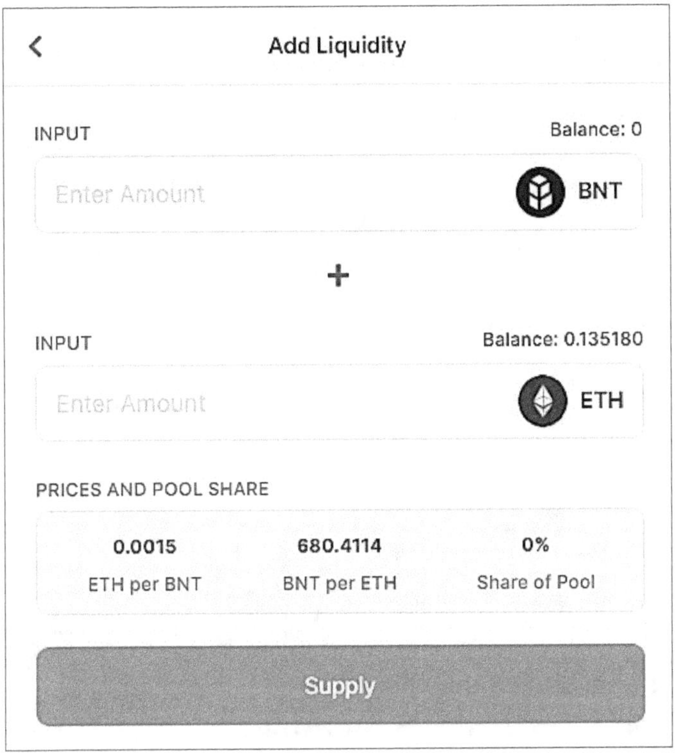

Figure 4.45

In this example, input the amount you wish to stake in ETH and the corresponding amount of BNT will appear, then proceed to supply.

If you do not own BNT yet, you can go to swap to get the token by clicking the Swap tab and bring up the Swap dialog box, as seen in Figure 4.46.

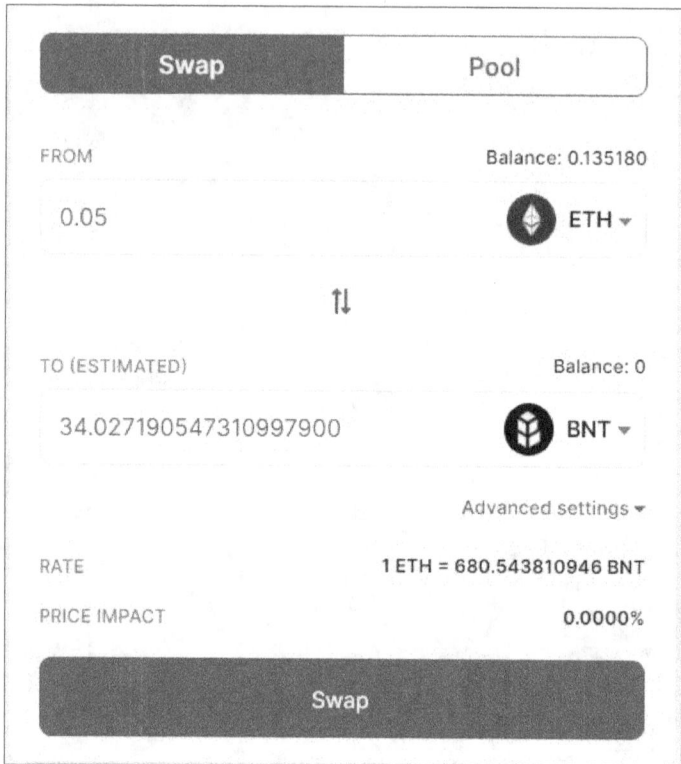

Figure 4.46

Clicking 'Swap' will trigger the next dialog box which requires you to confirm the swap, as shown in Figure 4.47.

Figure 4.47

Clicking 'Confirm' will launch your wallet that requires you to confirm the transaction. Once the transaction is verified, your BNT token will appear in your wallet. Now you can go back and contribute to the liquidity pool. Let us say you wish to contribute to the ETH/BNT pool and supply 0.03 ETH, as seen in Figure 4.48.

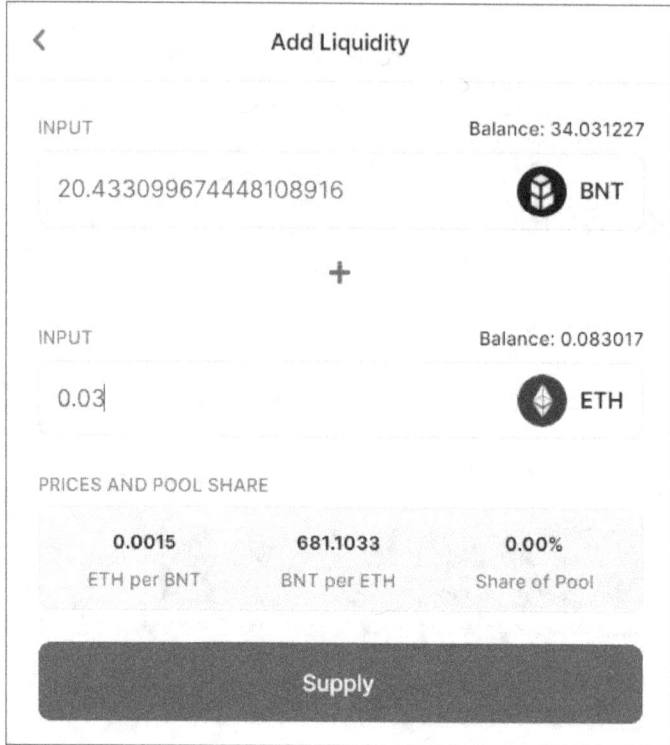

Figure 4.48

Clicking the Supply button launches the dialog box that requires you to confirm the amount, as shown in Figure 4.49.

Figure 4.49

Next, clicking the Confirm button will launch your wallet for final confirmation. When the transaction is verified, you can view your pool on Bancor network, as seen in Figure 4.50.

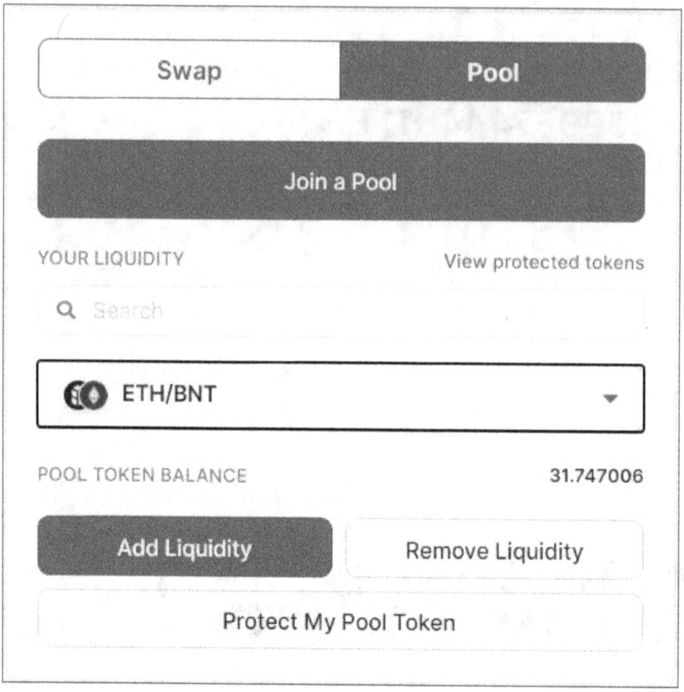

Figure 4.50

4.2.6 Synthetix- The Derivatives Liquidity Protocol

We have learned about Synthetix Exchange in Chapter 3. In this chapter, we shall learn how to can be incentivized by Synthetix Network Token (SNX). SNX holders are incentivised to stake their tokens as they are paid a pro-rata portion of the fees generated through activity on Synthetix.Exchange, based on their contribution to the network. It is the right to participate in the network and capture fees generated from Synth exchanges, from which the value of the SNX token is derived.

The link ot access synthetix staking protocol is

https://staking.synthetix.io/

The landing page is as shown in Figure 4.51.

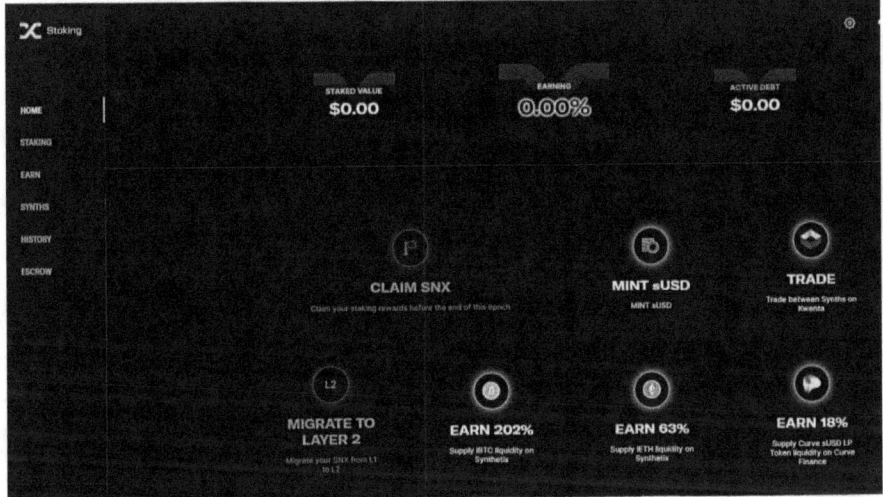

Figure 4.51

You can mint sUSD by staking SNX, earn APY by staking iBTC, iETH as well as Curve sUSD LP token.

Let us click Mint sUSD by staking SNX, as shown in Figure 4.52. If you do not have SNX, you can purchase It from any DEX like Uniswap.

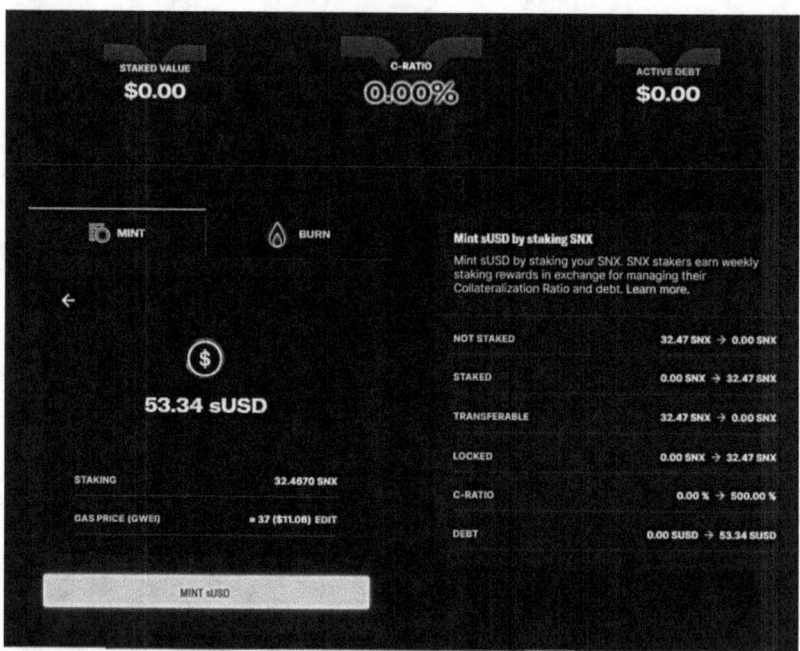

Figure 4.52

Once confirmed you will be able to see your position on the dashboard, as shown in Figure 4.53.

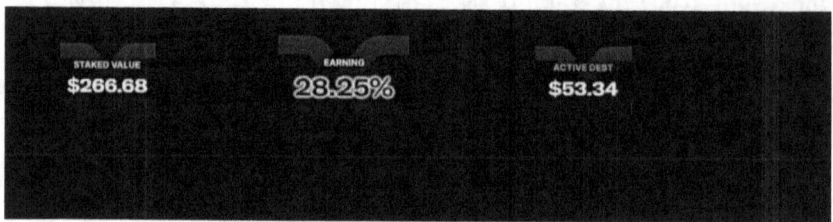

Figure 4.53

It shows your staked value, earning and active debt. If you are using Zapper, you can view your whole portfolio of synthetix, as shown in Figure 4.54. You may unstake SNX anytime by clicking the 'Burn' button to burn sUSD.

My Synths	Balance	Value
s| sUSD	53.3367	$53.34

Mintr Info		Estimated Weekly SNX Staking Rewards	
Collateral Ratio	518%	Exchange Fees	0.3014 sUSD
Collateral	32.4669 SNX	SNX Rewards	0.1566 SNX
Escrowed SNX	0.0000 SNX	*Based on exchange fees from the previous 3 days and a perfect c-Ratio	
Unescrowed SNX	32.4669 SNX		
Unlocked SNX	SNX		
SNX USD Price	$8.22		
Fees Available	0.0000 sUSD		
SNX Staking Rewards Available	0.0000 SNX		

Figure 4.54

In addition, Synthetix also allow you to earn rewards for staking tokens in several pools. To earn rewards by staking, click the 'Earn' tab on the sidebar to access the staking page, as shown in Figure 4.55.

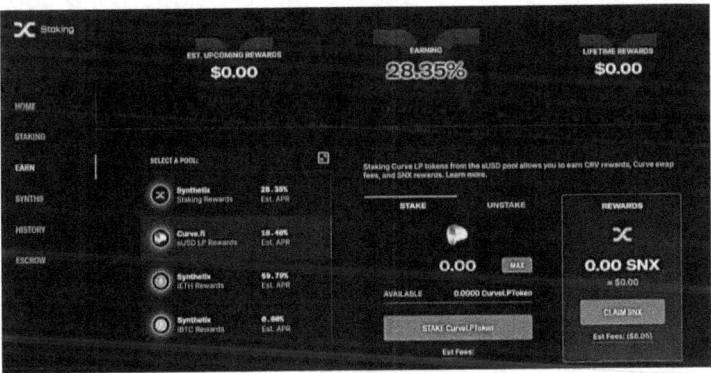

Figure 4.55

For example, you can stake Curve LP tokens from the sUSD pool and earn CRV rewards, Curve swap fees, and SNX rewards.

4.2.7 Alpha Homora

Alpha Homora, a product by Alpha Finance Lab, is a protocol for leveraging your position in yield farming and liquidity providing pools. ETH lenders can earn high interest on ETH. Yield farmers can get even higher farming APY and liquidity providers can get higher trading fees APY from taking on leveraged positions.

Alpha Homora offers the following features:

- CAN FARM WITH ONE TOKEN: Once you select a pool; you can farm with just one token. For instance, if you select ETH/DPI pool, users can farm by just supplying DPI. Alpha Homora will automatically and optimally swap the tokens to make sure users have equal value of both DPI and ETH to supply to ETH/DPI pool on Uniswap.
- UP TO 2.5x LEVERAGE: you can borrow ETH with up to 2.5x leverage to yield farm on supported leveraged yield farming pool to earn higher trading fees APY and farming APY.
- AUTO STAKING: Alpha Homora will automatically stake LP token to get farmed tokens for you. For instance, Alpha Homora will stake UNI-v2 ETH/DPI LP token on IndexCoop to farm INDEX for you.
- AUTO REINVEST: All the farmed tokens will be automatically converted to add onto your positions every 24 hours or will be automatically reinvested when you take action. This makes sure all yields are reinvested to further maximize user's profit.

To access Alpha Homora, use the following link:

https://homora.alphafinance.io/

The landing page is as shown in Figure 4.56.

Figure 4.56

4.2.8 Curve Finance

Curve finance is a great platform for staking, liquidity mining and yield farming. There are many liquidity pools available on Curve, as shown in Figure 4.57.

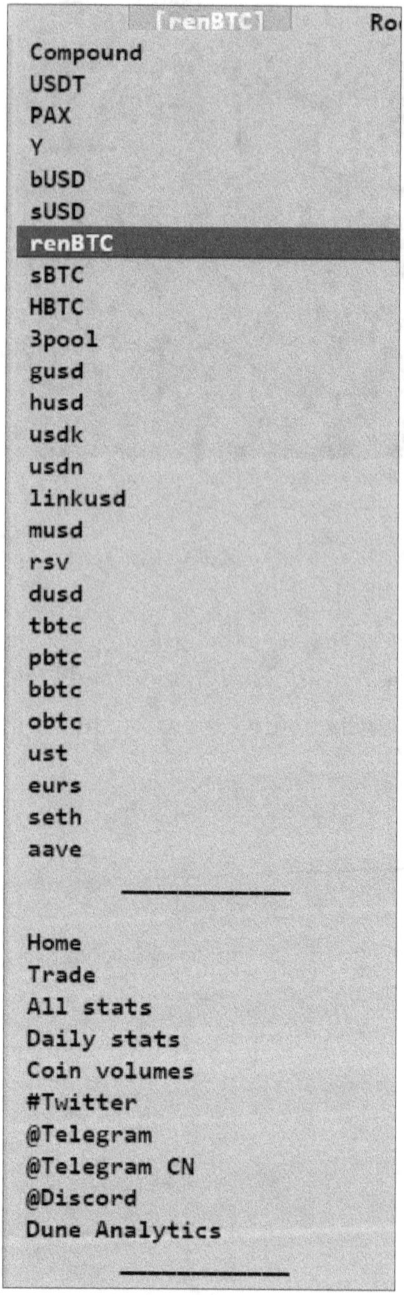

```
     [renBTC]        Ro
Compound
USDT
PAX
Y
bUSD
sUSD
renBTC
sBTC
HBTC
3pool
gusd
husd
usdk
usdn
linkusd
musd
rsv
dusd
tbtc
pbtc
bbtc
obtc
ust
eurs
seth
aave
         ─────────

Home
Trade
All stats
Daily stats
Coin volumes
#Twitter
@Telegram
@Telegram CN
@Discord
Dune Analytics
         ─────────
```

Figure 4.57

To start staking, click a pool such as 3pool and then click the 'Deposit' tab to launch the dialog box, as seen in Figure 4.58.

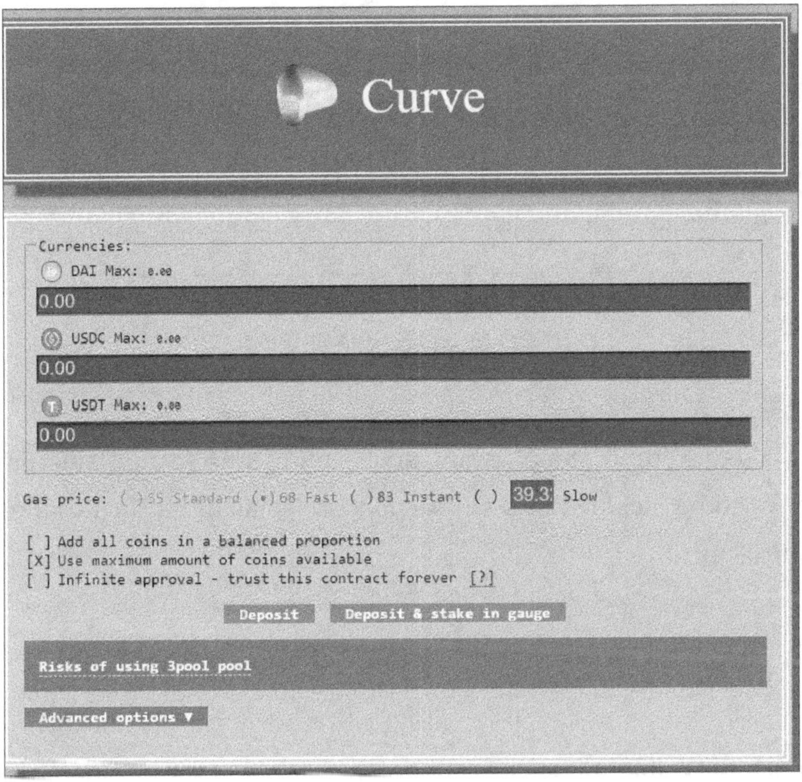

Figure 4.58

You may supply one, two or all three stablecoins comprising DAI, USD and USDT to the pool. Once deposited you will receive the LP token 3CRV and start to earn fees. However, you can further monetize via yield farming by staking 3CRV in Curve' gauge by clicking the 'Deposit & stake in gauge' button or visit the gauge website using the following link:

https://dao.curve.fi/

You must choose the relevant pool to stake. Assuming you have 3CRV token, you can stake at 3pool, as shown in Figure 4.59.

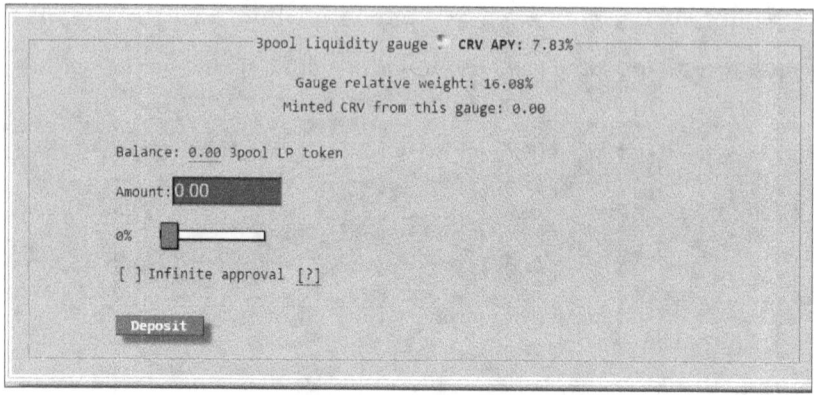

Figure 4.59

The next yield farming protocol I want to discuss is Sora Farm. However, it is too huge to be included as a subsection, so I shall describe it in the next chapter.

4.3 Impermanent Loss

Although liquidity mining seems to provide investors with lucrative returns, it also poses some risks. Among them, the most obvious one is the Impermanent loss. Impermanent loss occurs when the price of the digital assets that you have added to a liquidity pool changes compared to the time you deposited them (Binance Academy, n.d.). The bigger the change, the higher the impermanent loss. The loss means less dollar value at the time of withdrawal than at the time of deposit. Table 4.1 illustrates the percentage loss with respect to change in price.

Table 4.1

Change in Price	Percentage Loss
1.25x	0.6%
1.50x	2.0%
1.75x	3.8%
2x	5.7%
3x	13.4%
4x	20.0%

How does impermanent loss happen? Let me illustrate with the following example:

Let say you deposit 5 ETH and 3000 USDC in a liquidity pool with AMM fixing the weightage of the tokens at 50:50, which means the token pair must be of equivalent value (The price of ETH is 600 USDC at the time of writing). The dollar value of your deposit is 6000 USDC.

Next, assuming after added your tokens the total token in the pool became 50 ETH and 30,000 USDC which gave a total liquidity of 60,000.

Let say now the price of ETH increased to 800 USDC, which means now ETH has a higher weightage than USDC and the value of ETH in the pool became 40,000 USDC. As this is a 50:50 pool, the AMM must maintain the balance via some arbitrage traders to reduce the ETH and increase the USDC until the ratio is 50:50 again. Let say now we have 40 ETH and 32,000 USDC in the pool and you wish to withdraw your tokens from the pool. Since you own 10% of the pool, your profit is 4x800+32,00-6000=$400, seems not bad. However, what if you just hold the tokens, the profit will be 5x800+3000-6000=$1000, which means you have lost $600 by contributing to the pool.

It seems permanent loss is unavoidable, but the liquidity providers can be compensated with trading fees and mining rewards. Therefore, be extra careful when contributing to liquidity pools, avoid assets that are volatile in the pool as you will have higher chance of exposure to impermanent loss.

Chapter 5 Sora Farm-A Yield Farming Game

Sora Farm is another amazing DeFi project that promises good returns in yield farming. It is different from all previously discussed protocols because it is powered by a different blockchain network known as SORA V2 Network developed using Polkdadot's Substrate.

Polkadot is a network protocol that allows arbitrary data—not just tokens—to be transferred across blockchains (Polkadot, n.d.). This means Polkadot is a true multi-chain application environment where things like cross-chain registries and cross-chain computation are possible.

5.1 Farming PSWAP

The Sora Farm protocol features a yield farming game known as Sora Farming Game. It is a community-initiated game that allows you to earn a pool token called PSWAP by adding liquidity to the farm (Polkaswap, 2020). PSWAP is the native token of the Polkaswap DEX. Up to 2% of the PSWAP token supply (2 million PSWAP) is allocated for the SORA farm game!

Adding liquidity means you must contribute any three pairs of tokens comprising ETH-XOR, ETH-VAL and XOR-VAL on Uniswap or Paraswap. Please be aware that PSWAP will not be distributed on Ethereum but will be claimable on the SORA V2 Network after SORA V2 and Polkaswap launch. By the way, XOR is an ERC20 token.

Polkaswap is a non-custodial AMM DEX designed uniquely for the Polkadot ecosystem and hosted on the SORA V2 network. Near boundless liquidity through one of a kind **Aggregate Liquidity**

Technology (ALT) with the security and convenience of a DEX (Polkaswap, 2020). It is expected to launch in Q1 2021.

In fact, The SORA, Polkaswap, and Fearless Wallet projects are all closely related as they form integral parts of the SORA ecosystem. Fearless Wallet is a futuristic mobile wallet designed for the decentralized Finance on the Kusama and Polkadot networks, with support on iOS and Android platforms. Kusama is a scalable network of specialized blockchains built using Substrate and nearly the same codebase as Polkadot. Mobile apps are developed by Soramitsu, with support from the Kusama Treasury. Soramitsu is a Japanese technology company delivering blockchain-based solutions for enterprises, universities, and governments.

To access Sora Farm Game, use the following link:

https://sora.farm/

The landing page is stunningly beautiful that features a Japanese manga with the Sora logo and the farmland, as shown in Figure 5.1. Each tile of the farmland represents an amount of a token that can be deposited, as shown in its legend.

Figure 5.1

5.2 How to Farm PSWAP?

To farm PSWAP, you must Provide liquidity for any of XOR-ETH, VAL-ETH, or VAL-XOR pairs on Uniswap or Mooniswap:

- XOR-ETH Uniswap
- VAL-ETH Uniswap
- XOR-VAL Uniswap
- XOR-ETH Mooniswap
- VAL-ETH Mooniswap
- XOR-VAL Mooniswap

Track your gathered $PSWAP tokens on the SORA Farm website and claim your harvested tokens when $PSWAP token is released. Make sure to read the SORA Farm rules by clicking the 'SORA FARMING RULE' tab in the box as seen in Figure 5.2.

Figure 5.2

Clicking the tab will launch the dialog box that display the farming rules, as shown Figure 5.3.

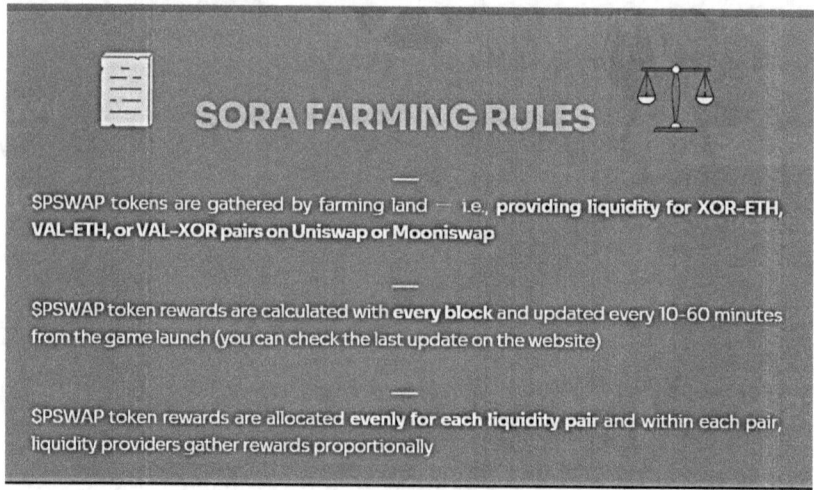

Figure 5.3

To start farming, click on any tile field and choose where you want to add liquidity:

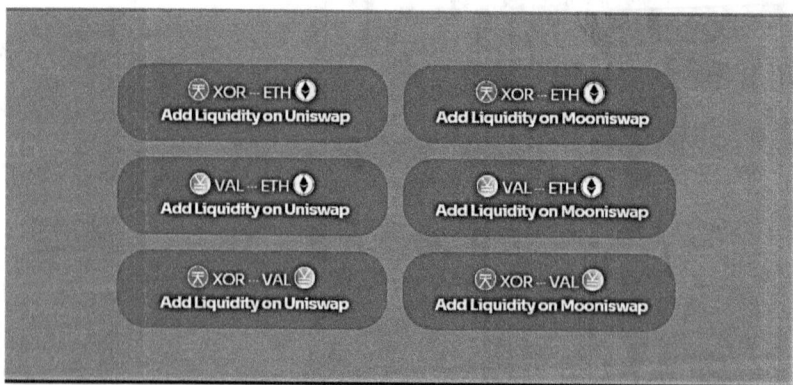

Figure 5.4

You will be redirected to the exchange and pair you chose to add liquidity to. Let say you wish to deposit XOR and ETH on Uniswap, click the 'Add Liqudity on Uniswap' button. At the Uniswap exchange platform, choose the amount of ETH and XOR you wish to deposit, as shown in Figure 5.5. If you do not own ETH and XOR yet, you can purchase them from the secondary markets like Uniswap.

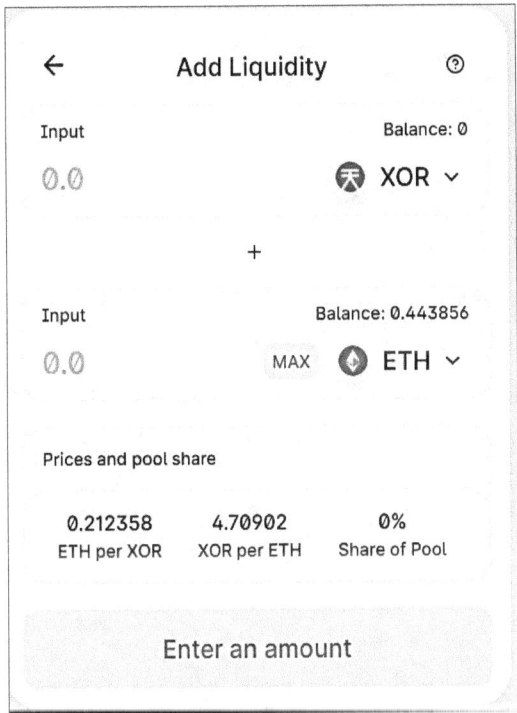

Figure 5.5

After adding the tokens, you can view your liquidity pool in Uniswap, as shown in Figure 5.6.

⊙ XOR/ETH	Manage
Your total pool tokens:	1.635
Pooled XOR:	4.6908
Pooled ETH:	0.998565
Your pool share:	0.02%
View accrued fees and analytics »	
Add	Remove

Figure 5.6

If you add XOR-VAL pair or ETH-VAL pair, you must import the pool and entering VAL to see the pool on Uniswap or Moonisawp. Next, you can connect your wallet and check collected PSWAP tokens on Sora Farm. The rewards are updated approximately every 10–60 minutes (depending on the number of users), so you need to wait to see the updates. If the load is too high, the server will process requests slowly, so you can try later. The PSWAP tokens will be displayed as seen in Figure 5.7. Besides that, you can also see your token pairs that you have added, and the percentage in the pool.

Figure 5.7

In addition to the XOR token, you can see another token VAL. What is it? VAL is a new token used to reward SORA network validators that secure the network, created by community governance; all contracts and executable code were released in a disabled form and could not be used until activation by a community member (by insertion of cryptographic proof of the referendum); now it is fully activated (Sora XOR, 2020).

VAL fully diluted supply will be 100,000,000. Only 33,900,000 VAL are circulating at the time of writing, and the supply is capped until SORA v2 network launch. VAL tokens were formerly known as v1 XOR tokens, but were turned into VAL with new tokenomics by November 2020, through community governance. VAL is a multichain token that lives on the SORA v1 Network and on Ethereum, with a trustless bridge — HASHI — that spans the two networks.

HASHI, is a trustless Hyperledger Iroha-Ethereum bridge, built on top of D3 Ledger technology (developed by Soramitsu), without a counterparty to render tokens interoperable with the Ethereum blockchain.

In addition, VAL will be airdropped per XOR to ERC-20 XOR holders, during the first year of the SORA v2 network. SORA v2 mainnet is expected to launch between December 2020 -February 2021.

5.3 Sora Tokonomics(SORAnomics)

Sora claimed to have created a new economic order known as Soranomics that is different from the conventional economic models. The conceptualization of Soranomics started on October 17, 2019, when the SORA v1 Network was launched, issuing approximately 1,618,033,988 XOR. By March of 2020, approximately 350,000 XOR were moved from the SORA v1 Network to the Ethereum Network and trading was started on Uniswap.

The goal of the initial launch on Uniswap was to perform preliminary price discovery and build the Sora community by incorporating users of the Ethereum network. However, as technology has improved, giving SORA the possibility to shape a new and more ambitious type of crypto ecosystem. Whereas the medium-term goal remains generating value for Sora community, the analysis of the SORA economy has led them to embrace the long-term goal of realizing a supranational world economic system.

The key concept of the SORA economic system is that for cryptoeconomic systems to be able to compete with contemporary, centralized economic systems, there needs to be a rational economic model. To create a rational economic model, the Sora team did a survey of various economic theories, starting in 2017. Over the course of this time they also employed an economist (Yokei Yamaguchi) to work with them in 2018, and he helped them with several key parts of the model. I shall not discuss the technical details of SORANOMICS, but you can read them in Appendix D.

The key takeaways of SORANOMICS are as follows:

- Supply of ERC-20 XOR is capped at 350,000 until the v2 launch.
- SORA v2 tokenomic model is proposed that uses a token bonding curve with an increasing price function. This means that as the token supply increases, the price also increases.
- Reserves held by the token bonding curve will provide liquidity for XOR.
- A new, staking reward token, tentatively called VAL is proposed.
- ERC-20 XOR trading on Ethereum will be the initial supply of v2 XOR. ERC-20 XOR holders will also receive airdropped VAL.
- SORA v1 tokens are proposed to be converted into VAL.

Chapter 6 DeFi Portfolio Management

As more and more DeFi products are emerging every now and then, you will face a huge challenge in managing your portfolio if you have invested in a dozen of them. The greatest issue is time and the complexity of the DeFi protocols.

Beside the need to spend time to understand the protocols you are investing in; you need time to track the price movement of the crypto assets and take profit or cut loss at the right timing. Besides that, you need to have enough time to re-balance your portfolio. In short, you need time and knowledge to manage your DeFi portfolio.

Fortunately, there are some DeFi portfolio management tools that provide solutions to these issues. One of them is DeFi Saver which you have learned about in Chapter 21. The others are TokenSets, Zapper.fi, Zerion and more. I shall only discuss Zapper and Zerion as they are the two more established ones.

6.1 Zapper.fi

Zapper is a platform for monitoring your DeFi portfolio, comprising assets, debts, liquidity pools, staking, claimable rewards, and yield farming activities (Dad, 2020). There is no KYC, you just need to connect your Ethereum wallet or paste in the ETH wallet address to use the services.

This platform is your gateway to investing in hundreds of DeFi strategies with just a few clicks. Zaps save time, effort, and gas fees by deploying capital in a single DeFi command control center. It works with the most trusted DeFi protocols like yearn.finance, Uniswap, Balancer, Curve, and more.

To access Zapper, use the following link: https://zapper.fi/

The landing page is as shown in Figure 6.1.

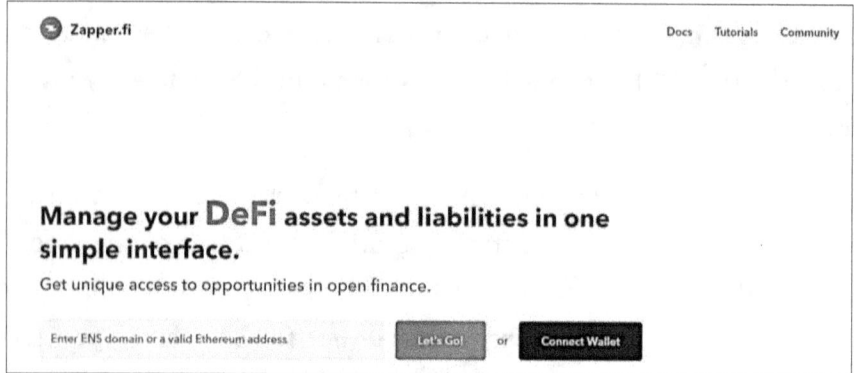

Figure 6.1

Next, proceed to connect your wallet to Zapper. Once your wallet is connected you can view your portfolio on the dashboard, as seen in Figure 6.2. Cool!

Figure 6.2

You can see your investment details too, as shown in Figure 6.3 and Figure 6.4.

Account Overview Don't see your assets?						Switch View
Wallet	$1,484.95	Deposits	$894.30	Investments	$20.03
Liquidity Pools	$116.07	Yield Farming	$0.51	Debt	$331.04

Platforms

Maker	$187.51	Uniswap	$43.98	dYdX	$217.03
PoolTogether	$150.00	Curve	$19.57	yEarn	$28.75
Balancer	$24.79	Mooniswap	$27.73		

Figure 6.3

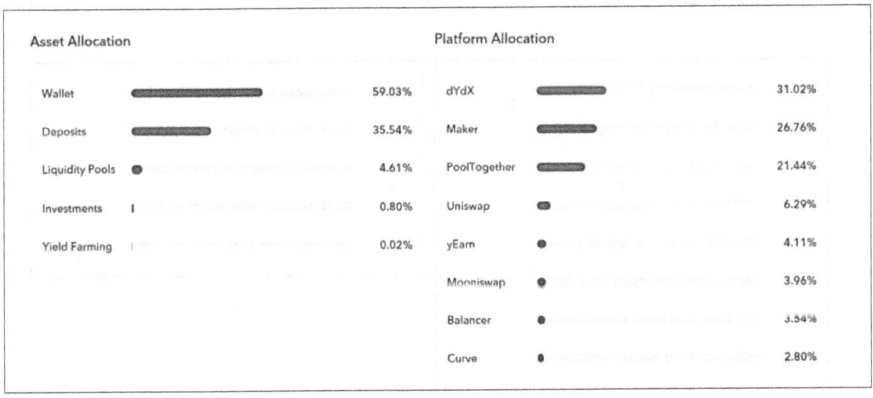

Asset Allocation		Platform Allocation	
Wallet	59.03%	dYdX	31.02%
Deposits	35.54%	Maker	26.76%
Liquidity Pools	4.61%	PoolTogether	21.44%
Investments	0.80%	Uniswap	6.29%
Yield Farming	0.02%	yEarn	4.11%
		Mooniswap	3.96%
		Balancer	3.54%
		Curve	2.80%

Figure 6.4

When you click the 'Invest' tab, you can see all your DeFi investments in one place (Figure 6.5) instead of having to go to every DeFi platform where you have invested. Super convenient!

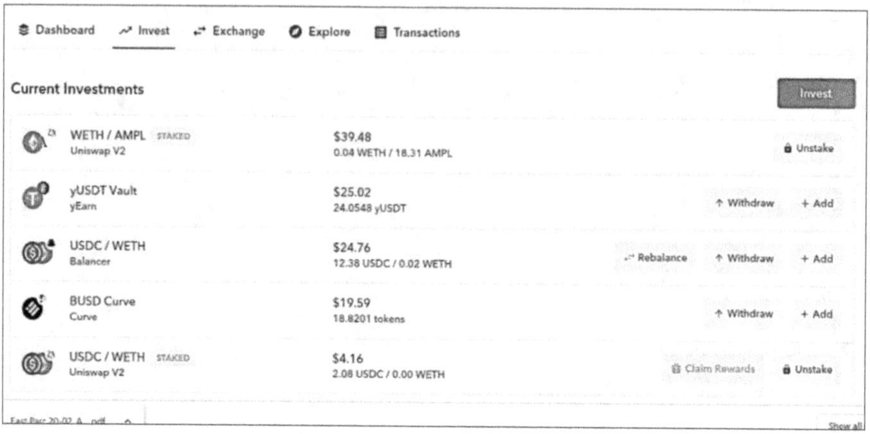

Figure 6.5

Best of all, you can execute several actions in this panel, like unstake, withdraw, claims rewards, add more tokens to existing pools and rebalancing by moving them to a different pool. It is extremely easy indeed. For example, if you wish to rebalance your investment at Balancer, you can simply click the 'Rebalance' button to open the panel as shown in Figure 6.6.

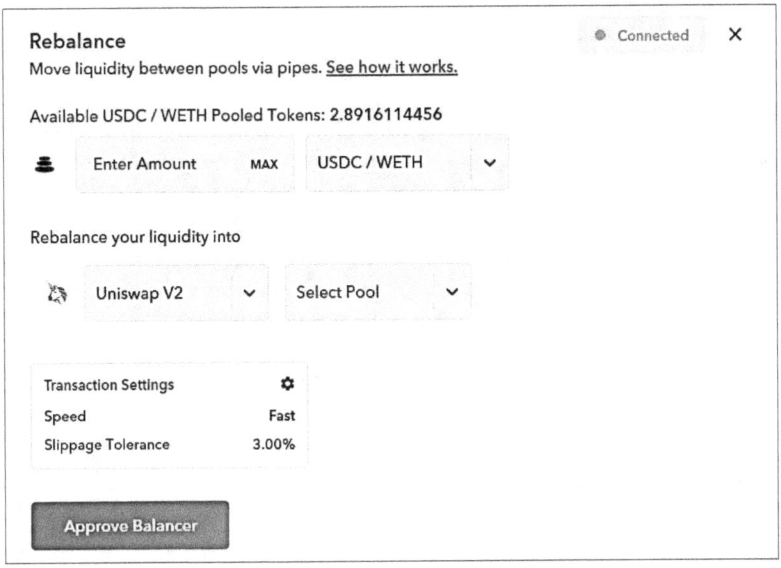

Rebalance
Move liquidity between pools via pipes. See how it works.

Available USDC / WETH Pooled Tokens: 2.8916114456

Enter Amount | MAX | USDC / WETH

Rebalance your liquidity into

Uniswap V2 | Select Pool

Transaction Settings
Speed — Fast
Slippage Tolerance — 3.00%

Approve Balancer

Figure 6.6

Next, you enter a certain amount of the pooled tokens, select a pool, and then move them to that pool by clicking the 'Approve Uniswap V2' button, as shown in Figure 6.7.

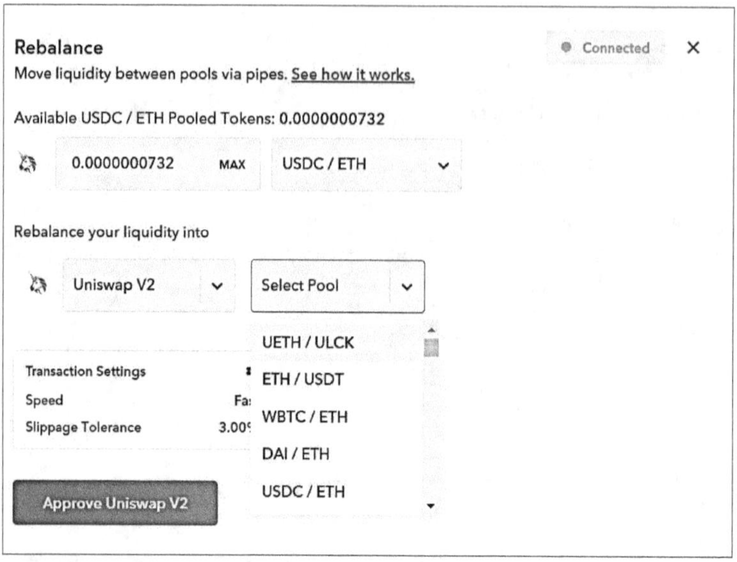

Figure 6.7

You can also add more liquidity by clicking the 'Add' button to bring up the dialog box, as shown in Figure 6.8. You just need to enter a token and the app will automatically configure the pool output.

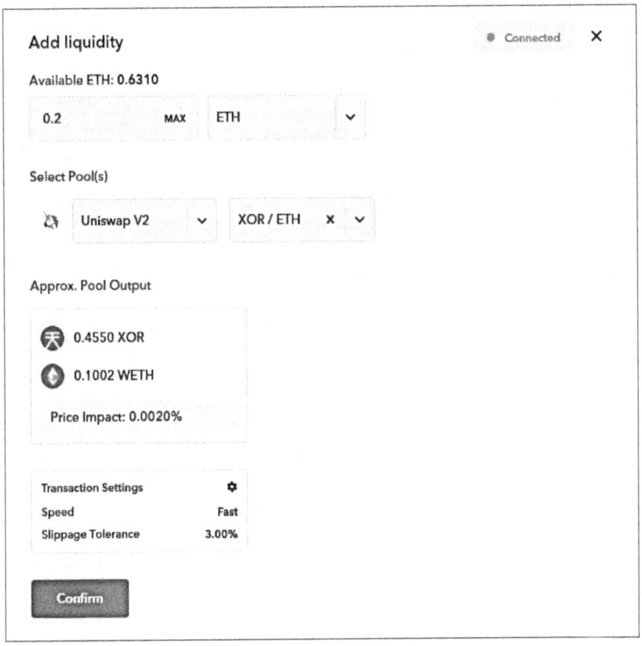

Figure 6.8

In addition, you can explore various investment opportunities under the Invest page, where you can pick and choose liquidity pools that you might want to invest, as shown in Figure 6.9.

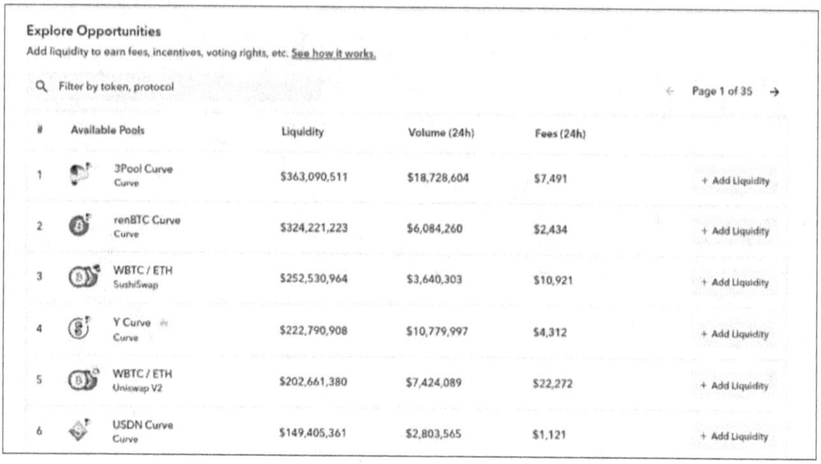
Explore Opportunities

Add liquidity to earn fees, incentives, voting rights, etc. See how it works.

Filter by token, protocol

Page 1 of 35

#	Available Pools	Liquidity	Volume (24h)	Fees (24h)	
1	3Pool Curve Curve	$363,090,511	$18,728,604	$7,491	+ Add Liquidity
2	renBTC Curve Curve	$324,221,223	$6,084,260	$2,434	+ Add Liquidity
3	WBTC / ETH SushiSwap	$252,530,964	$3,640,303	$10,921	+ Add Liquidity
4	Y Curve Curve	$222,790,908	$10,779,997	$4,312	+ Add Liquidity
5	WBTC / ETH Uniswap V2	$202,661,380	$7,424,089	$22,272	+ Add Liquidity
6	USDN Curve Curve	$149,405,361	$2,803,565	$1,121	+ Add Liquidity

Figure 6.9

For example, to invest in Curve's pools, just click the Add Liquidity button adjacent to 3Pool Curve to launch a dialog box where you can choose the pool you wish to invest, as shown in Figure 6.10.

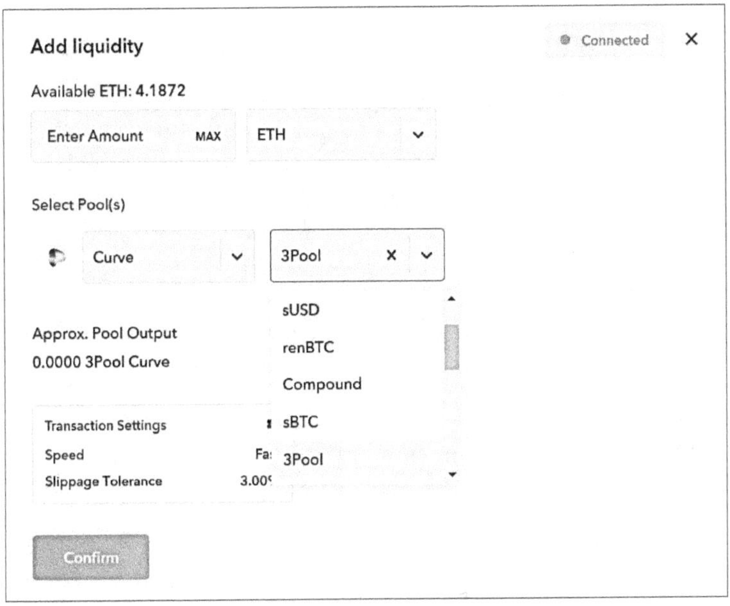

Figure 6.10

Let say you wish to invest in Curve 3Pool, one of the more popular Curve's pools, just select the pool and deposit a specific amount of token into the pool. Cure 3Pool only accepts stablecoins like USDC, DAI and USDT. Once you have contributed to Curve 3 Pool, you can further monetize it by yield farm the LP tokens in Harvest Finance earn interest.

You can also use its exchange to swap tokens, as shown in Figure 6.11.

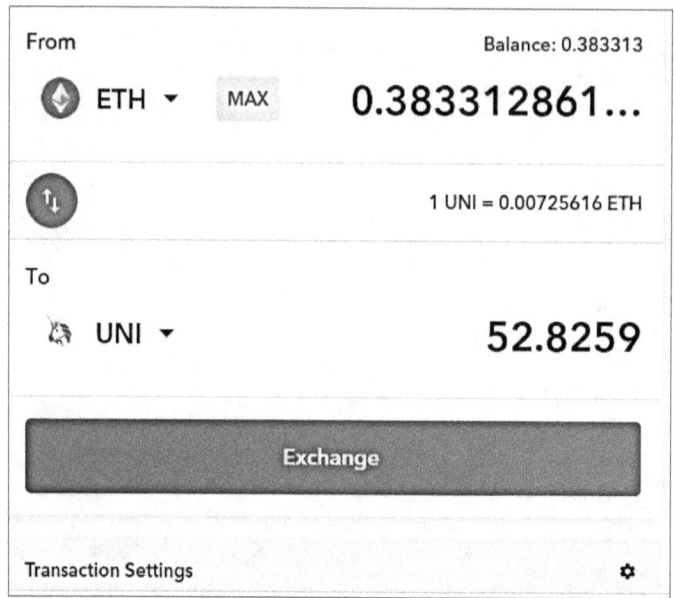

Figure 6.11

In addition, you can also explore your portfolios in all the DeFi platforms that you have invested, or yield farmed, as shown in Figure 6.12.

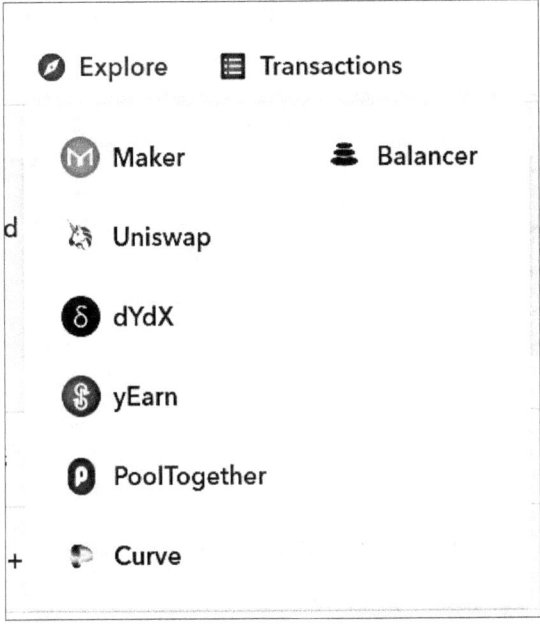

Figure 6.12

For example, if you click Uniswap, you can see your investments there, as shown in Figure 6.13.

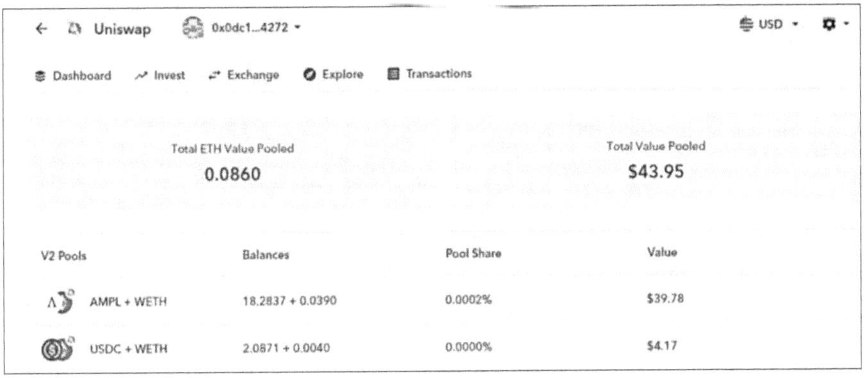

Figure 6.13

If you explore PoolTogether, you can see how much Dai you have added to the pool, as shown in Figure 6.14.

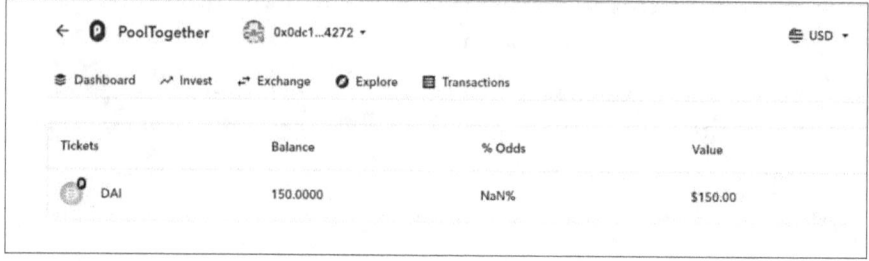

Figure 6.14

Besides that, you can also view the history of all the transactions you have conducted on the Ethereum blockchain, as shown in Figure 6.15.

Figure 6.15

You can also download the CSV file to see all the transactions.

Therefore, I recommend everyone use Zapper as your preferred DeFi portfolio management tool.

6.2 Zerion

Zerion is another fantastic DeFi portfolio management platform. It is one of the the simplest ways to track and manage your entire DeFi portfolios across different protocols from one place.

To access Zerion, use the following link:

https://app.zerion.io/

The landing is as shown in Figure 6.16.

Figure 6.16

The platform displays the portfolio performance comprising all your assets, your savings, and debts, as well as your staked assets and any other assets.

Besides providing information about your portfolios, you can trade tokens by clicking the 'Invest" and the 'Market' buttons. Clicking the 'Invest' button allows you to buy and sell tokens in different categories of DeFi tokens, as shown in Figure 6.17.

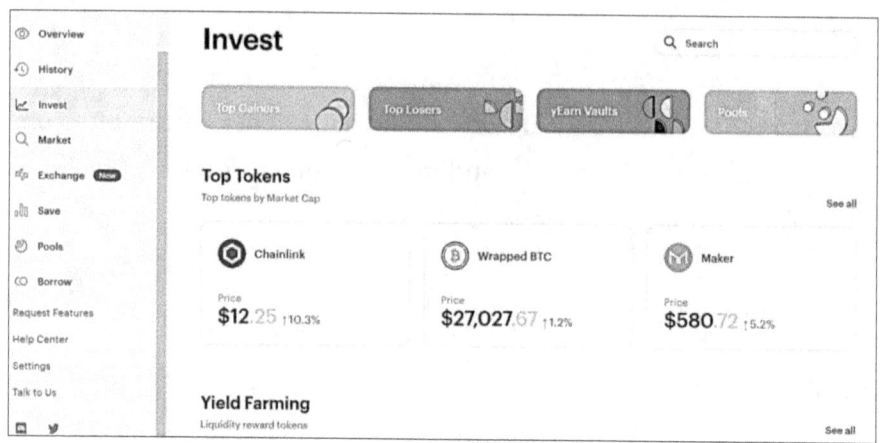

Figure 6.18

Clicking the 'Market' button allows you to trade all ERC20 tokens, as shown in Figure 6.19.

Figure 6.19

Clicking the 'Save' button allows you to deposit tokens and earn interest, as shown in Figure 6.20.

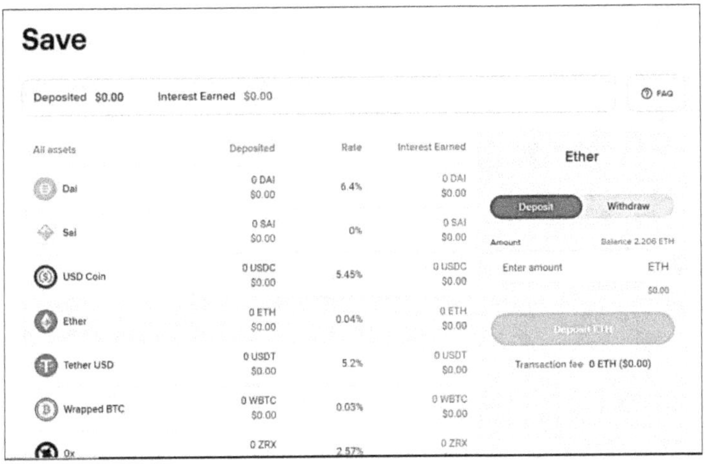

Figure 6.20

You can also participate in liquidity mining by clicking the 'Pool' button, as shown in Figure 6.21.

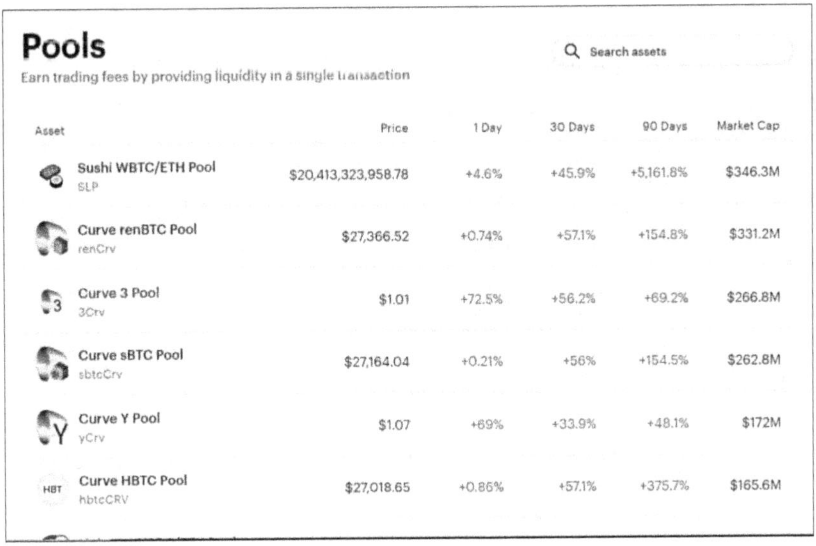

Figure 6.21

For example, if you want to participate om Curve 3 Pool, simply click the link to purchase the 3CRV LP token, as seen in Figure 6.22.

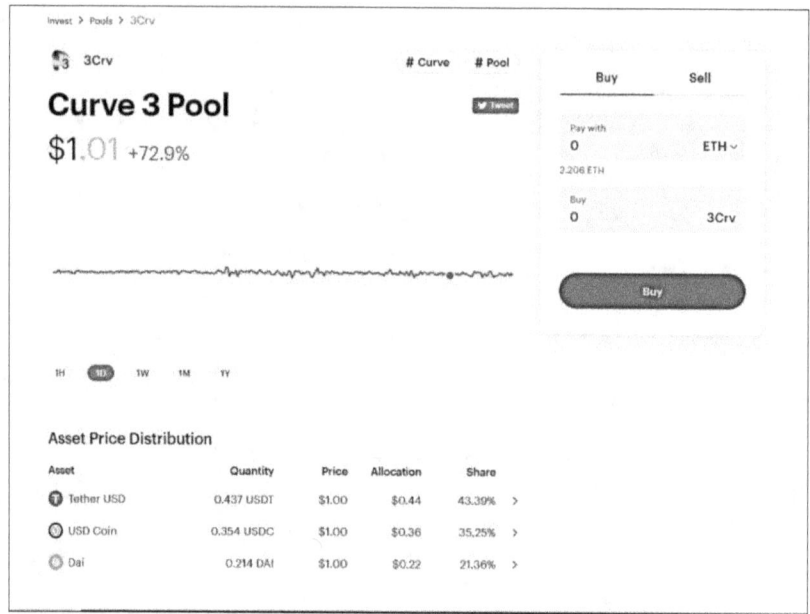

Figure 6.22

3Crv token represents a share in the Curve DAI-USDC-USDT pool. Liquidity providers earn 0.04% fee on every trade made through the protocol as well as yield generated by iEarn protocol on stablecoins. The fees are then split proportionally to your share of the pool. By purchasing 3Crv token, you become a liquidity provider of the Curve DAI-USDC-USDT pool. If you wish to obtain 3Crv token on Curve protocol, you need to deposit stablecoins comprising USDT, DAI and(or) USDC, but Zerion allows to get the token by purchasing it, so it is simpler and more convenient.

In addition, you can also swap coins using the Exchange app, as shown in Figure 6.23.

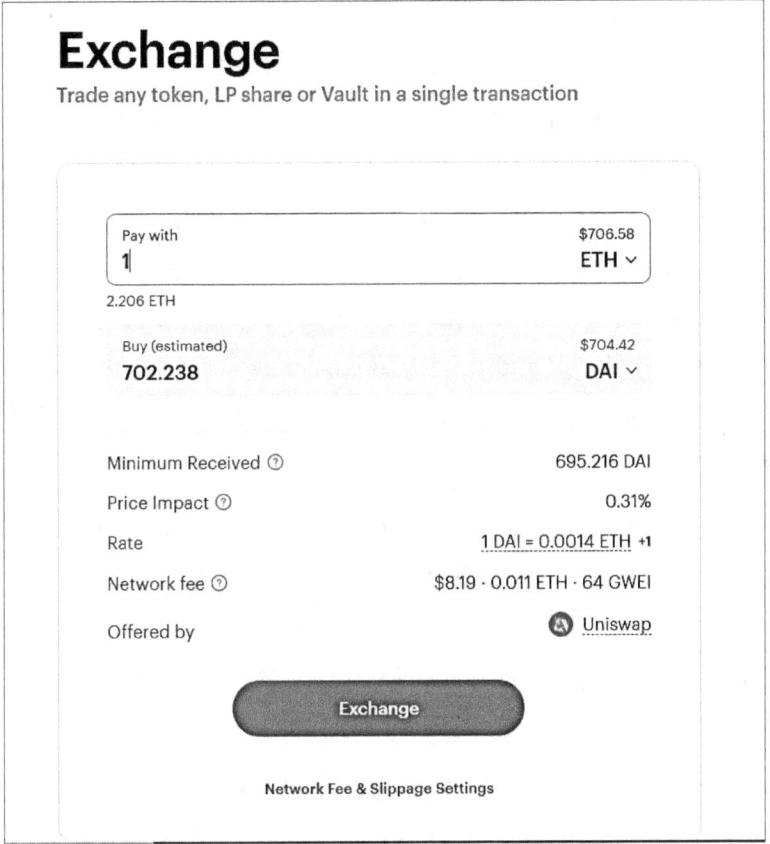

Figure 6.23

Finally, you can also borrow assets.

Chapter 7
DeFi Risk Management

As Defi is non-custodial in nature therefore we might assume investing in DeFi is risk free compared to investment in conventional finance. However, this is further from the truth. Although DeFi has low counterparty risk (Capital, n.d.) , custodial risk and other risks associated with centralized finance, it has its own set of risks pertaining to DeFi. The risks in DeFi will be more technical in nature rather than the non-technical ones.

Basically, DeFi risks consist of three types, namely procedural risk, technical risk, and financial risk (IREDALE, 2020).

7.1 Technical Risks

The threat of technical risks could be serious as they can endanger the functionality of the platforms, resulting in the loss of digital assets. Technical risks in DeFi usually occur due to issues related to protocols comprising smart contracts, software, and hardware.

As we know, all DeFi platforms are powered by smart contracts and users only interact with smart contracts rather than with another peer or middlemen. If smart contracts failed everything failed, there is no way to retrieve your lost digital assets. DeFi is simply a suite of software that includes smart contracts in the form of numerous lines of code, that supports a host of financial services (Lielacher, 2020).

Due to the complex nature of DeFi protocols, it is not uncommon for smart contact and associated code to contain bugs that can provide malicious parties with an attack vector through which they can steal funds.

Funds locked in DeFi are only as secure as the code of their underlying protocols written by the software developers.

For example, on February 14, 2020, the DeFi lending platform, bZx, was hacked while the development team was attending an Ethereum meetup in Denver. The hacker exploited several bugs across multiple bZx protocols, stealing 1,193 ETH, worth approximately $300,000 at the time. Although the development team shut down the affected protocol using a centralized master key, but a second attack happened just four days after the first hack, resulting bZx to lose another $633,000 (SFOX, 2020).

7.2 Financial Risk

Investors in DeFi are exposed to financial risk due to the volatility of cryptossets. Assets locked in liquidity pools could be profitable as many yield farming protocols promise high APY, but they may also lose money if the value of the locked assets depreciated.

In addition, investors may face the risk of Impermanent loss meaning that tokens held in an AMM protocol are seen to have a lesser value than they would if they were being held in their own wallet (Lielacher, 2020).

7.3 Procedural Risks

Basically, procedural risks refer to security risks associated with DeFi protocols and services. The most common security risks in DeFi includes phishing attacks. For example, a hacker may set up a fake website or service to lure users into sharing their sensitive information, especially their private keys.

Another form of phishing attack is by sending emails mirroring that of service providers to the unsuspecting users. As soon as the user clicks on the email, he or she will be redirected to a malicious website.

By using phishing techniques, the hacker will be able to use the personal information of the user such as the private key to transfer funds or conduct illegal transactions without the knowledge of the user. Recent incidents include a fake MetaMask website which look like the real MetaMask website that attempted to mislead users to install its app. Fortunately it was discovered by someone and the site was announced to the public.

To mitigate and manage the DeFi risks, besides being vigilant on our part like stay alert against phishing attacks as well as installing good antivirus software on your devices, you can rely on some online platforms that provide risk information on DeFi platforms, let us examine a few of them.

7.4 DeFi Score

DeFi Score is a platform for measuring risk in permissionless lending pools. The platform was created by a team at ConsenSys, the project is now open source and open for community contribution. It uses a single, consistently comparable value for measuring protocol risk, based on factors including smart contract risk, collateralization, and liquidity. The platform uses an easy to understand 0-10 score that can be presented to users or integrated into other systems.

To access DeFi Score, use the following link:

https://app.defiscore.io

The landing page is as shown in Figure 7.1.

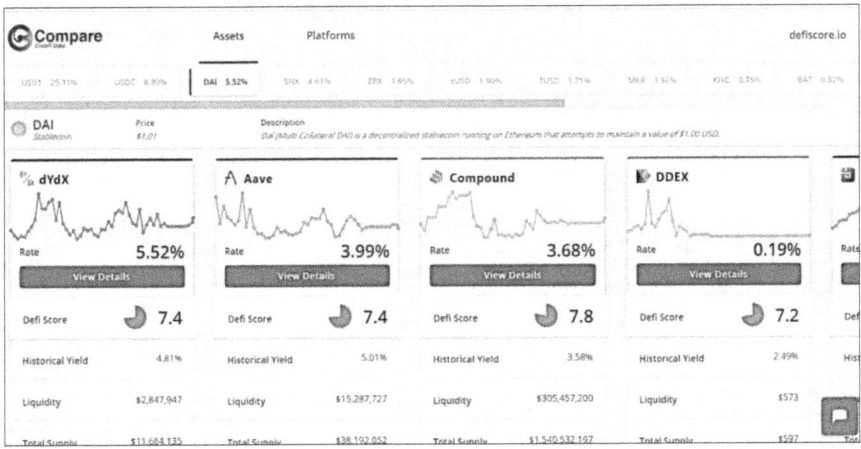

Figure 7.1

You can see the DeFi Score of each digital asset associated with the lending pools across some major DeFi platforms like dYdX, Aave, Compound, DDEX and more. On top of that, it is also providing data on historical yield, liquidity, total supply, and utilization rate, as shown in Figure 7.2. In our example, we examine lending DAI to the platforms.

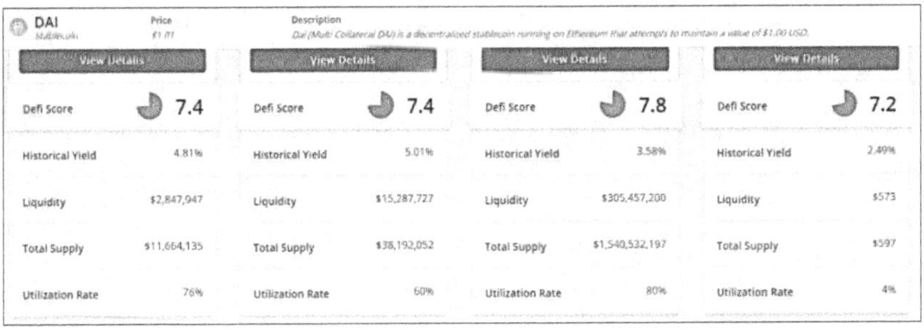

Figure 7.2

You may click the 'View Details' tab to see the detail information the DeFi score, as shown Figure 7.3.

The DeFi Score			
A metric to help users understand the risks associated with a particular DeFi lending opportunity. Learn more			
7.4 out of 10			
Bug Bounty	✓ Yes	Audited	✓ Yes
Time Index	○ 74%	Centralization Index	○ 62%
Utilization Index	○ 1%	Liquidity Index	○ 73%

Figure 7.3

The DeFi Score was calculated based on several elements comprising Bug Bounty, Time Index, Utilization Index, Audited, Centralization Index and Liquidity index. Each of the elements is explained as follows:

- Bug Bounty- Whether the protocol offers bug bounty program
- Time Index -How long has the protocol operated on the mainnet without an exploit (has a cyber-attack occurred that takes advantage of some vulnerability)?
- Utilization Index-Is the market sufficiently over-collateralized to protect collateral price volatility?
- Audited- Has a reputable security firm audited the smart contract code and published the results?
- Centralization Index-To what degree the platform is centralized? Who holds the admin key? Can the price oracle be manipulated?
- Liquidity Index- Is there sufficient liquidity to ensure that the lenders can exit their positions at will?

You can assess the risk further by looking at the market details, as shown in Figure 7.4.

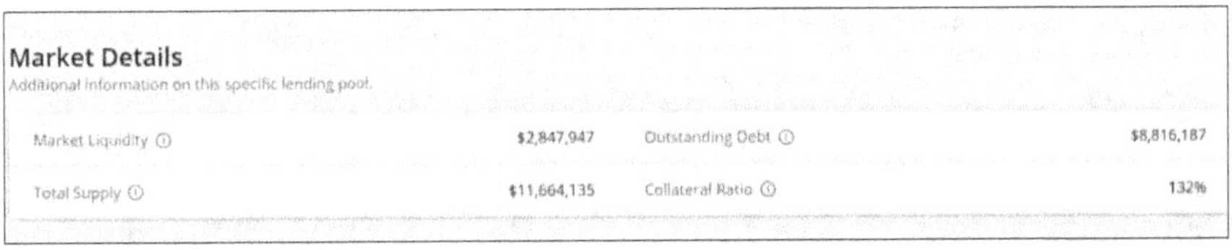

Market Details			
Additional information on this specific lending pool.			
Market Liquidity	$2,847,947	Outstanding Debt	$8,816,187
Total Supply	$11,664,135	Collateral Ratio	132%

Figure 7.4

The market details comprise of Market liquidity, Total Supply, Outstanding Debt and Collateral ratio. They are explained as follows:

- Market Liquidity-Represents the size of the lending pool. The bigger the size, the higher the liquidity therefore less risky.
- Total supply-Represents total funds supplied to the lending pool as collateral. Again, the more the total supply, the less risky.
- Outstanding Debt-Represents outstanding loans. It should not be too high so that the collateral to debt ratio does not exceed a certain limit to minimize the risk.
- Collateral Ratio-Represents the collateral to debt ratio. The higher the ratio, the more the platform is overcollateralized, and less risky.

In addition, you should also look at the platform details to evaluate the risk. The platform details are seen in Figure 7.5.

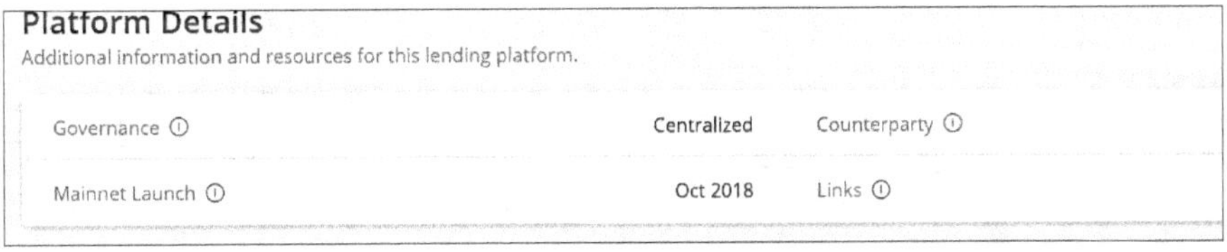

Platform Details		
Additional information and resources for this lending platform.		
Governance	Centralized	Counterparty
Mainnet Launch	Oct 2018	Links

Figure 7.5

The platform details are explained as follows:

Governance- How is the group behind the protocol organized? If it is governed by a small group in an autocratic way or governed by a community in a democratic decentralized way? Obviously the more centralized and autocratic the governance, the riskier the platform.

Mainnet Launch-When did this protocol release to the mainnet? Obviously the earlier the platform is released to the mainnet, the better as a proof of majority, and hence can be perceived to be less risky.

Counterparty-Peer to peer lending can be done by either direct matching or liquidity pool. Obviously lending via a liquidity pool is much safer than P2P lending as it does not involve a counterparty.

Links- Does the platform provide additional resources for the public to understand the protocol better? Providing additional resources such as websites, social media platforms, Github will increase transparency and hence can be perceived as less risky.

Table 7.1 compared the risk score and APY of some major platforms.

Table 7.1 DeFi Score and APY for Lending DAI

Platform	DeFi Score	APY
dYdX	7.4	5.52%
Aave	7.4	3.99%
Compound	7.8	3.68%
DDEX	7.2	0.19%
bZx	5.0	0.00%
Nuo	4.9	0.00%
MakerDao Oasis	9.7	0.00%

Based on the DeFi score, the safest platform for lending DAI is MakerDao Oasis and the riskiest is Nuo. Then again you need to look at the APY to determine which platform you can invest to obtain the optimum return.

Let us examine the DeFi score and the APY for lending USDT to the platforms.

Table 7.2 DeFi Score and APY for Lending USDC

Platform	DeFi Score	APY
dYdX	7.5	4.28%
Aave	7.2	5.54%
Compound	7.7	4.15%
DDEX	6.7	8.3%
bZx	4.9	1.75%
Nuo	5.0	0.04%

Other tokens are analyzed by DeFi Score are USDT, SNX, ZRX, sUSD, TUSD, MKR, KNC, BAT, ETH, WBTC, LINK, SAI, REP and LEND. You can compare the risks and the potential returns before making your decision to invest.

On the other hand, you can also select a platform and see the DeFi scores and the APY of the tokens that can be lent and borrowed, as shown in Figure 7.6.

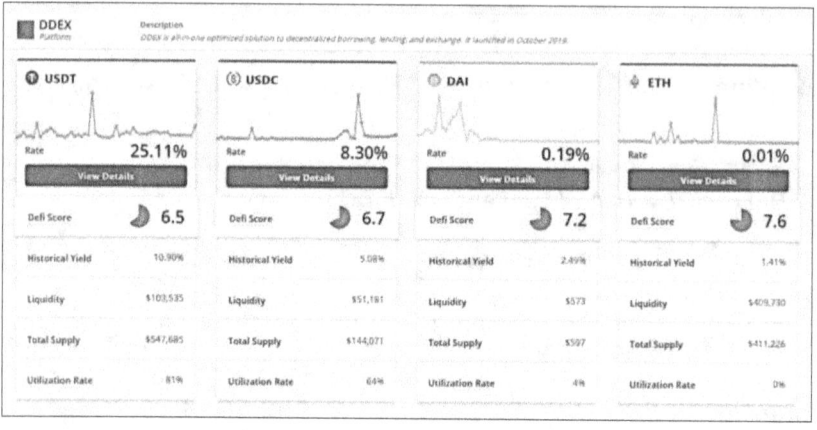

Figure 7.6

7.5 Swaprate.finance-Hegding Against Interest Rate Fluctuation.

Swaprate is a platform that allows hedging against the interest rate fluctuations by swapping interest rates on the DeFi money markets. Interest rate swap involves the exchange of a fixed interest rate for a floating rate, or vice versa, to reduce or increase exposure to fluctuations in interest rates or to obtain a marginally lower interest rate (Belyakov, Getting FIXED interest rate for DAI, 2019).

On Swaprate, you can swap interest rates for deposit as well as for borrowing for DAI and USDC. In other words, you can get an insurance for your existing DAI deposit and USDC deposit if the interest rates fluctuate.

How does Swaprate works? It is quite simple. Basically, there are two strategies you can use. First, you can choose to fix your floating rate on your deposit or loan by entering an interest rate swap (IRS), a kind of insurance contract that will pay out the difference between the promised fixed rate and the realised rate at the time of maturity.

For example, if the estimated swap rate for DAI on Compound for 12 months is 10%, but you think the variable rate will give you less, you can enter a swap in which you receive a guaranteed 10% fixed rate and the obligation to pay the floating interest of Compound over the next 12 months. Suppose you choose 1000 DAI as a nominal; you would only need to lock 100 DAI as collateral due to 10x leverage. After 12 months, three scenarios could occur:

Scenario 1:

The accumulated rate of 12 months is less than 10%, let us say 6%, you will get 30% return on your strategy. You will get your collateral 100 DAI back, and receive 4 % (10%-6%) over your nominal of 1000 DAI, i.e., 40 DAI.

Scenario 2:

The accumulated rate for the 12 months is more than 10%, let's say it is 13%. You will get your 100 DAI back minus 3% (13%-10%) over your nominal of 1000 DAI, or 30 DAI, which means you lose 30% on your strategy.

Scenario 3:

The rate is exactly 10%, you will just get your collateral back.

The second strategy is you pay for the fixed rate and receive variable rate if you believe that the variable rate will give you more return than the quoted fixed rate over the investment period. For example, the quoted swap rate for 12 months is 10% and you think the variable rate will give you more. After 12 months, three scenarios can occur:

Scenario 1:

The accumulated rate of 12 months is more than 10%, let us say 14 %, you will get 40% return on your investment. You will get your collateral 100 DAI back plus 4 % (14%-10%) over your nominal of 1000 DAI, i.e., 40 DAI or 40% profit.

Scenario 2:

The accumulated rate for the 12 months is less than 10%, let say it is 6%. You will get your 100 DAI back minus 4% (10%-6%) over your nominal of 1000 DAI, or 40 DAI, which means you lose 40% of your investment.

Scenario 3:

The rate is exactly 10%, you will just get your collateral back.

If you examine both strategies, the first strategy is indeed a going short strategy because you expect the rate to drop while the second strategy is going long because you expect the price to appreciate.

To use Swaprate, following the link below to access the website:

https://swaprate.finance/

The landing page is as shown in Figure 7.7.

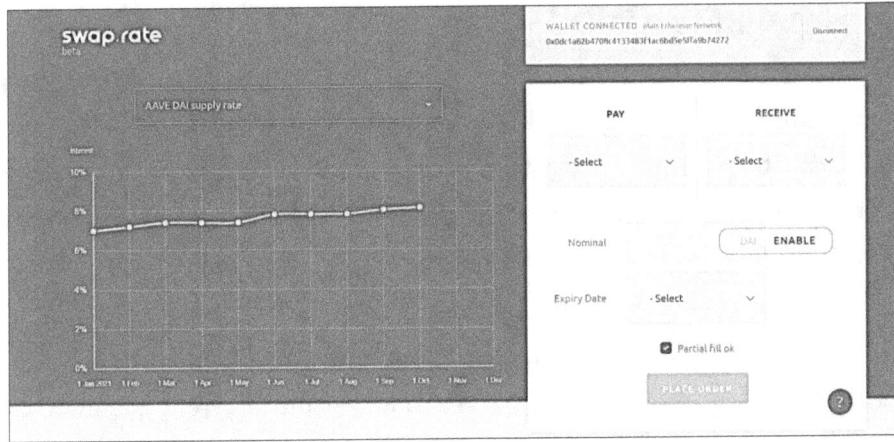

Figure 7.7

Currently the services are only available for DAI on Aave platform and DAI and USDC on the Compound protocol, as seen in Figure 7.8.

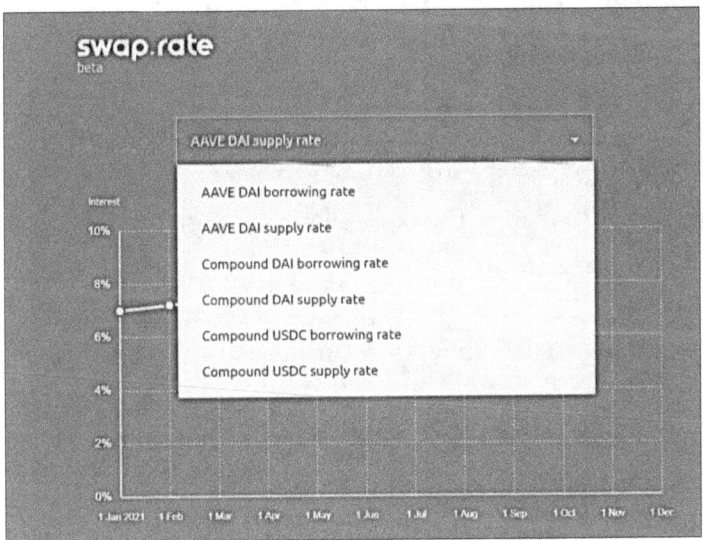

Figure 7.8

7.6 Nexus Mutual

Nexus Mutual is a decentralised version of insurance. It used the blockchain technology to create a mutual pool (a risk sharing pool) of insurance to the community. The platform is built on the Ethereum mainnet and serves only the Ethereum users. It is partially decentralised as you still must become a member to buy cover, so the usual KYC applied. However, it is different from the traditional insurance companies as it is wholly owned by the members. The model encourages engagement as members will get economic incentives for participating in risk assessment, claims assessment and governance.

What kind of cover does Nexus Mutual provide? Currently they only provide Smart Contract Cover. The main objective is to provide the Ethereum community with protection against hacking of smart contracts. In future they will develop insurance coverage for other risks. For further details, refer to its whitepaper at:

https://nexusmutual.io/pages/SmartContractCoverWordingv1.3.pdf

To buy the insurance cover, head to the buy cover page with the following link:

https://app.nexusmutual.io/cover/buy/select-project

The page UI is as shown in Figure 7.9. You may choose the supported platforms to buy the insurance cover.

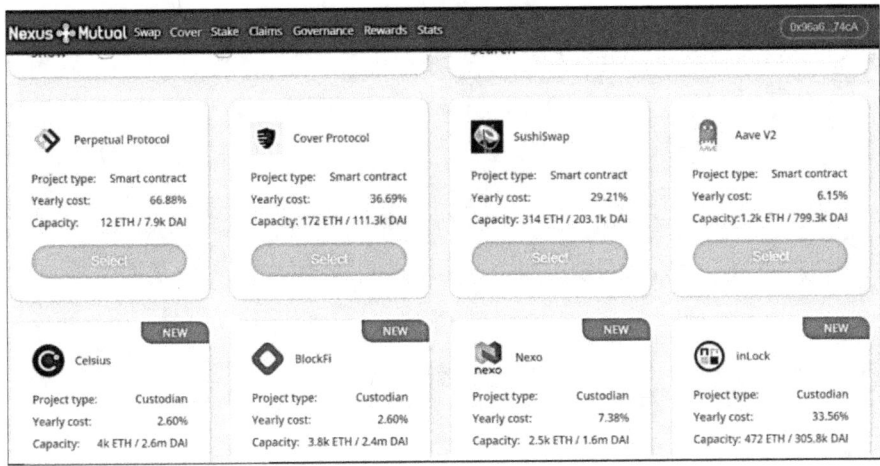

Figure 7.9

Let say you wish to cover Uniswap V1, so click it to get quote, as shown in Figure 7.10.

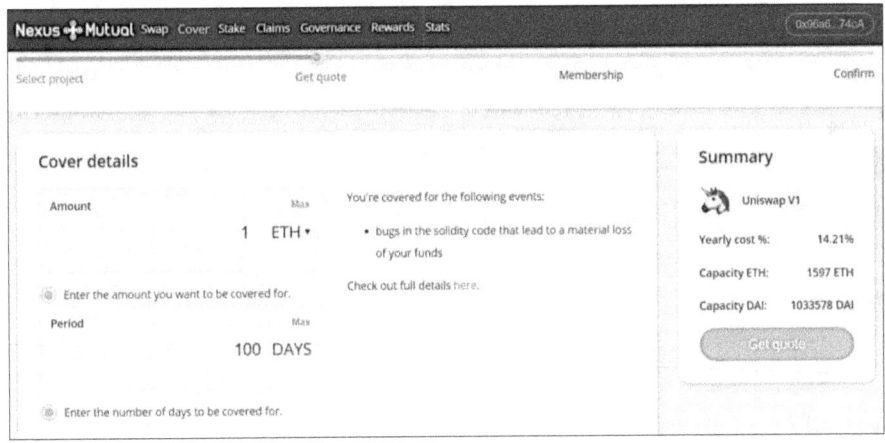

Figure 7.10

Upon clicking the 'Get quote' button, you must become a member and pay a membership fee of 0.002 ETH to continue, as shown in Figure 7.11.

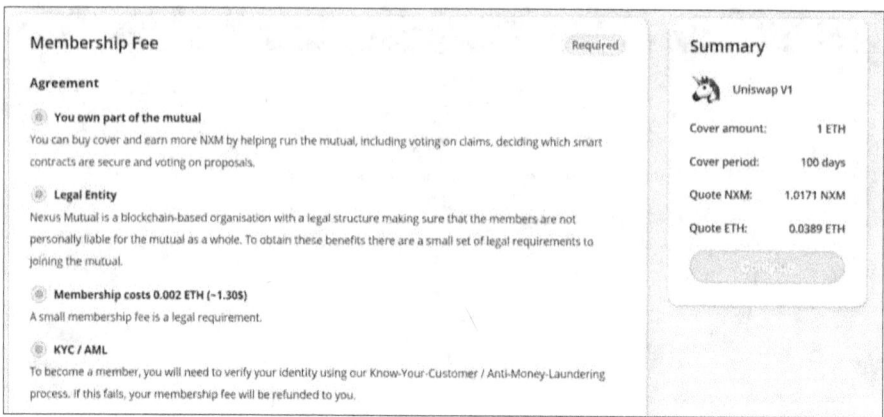

Figure 7.11

After your payment is confirmed, you must proceed with the KYC process, as seen in Figure 7.12. You may register as an individual or as a company.

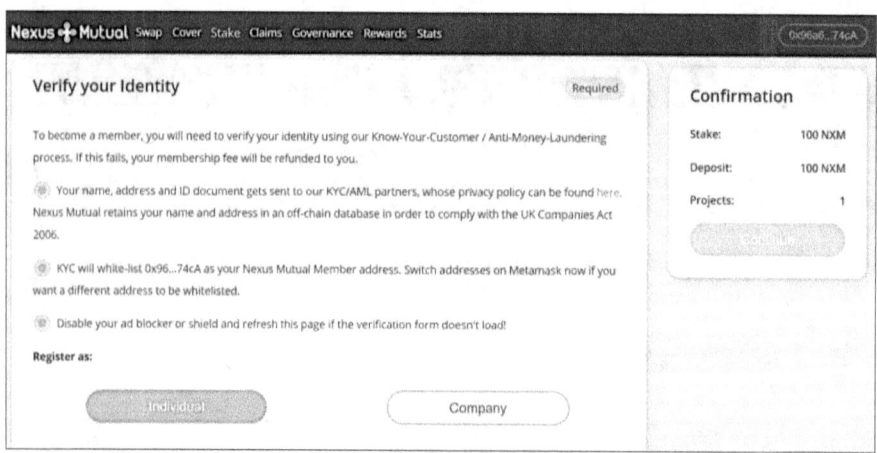

Figure 7.12

Chapter 8
DeFi Options Trading Protocols

Besides insurance, DeFi also allows investors to hedge risks via options trading. An option is a contract giving the buyer the right, but not the obligation, to buy or sell the underlying asset at a specific price on or before a certain date (Downey, 2020). Generally, people use options to hedge risk while looking for profit. Options are derivatives because they derive their value from an underlying asset.

There are two types of options, the call options and the put options. A call option gives the holder the right to buy and an asset whilst a put option gives the holder the right to sell a stock. If you have difficulty to understand the concepts of options, think of the call option as akin to paying a down-payment for a future purchase of a property and the put option as buying an insurance for protection for any untoward incident happens in the future.

For example, you foresee the price of Bitcoin is bullish and may rise to $19,500.00 in the future, you can hedge the risk of paying a high price by purchasing a call option to buy 1 BTC at $18,500.00, which is also known as the strike price. The cost you pay is like a down payment or a premium which will be forfeited if you do not exercise you right to purchase BTC within the contract period. However, if BTC price has risen to $19,500 within the contract, you can exercise your right to purchase the BTC at $18,500.00 and sell it in the open market at $19,500.00, you will make a handsome profit of $1000 minus the premium you pay.

On the other hand, you foresee the price of BTC is bearish and may fall to $17,500.00 in near future, you can hedge the risk of losing money by purchasing a put option to sell BTC at $18,000.00 when the current price is $18,500. In the event the BTC price has dropped to $17,500.00, you still can sell your BTC at $18,000.00, which means you just lose $500 minus the premium instead of losing $1000 if you did not use the put option. Additionally, if the price does not drop, you do not have to exercise your right to sell BTC and what you lose is the premium spent.

8.1 Opyn- Buying Protection Via Options

Opyn is a decentralized insurance platform built on Ethereum that allows users to protect themselves from the unique risks they face in DeFi. Opyn is built using Convexity Protocol, a generalizable options protocol that allows DeFi users to create put and call options (Opyn, n.d.).

What can you benefit from Opyn? Basically, you can buy or sell protections on Opyn. On one hand, you can buy options (oTokens) to protect yourselves against DeFi risks. On the other hand, you can also deposit collateral in a vault to mint and sell oTokens, earning premiums for protecting others, not unlike a liquidity provider.

At the time writing, Opyn allows users to insure Compound deposits, hedging ETH downside with protective put options on ETH, and hedge ETH upside with calls options on ETH. Opyn should be secure as its smart contracts have been audited by OpenZeppelin. To access Opyn, using the following link: https://v1.opyn.co/#/

The landing page is as shown in Figure 8.1.

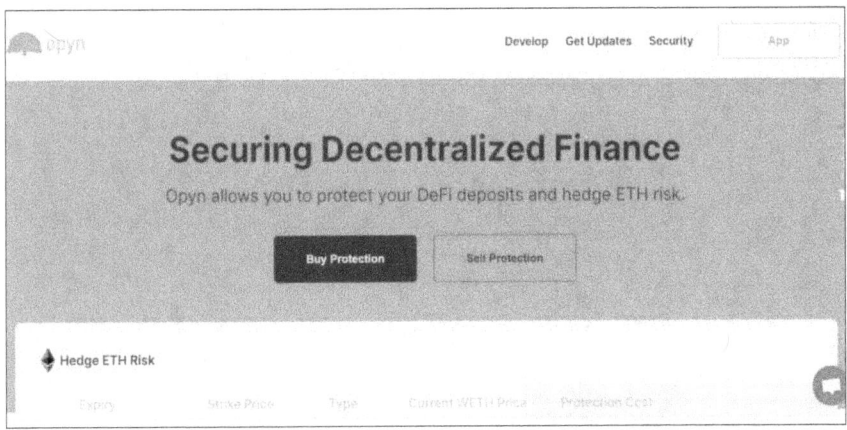

Figure 8.1

You can launch the app by clicking the App button on the top righthand corner of the landing page or simply click the 'Buy Protection' button or the 'Sell Protection' button. As usual, you must connect your wallet to use the app.

8.1.1 Purchasing Put Options for Downside Protection

On Opyn, you can secure downside protection for your cryptoassets by purchasing a put option. Currently you can buy protections for ETH (or rather WETH), DPI, UNI, WBTC and YFI.

To buy the ETH put options, click on buy to launch the buying dialog box which you can enter all the particulars, as shown in Figure 8.2.

Figure 8.2

The dialog box provides several key information comprising liquidity, protection cost, expiry date, current WETH price and the strike price.

In this example, the strike price is $560, if WETH dipped below $550, you could exercise your right to sell ETH to receive 560 USDC per ETH before the expiry date. Let us say the price is 500 USDC, your profit is 60 USDC minus the premium $25.7 which is $34.30. Be aware that you must exercise your right before the expiry date. Besides that, you must convert your ETH to WETH to exercise. To obtain WETH, you swap your ETH at some exchanges like Uniswap, 1inch Exchange and more.

Next, click the 'Confirm Purchase' button to launch the form that allows you to enter the amount of ETH you wish to protect, as shown in Figure 8.3.

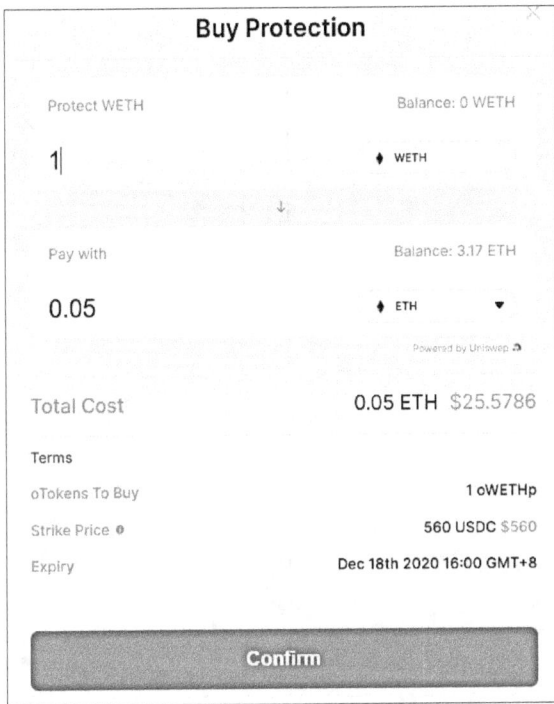

Figure 8.3

Once you click the 'Confirm' button you must confirm the transaction at MetaMask, as shown in Figure 8.4.

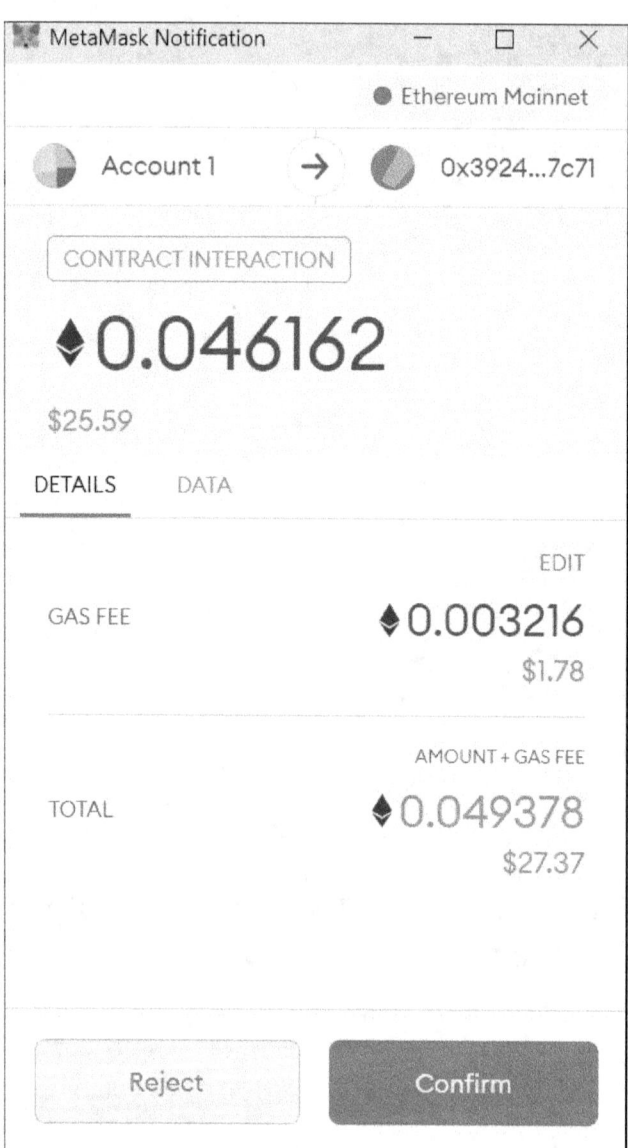

Figure 8.4

8.1.2 Purchasing Call Options for Upside Protection

To buy a call option, click the 'Sell Protection' tab to bring up the buy dialog box, as shown in Figure 8.5.

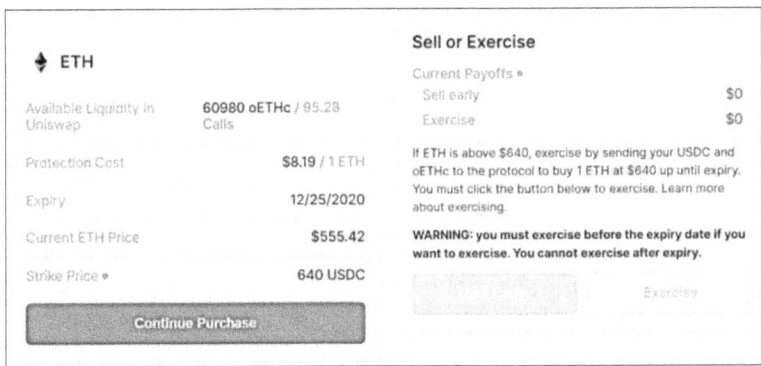

Figure 8.5

If you believe the market is bullish and the price of ETH will rise further, you can purchase a call option for upside protection. In this example, the call option strike price of 640 USDC, if ETH is above 640 USDC, you can exercise your right to buy 1 ETH per 640 USDC, instead of the current price. Let us say the current price is 680 USDC per ETH, you can buy the 1 ETH at 640 and sell it at 680 USDC, thus making a profit of 40 USDC minus the cost of $8.18, which gives you $41.82.

To confirm the purchase, click the 'Confrim Purchase' button and then confirm it on your wallet, as seen in Figure 8.6 and Figure 8.7.

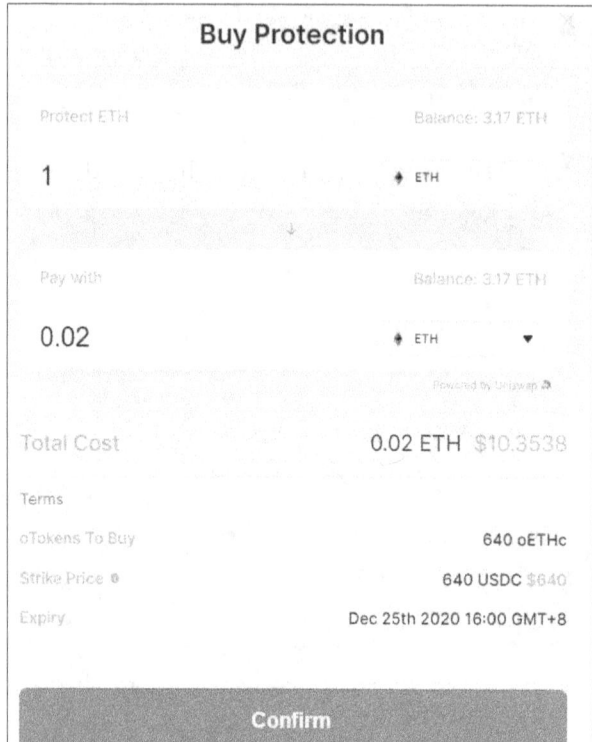

Figure 8.6

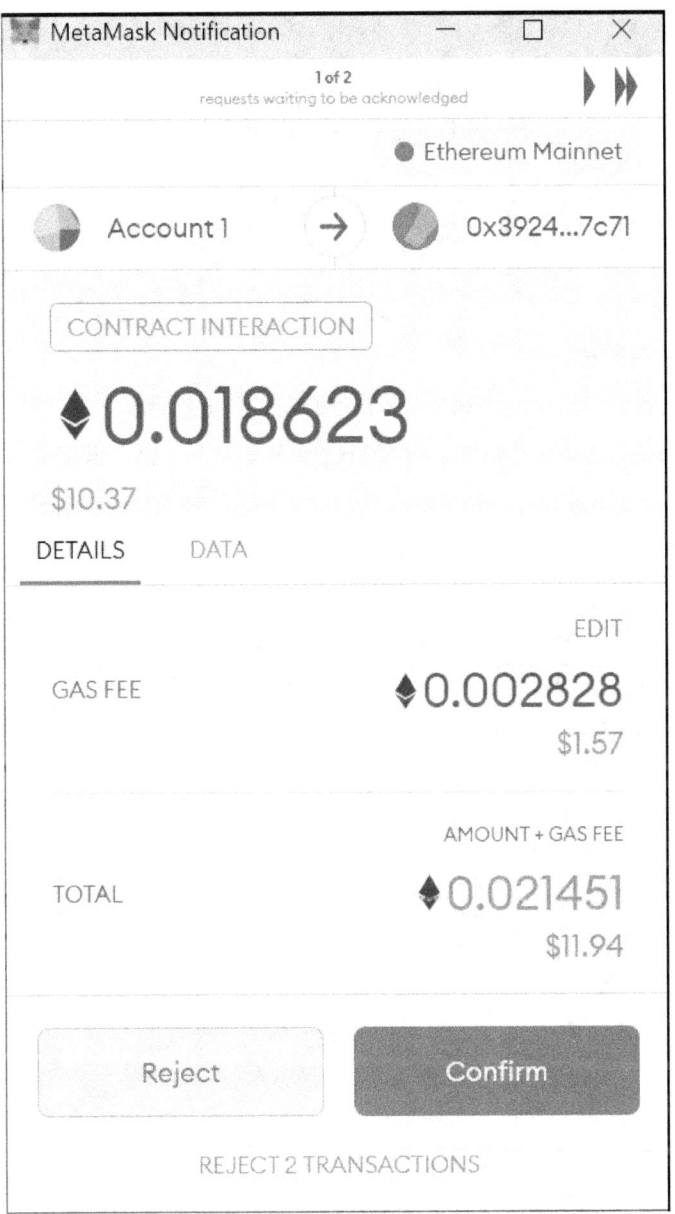

Figure 8.7

8.1.3 Compound Deposit Protection

- Opyn's Compound protection protects against several different risks:
    - Technical risks (eg. smart contracts hacks)
    - Financial risks (eg. liquidity crises)
    - Admin risks (eg. admin key compromise, governance vulnerabilities)
- Opyn's Compound protection does not protect against
    - Issues with Compound's ETH:USD oracle and Maker's ETH:USD oracle
    - Non-transferable ERC20 tokens

Opyn allows you to buy insurance for your USDC and DAI deposits on Compound. For example, you may want to buy insurance for your Dai deposit on compound, as shown in Figure 8.8.

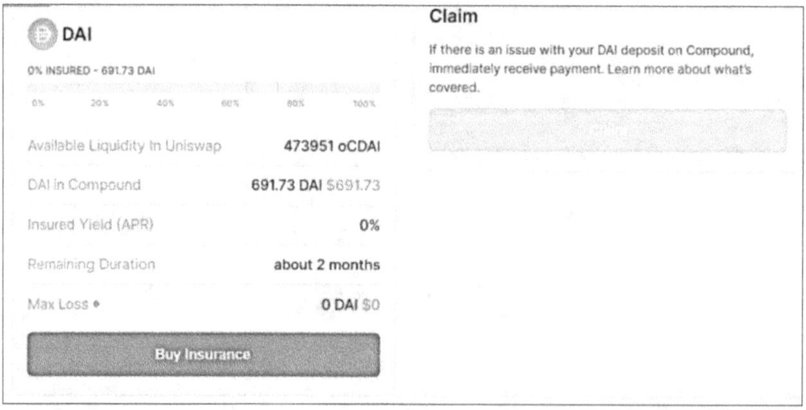

Figure 8.8

To proceed, click the 'Buy Insurance' button to launch the next dialog box that require you to confirm the purchase, as shown in Figure 8.9.

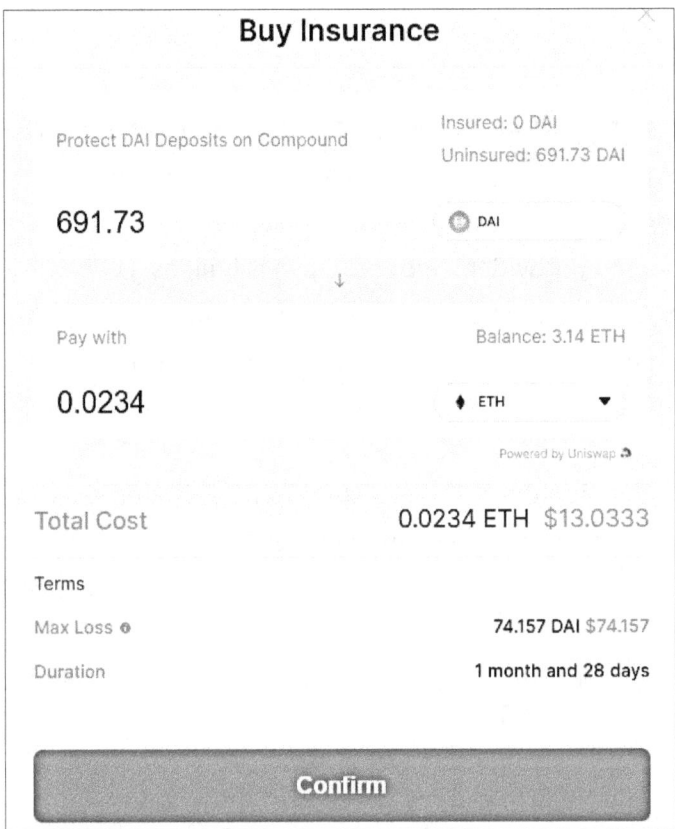

Figure 8.9

If you are satisfied with the pricing, you may proceed confirm the purchase and then confirm the transaction at MetaMask.

Additionally, you can also buy yield insurance for USDC and DAI deposits on Compound platform. Besides that, you can be an insurance provider by selling insurance.

8.1.4 Selling Protections

You may wonder which party is providing the protection for the insurance you bought? As Opyn is a DeFi platform, there is no single entity that provides the protection, instead, the claims are paid from a pool of funds contributed by the liquidity providers. Indeed, Opyn is built as a two-sided marketplace, so any individual who is interested in providing protection can do so by depositing a collateral and earn a premium in the process (Opyn, n.d.).

To sell the protections, click the 'Sell Protection' and browse the list of protections you wish to enter, as shown in Figure 8.10.

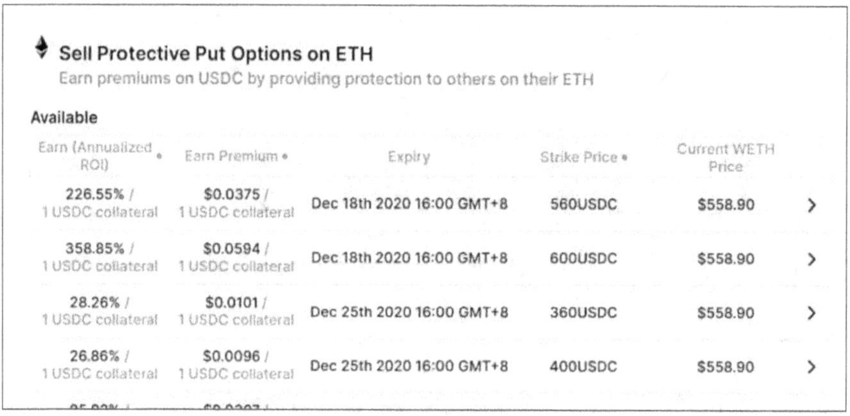

Figure 8.10

Let say you wish to sell protective put option on ETH, proceed to click one of the products, as shown in Figure 8.11.

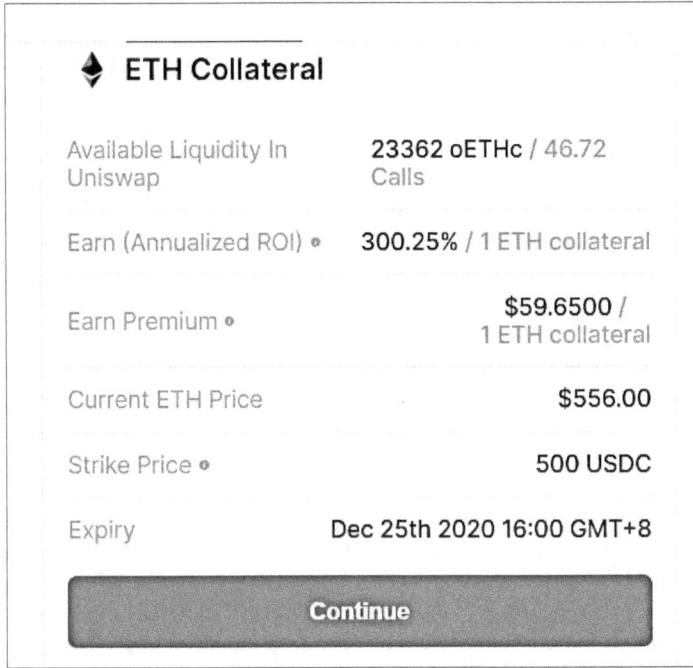

Figure 8.11

In this protection package, you pay ETH as a collateral and earn premiums paid by the protection buyer. If you are satisfied with the pricing, you may click the 'Continue' button and then click Confirm in the next dialog box to confirm the purchase, as shown in Figure 8.12.

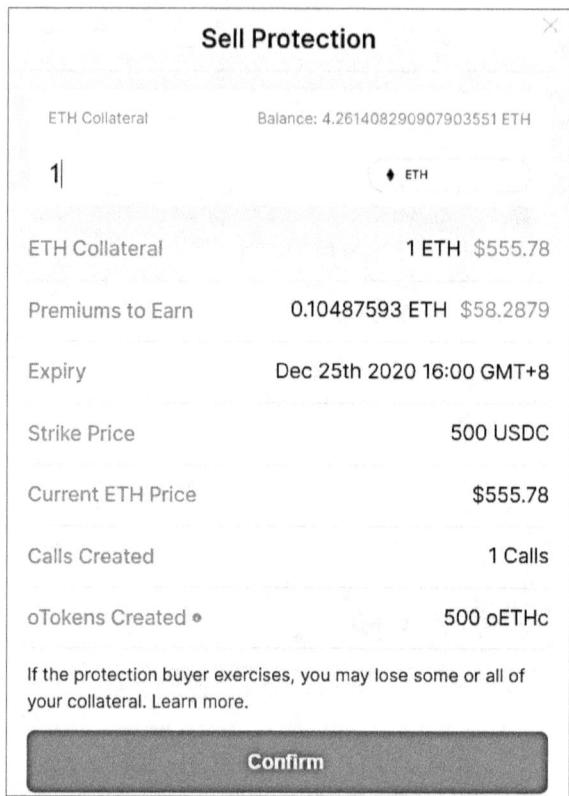

Figure 8.12

Finally, confirm the transaction on MetaMask, as shown in Figure 8.13.

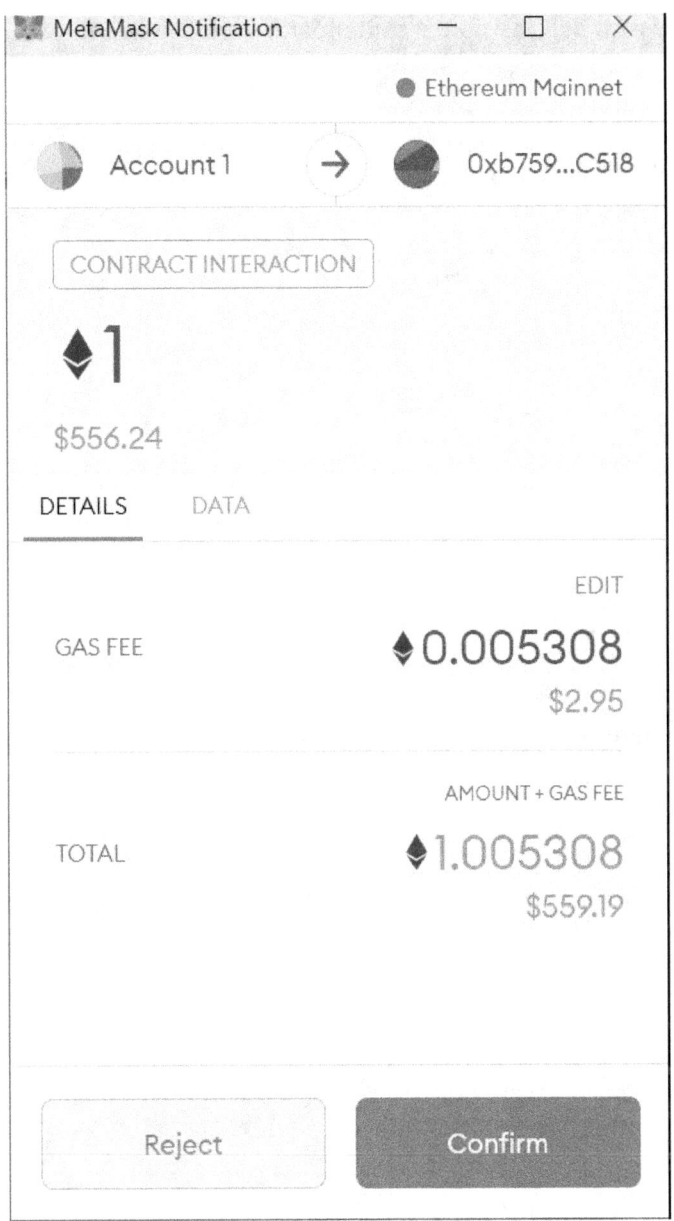

Figure 8.13

In addition, you may also sell insurance to depositors of Compound who purchased insurance for their DAI or USDC deposits, as shown in Figure 8.14.

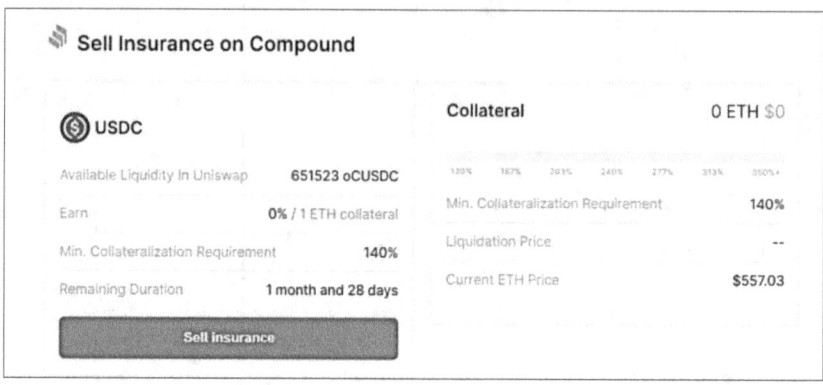

Figure 8.14

You must provide collateral using ETH, as shown in Figure 8.15. In return, you earn a premium in ETH.

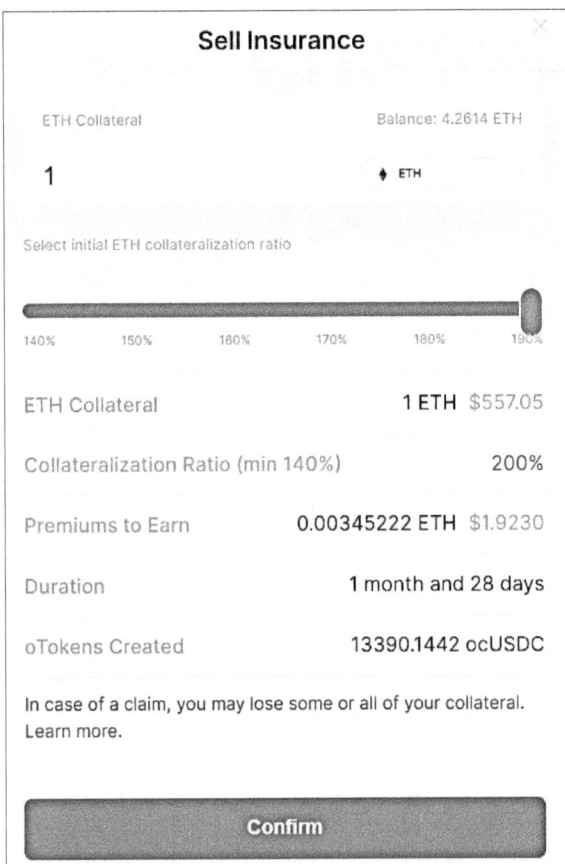

Figure 8.15

Finally, you must confirm the transaction on your wallet, as shown in Figure 8.16.

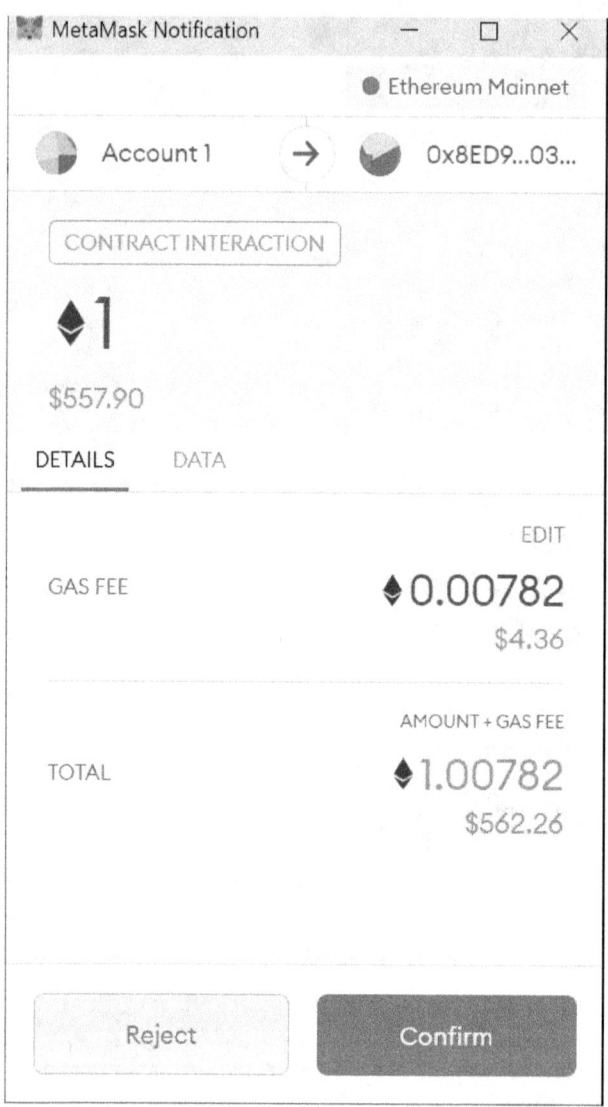

Figure 8.16

8.1.5 What are oTokens?

In Opyn, every option supported by the Convexity Protocol is integrated through an oToken smart contract which is representation of options issued by the protocol. Options sellers create options by locking up collateral for some period and minting oTokens. Each oToken protects a unit of the specified underlying ERC20 asset. The Options seller can sell these oTokens on an exchange to earn premiums. The oToken marketplaces deployed for the purpose of insurance are ocDai and ocUSDC.

oToken can be purchased on Uniswap and its pricing is determined by the market price of oTokens on Uniswap. However, due to limited liquidity, the otokens will not appear in the Uniswap's default list, you must add the oTokens manually by searching for the token address on Etherscan or other platforms like Coingecko, then copy and paste it in Uniswap. For example, the contract address for OCUSDC can be found on Coingecko, shown in Figure 8.17.

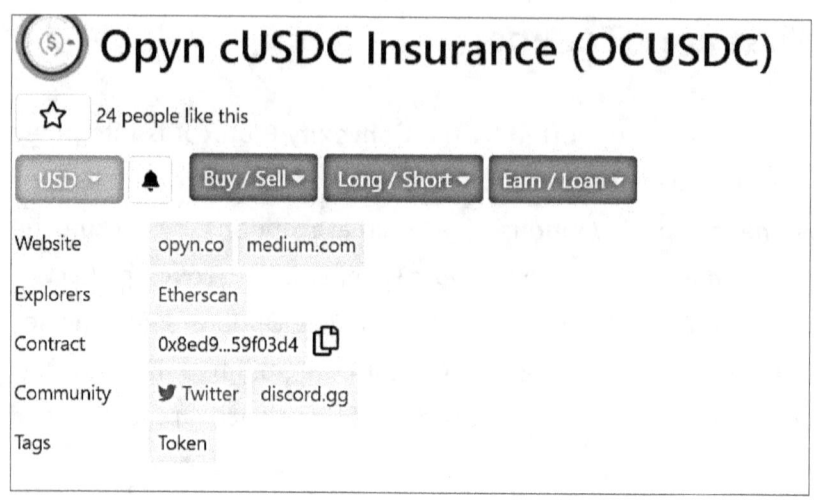

Figure 8.17

Next, select the exchange or platform list by clicking the change button on Uniswap, browse the list and select Coingecko, as shown in Figure 8.18. and Figure 8.19.

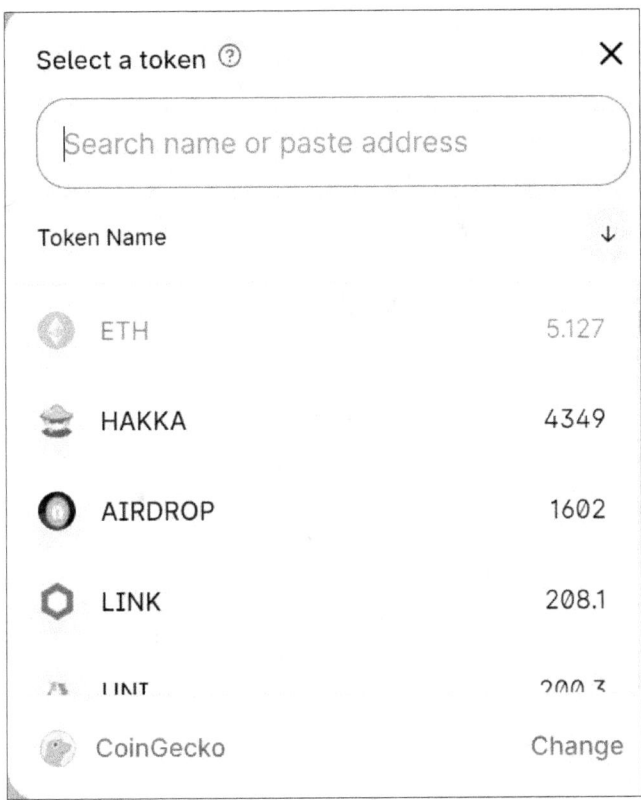

Figure 8.18

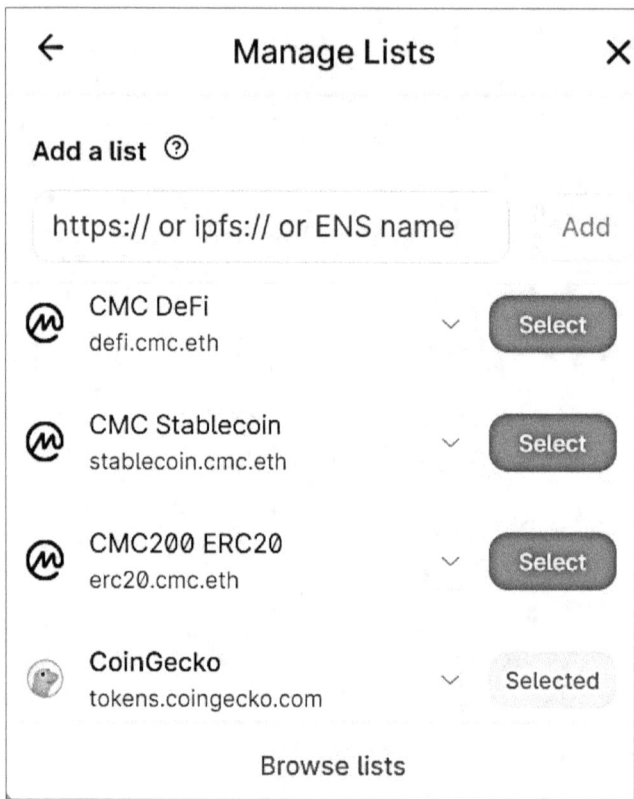

Figure 8.19

Now go back to the main panel and paste the contract address and add it to Uniswap, as shown in Figure 8.20.

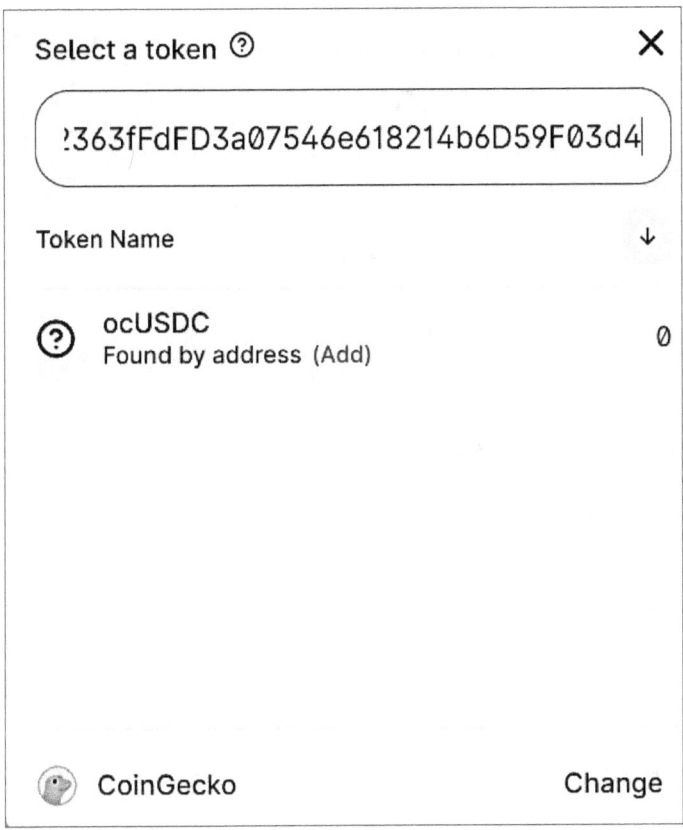

Figure 8.20

You will find that trying to buy OCUSDC on Uniswap V2 is not possible due to insufficient liquidity, as shown in Figure 8.21.

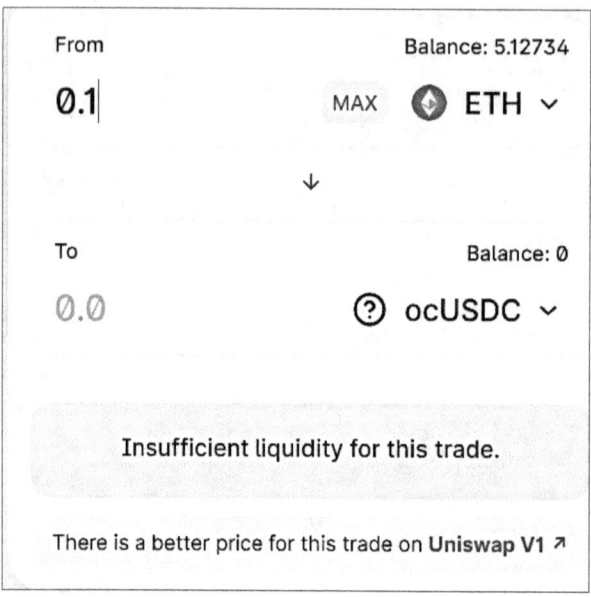

Figure 8.21

However, you can try to trade on Uniswap V1 by clicking the hyperlink below, then you can trade OCUSDC, as shown in Figure 8.22.

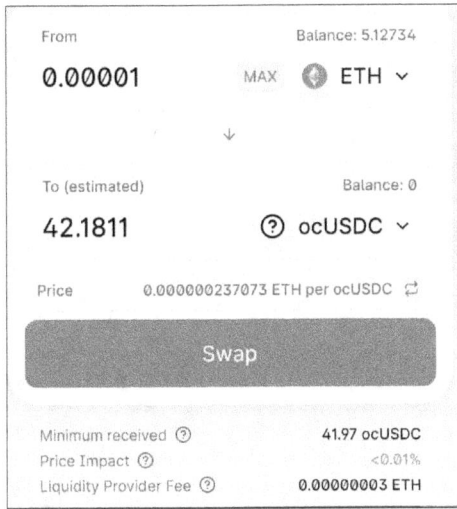

Figure 8.22

As for OETH, you can find the contract address on Etherscan, which is 0x1bc76312a8549204b23c19ad82bab8079c64c265 . Simply copy the address and paste it to Uniswap, the token should appear, as shown in Figure 8.23.

Figure 8.23

OETH also cannot be traded on Uniswap V2, so you can try to trade on Uniswap V1, as shown in Figure 8.24.

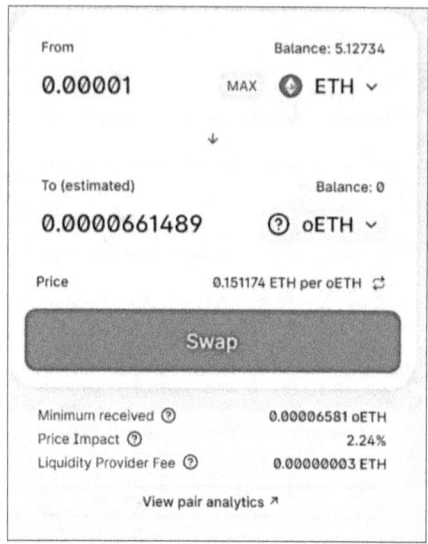

Figure 8.24

Besides that, you can also find OCDAI on CoinGeckgo, so you can copy the contract address and add it to Uniswap, as shown in Figure 8.25.

Figure 8.25

You may also swap OCDAI on Uniswap V1, as shown in Figure 8.26.

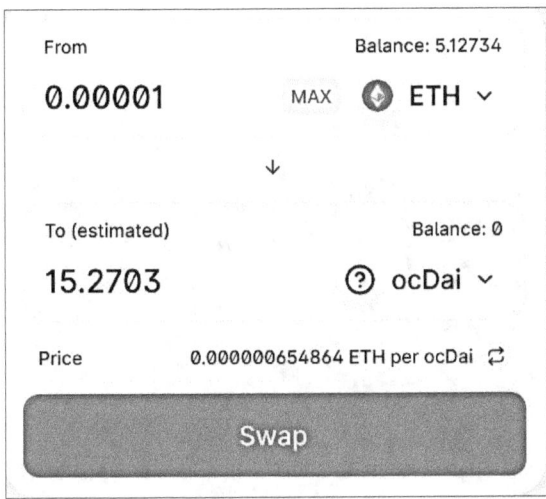

Figure 8.26

Last, you may want to know how to make claims in Opyn. Well, the process is a bit technical, please refer to Appendix C.

8.2 Hegic-An On-chain Options Trading Protocol

Hegic is an on-chain options trading protocol on Ethereum powered by hedge contracts and liquidity pools. In contrast to traditional options contracts, hedge contracts are non-custodial, trustless and censorship resistant. According to Hegic whitepaper (Wintermute, 2020), the hedge contract is a system of Ethereum contracts that accumulate and hold liquidity in a non-custodial way, write (sell) hedge contracts to the holders, accumulate, and distribute premiums between the liquidity providers (writers) and conduct on-chain settlement of the contracts.

To access Hegic , use the following link:

https://www.hegic.co/

The landing page is as shown in Figure 8.27.

Figure 8.27

8.2.1 Buying Options

To buy a call option or a put option, click the 'HOLDERS' tab. If you are bullish on WBTC or ETH, buy a call option which you will be given the right to buy the option at a fixed price even if the future price increased above the strike price.

For example, if you wish to buy a call option for WBTC, you can enter the pricing and select the period from 1 day to 4 weeks, as shown in Figure 38.28.

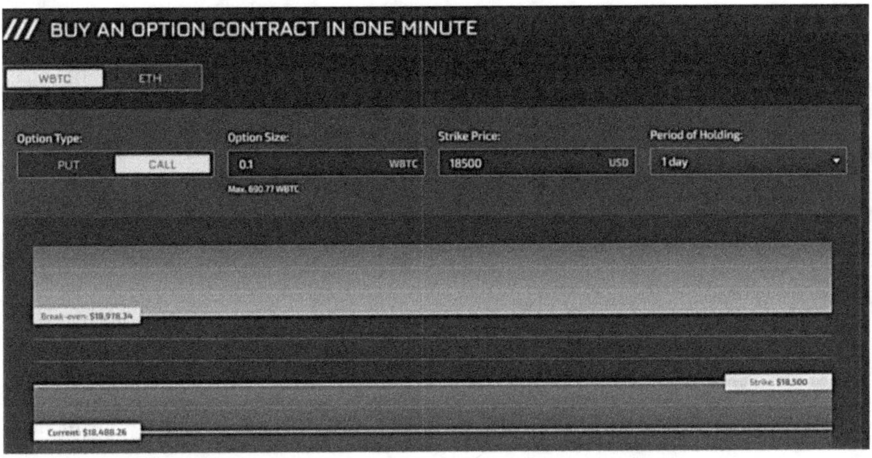

Figure 8.28

In this contract, your option size is 0.1 WBTC and set the strike price at 18,500 and the period of holding for one day. It will show you the current price at $18,488.26. You need to scroll down further to check the cost you must pay, as shown in Figure 8.29.

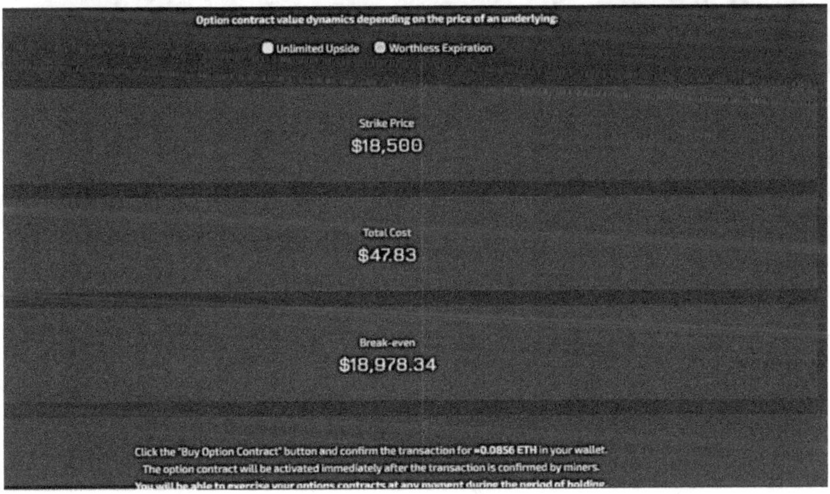

Figure 8.29

For a call option buyer, the breakeven point is reached when the underlying is equal to the strike price plus the premium paid. In this example, you bought 0.1 BTC for a strike price of $18,500.00 per one BTC, and the cost is $47.83, so the amount you pay is $1850.00+$47.83 which is $1897.83. So the BEP(Break Even Price) for one BTC is $18978.30. The figure shown in the app is $18,978.34 which may be due to decimals correction. If the price rose more than the BEP , say $19,200.00, then your profit is $1920.00-1850.00-$47.83=$22.47

In addition, you may want to change the period to one week by selecting from the drop-down list for the period of holding, as shown in Figure 8.30.

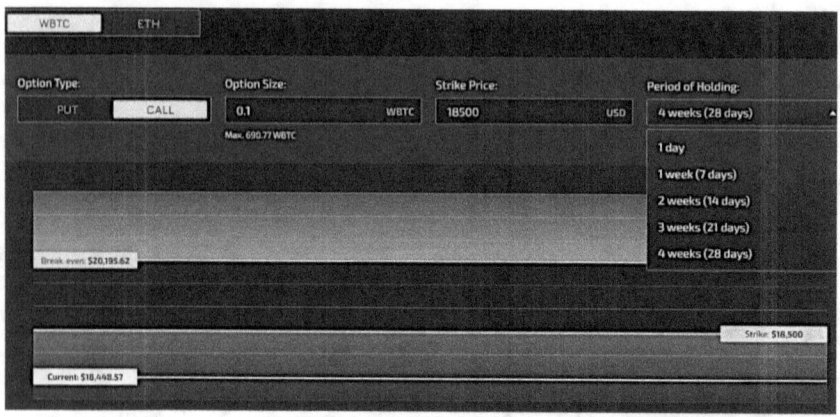

Figure 8.30

Let say you choose 2 weeks with similar strike price for 0.1 WBTC. Now the cost and the BEP will be different, as shown in Figure 8.31.

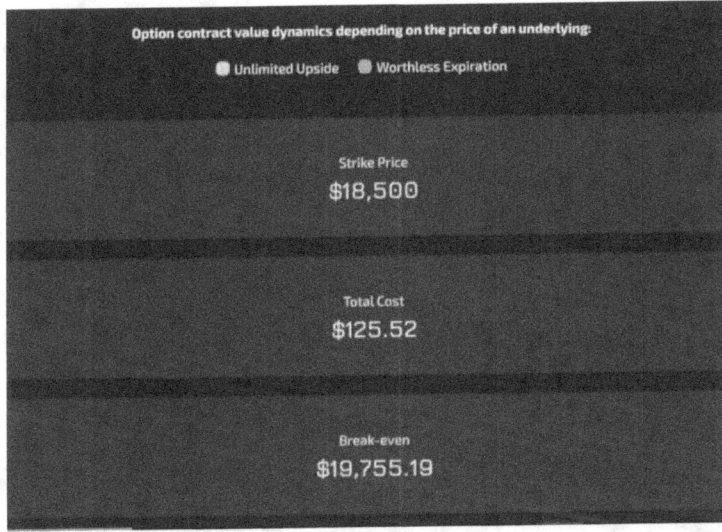

Figure 8.31

Now, let say you expected the price of Ethereum is bearish, so you wish to buy a put option to hedge the risk of the price crash. To buy the put option, select ETH, and click the 'PUT' tab, and enter the option size and the strike price, as shown in Figure 8.32.

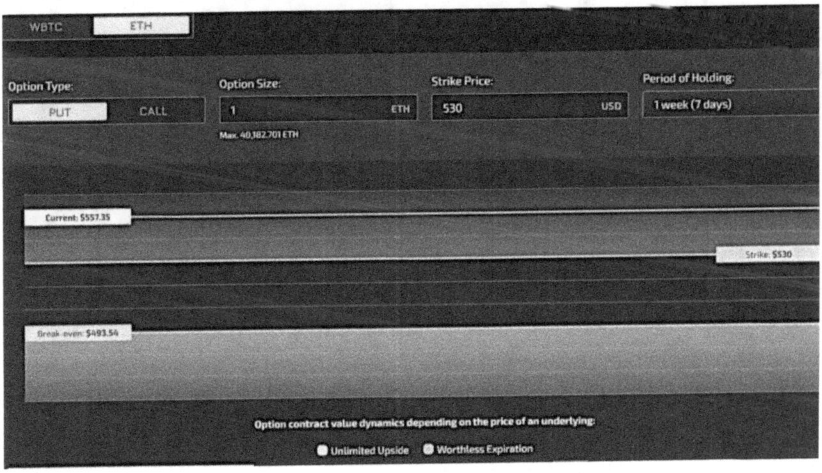

Figure 8.32

A put option allows you to sell the option at the strike price if the price of fell below the strike price. Next, scroll down to view the cost and the breakeven price (BEP), as shown in Figure 8.33.

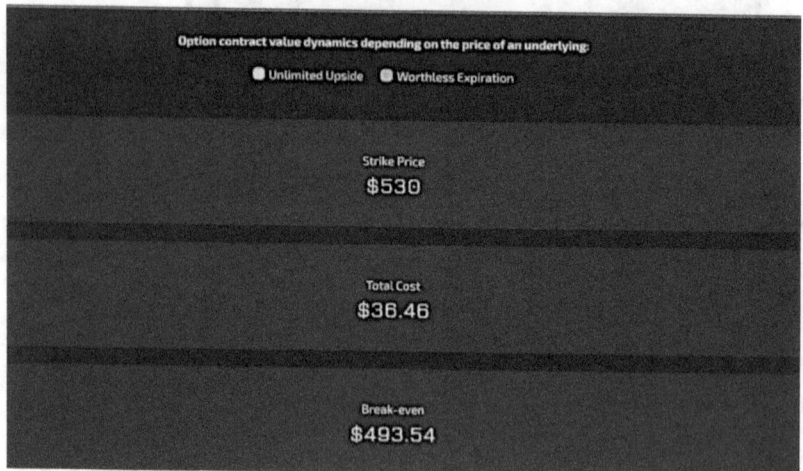

Figure 8.33

The BEP of a put option is equal to the strike price minus the cost. In our example, the strike price is $530 and the cost is $36.46, so the BEP is $530-$36.46=$493.54. So, when the ETH price is $493.54, you just manage to break even. If the price is lower than the breakeven price, say $480, then your profit is $530-$480-$36.46=$13.54

8.2.1 Selling Options

Another way to monetize on Hegic is to become an option seller or rather a liquidity provider. Hegic depends on the non-custodial liquidity pool to sell options. There are two types of pool, the WBTC pool and the ETH pool. The WBTC pool is for selling WBTC call and put options whilst the ETH pool is for selling ETH call and put options.

As a liquidity provider, you are also known as an options writer. As a writer (liquidity provider) you receive writeWBTC tokens (a kind of ERC20 token) or writeETH tokens that give you a share in the pool's premiums that are distributed to you upon the options contracts' expiration date. When you wish to receive your WBTC or ETH back, you must call the Withdraw function of the contract and burn writeWBTC tokens or writeETH. WBTC or ETH will be sent to the writer's Ethereum address.

Let say you wish to provide 0.1 ETH to the ETH pool, select ETH and enter the amount of ETH you wish to deposit, as shown in Figure 8.34.

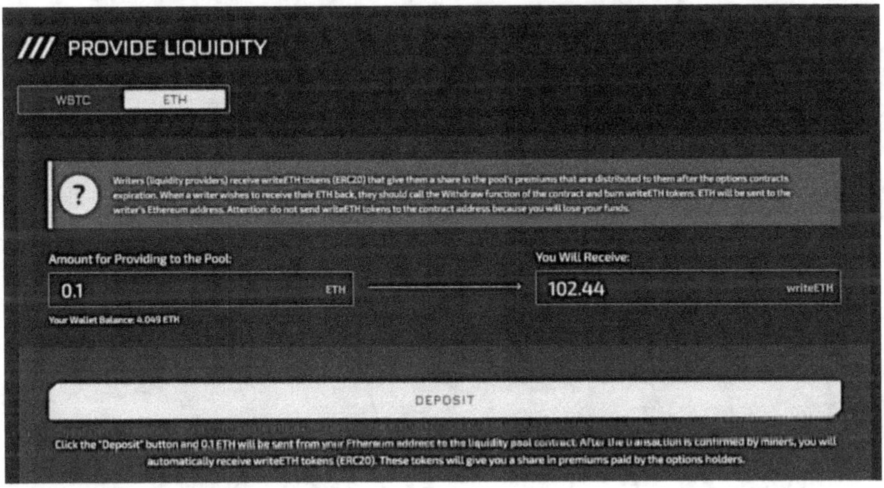

Figure 8.34

To proceed, click on the 'DEPOSIT' button and confirm the transaction on your wallet.

Your earnings will be shown in panel as shown in Figure 8.35.

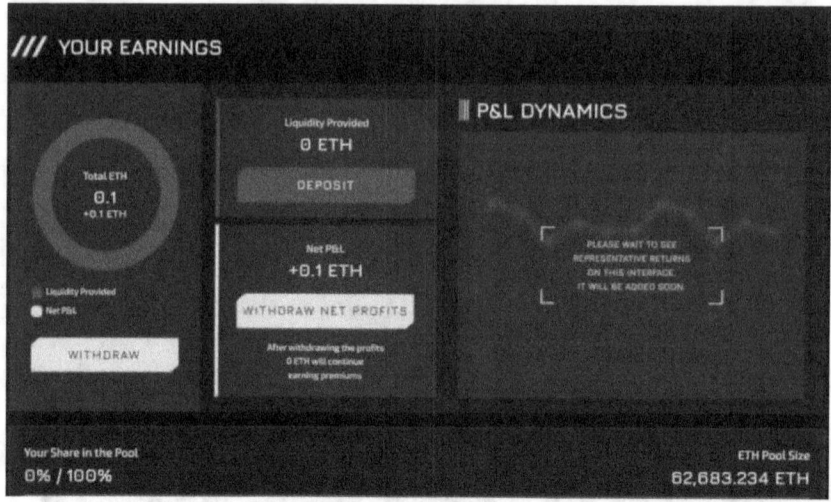

Figure 8.35

8.2.3 HEGIC Token

The third way you can monetize on Hegic platform is by becoming a HEGIC token holder. HEGIC is the native ERC20 token of HEGIC. There are four types of income you can earn from HEGIC:

I. Liquidity mining rewards

Liquidity providers can claim rewards in HEGIC. After providing WBTC or ETH to one of the pools you will receive writeWBTC or writeETH tokens. You can lock these write tokens to start receiving rewards in HEGIC tokens. After locking them your share in rewards will be increasing each block. You will need to manually claim HEGIC.

The interface is as shown in Figure 8.36.

Figure 8.36

For example, after contributing to the ETH pool, you can lock your rewards writeETH and earn rHEGIC which you can convert into HEGIC. To do this, click on the 'Liquidity Mining Rewards' button to stake your writeETH, as shown in Figure 8.37.

Figure 8.37

Next, click 'Lock Tokens' to lock writeETH. After confirmation, you will start to earn your rewards, as shown in Figure 8.38.

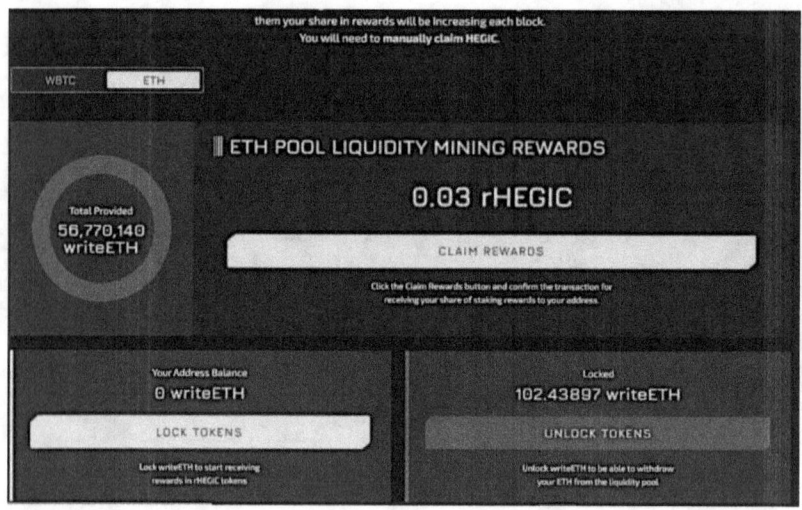

Figure 8.38

You may unlock your tokens or claim your rewards by clicking the relevant buttons.

II. Liquidity utilization rewards

Options buyers can claim rewards in HEGIC. After buying ETH or WBTC options you will be able to claim your rewards. Reward's size depends on the size and period of an option.

III. Hold Staking Lots to Earn WBTC or ETH

You need 888,000 HEGIC for a staking lot. You can buy a staking lot by converting 888,000 HEGIC into a staking lot that you will be able to stake for receiving a share of staking rewards distributed among lots holders. One lot can be used to receive rewards in WBTC or ETH. Current rewards size: 1% of each option's size.

You can see that staking lots is expensive as 888,000 lots is equivalent to a whopping $159,840.00. However, there are other third-party platforms like Jmonteers Hegic Staking (https://www.hegicstaking.co/) and zLots Hegic Pools(https://zlot.finance/) allow you to join the pool with any amount of HEGIC available. You can access them from Hegic website, as shown in Figure 8.39.

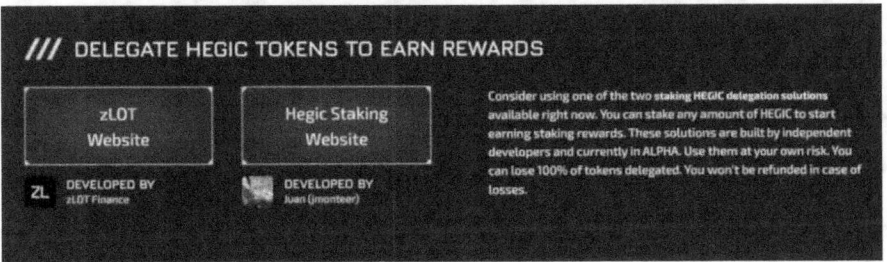

Figure 8.39

However, Hegic warned that these pools have been independently developed and are not directly associated with Hegic so you should do your own risk analysis before providing funds to any of these pools. Lost funds from bad staking pools have nothing to do with Hegic.

Let say your risk appetite is high and willing to take the risk, then you can visit Jmonteers to stake your HEGIC, as shown in Figure 8.40.

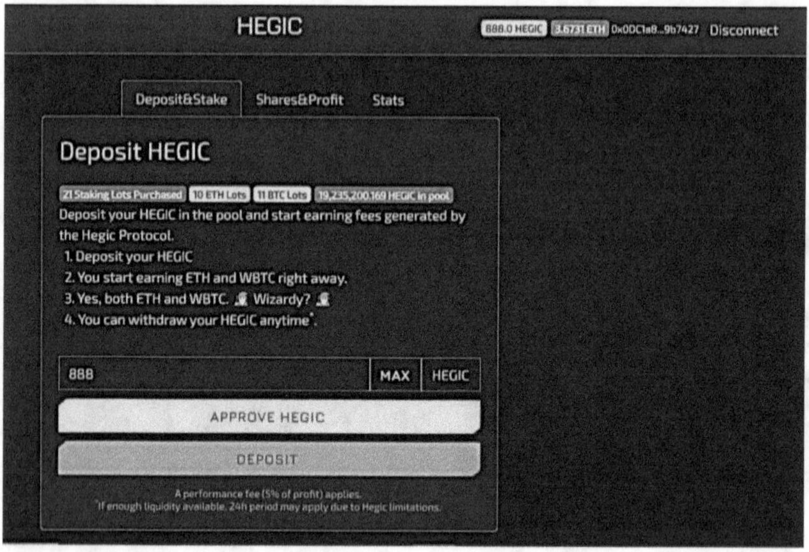

Figure 8.40

Click the 'APPROVE HEGIC' button to approve spending of your Hegic and then deposit it. You Stake will be represented as sHEGIC and you can start earning WBTC and ETH , as shown in Figure 8.41.

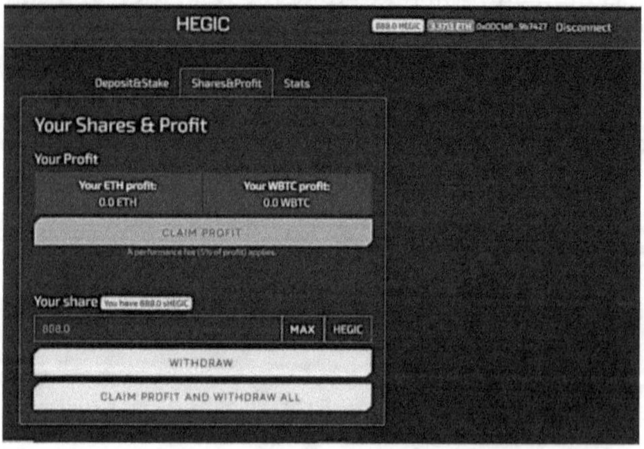

Figure 8.41

The Interface for zlot.finance is as shown in Figure 8.42.

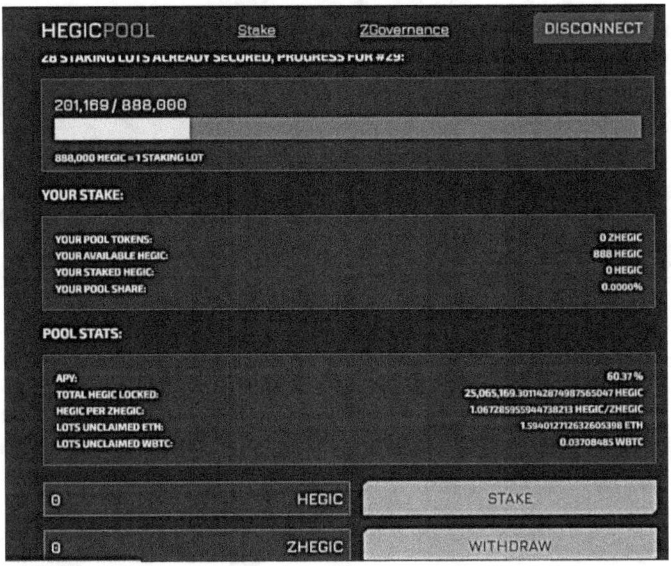

Figure 8.42

On Zlot, you will be given ZHEGIC as a representation of your HEGIC tokens, as shown in Figure 8.43.

Figure 8.43

ZHEGIC will also appear in your wallet as seen in Figure 8.44.

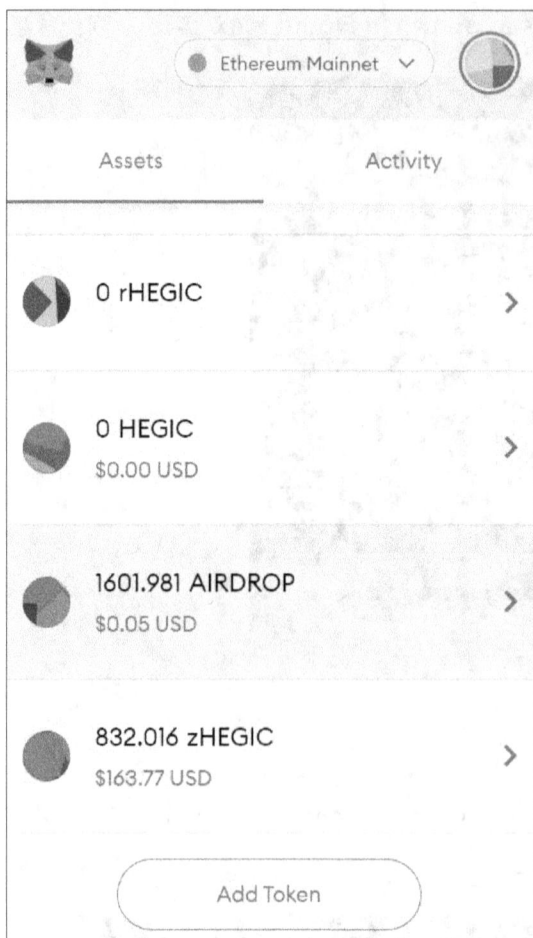

Figure 8.44

In addition, you also won a Citadel collectible Rabbi, as shown in Figure 8.45.

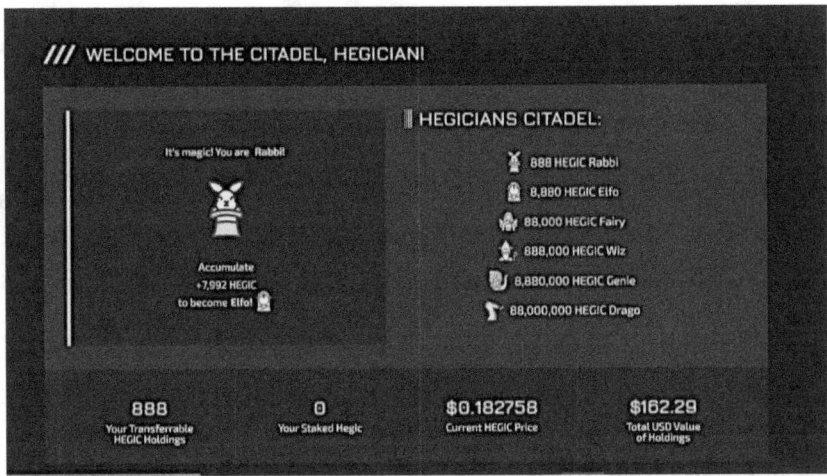

Figure 8.45

Collectible is a kind of NFT (Non-Fungible Token) which means every asset is unique and cannot be divided like cryptocurrencies. These collectibles are the first of its kinds on a DeFi platform as Hegic has launched a new NFT collection in partnership with Toxic Poeth (Khaitan, 2020). This is in celebration of the Hegic protocol nearing $100 million in cumulative trading volume.

There are six different NFTs that you buy from this collection. Each card offers holders a unique piece of art as well as rewards. The price ranges from 0.0088 ETH for the cheapest artwork to a staggering 888.8 ETH for the most expensive. You can get it by holding HEGIC or you can purchase them from Toxix Poeth website, the link is :

https://app.rarible.com/toxicpoeth/onsale

IV. Buying and Selling

The HEGIC token price increases as the supply of the token increases. When a new buyer has acquired the HEGIC token, each subsequent buyer will have to pay a slightly higher price for each token. As more people will discover Hegic protocol and buying continues, the value of each token gradually increases along the bonding curve.

Each time HEGIC tokens are acquired using the bonding curve contract, the ETH-HEGIC swap transaction increases the price of HEGIC token for a fixed value of 0.00000000001 ETH. The contract itself is used as a price oracle. If a token holder wants to swap HEGIC tokens for ETH using the bonding curve contract, she will pay a 10% swap fee on this transaction.

The bonding curve represent the changes of the price of a newly minted token as its supply increases over time. The price of a token is determined by its supply. The more tokens that have been distributed, the higher the price.

Hegic has conducted its IBCO (Initial Bonding Curve Offering) to distribute its native token HEGIC in September 2020. It start price was 0.0027 but trading at $0.182207 in December, nearly 7000 % appreciation.

IBCO is the new primitive for crypto projects fundraising, eliminating the main issues of ICOs such as lack of accountability, lack of liquidity and flawed price discovery mechanics for the token itself (Tommaso, 2020). Some recent interesting IBCO projects are OVR, DIA and PERP.

At the time of writing, the selling price on Hegic bonding curve contract is 0.000358, or 0.202, higher than the open market. To buy HEGIC on the bonding curve contract, simply enter the amount you wish to purchase, as seen in Figure 8.46.

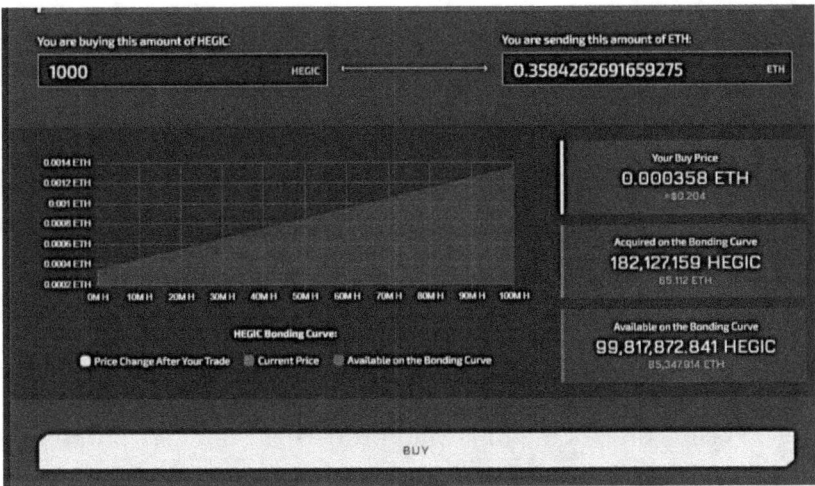

Figure 8.46

Chapter 9 Flash Loan

Flash loan is a loan that can be borrowed and repaid in one single transaction offered by DeFi protocols AAVE and dYdX. Flash loan allows users to borrow any amount up to the total liquidity available without any collateral if it is paid back in the same transaction. However, If the loan is not paid back, the transaction will be reverted, and you will lose some gas fees and transaction fees.

In a nutshell, Flash loan has the following properties (GAURAV, 2020):

- Borrow and repaid in a single transaction
- No collateral required
- The borrower must return the original borrowed amount + a small fee (0.09% currently)
- The transaction needs to be completed successfully otherwise everything will be reverted, and you need to pay the only Gas fee.

Currently the flash loan feature is not user friendly as you must write smart contract code to execute it, so it caters more for software programmers to play with this feature. However, some programmers have exploited this feature to swindle money unethically. In fact, some sophisticated programmers have executed what we call 'Flash loan attack' that can cause a loss of millions of dollars. The most famous case was the flash loan attack on Harvest Finance that resulted in a loss of $24 million (Foxley, 2020).

Although there is threat of flash loan attack, there are many use cases which can benefits the investors. Among them, arbitrage is the most common use case. Arbitrage means capitalizing on price differences between markets to make a profit. Since Decentralized AMM are not perfect markets, you can often gain profit by selling low at one DEX and sell high at another exchange. Using flash loan, you can borrow one crytoasset without a collateral and then swap it for another collateral for a profit and repay the loan in the same transaction.

Let me illustrate the use case with an example:

Step 1 You borrow 1000 USDC from Flashloan
Step 2 You swap 1000 USDC to 1050 DAI on Uniswap
Step 3 Swap 1050 DAI to 1048 USDC on Kyberswap
Step 4 Repay 1000 USDC to Flashloan
Step 5 You keep 48 USDC profit.

** You will earn less than 48 USDC as I have omitted transaction fees and gas fees.

It is impossible to execute the transactions manually so you must write smart contract codes to auto execute them. Fortunately, there is a third-party app that make it easier for you to execute the flash loan, this app is called Furucombo.

For arbitrage traders, Furucombo lowers the barriers-to-entry for building money legos, a user-friendly app providing all the necessary elements to create arbitrage strategies including the so far coder-only flashloans. However, Furucombo does NOT find arbitrage opportunities for you, you must do a bit of homework to find them yourself.

Besides flash loan, Furucombo is a tool built for end-users to optimize their DeFi strategy simply by drag and drop, super easy and convenient. It visualizes complex DeFi protocols into cubes. Users simply need to set up inputs/outputs and the order of the cubes (a "combo"), then Furucombo bundles all the cubes into one transaction and sends out.

To access Furucombo, use the following link:

https://furucombo.app/

The landing page is as shown in Figure 9.1.

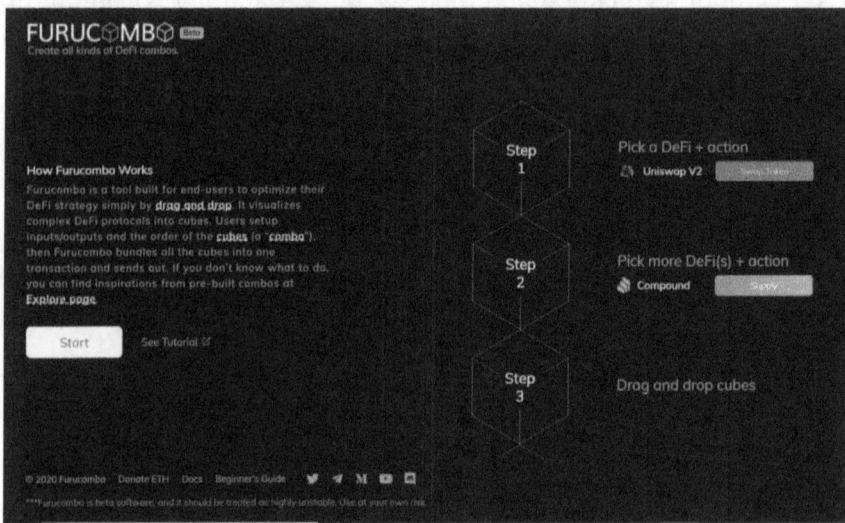

Figure 9.1

To start using Furucombo, click the start button and connect it to your wallet. The app UI that shows an empty cube is as seen in Figure 9.2.

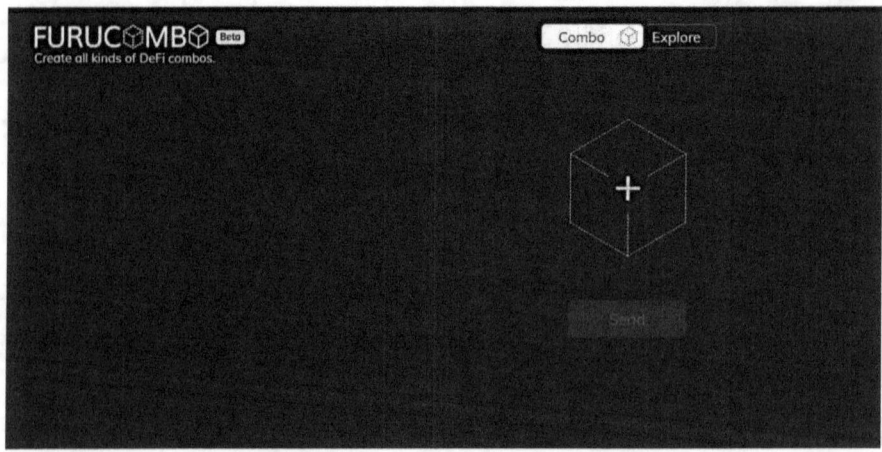

Figure 9.2

To create the first cube, click the + button to launch the app the display a host of protocols and the actions that you can execute, as seen in Figure 9.3.

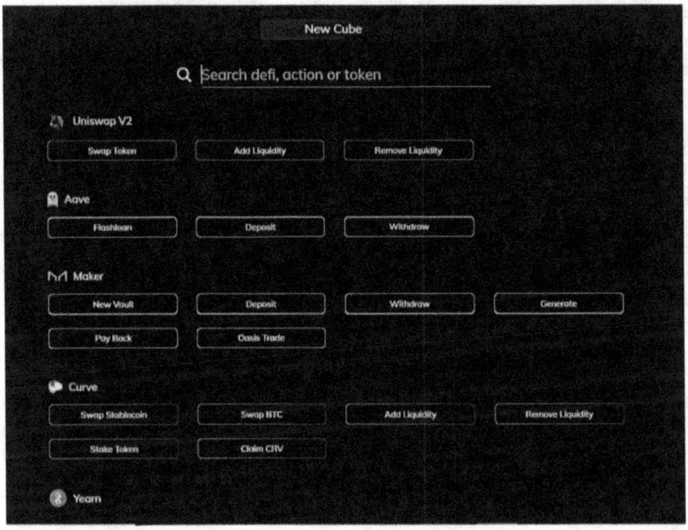

Figure 9.3

As seen from Figure 9.3, you can swap tokens, supply tokens, borrow flash loan, add liquidity, remove liquidity, withdraw funds, create CDP vault in Maker, trade, stake tokens and more.

For example, if you want to swap ETH for sUSD on Uniswap, simply click the 'Swap token' under Uniswap to launch the following dialog box, as seen in Figure 9.4.

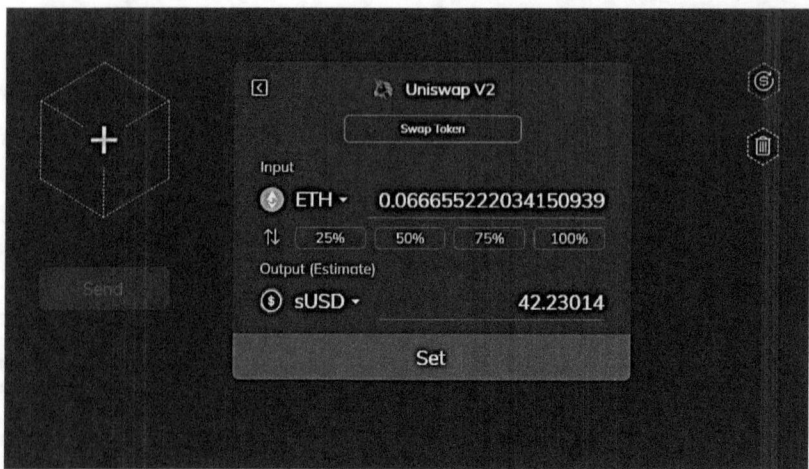

Figure 9.4

After clicking the 'Set' button, you have created the first cube, as shown in Figure 9.5.

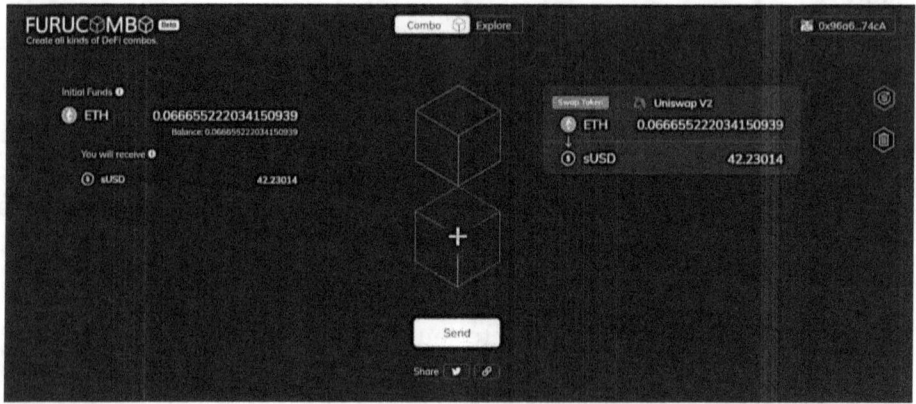

Figure 9.5

It shows the initial funds you must provide for the execution and the funds you will receive. If you are satisfied with the rate, click 'Send' to complete the execution. But wait! You might want to add more actions and executive all in one go. Let us add another cube which is to trade tokens at Oasis and one more to supply tokens to Compound. You will see that two additional cubes added to the money Lego, as seen in Figure 9.6.

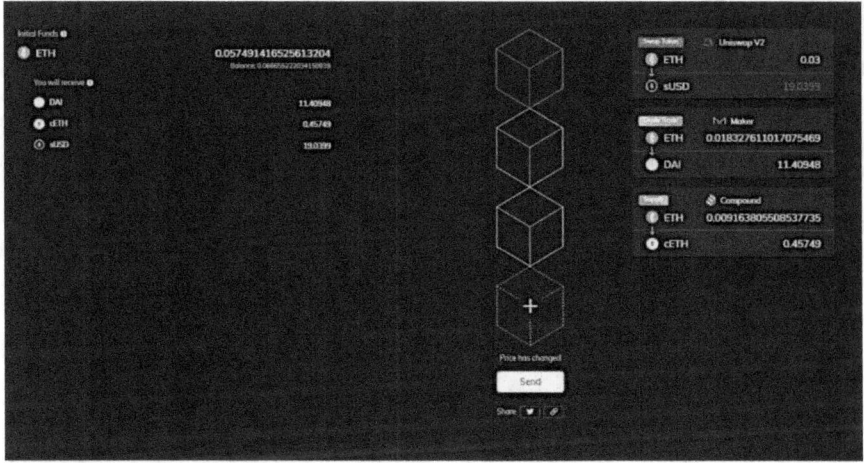

Figure 9.7

To complete the batch actions, click the 'Send' button which confirm the transactions on your wallet. Done, it is that easy.

In addition, you can remove or edit the cubes before finalizing the actions you wish to execute. To remove or edit a cube, hover the mouse over it to bring up the bin and the pen icon, as seen in Figure 9.8.

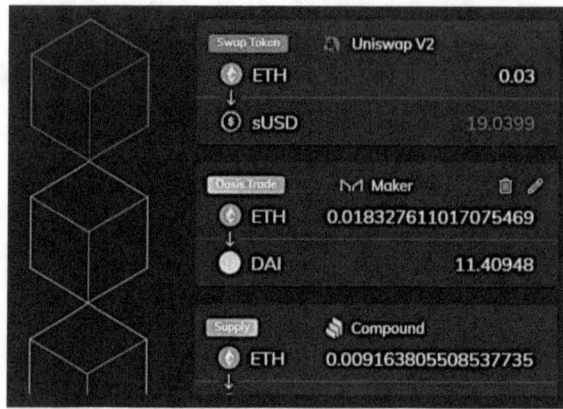

Figure 9.8

Next, let see how we can borrow flash loans using Furrowcombo. First, select a pair of tokens you wish to swap on a platform, for example, swapping sUSD with DAI on Balancer. Click 'Swap token' on Balancer and swap 1000 sUSD with DAI, which was 1001.0437 on Balancer at the time of writing. Next, swap 1001.0437 DAI with sUSD on 1Inch, which was 1002.10612 at the time of writing. You can see that you have a small arbitrage opportunity at the time because you can borrow 1000 sUSD and get 1002.10612 with a profit of 2.10612, as seen in Figure 9.8.

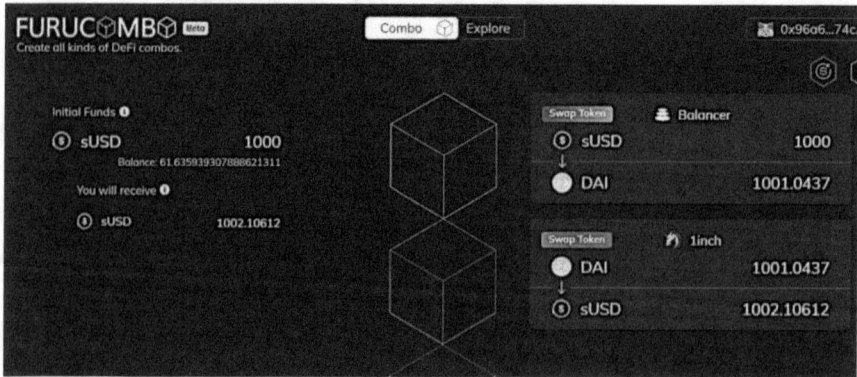

Figure 9.8

Next, you need to borrow 1000 sUSD flash loan as your wallet do not have enough sUSD. Proceed to click 'FlashLoan' on AAVE to add two cubes, one to borrow loan and the other one to pay (remember that flash loan means you borrow and pay back in one transaction). You need to pay back 1000.90 sUSD as AAVE charge a 0.09% on flash loans. The new combo is as shown in Figure 9.9.

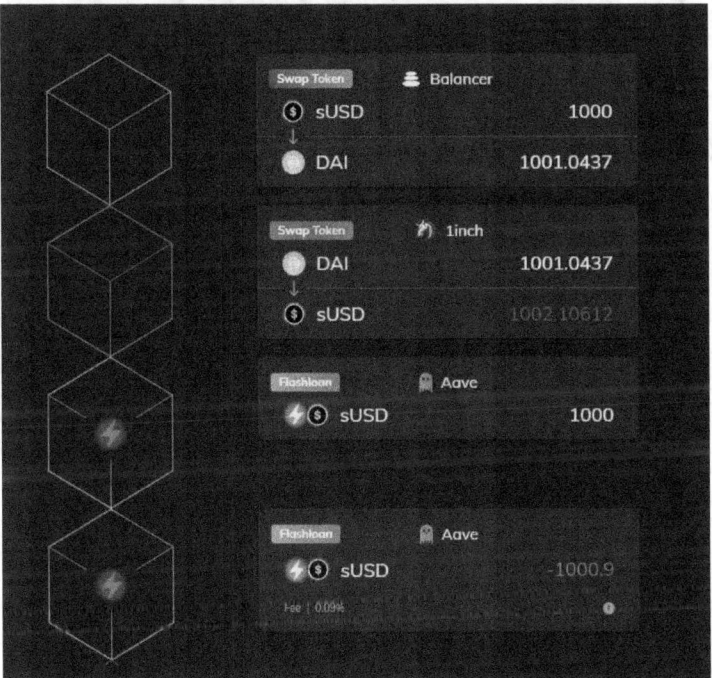

Figure 9.9

Next, you must drag the first flash loan cube to the top as you must borrow the funds first before you can start the procedure. The execution starts from the top. The final combo is as shown in Figure 9.10.

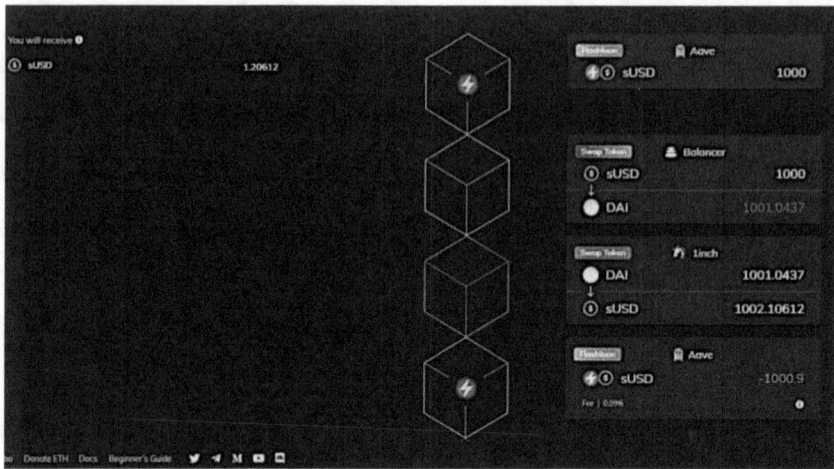

Figure 9.10

You can see that your profit is a meagre 1.20612 sUSD because the difference in pricing is small. This is just a demonstration of how you can make a profit using flash loan and arbitrage opportunities. You might want to explore more opportunities before making the decision to execute the transaction. If you are satisfied with the profit, proceed to click the 'Send' button and confirm it on your wallet, as shown in Figure 9.11.

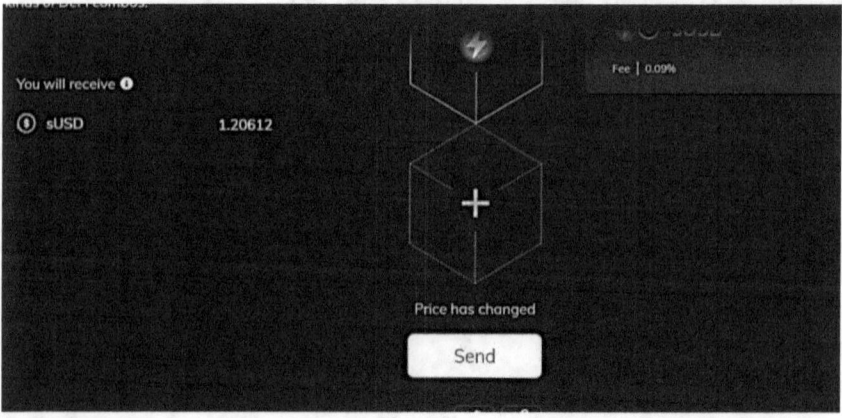

Figure 9.11

Clicking 'Send' with initiate borrowing sUSD from AAVE, swap sUSD for DAI on Balancer, swap DAI for sUSD on 1Inch and finally pay back the loan to AAVE, all in one transaction. If you check the transactions on Etherscan, you will see that this is a batch action as shown in Figure 9.12.

Figure 9.12

Glossary

AMM	Automated Market-Maker
APY	Annual Percentage Yield
Cold Wallet	Cold Wallet is also known as offline wallet. Cold wallets usually rely on "cold" devices (non-networked computers, mobile phones, hardware wallets, paper wallets etc.) to ensure the security of the cryptocurrency private key.
CDP	Collateralized Debt Position
DApp	DApp is an abbreviation for decentralized application.
DEX	Decentralized Exchange
DSR	Dai Savings Rate is a mechanism for the MakerDAO to control the demand side of the supply and demand equation by offering an interest rate for locking in some of the total Dai supply.
Electrum	Electrum is a lightweight Bitcoin client, based on a client-server protocol.
ERC20	ERC20 is an official protocol for proposing improvements to the Ethereum (ETH) network. ERC stands for Ethereum Request for Comment, and 20 is the proposal identifier. This is a common standard for creating tokens on the Ethereum blockchain.
EVM	Ethereum Virtual Machine ("EVM") is the core engine that runs the Ethereum Platform.

Gas	Gas is a unit that measures the amount of computational effort that it will take to execute certain operations on the Ethereum blockchain.
Hash	A hash or hash value is the result of a hash function.
IEO	Initial Exchange Offering
IBCO	Initial Bonding Curve Offering
Impermanent loss	Impermanent loss happens when you provide liquidity to a liquidity pool, and the price of your deposited assets changes compared to when you deposited them.
KYC	Know Your Customer
Liquidity Mining	Liquidity mining is a process where users supply liquidity to decentralized financial applications and receive rewards in the form of DeFi tokens.
Liquidity Pool	It is basically a smart contract that contains funds. In return for providing liquidity to the pool, LPs get a reward. That reward may come from fees generated by the underlying DeFi platform, or some other source.
MakerDAO	MakerDAO is a decentralized credit platform on Ethereum that supports Dai.
Margin trade	Margin trade means to use money borrowed from a broker to purchase securities.
Merkle tree	Merkle tree is one of the metadata in a block of the blockchain.

MetaMask	MetaMask is an extension for accessing Ethereum-enabled distributed applications, or "Dapps" in your browser.
Mining	Mining is the process by which transactions are verified and added to the blockchain, and the means through which new coins are released.
Nonce	A nonce is a random number that miners use to solve a mathematical puzzle in the mining process, which is also known as proof of work.
Proof of Work	Mining involves the process of producing a hash whose value is less than the target value. When this hash has been found, it is called a valid hash and hence proof of work is achieved.
Rebasing	Rebasing is a mechanism generally used to promote price stability by increasing the supply when the price is above the target price and decrease supply when price is below the target.
Solidity	Solidity is a high-level programming language that is used to create and implement smart contracts on the Ethereum platform.
STO	Security Token Offering
Total Value Locked (TVL)	TVL measures how much crypto is locked in DeFi lending and other types of money marketplaces. It is a way to measure the overall health of DeFi yield farming.

Yield Farming	Yield farming is an activity that uses crypto assets to maximize return on those assets.

Appendix A

List of DeFi Platforms for Quick Reference

I. Decentralized Finance

Name	Description
Aave	Aave is a decentralized non-custodial money market protocol in which users can participate as depositors (lenders) or borrowers. URL: https://aave.com
Compound	Compound is a protocol on the Ethereum blockchain that creates a money market comprising a group of assets with algorithmically earned interest rates URL: https://app.compound.finance
Curve	Curve Finance is a decentralized exchange liquidity pool on Ethereum designed for trading stablecoins. URL: https://www.curve.fi
DeFi Saver	DeFi Saver is a one-stop management app for decentralized finance protocols. It consolidates DeFi protocols comprising MakerDAO, Compound, dYdX and Fulcrum all into one place. URL: https://defisaver.com
MakerDAO	MakerDAO is a decentralized credit platform on Ethereum that supports Dai,

	a decentralized, unbiased, collateral-backed stablecoin whose value is pegged to USD. URL: https://oasis.app
Yearn Finance	Yearn Finance is a decentralized ecosystem of aggregators that utilizes decentralized lending services such as Aave, Compound, Dydx, and Fulcrum to optimize your token lending. https://yearn.finance/
Zapper.fi	This is a DeFi app that manages your DeFi assets and liabilities in one simple interface.

II Decentralized Exchanges

Name	Description
1inch	1inch is a decentralized exchange Aggregator with the best prices on the market. https://1inch.exchange/#/
AirSwap	According to Decrpt (Tran K. C., 2019), AirSwap is a peer-to-peer trading platform for ETH and ERC20 tokens. https://www.airswap.io/
Balancer	Balancer is a decentralised crypto exchange that allows you to swap ERC20 tokens. https://balancer.exchange/

Bancor	Bancor is a protocol on Ethereum for non-custodial token exchange using pooled liquidity. https://app.bancor.network/
Dex.Ag	Dex.ag is another DEX aggregator that has aggregated some popular decentralized exchanges. https://dex.ag/
dYdX	dYdX is a decentralized trading platform that supports margin trading, spot trading, lending, and borrowing. https://dydx.exchange/
Kyber Swap	Kyber is a blockchain-based liquidity protocol that aggregates liquidity from a wide range of reserves into a single pool, which provides the best rates for users. https://kyberswap.com/
Matcha	Matcha is a decentralized exchange powered by the 0x protocol. https://matcha.xyz/
Radar Relay	Radar Relay is a decentralised token exchange that provides a wallet-to-wallet trading platform for Ethereum tokens. https://relay.radar.tech/
Tokenlon	Tokenlon is a decentralized exchange based on 0x protocol that enables decentralized atomic token exchange. https://tokenlon.im/#/
Totle Swap	Totle Swap is another DEX aggregator that combines decentralized exchanges and synthetic asset providers into a set of

	tools that makes it easy to trade DeFi assets at the best price. https://swap.totle.com/
Uniswap	Uniswap is a decentralized ERC20 token exchange that supports Ethereum and ERC20 tokens. https://app.uniswap.org/#/

Appendix B

List of Top 20 DeFi Tokens

No	Token Name	Price	Market Cap
1	LINK	$14.82	$5,829,857,022
2	WBTC	$18307.11	$2,274,847,867
3	DAI	$1.00	$,101,2286,143
4	UNI	$3.81	$836,348,417
5	AAVE	$63.74	$748,941,883
6	YFI	$17,394.43	$521,265,493
7	MKR	$512.65	$514,263,945
8	COMP	$118	$489,804,049
9	UMA	$8.32	$461,321,127
10	SNX	$4.10	$432,906,404
11	RENBTC	$15,722.54	$298,405,929
12	REN	$0.304578	$269,409,391
13	ZRX	$0.349079	$259,692,981
14	LRC	$0.175529	$201,153,451
15	SUSHI	$1.19	$180,792,135
16	KNC	$0.883293	$177,133,780
17	RSR	$0.015265	$142,731,969
18	AMPL	$1.02	$141,138,454
19	RUNE	$0.845803	$134,002,284
20	NXM	$23.91	$126,312,252

To check the most current list, visit:

https://coinmarketcap.com/DeFi/

Appendix C

Making a Claim (Exercising) on Opyn through Etherscan

This is a step-by-step guide on how to make claims if you purchased protections through Opyn.

Exercise oETH

1. Go to the Write Contract Tab on the oETH contract page on Etherscan.

The web link is:

https://etherscan.io/address/0x48ab8a7d3bf2eb942e153e4275ae1a8988238dc7#writeContract

You will open a webpage as shown in Figure AC1.

Figure AC1

You must connect your Web3 wallet which is MetaMask to be able to write the contract. When you click on the 'Connect Web3' button, you will be prompted will a dialog box that asked you to connect to a wallet, as shown in Figure AC2.

Figure AC2

Once connected, you will notice that your wallet address appears at the bottom left corner of the webpage, as shown in Figure AC3.

Figure AC3

2. Approve the contract to transfer your oETH

- In the write contract tab, search for the function approve
- Enter the oETH address 0x48AB8A7d3Bf2EB942e153e4275Ae1a8988238dC7 and Key in an amount in WEI to approve the contract to transfer. The recommended amount is 1000000000000000000000000000000, as shown in Figure AC4.

Figure AC4

- Click write and confirm the transaction through your wallet, as shown in Figure AC5.

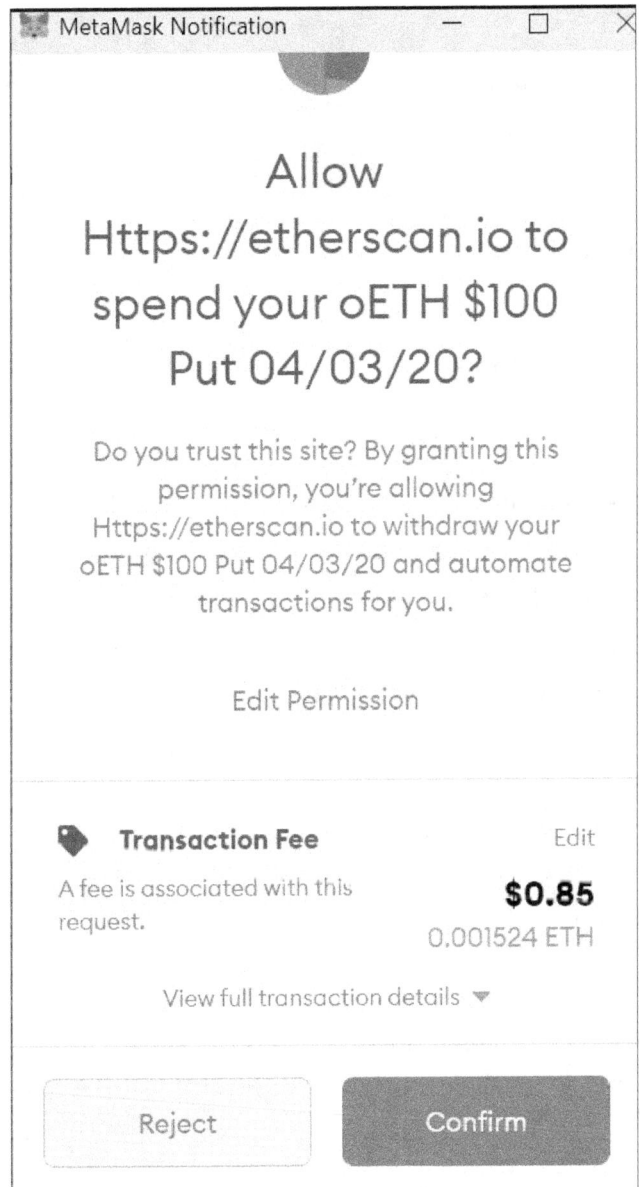

Figure AC5

Other claims also follow the same procedure, please refer to the following link to read the details:

https://opyn.gitbook.io/opyn/making-a-claim-through-etherscan

Appendix D
Source: **SORA: The New Economic Order**
https://medium.com/sora-xor/sora-the-new-economic-order-3ec3f0327e5a

SORA TONONOMICS

Sora token economics model derived from the large amount of empirical evidence that suggests that it is the change in the allocation of money in an economy that is a necessary and sufficient determinant of growth. This was shown by Richard Werner in his disaggregated quantity theory of money, where he disaggregated Fisher's equation of exchange(MV = PY; a good way to think about this is also that MV equals nominal GDP viewed from the perspective of buyers, whereas PY equates to nominal GDP viewed from the perspective of producers/sellers) into *real* (R) and *financial* (F) transactions:

$$V_R \Delta M_R = \Delta(P_R Y)$$
$$V_F \Delta M_F = \Delta(P_F Q_F)$$

Where:

$V :=$ velocity of money[5]
$M :=$ quantity of money
$P :=$ price index
$Y :=$ output of goods/services
$Q :=$ quantity demanded

---

[5] The velocity of money is the measurement of the rate at which money is exchanged in an economy. It is the number of times that money moves from one entity to another. It also refers to how much a unit of currency is used in each period. Simply put, it is the rate at which consumers and businesses in an economy collectively spend money (Investopedia, n.d.).

It is helpful to think of the above equations as a dynamical system, such that if the quantity of money, M, changes on the left-hand side of the equation, there must be some change on the right-hand side to balance out this change (this is because V is typically stable in large economies).

For transactions in the real economy, this means that new money put into circulation is balanced out by new goods and services that consume this new purchasing power. However, for financial transactions, there are no new goods or services being created with the new money put into circulation, so this causes a rise in asset prices to compensate (which is not what you want in your economic system). Additionally, it is also important to understand the importance of expanding M to produce new goods and services.

As Shimomura wrote about extensively and Kurihara distilled to a simple, linear programming model, expanding the quantity of money for new goods and services expands the economic output because latent resources (especially human resources) are mobilized, and existing resources are upgraded by the creation of new capital for production.

What all this means is that for SORA to become a successful decentralized economy, we must create new tokens explicitly for creating new goods (like wine) or services (like DEX). This is where the research of Yamaguchi paid off again, as back in 2018, he suggested that SORA use a **token bonding curve** to autonomously manage the issuance and de-issuance of XOR in the economy. In other words, They found a way to manage the supply of tokens in a rational way, without involvement of humans, which will create a system that avoids the boom-bust problems of traditional economies and the deflationary economics of many cryptocurrencies.

Token Bondage

A **token bonding curve** is a smart contract that takes as input some token and outputs a new token. There are many possible variations, but SORA uses a simple model where there are two linear functions: a **buy-price function** and a **sell-price function**, as shown in Figure AD1

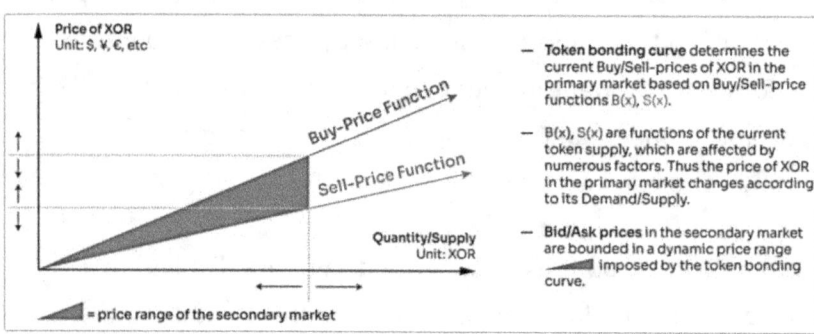

Figure AD1 Source: Image courtesy of Sora

XOR supply in the SORA mainnet will be backed by acceptable liquid cryptocurrencies, and each network transaction of XOR will require the burning of a small fee, the rate decided by the community (e.g., 0.01– 0.10 USD equivalent). To buy XOR on the token bonding curve, one of the acceptable currencies must be used. After launch, SORA plan to include these tokens that you can use to buy XOR from the token bonding curve:

- DOT (at launch)
- KSM (at launch)
- BTC
- ETH

- USDT
- USDC
- TUSD
- DAI
- VAL
- PSWAP

The token bonding curve will be built directly into Polkaswap such that if the secondary market price of XOR is exceeded for one of the above trading pairs, the token bonding curve will automatically be executed so that new XOR will be put into circulation, 20% of the buying currency will be put into a pool to buy back and burn XOR, and 80% of the buying currency will go to reserves, held by the token bonding curve. As reserves are in multiple currencies, future releases of the system should provide for ways to balance between the currency reserves to provide liquidity in a variety of tokens. The close integration of the SORA economic model with Polkaswap will allow this process to be automated at some point in the future.

The buy-price function will start at a discount (accounting for the initial price of VAL on mainnet launch) to the Uniswap XOR price at launch (but do not panic if you have ERC-20 XOR now; there will be a new token, VAL, that will be airdropped to ERC-20 holders to make up for this). The buy-price function uses an oracle to find out the current price that XOR should be with respect to a fiat currency.

The sell-price function will, in turn, be 20% less than the buy-price function. The 20% spread between the buy and sell functions will have different uses. A new SORA Parliament (multi-body sortition governance system), will provide a methodology for rationally allocating these XOR to create new goods and services in the SORA ecosystem, in accordance with the SORA economic model. All XOR that are created are given for free to the SORA Parliament, which then manages the token supply using the token bonding curve; specifically, the Financial Markets Authority, a standing body of the SORA Parliament will be the entity that buys and sells XOR via the primary market maker, as shown in Figure AD2.

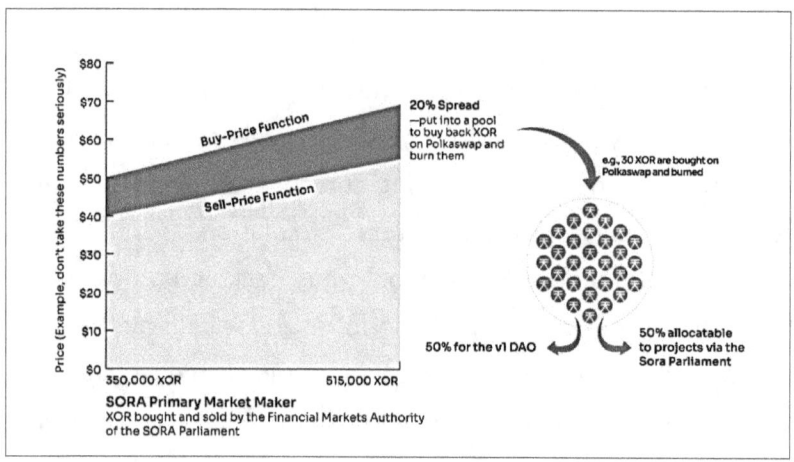

Figure AD2 Source: Image courtesy of Sora

Because the token bonding curve is essentially an infinitely liquid, decentralized central bank, the price cannot go above or below the buy and sell functions, respectively. This is especially true because the SORA primary market maker will be built into Polkaswap and executed automatically when within range. Furthermore, because the token bonding curve's pricing functions slope upwards, the price increases with the token supply. This gives the following properties:

- **Autonomous Management of Token Supply to Match Demand (Elastic Supply)** — The token bonding curve introduces and removes XOR from circulation to meet the demand of the market. This ensures sustainable economic growth and price stability of the token economy, as the system can adapt to the changing needs.

- **Deterministic Price Calculation** — The buy and sell prices of tokens in the primary market increase and decrease with changes in the supply of token. It is therefore **NOT** a fixed exchange rate system. The buy-price function starting price will be determined closer to the v2 launch and increase by $0.01 for each 5000 XOR sold, even if this is not final and may change before launch.
- **Continuous Price Dynamics** — Given that the price of token N is inferior to token N+1 and superior to token N-1, calculating the number of tokens minted for a given amount of buy or sell orders requires integral calculus.
- **Deep and Immediate Liquidity** — The bonding curve contract is the counterpart of the transaction and always holds enough buyback reserves (if investors want to sell tokens back at the current sell-price).

Features specific to the SORA token bonding curve-based economic design:

- **Separation of primary & secondary markets:** Primary market — issuance/withdrawal, Secondary market — exchange rates, arbitrage trading.
- **Mitigate influences of pump-and-dump/market-manipulation attacks** while the token is in its nascency and its economy constitutes only a fraction of the world nominal GDP (US $88 Trillion as of 2019).
- The token bonding curve naturally rewards early buyers of XOR, **encouraging word of mouth marketing.**
- The decentralized monetary policy of XOR offers **protection from abuse by authorities and full transparency for users.**

- Primary market buy-back reserve puts a limit on ability of governments or short-sellers to manipulate the market.
- The overall incentive mechanism works to **align interests of all stakeholders,** and help ****to **sustain continuous development of the Sora Ecosystem as a global decentralized autonomous economic organization.**
- The SORA v2 monetary system is neither debt-based nor debt-driven, and new tokens are always allocated under democratic supervision, which works to **eliminate the unsustainable boom-bust cycles in contemporary economic systems.**

Bid/ask prices in the secondary market are bounded in a dynamic price range imposed by the token bonding curve. Therefore, the current buy/sell-prices offered by the token bonding curve provide support & resistance levels, or the confidence range of XOR in the market, with forward guidance, as shown in Figure AD3

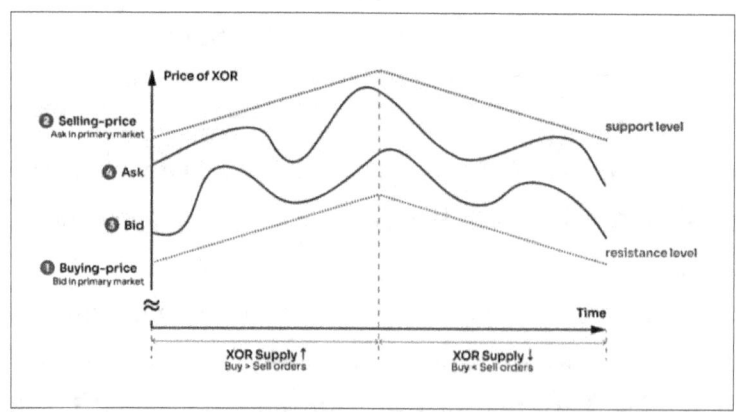

Figure AD3 Source: Image courtesy of Sora

Price uncertainty has been a major cause of low cryptocurrency adoption for payments. However, with real-time token supply data available on a public blockchain and a globally known token bonding curve, all users can observe current trends related to the token price and make informed expectations on the future levels. As illustrated below, buy/sell-prices offered by the token bonding curve and bid/ask prices in the secondary market change continuously since buy/sell-orders continuously change(Figure AD 4). Observability of the XOR supply together with the properties of the token bonding curve thus act as a built-in forward guidance on the XOR exchange rate, reducing uncertainty and enhancing its store-of-value property while the token is in its nascency. Once the self-circulating economy based on XOR matures, the token bonding curve mechanism can be eased out or disengaged, but this is likely to be several decades into the future.

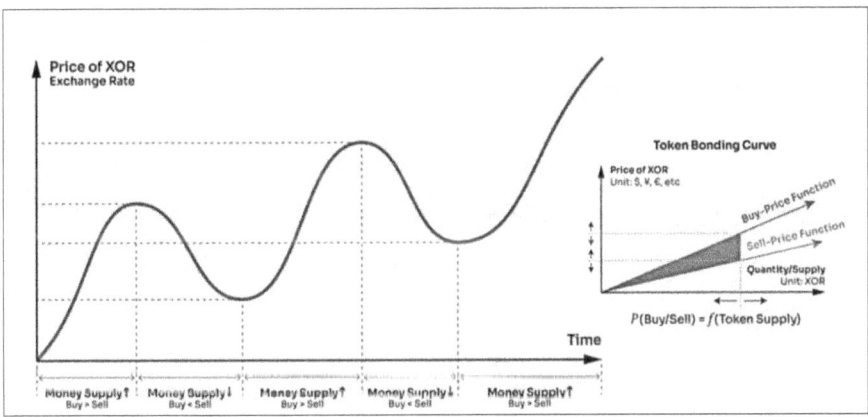

Figure AD4 Source: Image courtesy of Sora

While the SORA economy is in its infant phase, the token bonding curve plays a crucial role in maintaining the store-of-value property of XOR. The ability to set confidence ranges of token price movements lowers the psychological boundary in accepting XOR for payments. Since its price changes continuously, the token bonding curve is NOT a fixed exchange rate mechanism, though its policy rationale shares similarity with that of FX market intervention by central banks, especially in developing economies.

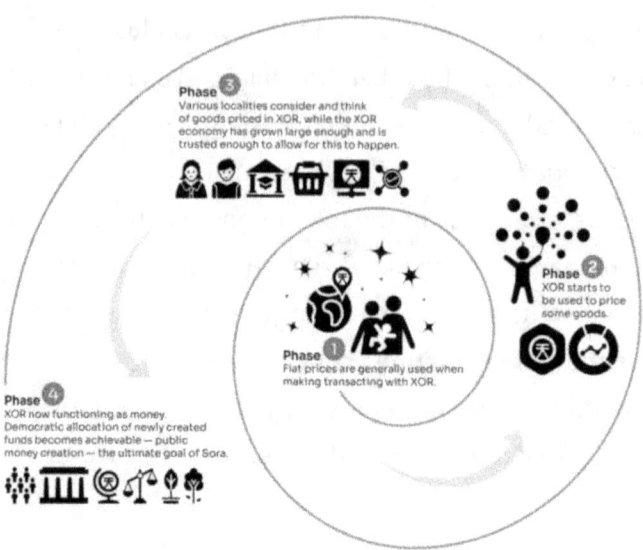

Figure AD5 Source: Image courtesy of Sora

In addition to XOR, there is going to be a new token, tentatively called VAL, that will play a role in incentivizing validators on the SORA v2 Network.

A New Token: VAL

As XOR is becoming a token that has forward price guidance, a new token has been added to the ecosystem that captures value related to the growth and use of the ecosystem. This token is tentatively called VAL and is a staking reward token, that incentivizes validators to join the SORA v2 Network. Economically, this also adds the ability to determine long and short sentiments as the market, as price trends for VAL can reveal the preferences of market participants.

VAL tokens are given to validators and nominators as a reward for staking. VAL is a complex model in and of itself and will be fully explained in a future article, along with the initial rules and parameters for staking and validation on the SORA v2 Network.

V1→V2 Migration Plan: The Basics

The SORA v2 Network is a profound change, both technologically and economically. Whereas the v1 network uses Hyperledger Iroha v1, SORA v2 will use Substrate and will become a parachain for the Kusama and Polkadot networks. This will allow XOR, VAL, and other tokens of the SORA network to move to other blockchains in the Polkadot ecosystem, as well as to Ethereum, using bridging contracts, as shown in Figure AD6.

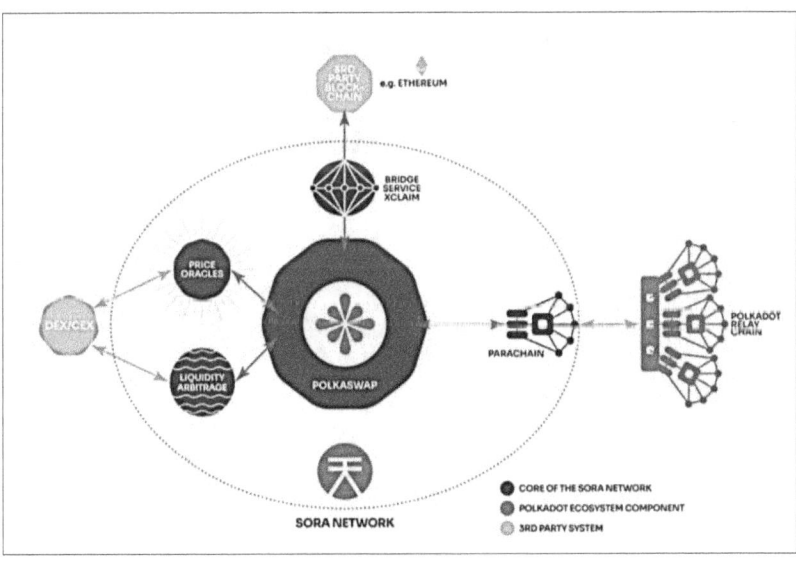

Figure AD6 Source: Image courtesy of Sora

In addition to the compelling technological vision, v2 requires that we completely change the economic model of a running network. As explained above, all v2 XOR should be backed by reserves of the token bonding curve. Because many v1 XOR currently exist, this poses a difficultly to transition them directly to the v2 network. Instead, v1 XOR will be replaced with a new token, VAL.

In summary, the key parts of the migration plan are:

- SORA v1 Network XOR tokens will be transformed into VAL, based on a specific ratio that will be explained in a future article. An important implication of this proposal, however, is that no SORA v1 Network XOR tokens will dilute the v2 network, while at the same time v1 Network XOR token holders will receive value and self-deterministic governance.

- All ERC-20 XOR becomes v2 XOR automatically. This initial supply will be capped at 350,000 XOR. Because they will not be backed by reserves of the primary market maker at launch, the token bonding curve will prioritize building up reserves at the beginning.

- All ERC-20 XOR token holders will be airdropped VAL at v2 launch, proportionally for each XOR they hold at a snapshot event (will be defined later, but most likely the instant of v2 launch). So the ERC-20 XOR holders will have VAL and v2 XOR (1 ERC-20 XOR is equal to 1 v2 XOR). To be clear, ERC-20 XOR will not change in any way.

References

CoinMarketCap. (n.d.). *About CoinMarketCap*. Retrieved from https://coinmarketcap.com/about/

0x. (n.d.). *Powering Decentralized Exchange*. Retrieved from https://0x.org/

1inch. (n.d.). *About 1inch*. Retrieved from https://1inch-exchange.medium.com/about

AAVE FAQ. (n.d.). Retrieved from https://docs.aave.com/faq/

Adam B. Levine, J. B. (2020, February 20). *The Flash Loan Attacks Explained (for Everybody)*. Retrieved from https://www.coindesk.com/the-flash-loan-attacks-explained-for-everybody

ADolmatov. (n.d.). *Wrapped Ether (WETH)*. Retrieved from https://academy.binance.com/en/glossary/wrapped-ether

Ampleforth. (n.d.). *The Basic*. Retrieved from https://www.ampleforth.org/basics/

Balakrishnan, A. (2020, July 15). *What Is Ampleforth? How AMPL Is Redefining Decentralized Money*. Retrieved from https://cryptobriefing.com/what-ampleforth-how-ampl-redefining-decentralized-money/

Bancor. (2020, January 9). *Guide: How to Stake Liquidity in Bancor Pools*. Retrieved from https://blog.bancor.network/how-to-stake-liquidity-earn-fees-on-bancor-bff8369274a1

Bancor. (n.d.). *Welcome to Bancor's Help Center.* Retrieved from https://support.bancor.network/hc/en-us

Bavosa, A. (2020, February 13). *Supplying Assets to the Compound Protocol.* Retrieved from https://medium.com/compound-finance/supplying-assets-to-the-compound-protocol-ec2cf5df5aa

Belyakov, A. (2019, November 6). *Getting FIXED interest rate for DAI.* Retrieved from https://medium.com/opium-network/getting-fixed-interest-rate-for-dai-bbc4a5cea9b

Belyakov, A. (2020, March 12). *How to: make 10x returns on Compound.finance.* Retrieved from https://medium.com/opium-network/how-to-make-10x-returns-on-compound-finance-9bf8914dbd21

Binance Academy. (2020, October 12). *What Are Perpetual Futures Contracts?* Retrieved from https://academy.binance.com/en/articles/what-are-perpetual-futures-contracts

Binance Academy. (n.d.). *Impermanent Loss Explained.* Retrieved from https://academy.binance.com/en/articles/impermanent-loss-explained

BitMEX. (n.d.). *Perpetual Contracts Guide.* Retrieved from https://www.bitmex.com/app/perpetualContractsGuide#:~:text=A%20Perpetual%20Swap%20is%20an,the%20underlying%20reference%20Index%20Price.

BitShadow. (2020, April 2). *What is DeFi (Decentralized Finance) and Which Types of DeFi Product available in Market.* Retrieved from https://medium.com/@bitsshadow/what-is-defi-decentralized-finance-and-which-types-of-defi-product-available-in-market-f6b7b453354#:~:text=There%20are%20a%20total%20of,Dexes%2C%20Assets%2C%20and%20Payments.

Burgess, M. (2020, September 19). *Bringing Bitcoin to DeFi: A Complete Beginners Deep Dive Into RenVM.* Retrieved from https://coinmarketcap.com/alexandria/article/bringing-bitcoin-to-defi-a-complete-beginners-deep-dive-into-renvm#:~:text=The%20REN%20token%20is%20used,the%20sMPC%20network%20(RenVM).&text=This%20prevents%20malicious%20adversaries%20from,the%20network%20wit

businesswire. (2019, February 29). Retrieved from https://www.businesswire.com/news/home/20190225005174/en/Synthetix-Releases-sBTC-Ethereum%E2%80%99s-First-Synthetic-Bitcoin#:~:text=Synthetix's%20synthetic%20Bitcoin%20(sBTC)%20provides,others%20available%20on%20the%20blockchain.

bZx. (n.d.). *Lending.* Retrieved from bZx Documentation: https://docs.bzx.network/fulcrum-integration/lending

bZx. (n.d.). *What are iTokens?* Retrieved from https://bzx.network/itokens

Capital, T. (n.d.). *DeFi Risk Management.* Retrieved from https://techemy.capital/wp-content/uploads/2020/06/Techemy-Capital-DEFI-RISK-MANAGEMENT-Insurance-Put-Options-Ratings.pdf

Cavicchioli, M. (2020, March 8). *DeFi: what is Fulcrum and the differences with other projects.* Retrieved from https://en.cryptonomist.ch/2020/03/08/defi-what-is-fulcrum/

Chainlink. (2020, January 16). *Analyzing the DeFi Ecosystem and The Many Ways Chainlink Can Accelerate Adoption.* Retrieved from https://blog.chain.link/analyzing-the-defi-ecosystem-and-the-many-ways-chainlink-can-accelerate-adoption/

Chainlink. (2020, October 14). *DeFi Yield Farming Explained*. Retrieved from https://blog.chain.link/defi-yield-farming-explained/

Chipolina, S. (2020, December 14). *Hacker Steals $8 Million From Nexus Mutual CEO*. Retrieved from https://decrypt.co/51355/hacker-steals-8-million-from-nexus-ceo-by-remotely-changing-metamask

Coelho-Prabhu, S. (2020, January 7). *A Beginner's Guide to Decentralized Finance (DeFi)*. Retrieved from Coinbase: https://blog.coinbase.com/a-beginners-guide-to-decentralized-finance-defi-574c68ff43c4

Coinbase. (2020, October 16). *Wrapped Bitcoin (WBTC) is launching on Coinbase Pro*. Retrieved from https://blog.coinbase.com/wrapped-bitcoin-wbtc-is-launching-on-coinbase-pro-48804a13aa35

Coindesk. (2020, September 19). *What isDeFi?* Retrieved from https://www.coindesk.com/what-is-defi

Consenlabs. (2020, November 12). *How to use Tokenlon*. Retrieved from https://support.token.im/hc/en-us/articles/360002147214-How-to-use-Tokenlon#:~:text=Tokenlon%20is%20a%20collection%20of,making%20assets%20transaction%20more%20convenient.

Coutts, V. (2019, August 2). *An introduction to bonding curves, shapes and use cases*. Retrieved from https://medium.com/linum-labs/intro-to-bonding-curves-and-shapes-bf326bc4e11a

Crypto Wisser. (n.d.). *IDEX Review*. Retrieved from https://www.cryptowisser.com/exchange/idex/#:~:text=IDEX%20is%20a%20%E2%80%9Cdecentralized%20exchange,to%20suppor t%20real%2Dtime%20trading.&text=The%20smart%20contract%20is%20responsible,using%20the%20user's%20private%20keys.

Curve Finance. (n.d.). Retrieved from https://defipulse.com/curve-finance

Cusack, L. (2019, July 24). *Absolute Beginners Guide to Using PoolTogether*. Retrieved from https://medium.com/pooltogether/absolute-beginners-guide-to-using-pooltogether-c3c91f8df3bb#:~:text=Note%20that%20PoolTogether%20is%20built,use%20it%20in%20your%20wallet.

Dad, D. (2020, October). *What is Zapper?* Retrieved from https://zapper.crunch.help/zapper-fi-faq/what-is-zapper-fi

Dale, B. (2020, September). *What Is Yearn Finance? The DeFi Gateway Everyone Is Talking About*. Retrieved from https://www.coindesk.com/what-is-yearn-finance-yfi-defi-ethereum

David. (2019, September 17). *Radar Relay DEX – Complete guide*. Retrieved from https://coinpedia.org/decentralized-exchange/radar-relay-dex/

DDEX Exchange Review. (2019, December 12). Retrieved from http://defipicks.com/2019/12/12/ddex-exchange-review/

De, N. (2018, August 1). *Decentralized token exchange Radar Relay has completed a $10 million Series A funding round*. Retrieved from Coindesk: https://www.coindesk.com/blockchain-capital-leads-10-million-radar-relay-funding-round

DeBank. (n.d.). *What is DEX.AG?* Retrieved from https://debank.com/projects/dexag

Decrypt. (n.d.). *What is Uniswap and How Does It Work?* Retrieved from https://decrypt.co/resources/what-is-uniswap

Defi Pulse. (n.d.). Retrieved from Defi Pulse: https://defipulse.com/

DeFi Score. (n.d.). *What is the DeFi Score?* Retrieved from https://defiscore.io/overview

defiprime. (n.d.). *DeFi Saver.* Retrieved from https://defiprime.com/product/defi-saver#:~:text=DeFi%20Saver%20is%20a%20management,as%20Compound%2C%20dYdX%20and%20Fulcrum.

Defiprime. (n.d.). *Fulcrum.* Retrieved from https://defiprime.com/product/fulcrum#:~:text=Fulcrum%20is%20the%20platform%20for,Trade%20%24BZRX%20on%201inch.exchange

Dharma. (n.d.). Retrieved from https://www.dharma.io/

Dharma Review. (n.d.). Retrieved from DeFi Rate: https://defirate.com/dharma/#:~:text=Dharma%20is%20a%20user%2Dfriendly,participate%20in%20DeFi%20lending%20markets.&text=Dharma%20has%20previously%20offered%20their,their%20business%20model%20in%202019.

Don Tapscott, A. T. (2017). *Blockchain Revolution: How the Technology Behind Bitcoin and Other Cryptocurrencies Is Changing the World.* Portfolio.

Downey, L. (2020, July 14). *Essential Options Trading Guide.* Retrieved from https://www.investopedia.com/options-basics-tutorial-4583012#:~:text=Call%20and%20Put%20Options,-Options%20are%20a&text=A%20call%20option%20gives%20the,payment%20for%20a%20future%20purchase.

dYdX. (n.d.). Retrieved from https://docs.dydx.exchange/

Eichholz, L. (2020, October 15). *AAVE Token: An Analysis of Migration and Staking.* Retrieved from https://insights.glassnode.com/aave-token-analysis-migration-staking/#:~:text=The%20migration%20went%20live%20on,been%20voluntarily%20migrated%20to%20AAVE.&text=As%20the%20migration%20takes%20place,holding%20AAVE%20is%20increasing%20rapidly.

Foxley, W. (2020, October 27). *Harvest Finance: $24M Attack Triggers $570M 'Bank Run' in Latest DeFi Exploit.* Retrieved from https://www.coindesk.com/harvest-finance-24m-attack-triggers-570m-bank-run-in-latest-defi-exploit

Furucombo. (2020, May 29). *Tutorial: Create Flashloan Combo on Furucombo.* Retrieved from https://medium.com/furucombo/create-flashloan-combo-on-furucombo-c7c3b23267f0

Futures. (n.d.). Retrieved from Investopedia: https://www.investopedia.com/terms/f/futures.asp

GAURAV. (2020, February 21). *Flash Loans – Borrow Without Collateral.* Retrieved from https://blog.coincodecap.com/what-are-flash-loans-on-ethereum#h-what-is-a-flash-loan

Gemini. (n.d.). *What Is Chainlink in 5 Minutes.* Retrieved from https://gemini.com/learn/what-is-chainlink-and-how-does-it-work

Gemini. (n.d.). *What Is Compound in 5 Minutes.* Retrieved from https://gemini.com/learn/what-is-compound-and-how-does-it-work

Goldfarb, S. (2019, September 2). *A guide to financial risk in DeFi.* Retrieved from https://defiprime.com/risks-in-defi

Hakka Finance. (n.d.). Retrieved from https://hakka.finance/doc/whitepaper_v3.pdf

Hegic. (2020, September 10). *HEGIC IBCO IS LIVE! A Step-by-Step Guide On How To Participate.* Retrieved from https://medium.com/hegic/hegic-ibco-is-live-a-step-by-step-guide-on-how-to-participate-6989e36129c7

Hu, E. (2019, July 9). *Getting Started With dYdX — Lending.* Retrieved from https://medium.com/dydxderivatives/getting-started-with-dydx-part-1-c655a6a48b32

Hu, E. (2020, April 17). *Getting Started With dYdX — Margin Trading (Part 1).* Retrieved from https://medium.com/dydxderivatives/getting-started-with-dydx-margin-trading-part-1-fe43789c2368#:~:text=Liquidation%20Price%20%E2%80%94%20When%20margin%20trading,trading%20with%20your%20own%20funds.

Hu, E. (n.d.). *Getting Started With dYdX — Borrowing.* Retrieved from https://medium.com/dydxderivatives/getting-started-with-dydx-part-2-borrowing-d7d1236a572d

Hu, E. (n.d.). *Getting Started With dYdX — Margin Trading (Part 1).* Retrieved from https://medium.com/dydxderivatives/getting-started-with-dydx-margin-trading-part-1-fe43789c2368

Hugh Karp, R. M. (n.d.). *NEXUS MUTUAL-A peer-to-peer discretionary mutual on the Ethereum blockchain.* Retrieved from https://nexusmutual.io/assets/docs/nmx_white_paperv2_3.pdf

Idle. (n.d.). *Idle-The Best Place for Your Money*. Retrieved from https://idle.finance/#/

Investopedia. (n.d.). *Spot Trade*. Retrieved from https://www.investopedia.com/terms/s/spottrade.asp

IREDALE, G. (2020, October 17). *A Guide to Risks in DeFi and How to Manage them*. Retrieved from https://101blockchains.com/risks-in-defi/#:~:text=The%20three%20common%20types%20of,and%20management%20of%20the%20opportunities.&text=Technical%20risk%20directly%20relates%20to,of%20DeFi%20products%20or%20services.

Jankovic, N. (2020, October 2). *How does CDP Automation work*. Retrieved from https://help.defisaver.com/makerdao/how-does-cdp-automation-work

Kalani, C. (2020, July 1). *Say Hello to Matcha!* Retrieved from https://blog.0xproject.com/say-hello-to-matcha-1a399251451e

Khaitan, T. (2020, December 7). *Hegic Celebrates $100M Volume, Launches Cypherpunk NFTs*. Retrieved from https://cryptobriefing.com/hegic-100m-launches-cyberpunk-nft/

Kistner, K. J. (2019, March 26). *Introducing Fulcrum: Tokenized Margin Made Dead Simple*. Retrieved from https://medium.com/bzxnetwork/introducing-fulcrum-tokenized-margin-made-dead-simple-e65ccc82393f

Kulechov, S. (2020, July 30). *Aavenomics*. Retrieved from https://medium.com/aave/aavenomics-eeab650cccc2

Kuznetsov, N. (2020, March 18). *Crypto Synthetic Assets, Explained*. Retrieved from https://cointelegraph.com/explained/crypto-synthetic-assets-explained#:~:text=The%20term%20%E2%80%9Csynthetic%20asset%E2%80%9D%20refers,indexes%2C%20currencies%20or%20interest%20rates.

Kyber Network. (n.d.). *Seamless Token Swaps, Anywhere.* Retrieved from https://kyber.network/?lang=en

Lielacher, A. (2020, October 4). *Top 4 Risks DeFi Investors Face.* Retrieved from https://cryptonews.com/exclusives/top-4-risks-defi-investors-face-7892.htm

Loong. (2020, January 10). *How RenVM Actually Works.* Retrieved from https://medium.com/renproject/how-renvm-actually-works-c2f76a2630c4

MakerDAO. (n.d.). Retrieved from https://makerdao.com/en/

MakerDAO. (n.d.). *Liquidation.* Retrieved from https://community-development.makerdao.com/en/learn/vaults/liquidation/#:~:text=The%20Liquidation%20Ratio%20is%20the,their%20Liquidation%20Ratio%20is%20breached.

MakerDAO. (n.d.). *The Maker Protocol: MakerDAO's Multi-Collateral Dai (MCD) System.* Retrieved from https://makerdao.com/en/whitepaper#in-mcd-we-trust

MakerDao Whitepaper. (n.d.). Retrieved from https://makerdao.com/en/whitepaper

Nick, S. (2019, April 1). *About DeFiPrime.* Retrieved from https://defiprime.com/about

Opyn FAQ. (n.d.). Retrieved from https://opyn.gitbook.io/opyn/faq#what-risks-are-covered

Opyn. (n.d.). *Getting Started.* Retrieved from https://opyn.gitbook.io/opyn/

OVR. (2020, October 13). *https://medium.com/ovrthereality*. Retrieved from https://medium.com/ovrthereality

Polkadot. (n.d.). *A scalable, interoperable & secure network protocol for the next web*. Retrieved from https://polkadot.network/technology/

Polkaswap. (2020, December 3). *SORA Farm Game*. Retrieved from https://medium.com/polkaswap/sora-farm-game-193f74d8e91f

Polkaswap. (n.d.). *The DEX for the Interoperable Future*. Retrieved from https://polkaswap.io/

pooltogether. (n.d.). *Qustions and Answers*. Retrieved from https://pooltogether.com/faq

Ren. (n.d.). Retrieved from https://renproject.io/renvm

Sassano, A. (2020, January 22). *Set Social Trading is Now Live on TokenSets*. Retrieved from https://medium.com/set-protocol/set-social-trading-is-now-live-on-tokensets-c981b5e67c5f#:~:text=Set%20Social%20Trading%20is%20a,single%20action%20the%20trader%20enacts.

Sawinyh, N. (2020, July 7). *What Are Perpetual Contracts for Bitcoin? dYdX Perpetual Futures Explained*. Retrieved from https://defiprime.com/perpetual-dydx

SFOX. (2020, November 2). *Risk in Decentralized Finance: Is the DeFi Boom Another Bubble?* Retrieved from https://www.sfox.com/blog/risk-in-decentralized-finance-is-the-defi-boom-another-bubble/

Sora XOR. (2020, November 27). *SORA Validator Reward Token: $VAL*. Retrieved from https://medium.com/sora-xor/sora-validator-reward-token-val-c96a8afb8541

Synthetix System Documentation-Litepaper. (2020, March). Retrieved from https://docs.synthetix.io/litepaper/

Synthetix.Exchange Overview. (2019, Feb 15). Retrieved from https://blog.synthetix.io/synthetix-exchange-overview/#:~:text=Exchange%3F-,Synthetix.,Synths%20seamlessly%20without%20liquidity%20restrictions.

Team, D. S. (2020, June 11). *Introducing our completely new Compound dashboard.* Retrieved from https://medium.com/defi-saver/introducing-our-completely-new-compound-dashboard-30a19c5486ad

Tech, I. o. (2020, October 13). *Top 10 DeFi Platforms You Need To Know About: Breaking Down Defi Pulse.* Retrieved from https://academy.ivanontech.com/blog/top-10-defi-platforms-you-need-to-know-about-breaking-down-defi-pulse

Tokenlon. (2020, October 20). *Instant Exchange Tutorial.* Retrieved from https://tokenlon.zendesk.com/hc/en-us/articles/360037732371

Tokensets. (2020, January 28). *WHAT IS TOKENSETS AND HOW TO USE IT TO TAKE CONTROL OF YOUR CRYPTO.* Retrieved from https://www.markethodl.com/blog/what-is-tokensets-and-how-to-use-it-to-take-control-of-your-crypto

Tommaso, D. D. (2020, October 30). *Understanding IBCO: Can Another Crypto-Funding Mechanism Yield Accountable Results?* Retrieved from https://hackernoon.com/understanding-ibco-can-another-crypto-funding-mechanism-yield-accountable-results-qb4a3zi5

Trade, borrow, and save using Dai. (n.d.). Retrieved from https://oasis.app/

Tran, K. C. (2019, October 9). *What is AirSwap?* Retrieved from https://decrypt.co/resources/what-is-airswap

Tran, M. H. (2020, April 27). *What is dYdX?* Retrieved from https://decrypt.co/resources/dydx-ethereum-margin-trading-platform-explained-learn

Uniswap. (n.d.). *Uniswap Documentation*. Retrieved from https://uniswap.org/docs/v2

Warlmertt. (2020, April 17). *Chainlink — A top 3 token investment for 2020/21*. Retrieved from https://marwolwarl.medium.com/chainlink-the-1-token-investment-for-2020-21-3bd9229cad4

What Are Yearn Vaults And How To Invest In Vaults? (2020, September). Retrieved from https://coinmarketcap.com/headlines/news/yearn-vaults/

Wintermute, M. (2020, February 2). *Hegic: On-chain Options Trading Protocol on Ethereum Powered by Hedge Contracts and Liquidity Pools*. Retrieved from https://ipfs.io/ipfs/QmWy8x6vEunH4gD2gWT4Bt4bBwWX2KAEUov46tCLvMRcME

YAM Finance. (n.d.). *YAM FAQ*. Retrieved from https://yam.finance/faq

yearn.finance. (n.d.). *Introduction to Yearn*. Retrieved from https://docs.yearn.finance/

Yin, Z. (2019, July 11). *Utilizing Margin and Leverage on dYdX*. Retrieved from https://medium.com/dydxderivatives/utilizing-margin-and-leverage-on-dydx-60b34ca8f3cb

YOUNG, M. (2020, August 12). *Surging Interest in 'Yam' Yield Farming — But Is It Too risky?* Retrieved from https://cointelegraph.com/news/surging-interest-in-yam-yield-farming-but-is-it-too-risky

Young, M. (2020, November 13). *Uniswap farming ends in 4 days, potentially freeing up $1.1B in Ether*. Retrieved from https://cointelegraph.com/news/uniswap-farming-ends-this-week-potentially-freeing-up-1-1b-eth

Yurtaev, E. (2020). *What is Zerion?* Retrieved from https://help.zerion.io/en/articles/4053536-what-is-zerion

INDEX

$

$BZRX · 53

.

. Kusama · 264

0

0x · 81, 137, 181, 186, 196, 362

1

1inch · 167, 170, 361

3

3pool · 259

A

Aave · 16, 41, 42, 43, 69, 70, 93, 95, 212, 291, 294, 295, 299, 360, 361
AAVE · 41, 364
aggregator · 193, 196, 362
AirSwap · 173, 174, 178, 361
Alpha Finance Lab · 256

Alpha Homora · 256
AMM · 18, 19, 132, 210, 356
AMPL · 364
Annual Percentage Yield · 25, 210, 356
APY · 23, 25, 43, 63, 144, 210, 212, 213, 215, 223, 253, 256, 289, 294, 295, 356
Arbitrage · 346
asset management · 15
automated market-maker · 132
automatic market maker · 18

B

Balancer · 132, 133, 136, 210, 232, 233, 234, 237, 361
Bancor · 147, 243, 251, 362
Bancor Network · 147
BEP · 332, 334
Binance · 12, 233
Bitcoin · 154, 232, 356
Bittrex · 12
blockchain · 3, 11, 28, 357, 358
Blockchain · 3
BNT · 147, 247, 249
BOOST · 80, 81, 90, 91, 96
borrowing · 20, 27, 38, 41, 52, 57, 59, 61, 69, 109, 114, 118, 204, 296, 355, 362
breakeven price · 334
Bug Bounty · 292
BUSD · 158

bZx · 53, 54, 57, 289, 294, 295

C

C.R.E.A.M. Finance · 50
call options · 303, 304
CDP · 28, 38, 40, 72, 73, 74, 75, 80, 81, 83, 84, 87, 103, 104, 349, 356
Chainlink · 211
client-server protocol · 356
Coinbase · 12
Coingecko · 321, 322
CoinMarketCap · 212
Cold Wallet · 356
collateral · 21, 28, 29, 41, 61, 65, 66, 110, 115, 118, 122, 123, 154, 156, 361
Collateral Ratio · 293
collateral. · 21, 28, 41, 88, 118, 122
collateralization ratio · 28, 74, 80, 81, 82, 93, 114
collateralization threshold · 61
Collateralized Debt Position · 28, 72, 356
COMP · 21, 364
Compound · 4, 16, 20, 21, 22, 23, 25, 26, 45, 50, 69, 70, 88, 100, 105, 158, 210, 212, 291, 294, 295, 297, 299, 304, 312, 313, 318, 350, 360, 361
ConsenSys · 290
Convexity Protocol · 304, 321
Cover · 300
Cross margin trading · 118
CRV · 158
CRV-BUSD · 215, 221

crypto assets · 12, 60, 122, 142, 210, 359
crypto hedge fund · 3
cryptoasset · 38, 51, 52
cryptoassets · 16, 18, 41, 65, 154
cryptocurrency · 3, 41, 356
cTokens · 21
Curve · 158, 159, 161, 181, 196, 271, 360
Curve 3 Pool · 279, 286
Curve finance · 257
Curve Finance · 158, 360
Curve platform · 158
Curve pool · 158, 159
cUSDT · 210

D

DAI · 21, 24, 28, 30, 32, 33, 34, 35, 36, 38, 40, 47, 48, 53, 59, 60, 61, 62, 63, 66, 67, 73, 74, 75, 78, 79, 80, 82, 83, 84, 100, 101, 109, 110, 111, 112, 114, 139, 140, 160, 170, 174, 176, 200, 208, 223, 259, 279, 286, 291, 294, 296, 297, 298, 299, 312, 313, 318, 347, 352, 355, 357, 360, 364, 373
DApp · 150, 356
DApps · 3
DDEX · 204, 207, 291, 294, 295
decentralizations · 13
Decentralized exchanges · 18
Decentralized finance · 11
Decentralized Finance · 11
decentralized ledger technology · 12
decentralized platform · 11

decentralized platforms · 12
DeFi · 4, 11, 12, 13, 14, 15, 16, 21, 28, 69, 70, 71, 102, 193, 211, 212, 233, 271, 273, 280, 282, 357, 358, 360, 361, 363, 364
DeFi coins · 12
DeFi protocols · 12, 211
DeFi Saver · 69, 70, 71, 271, 360
DeFi Score · 290, 291, 292, 294, 295
DEX · 137, 142, 158, 181, 186, 193, 196, 356, 362
DEX, · 137
Dharma · 16
digital assets · 4, 11, 12, 13, 14, 23, 26, 28, 41, 61, 110, 122, 136, 210, 211
DPI · 256, 305
dYdX · 16, 59, 60, 61, 63, 66, 69, 100, 101, 109, 110, 111, 115, 118, 122, 123, 124, 126, 291, 294, 295, 346, 360, 362

E

Earn · 142
EOS · 147
ERC20 token · 41, 127, 158, 233
ERC20 tokens · 41, 127, 132, 154, 238
ETH · 16, 21, 28, 38, 39, 40, 52, 53, 58, 59, 60, 61, 62, 65, 66, 67, 72, 73, 74, 75, 79, 80, 81, 82, 83, 84, 90, 96, 99, 103, 104, 109, 110, 111, 123, 129, 134, 139, 140, 148, 156, 165, 173, 176, 200, 201, 202, 204, 205, 211, 222, 224, 225, 226, 227, 228, 233, 234, 235, 238, 245, 247, 249, 256, 261, 263, 265, 266, 268, 271, 289, 295, 301, 304, 305, 306, 309, 312, 314, 315, 318, 330, 333, 334, 335, 336, 337, 338, 340, 343, 344, 349, 352, 356, 361, 372
Ethereum · 3, 13, 18, 21, 28, 41, 62, 122, 127, 132, 135, 137, 147, 154, 158, 232, 356, 357, 358, 360, 362, 363
Ethereum Virtual Machine · 356
EVM · 356
exchange · 3

F

FARM token · 213, 215
FCRV-BUSD · 216, 217, 218
financial risk · 288, 289
Flash loan · 346
Fulcrum · 53, 54, 163, 164, 167, 360, 361
Furucombo · 347, 348
futures · 121, 123, 126

G

Gas · 357
gas fee · 61, 76, 77, 81, 88, 94, 97, 131, 192, 199

H

hacking · 13
hardware wallets · 356
Harvest.Finance · 213

hash function · 357
Hegic · 329, 334, 336, 339, 340, 343, 344
HEGIC token · 336, 344
Huobi · 12, 156

I

IBCO · 344, 357
iBTC · 253
ICO · 41
Idle Finance · 45
iearn.finance · 158
IEO · 3
iETH · 53, 253
Impermanent loss · 260, 289, 357
Initial Bonding Curve Offering · 344, 357
InstaDApp · 105
interest rate · 41, 115, 122
intermediary · 14, 137, 154
ISOLATED margin · 111
iUSDT · 53, 57
iUSDT, · 53, 57

K

KNC · 150, 153, 364
Kyber · 150, 151, 362
Kyber, · 81, 181
KYC · 13, 127, 357

L

LEND token · 41

Lending · 20, 30, 41, 53, 59, 60, 69, 204, 294, 295
leverage · 74, 81, 110, 112, 165, 166
leverage. · 112
LINK · 123, 167, 169, 189, 192, 364
LIQUDATION PRICE · 113
liquidation fee · 66, 115
liquidation threshold · 66, 115
liquidators · 21
liquidity · 21, 41, 122, 127, 128, 132, 136, 147, 150, 154, 158, 210, 211, 229, 230, 231, 232, 235, 237, 238, 241, 242, 243, 249, 357, 360, 362
Liquidity Index · 292
liquidity mining · 162, 210, 229, 238, 243, 257, 260, 285
Liquidity Pool · 127, 357
liquidity provider · 127
Loan Shifter' · 103
LP token · 215, 217, 228, 253, 256, 259, 286

M

Maker CDP Vault · 38
Maker DSR · 100
Maker Governance · 28
Maker Protocol · 28
MakerDao · 29, 30
MakerDAO · 4, 16, 20, 28, 69, 70, 71, 72, 74, 83, 105, 212, 356, 357, 360
margin account · 61, 109, 123
Margin deposit · 114